PAT.16

ALL WE
KNOW

ALL WE KNOW

THREE LIVES

LISA COHEN

FARRAR, STRAUS AND GIROUX

NEW YORK

Farrar, Straus and Giroux
18 West 18th Street, New York 10011

Distributed in Canada by D&M Publishers, Inc.
Printed in the United States of America
First edition, 2012

Grateful acknowledgment is made to the Society of Authors for permission to print an unpublished excerpt from Virginia Woolf's *Diary* and excerpts from "The New Dress" and to Houghton Mifflin Harcourt Publishing Company for permission to quote Woolf's *Diary* and *Letters*; to the Estate of Edmund Wilson for permission to quote his letters, diaries, and essays; to Bruce Kellner and the Estate of Carl Van Vechten for permission to reproduce Van Vechten's photographs of Esther Murphy and Muriel Draper; to the estate of Dawn Powell, with thanks to Peter Skolnik, for permission to quote excerpts from Powell's diaries, published and unpublished correspondence, *A Time to Be Born*, and *The Happy Island*; and to Houghton Mifflin Harcourt Publishing Company for permission to quote *Memories of a Catholic Girlhood* by Mary McCarthy.

Library of Congress Cataloging-in-Publication Data
Cohen, Lisa, 1962–
    All we know : three lives / Lisa Cohen. — 1st ed.
        p.   cm.
    Includes bibliographical references.
    ISBN 978-0-374-17649-5 (alk. paper)
    1. Murphy, Esther, 1898–1962.   2. Acosta, Mercedes de, 1893–1968.
3. Garland, Madge, 1896–1990.   4. Women—Biography.   5. Biography—
20th century.   6. Modernism (Aesthetics)—History—20th century.
7. Women intellectuals—Biography.   8. Socialites—United States—Biography.
9. Women authors, American—19th century—Biography.   10. Women
fashion designers—England—Biography.   I. Title.

CT3235 .C64 2012
920.72—dc23

                                                                    2011041055

Designed by Jonathan D. Lippincott

www.fsgbooks.com

1   3   5   7   9   10   8   6   4   2

In memory of Sybille Bedford

CONTENTS

ALL WE
KNOW

THREE LIVES

For five decades, Esther Murphy built a wall of words around
herself. A profusely erudite New York intellectual of the first
half of the twentieth century, she talked and talked, dazzling
her listeners with her vast memory, her extravagant verbal style,
and her inventive renderings of the past—and driving them to despair with her inability to finish the books she was contracted to
write, biographies of remarkable women in history. A privileged
insider and awkward outsider, she was a brilliant witness to her
own time and both an analyst and an example of "failure" as an an-
imating American conceit.

To the end of her life, Mercedes de Acosta saved a florist's card
that had come with flowers she received from Greta Garbo—a card
on which Garbo had written nothing. Seductress and seduced, de
Acosta was consumed by her intimacies with some of the most celebrated actresses and dancers of the twentieth century: Isadora Duncan, Marlene Dietrich, and Garbo, to name just a few. She amassed a
collection—letters, playbills, clothing, photographs, clippings, more—
that testifies to these intimacies, as well as to the ephemeral yet enduring relationships between fans and stars, and to the intersections of
popular celebrity and high modernism. In the process, she also preserved and prolonged for herself and for us a particular set of emotions: the self-abnegation and self-aggrandizement of the devotee; the
irrational, limitless passion of the collector; the socially inopportune
ardor of one woman for another.

Madge Garland played a defining role in almost every aspect of
the fashion industry in England in the interwar and postwar years
and she embodied the fleeting world of haute couture with sophis-

tication, steely fragility, and visceral pleasure. Yet she also approached her profession with a wry distance and longed to work in a more respected field of design. At once critical of and enraptured by fashion, she made sense of it by seeing it as allied with her feminism, and by living the connections among fashion, feminism, and modernist art, design, and literature. In old age, she was encouraged by friends to tell her story, but she found it almost impossible to think of her life as worth recording. Well into her eighties and almost blind, she scrawled several barely legible, emotionally veiled, but heated pages about clothing, career, and love—thick pencil on pale blue airmail paper.

Each of these women is now largely forgotten. Yet each was a dazzling figure of her time: independent, accomplished, and conflicted; scintillating and rebarbative; characteristic and exceptional. Esther Murphy played an integral part in literary New York in the 1920s and '30s; Edmund Wilson, Dorothy Parker, and Scott Fitzgerald were among her close friends. Mercedes de Acosta made her way in the New York theater world in the teens and twenties, worked as a screenwriter in Hollywood in the 1930s, and cherished her rare friendships. As an editor, writer, collaborator, and comrade, Madge Garland was associated with many of the writers and visual artists who have come to stand for the creative work of the interwar years in London and Paris.

All three women knew each other well and were commentators on one another's lives. Their stories reveal vital, rarely explored networks of friends, colleagues, and lovers. All three married, but were committed primarily to other women; all participated in the close-knit, fractious lesbian networks of New York, London, and Paris. *Sexual identity* is an anachronistic term for that context and is in any case too static to convey how the feelings and acts it refers to changed for these women throughout their lives. But for all three, sexual freedom, difference, and censure were crucial to their experiences of modernity and to their work as thinkers about modernity. Each in her own way was also shaped by a struggle between fact and fiction, or fantasy—a potent combination for a biographer.

All of which made it logical for me to write about them collectively. But that was not what drove me. It was something more elusive, to do with the challenge each woman posed. Esther Murphy,

Mercedes de Acosta, and Madge Garland inhabited centers of cultural production in England, Europe, and the United States, and they worked precariously at the edges. While each one published, each also produced a body of thought that was not and could not be worked out fully on paper. As a result, each has been seen as not quite part of history, when seen at all. Juxtaposing their lives was a way to illuminate work that has not been recognized as such: in Murphy's case, prolific conversation; in de Acosta's, the fervent, even shameful acts and feelings associated with being a fan and collector; in Garland's, a career in the ephemeral, often trivialized world of fashion.

Esther Murphy's immersion in history, literature, and politics, her uncanny memory, and her obsessive talking; the flotsam and jetsam of Mercedes de Acosta's fandom; Madge Garland's brilliantly clothed surfaces and her apparently impersonal writings on fashion—all are forms of evidence, of production, and of autobiography. All are ways of thinking about history. All are archives, formal and intimate.

In one of her essays on biography, "Lives of the Obscure," Virginia Woolf writes that "one likes romantically to feel oneself a deliverer advancing with lights across the waste of years to the rescue of some stranded ghost . . . waiting, appealing, forgotten, in the growing gloom." This romance has its appeal. I have wanted to make these three women visible again, albeit in new ways, and I have spent years tracking them. But none of them thought herself in need of rescue. Each memorialized herself and colluded in her own invisibility; each lived imagining what should, or might, or could never be, saved or jettisoned. Their lives also continually raised such questions about value for their friends and other observers. And so documenting Murphy, de Acosta, and Garland's lives has meant paying attention to the ways that each was, for the people around her, a storehouse of modern anxieties about what we call failure, irrationality, and triviality.

These are three stories, then, about how history is lived, written, and imagined—three lives in which what it meant to be modern was an urgent question. They are also stories about the meaning and uses of style: rhetorical, sexual, sartorial. "What is style?" the American modernist Marguerite Young has asked. Her own reply:

"Style is thinking." A riddle of unconscious excitements and conscious choices, style is a way to fascinate oneself and others—and to transform oneself and the world. It is an attempt to make the ordinary and the tragic more bearable. Style is a didactic impulse that aspires to banish doubt, a form of certainty about everything elusive and uncertain. Style is at once fleeting and lasting, and it has everything to do with excess—even when its excesses are those of austerity or self-denial. It is too much and it is nothing at all, and it tells all kinds of stories about the seams between public and private life. As a form of pleasure, for oneself and for an audience, and as an expression of the wish to exceed and confound expectations, to be exceptional, style is a response to the terror of invisibility and isolation—a wish for inclusion. Above all, it is a productive act that, although it concerns itself with the creation and experience of brilliant surfaces, is powerful because it unsettles what we think we know about the superficial and the profound.

A PERFECT
FAILURE

When you met Esther Murphy she told you about the history of people and things you knew and the history of things you had never considered. Six feet tall, regal in bearing, yet irremediably awkward, she was all energy, compulsion, and excitement about ideas, and she was excited above all about the past. She would command the floor with long monologues about the intricacies of the American presidency and of the Hanseatic League, the courts of Louis XIV and Louis XV, the building you were living in, the ancestors you thought you had forgotten. She would quote François Fénelon, Saint-Simon, Jane Austen, and Henry Adams while smoking two cigarettes at once, drinking nonstop, letting food congeal on her plate, gesticulating grandly, then stubbing her cigarettes out on her lapels. She would pull great swathes of human history out of her memory, exhilarated by its ironies, its neglected crevices, and its meaning in the present, stopping time and prolonging it while she explored its recesses, fascinating her listeners and overwhelming them, drawing them in and keeping them at bay, unaware of what she was doing, aware only of what she was thinking.

At age nine she was already "a nonstop conversationalist." When she was eleven years old, her father pronounced her "a wonder." Patrick Murphy, a famous public speaker in the first decades of the twentieth century and the owner of the luxury leather goods company Mark Cross, thought so highly of Esther that he would seat her at his dinner table so she could listen to the conversation of New York politicians, judges, writers, and businessmen. "Never have I seen such a mind," he crowed to his son Gerald, her elder brother; "everybody who meets her stamps her as a 'genius.'" Preternaturally well-read, Esther seemed able to glance at a book and absorb it all, verbatim. By her teens, her conversation and correspondence were crammed with references to the history, literature, and philosophy she incorporated with such ease. She "utterly demolished" the actor Monty Woolley, a friend of Gerald's, when she turned to him "with a dissertation on the difference between Dostoevski and Turgenev." When Gerald submitted a poem of hers "to several magazines (for criticism only)," the editors "pronounced it 'mature genius', etc." As Gerald boasted, "Moreover, she *wants* to write!"

In her twenties, which spanned the 1920s, she found her place and contemporary affinities in hard-drinking, haute bohemian New York and Paris, where her excesses, social and intellectual, were noteworthy even during that period of furious excess. Arriving at a party thrown in her honor in May 1928, Carl Van Vechten "ask[ed] why in heaven's name a party should be given for Miss Esther Murphy, who attended more parties than any living woman, never going to less than three a night." In Djuna Barnes's 1928 *Ladies Almanack*, a satire of the Paris salonnière and Sapphist Natalie Barney and her circle, Esther appears as "Bounding Bess, noted for her Enthusiasm in things forgotten," absorbed by "great Women in History," and "last seen in a Cloud of Dust, hot foot after an historic Fact." When Scott Fitzgerald published *Tender Is the Night*, for which he initially used Gerald Murphy and his wife, Sara, as models for the protagonists, a mutual friend wrote to Fitzgerald, "I don't remember talking to anyone in New York about the novel except Esther and she did all the talking." She talked all through lunch one day with the novelist Dawn Powell, then finally paused and said to Powell, "But you were going to say something." Powell replied: "I was going to say, 'Hello, Esther.'" Even when Esther Murphy couldn't speak, she was compelled to perform—and others were equally compelled to assist at the performance. Guests arriving late to a party one evening found everyone else sitting in silence with Esther standing before them "going through all the motions of holding forth, but with no audible sound. She had completely lost her voice, yet commanded the attention of her audience."

The charisma was real, and it was allied to a gentleness and gen-

erosity that often survived even when she was at her most dissipated. It was also allied to a profound insecurity. Dawn Powell
described Esther as "personally and professionally frightened, shy,
and arrogant without confidence, which is no way to profit by arrogance." Still, it seemed obvious to everyone around her that she
would turn her perorations into important books. Attracted to and
confounded by women of previous centuries who had been socially
mobile and had played contested roles in political history, Esther
planned to write several biographies and had contracts from publishers to do so. Instead, she kept talking. If she is remembered at all
today it is as Gerald Murphy's eccentric, pathetic sister, a marvel
who became a spectacular disappointment.

She could not live without books, but it seemed that she also
needed a live audience. If you asked her a question—"it could be a
question about a seventeenth-century Florentine economist, a question about almost anything"—she would lean back, take several
staccato puffs on her cigarette, say: "All we know is"—and then
launch into a long disquisition on the subject.

All we know. The phrase announces the partial, human quality
of that knowledge—collective and individual—and the encyclope-
dic discourse that would follow. It is at once "everything we know"
and "the very little we know," a declaration of comprehensiveness
and incompletion.

Esther Murphy's history is itself a portrait of comprehensiveness and incompletion: stunning accomplishment and prodigious
limitation, promise and defeat, writing and not writing, originality
and obsessive citation, fact and fantasy, performance and painful
reticence, uncanny memory and oblivion. She talked more than anyone, drank more than anyone, was bigger, more brilliant, kinder—
and yet her life seemed to her friends to hang in midair, unfulfilled.
She became a figure whose inability to complete her planned long
works both pained her writer friends and reassured them about
their own productivity and success.

"There has never been an American tragedy," said Scott Fitzgerald
in 1927. "There have only been great failures." "I am certain that
what makes American success is American failure," wrote Gertrude

Stein, who also described herself as "fond of saying that America, which was supposed to be a land of success, was a land of failure." To be seen as a failure in America and in American letters, as Stein and Fitzgerald knew, is to occupy a special place in the imagination of a culture that celebrates success and abhors its opposite to an uncommon degree. "I am an American," Esther would declare, drawing herself up to her full, considerable height. She said it in England, in Mexico, in Italy, and in France. It was not a declaration of patriotism, she averred, but "something much deeper." The America with which she identified consisted of an idea, an ideal, about the fruitful conjunction of democracy and intellect, a story— her father's and the nation's—of meritocratic rise. This America was a place where her experience of financial privilege and cynicism about the power of capital could coexist. It was a place of limitless violence and mendacity that produced and accommodated her pride, her agnosticism, her oddness, her pragmatism, and her belief in rational debate. It was a place where she could see Scott Fitzgerald demonstrate spectacularly the costs of literary success and defeat, acclaim and "crack-up," and where her acute sense of difference, her feeling of being at once exceptional and aberrant, was peculiarly at home. It was a place asking its own questions about the correct use of extraordinary talent—and telling, with every move, a story about the squandering of great resources. And it was a place whose historical amnesia Esther fought with her capacious memory, her profound engagement with the past, and her sense of obligation to politics in the present.

The issue of how the United States should come to maturity was a live issue as Esther came of age. The ruptures of the Civil War were a living memory; identity was often conceived in more local than national terms, yet still shaped in reaction to Europe; new waves of immigration were changing the country in profound ways; and "the speeded-up pace of American life, the constant changing-hands of money," in Edmund Wilson's words, and the resulting pressure to produce—which is to say, to succeed—was overwhelming some middle-class, white, Protestant men and sending them into retreat from work and the work ethic. It was at this fraught moment that an American woman could first be said to have failed at something other than femininity and motherhood.

In fact, failure was part of Esther Murphy's intellectual purview: She loved to think about wasted effort and lost causes, on the American scene and in Europe. She called Ramsay MacDonald's Labour government of 1929–31, with which she was briefly associated as the wife of the English politician John Strachey, "the most important failure since the Wall Street crash." She renounced Catholic doctrine at a young age, but was forever rehearsing the machinations of the Church, including the French suppression of Protestantism and the struggles between Jesuits and Jansenists there. She delighted in the fact that Charles Augustin Sainte-Beuve had "rescued the forgotten tragedy of the Jansenists" in his six-volume history of seventeenth-century France, *Port-Royal*. And then there was her long obsession with Madame de Maintenon, the biographical subject who was most important to her and about whom she left an unfinished manuscript. All of these interests had to do with her fascination with the ruins that are always part of the workings of power—with the ways that one strain of thought, faith, or behavior becomes dominant and another subsidiary. Madame de Maintenon was born in poverty, the granddaughter of a famous Huguenot writer and soldier, but became the second, secret wife of Louis XIV. Writing about Maintenon's dramatic renunciation of her Protestant faith and acceptance of Catholicism, Esther speculated, "Did she realize that the French reformation was one of the greatest failures in history and did she dislike failure?"

But while Esther believed that wasted effort was not a waste, or that such waste forever had meaning, she was not interested in simple acts of reclamation. Seeing her again after a long absence, Edmund Wilson relished her talking "with her usual historical gusto." History for her was what could not be contained: herself, her volubility, her pleasure in thinking about those who had preceded her, her desire to make herself the vehicle for the chasms and correspondences between now and then, the way the achievements and disasters of the past continually made themselves felt in the present—all of the sparkling facts. History was a dead woman—and a living one to whom she wanted to say something. She "was all about ideas and marvelous sentences, not about research," said the writer Sybille Bedford, one of those living women.

"Statistics," wrote Dawn Powell, after an evening with Esther,

"occupy her as if they were rare jewels." But if the facts were radi-
ant, glamorous, and meaningful to her, so was their absence and
fabrication—the missing, forgotten, and invented. And it was equally
her habit to see the world in literary terms. Some of her most elaborate discourses on the past turned out to be carefully wrought
fictions masquerading as fact. Analyzing public figures and friends,
she thought of them as characters from novels and plays as well as
actors in history. She loved odd juxtapositions of the actual and
invented. "I will now proceed to deliver a few comments on the general world situation," she wrote to a friend in 1933, then went on to
consider the French reaction to FDR's economic policies by quoting Samuel Richardson's *Clarissa*. " 'Fits upon fits upon fits, and the
loss of her intellects for days at a time,' is the only adequate description of what the French press and official classes have been going
through," she wrote, citing the histrionics of Richardson's heroine.
Projecting herself and others back in time, compounding the gesture with reference to literature: This was Esther Murphy's constant practice.

The genre of biography has itself, for approximately the past
eighty years, been said to lie at the intersection of history and literature, of fact and imagination. Esther Murphy did not write a biography. She did leave a record of her attempts to do so: of the archival
lacunae that hampered her writing; of the psychological inscrutability of her subjects; of the ebb and flow of her own admiration for,
identification with, and disgust at these figures—a pattern that often characterizes biographers' work. Her brother Gerald has become
known for his devotion to "living well," for the way he harnessed
his aesthetics as a painter, as a businessman, and as a creator of
perfect moments in the present for his family and friends, for many
of whom his taste represented the spirit of the 1920s. Esther responded to and shaped the first part of the twentieth century with
ideas rather than objects. She moved through her time fueled by
insecurity, alcohol, and relentless intellectual energy, promulgating
a vision that made that era new and old at once. Her expert, idiosyncratic engagement with history was as informed by her sense of not
quite belonging to her own time as it was by her perceptive understanding of the contemporary scene. She held that anachronism
was at least as important as novelty in thinking about modernity,

and that modernity was something far more complex than either rupture with the past or reversion to a remote past (the latter being the gestures that Ezra Pound and H.D. made, for example, in their turns to antiquity).

It is a cliché of American life that we like our brilliance to flare up and die young, we like it to crash and burn. This is not that tale— nor is it the nineteenth-century counternarrative of abdicating ambition: preferring "not to." This is a story about a life in which past and present, fact and fiction, history and failure, collide. It is a story about someone who made history and politics a literary occasion, whose sense of the politics of literature was acute, and who understood and embodied American success and American failure.

NO SUCH WORD AS FAIL

E sther is without a doubt the most widely read and best informed woman in New York," wrote a friend of hers in 1927,
"and her father's admiration for her and devotion to her is one
of the rarest things to behold . . . Mrs. Murphy, very patrician with
beautiful white hair and many jewels, sits back and smokes her cigarettes without interesting herself very much in her husband's and
her daughter's very brilliant dialogue."

Patrick Murphy bullied his sons, Frederic and Gerald, but he
was Esther's champion—"so proud," in his wife's words, "that he
[could] hardly see straight." Part of the first group of Irish Catholics
to find acceptance in New York society, Murphy raised his children
in a muddled combination of privileges deriving from his success
and scorn for the fact that they could not repeat his trajectory. Esther, whom he called Tess, was exempt from some of the expectations that haunted her brothers, such as success in business, and
she exceeded others, with her scholarly acumen. Still, like her
brothers, she grew up steeped in an atmosphere of opportunity and
exclusion and in the myth and fact of Patrick Murphy's professional
and social climb.

She also absorbed or inherited some of her mother's nervous-
ness and depression. Anna Murphy's letters to her children often
report her bad dreams and anxieties. She took "life and the living
of it so tragically," Gerald wrote in 1915. In the late 1950s, more
than a quarter of a century after their parents' deaths, he wrote to
Esther: "Mother was devoted, possessive, ambitious, Calvinistic,

---

Esther posed with a newspaper (Esther Murphy's photo album, AFP)

superstitious, with a faulty sense of the truth. She was hypercritical and as I recall it, ultimately resigned from most of her friendships." He remembered their father as a man who "avoid[ed] . . . close relationships including family ones . . . a solitary [who] managed, though he had a wife and children, to lead a detached life." Esther adored her father, but as the girl in the family and the youngest child, she found her place was with her mother and spent long stretches of time alone with Anna Murphy, at home and at the watering holes of the wealthy in Europe and the United States. Every once in a while, Patrick Murphy would appear from Paris or London, where he spent half of every year supervising the Mark Cross factories, procuring the fittings of upper-class European life for American consumption, and maintaining a mistress. "Our father who art in Europe," Gerald would say.

Born in Boston in 1855 or '56, the eldest of thirteen children, Murphy had gone to work for the saddler Mark W. Cross in the mid-1870s, first as a bookkeeper and then as a salesman. He eventually bought the company, relocated it to fashionable Tremont Street, and transformed it into a purveyor of small leather goods, including bags, cigar cases, tea baskets, gloves, and stationery cases. In 1892 he moved his business and family to Manhattan—the former to a shop on Lower Broadway, opposite City Hall and near the Financial District, the latter to a brownstone on lower Fifth Avenue. He had married Anna Ryan in 1884; Fred and Gerald were born in Boston in 1885 and 1888. Esther was born in New York on October 22, 1897. Murphy weathered the financial panics of 1890 and 1892–93, and in 1902 he opened another Mark Cross shop, at Fifth Avenue and Thirty-seventh Street. He also had a shop on Regent Street in London and a glove factory in Wiltshire, and he eventually bought the leather factory in central England that produced much of his inventory. Mark Cross still made luggage, equestrian supplies, and writing accessories, but Murphy also brought the thermos, the hot-water bottle, Minton china, English crystal, Scottish golf clubs, the demitasse, the highball glass, and the cocktail set (later subjects of Gerald's paintings) to market in the United States.

His political life was at least as important to him as his business. He had served in the Massachusetts Legislature as a Democratic representative of Boston's Twelfth District in 1878–79; in New York he associated with the reforming wing of Tammany Hall and was a friend of Al Smith, the progressive Irish-Catholic governor and 1928 presidential candidate. By the time Esther was a young child, he had also begun to move toward the circles of ruling-class power in Manhattan. In the late nineteenth and early twentieth centuries, New York society "was still a closed circle to which one either did or did not belong," wrote one critical insider. Religious, racial, and ethnic prejudice went without saying, as did a rigid "social hierarchy, from which all random elements were rigorously excluded." The Four Hundred, that group of families identified as "Society," would also "have fled in a body from a poet, a painter, a musician, or a clever Frenchman." But by the turn of the twentieth century there was room for an anomaly or two, and Patrick Murphy's controlled wit made him a celebrated speaker at the enormous banquets that were part of the public life of the city's elite. He made his debut in 1903 at one of its premier rituals, the National Horse Show Association dinner, held in the old Madison Square Garden, where his audience was composed of Astors, Harrimans, Vanderbilts, Schermerhorns, and Hamiltons. He came "to be regarded as the official orator of the . . . Association" and was in such demand as an after-dinner speaker, to business groups and private clubs, that he spent most of his evenings out.

Bald, clean shaven, meticulously tailored, he would hold himself rigid, clasp his hands behind his back, and speak in a "clear fluent monotone." His talks were a series of epigrammatic utterances, strung together cleverly and recycled frequently, with just a glancing mention of the group he was addressing. He timed himself ruthlessly. His themes were government, business, history, alcohol, and taxation. (The excise tax on business income and the graduated personal income tax were introduced in 1913.) He cited Macaulay, Shakespeare, the Bible, and the Greeks. The need to pay tribute to a prominent man of the day, often the guest of honor at such occasions, meant that he spent a certain amount of time musing about success and flattering his audiences. "He who breeds thoroughbreds must be a thoroughbred himself" was "an aphorism that elicited the liveliest applause" at the Horse Show banquet of 1904. He was compared to Mark Twain and other entertaining orators of the pre-

vious century. His characteristic rhetorical gesture was an ostensibly serious or paradoxical statement followed by a deflating quip.
"The art of speaking is to say nothing—briefly," he observed, more
than once. "But the tragedy of it is the less a man has to say the more
difficult he finds it to stop." Paradox and didacticism were also the
style of the advertising copy for his firm, which he wrote. "Buying
inferior articles to save money is like stopping the clock to save
time," ran one.

Esther's prolix and imaginative verbal style shared little with
her father's disciplined and formulaic method. Even as a child, she
performed constantly, testing her own and others' authority. On a
transatlantic voyage with her parents, age eleven, she initiated a trial
on behalf of a passenger after she overheard him complain about
his wife's cigarette smoking, appointing herself prosecutor and
choosing a jury. "Before we knew it there were a hundred people
around her," her mother wrote from on board the *Amerika* in
June 1909. That summer, at the Beau-Rivage Palace hotel in Lau-
sanne, a pinnacle of prewar leisure, Esther "instigated" a baseball
game, corralling the guests into two teams, coaching those who did
not know the game, again attracting a crowd. At home in New York,
when her elderly nanny took her to Central Park for exercise, Esther would skate off, a gawky girl Pied Piper, pulling a group of children after her and mesmerizing them with terrifying "Edgar Allan
Poe–ish" stories.

But if her style was unlike her father's, she was shaped by his
preoccupations and riveted by his political savvy. "History is simply a record of the failures of government," Patrick Murphy told
one audience. And: "History teaches us one thing only, and that is
no statesman has ever learned anything from history." At the Horse
Show in 1907, he addressed the financial crisis of the preceding
month. "We have had explosive financial fireworks," he said of
Theodore Roosevelt's attempts to regulate big business, the collapse of confidence in the banking system, the failure of the trust
companies, and J. P. Morgan's rescue of these institutions after negotiations in Morgan's home with a consortium of bankers.

Esther with the actor John Drew (Esther Murphy's photo album, AFP)

Happily . . . American difficulties have produced the great
Americans. It is not alone in the battlefield that valor is displayed; courage may be shown even in an art library. No
sounder pieces of American manhood have been put together than the group of financial statuary that defended
American credit . . . In the lexicons of Morgan's library
there is no such word as fail.

For Murphy, too, there was no such word. But his success, which
stemmed from his accomplishments in business, was seldom attributed to them. He was a well-to-do merchant who catered to wealthy
New Yorkers, and he was on the board of directors of at least one
bank in the course of his career; yet when his speeches were reported in the newspapers, as they often were, he was not identified
as the president of Mark Cross. It was important to him and others
that he never "appeared the business man." In the words of one acquaintance, "He looked like a gentleman and he was a gentleman."
The reporter added: "He always carried a cane and gloves." Membership in the Manhattan, Pilgrims, and Lambs clubs; a move
uptown to West Fifty-seventh Street, then to an enormous apartment at 525 Park Avenue; the purchase of a summer house in Southampton and membership in the Southampton Club (of which
Nicholas Murray Butler, the president of Columbia University, was
president)—all signaled and facilitated his rise.

And so, as Esther grew up, a number of the "distinguished and
remarkable . . . American women" she knew were members of New
York's elite families. One, Margaret "Daisy" Chanler—broad-minded,
kind, and married into the Astor family—was also a sharp analyst
of New York society, and her children became Esther's friends. The
travel and political writer Edith O'Shaughnessy—"a clever and pon-
derous dowager and a great crony of my Ma's"—was another fixture
of Esther's childhood. But the heroine of Esther's youth and young
adulthood was Edith Wharton. A voracious scholar, largely self-
educated, Wharton was at once a serious artist and a commercial
success who had also been a pawn in the marriage market. For a
bookish young woman who was studying her own awkward social

Patrick Murphy (Esther Murphy's photo album, AFP)

position, Wharton was an inspiration and a caution, and Esther read her closely. In *The House of Mirth*, Wharton's first major novel, her protagonist's failure is one of reputation—the old story. But Wharton also exposes exactly what Lily Bart's fall has to do with money—with her carefully calibrated yet blind accountings of expenditure and indebtedness—and she shows how a social system that offers meager alternatives to selling oneself in marriage is itself a failure. Through Margaret Chanler, Wharton's closest friend, Esther eventually met Wharton, and she continued to encounter and admire her as an adult.

Despite her father's delight in her, Esther also grew up with a heightened awareness of her physical and psychological imperfections, just as her brothers had. Fred was diagnosed with mastoiditis and bleeding ulcers as a young man and he had several surgeries when such procedures were extremely dangerous. Gerald suffered from depression, which he called "the Black Service," and understood himself as having "a defect over which I have only had enough control to scotch it from time to time"—his attraction to men. When he announced his engagement to Sara Wiborg, the daughter of multi-millionaire Frank Wiborg, Patrick Murphy castigated him about his poor work ethic and "fail[ure] to grasp the fundamental duty in life, i.e.: self-support,—and financial independence" and told him he "did not deserve to be married." Esther was an attractive child with long hair and her mother's wide face, but she did not grow into a beautiful young person; she had no interest in the conventional pastimes of girls of her social class—dancing, clothes, marriage; her enormous height was beyond the pale for a woman at the time; and she had a lazy eye, which heightened the impression of peculiarity. She was conveyed constantly to eye specialists in New York and Europe as a child and had at least one surgery to correct her vision as an adult. It was still ordinary, moreover, for a girl's scholarship to be seen as freakish and physically destructive. When Esther was eight, a doctor diagnosed her as suffering from "a peculiar form of 'Hives'" brought on by what he called "intellectual indigestion."

By her late teens, she had developed an ironically inflated, self-deflating way of speaking about her body: "My appearance is more than usually attractive owing to the gargantuan proportions of one cheek," she wrote Gerald. "An ulcerated tooth does not add to one's attractions." From the Maine resort where she and her mother stayed in the summer of 1915, she asked him to send her a set of golf clubs, the doctor having ordered exercise. She wanted equipment that was "as light in weight as possible, because although my height might impress the casual observer to the contrary, I am *not* an Amazon." Her body and her books were in constant conversation: "I assure you I shall probably be fairly apoplectic with physical well being when I leave here," she wrote. "I brought with me among my books a new and formidable French biography of the reign of Louis XIII, and so far have only read eight chapters . . . so you see down what alien byways I have wandered." Later, some would say that Esther looked like Gerald—only less pretty. "All the masculine traits seem to be concentrated in Esther," wrote Edmund Wilson, quoting John Dos Passos, "and the feminine ones in Gerald."

The message about inadequacy was general in the family; it was an upbringing in which one was encouraged to think of oneself both as exceptional and a failure. Patrick Murphy sent his sons to Yale, expected them to excel, took it for granted that they would then work for Mark Cross, and gave them executive positions when they graduated, but his dissatisfaction with them was constant. "Come, brace up," he wrote to Gerald during his second year at Yale. "You can't afford to let this thing [his studies] go *now*. It means *failure*." Although Gerald never resigned his position on the board of directors of Mark Cross, he stopped working for the company for almost twenty years when he enlisted in the army in 1918. His allergy to his father and to the commercialism of American life propelled him to Europe in 1921, where he spent the next decade, partly in the South of France that he and Sara Murphy helped to popularize, painting, living a carefully arranged life of the senses, and trying to be the kind of father he had not had—funded, of course, by his father and father-in-law's enterprises.

Fred, who was Esther's favorite, worked for the company, then enlisted as a private in the army at age thirty-two, over a doctor's objections, as soon as the United States entered the First World War. Commissioned as a lieutenant several months later, he fought at the battles of the Somme, Saint-Mihiel, and the Argonne Forest and served as a liaison officer between the French and American armies. He had his thigh shattered by machine-gun fire and his politics rad-

icalized by what he saw on the battlefield, and was awarded the
Croix de Guerre by the French. He had dabbled in the theater when
he was younger and in 1920 he married Esther's close friend Noel
Haskins, a Park Avenue debutante and trained lieder singer who
had acted with the Provincetown Players. For a short time after
the war, Fred continued to work for Mark Cross, in New York and
England. But his old ailments, war injuries, shell shock, and dis-
agreements with Patrick Murphy about how to run the company
soon made work impossible, and he and Noel moved to France. He
died in 1924 at age thirty-nine, from complications of his ulcer or
his war wound. Six months earlier, the French government had
made him a Chevalier of the Legion of Honor for his wartime work.
He died without being reconciled to his father.

Just as Patrick Murphy subjected his sons to pressures that he
would not have dreamed of imposing on Esther, Anna Murphy made
demands on her daughter that she did not make on Fred or Gerald.
She had longed for a girl (another child, Doris, had died young) and
she was overjoyed when Esther was born. But her dissatisfaction
was soon profound and expressive. It was always clear to Esther that
she had failed her mother by being the wrong kind of girl, intellectual
and ungainly. It is a truth not universally acknowledged, moreover,
that a girl in possession of a mother whom she has disappointed often feels responsible for that parent. When her mother telephoned
"in a bad condition . . . so depressed," saying "she was always alone,"
Esther proposed leaving school to keep her company. When Fred
was dying, Esther stayed in New York with Anna Murphy, instead
of sailing to France to be with him, and she cancelled plans to go to
France later that summer to comfort Noel.

Esther's education was often a site of family conflict. Although
her father was a worldly, Irish-Catholic atheist, her mother was apparently a pious Protestant who nevertheless felt it her duty to raise
her children in her husband's tradition. Esther was first enrolled at
the Sacred Heart, on East Fifty-fourth Street, the international
school for the daughters of well-to-do Catholics, where Mercedes
de Acosta was one of her classmates. But when she tested the nuns
with the "paradox of the stone"—the series of questions about God's

Esther and her mother (Esther Murphy's photo album, AFP)

omnipotence that asks if it is possible for God to create a stone that
is too heavy for God to lift—her teachers deemed the line of inquiry
blasphemous, told her to sit in the corridor, and notified her parents.
Thirty years later, Esther wrote that while she could not imagine

> a more *completely relapsed* Catholic being than myself, I freely
> admit that my whole view of life and of men is coloured by
> the fundamental philosophy of Catholicism . . . Their atti-
> tude towards life and men, half pessimistic, half cynical, is
> the only thing in the Catholic religion to which I can still
> subscribe, since their theology seems to me an ingeniously
> concocted farrago of nonsense and their ritual (unless seen
> with the setting of a place like Chartres) a pretty tedious
> piece of trial mummery. The Roman Catholic Mass and Wag-
> ner's Parsifal are two things I do not intend to go to again.

Yet, as she noted, she was strongly marked by her Catholic education. Mary McCarthy, writing about her own—and writing when
she had become a close friend of Esther's—observed that "if you
are born and brought up a Catholic, you have absorbed a good deal
of world history and the history of ideas before you are twelve, and
it is like learning a language early, the effect is indelible." But, she
added,

> it is also a matter of feeling. To care for the quarrels of the
> past, to identify oneself passionately with a cause that be-
> came, politically speaking, a losing case with the birth of
> the modern world, is to experience a kind of straining
> against reality, a rebellious nonconformity that, again, is
> rare in America, where children are instructed in the vir-
> tues of the system they live under, as though history had
> achieved a happy ending in American civics.

This training also taught, "together with much that proved to be
practical, a conception of something prior to and beyond utility . . .
an idea of sheer wastefulness that is always shocking to non-
Catholics." Both that sense of wider engagement with the world—
"knowing the past of a foreign country in such detail that it becomes

one's own"—and the devotion to a beautiful uselessness were legacies that Esther carried.

Patrick Murphy responded to the nuns' punishment of his daughter by enrolling her in the Brearley School, founded in 1884 to give upper-class New York girls a secular education comparable to what was then available to their brothers. Esther was at Brearley from 1910 to 1913, made lifelong friends, and was in the company of young women who went on to Bryn Mawr. At the Swiss finishing school that Anna Murphy then insisted on, Esther was too studious to fit in and was devastated by the social aggression of the other girls. Back in New York during the Great War, at a school just outside the city, she participated in every social, athletic, and dramatic activity. Her father then offered to send her to college, but her experience in Switzerland and sense of obligation to her mother deterred her. Instead of enrolling her at Bryn Mawr, he arranged for her to follow the Harvard curriculum at home.

To Patrick Murphy, who was inclined to retreat to his study to read Macaulay's *History of England* and Pascal's *Pensées*, Esther's intellectual achievements were one of his own successes, helping to fulfill his idea of himself as something more than a triumphant entrepreneur. For Esther, immersion in history and politics was a way to be close to him, to find some purchase in the miasma of depression and fear of withdrawn favor that was the family climate. But reading was not an achievement for her; it was life. And it had as much to do with imagining a relationship to the women who had preceded her as it did with connecting to and escaping from her family.

TO FILL UP HER KNOWLEDGE
IN ALL DIRECTIONS

By age nineteen, Esther was already writing the kind of criticism that she pursued for the rest of her life: self-conscious, dense with historical allusion, attuned to the politics of gender and to conditions of publication. " 'The American Woman' whom Edith Wharton pursues with unusual malevolence under the guise of Undine Spragg and Lily Bart was also Mr. Phillips' pet preoccupation," she observed to Gerald of David Graham Phillips, after she "cast an astigmatic eye over the two volumes" of his popular novel *Susan Lenox: Her Fall and Rise*, in the spring of 1917. "He seriously believed that she ['the American woman'] was the cancer at the heart of modern civilization," she wrote. "Every one of his novels is on the theme and they all are written with the venom of a 16th century Calvinist Pamphleteer writing upon the Pope. It was in a kind of blind savage anger against our fictional tradition of the deification of woman and sentimental falsehood about life, that he wrote his story," she noted. "And yet the story itself is one of the most wildly unreal, fantastic and romantically false novels ever written. In vain did he try to destroy the Hearst Magazine conception of life: his effort was doomed to be published in a Hearst Magazine!" The interest in American popular culture, the surprising historical analogy, the fascination with genre, the delight in contradiction, the use of Wharton as a touchstone—all were characteristic of Esther's style.

She was working her ideas out in letters, not yet publishing. Her correspondence often exceeded the space allotted to it, covering twenty pages, then filling the margins of the final page. In 1916,

writing to Gerald, she noted, "I will limit myself to normal note-
paper this time and normal length." What followed was another mis-
sive that mingled history; contemporary politics (America's stalled
involvement in the Great War); sixteenth- and seventeenth-century
dogma, texts, and events; and scholarly and sexual desire—all of it
powered by quotation. "One somehow realizes," she wrote, "how
entirely blind all the course of human events is from a contemporary view point. It's all such a tangle that one feels that the sixteenth
century's attempts to probe the whole matter with horoscopes and
astrologers, was not . . . transparently ridiculous." In the midst of
this letter, Esther recorded what seems to be her first encounter
with Madame de Maintenon and quoted Maintenon's comment on
her rise to power as the intimate of Louis XIV:

> "Yesterday, I was nothing. Today, I am great . . . Poverty I
> grew up in; winter has frozen me; hunger I have tasted; con-
> tempt I have suffered; shame I have drunk of. Now I am a
> wretched being carved out of the stuff of which the great are
> made, for such was the pleasure of a king."
>
> Rather a testimony! The past is so satisfactory to me. And
> it grows more and more so. Ah! Why could I not have lived at
> Versailles under Louis XIV! It is my one poignant regret.
> I would so like to have been the Duchesse de Bourgogne,
> wife of the king's eldest grandson. I would willingly have
> endured the Duc de Bourgogne—"the Saint Anthony of the
> Bourbons"—and dying rather painfully of small pox at the
> age of 28. I really would have filled the position well. I would
> have put my heart into it and been far more discreet than
> the original Duchesse de Bourgogne. It seems too bad, I'm
> afraid no other destiny will be quite as suitable. Everything
> would have been so completely satisfactory. The Duc de
> Bourgogne and I would have got on admirably. Celibacy
> really stares me in the face as I have missed all my affinities
> by several centuries. Please let me know anything you hear
> about Fred that is in any way definite . . . I have not really
> been able to talk to you for ages because in my letters my
> style is always inflated. I do so want to.

In this extraordinary testimony of her own, Esther grappled
with her contemporary viewpoint and with the emotional and intellectual uses to which she could put the past, confronting the idea
of greatness and the constraints of her body. It was, in effect, an attempt to marry history. Here is her vigorous sense of herself as an
instrument of excess, a continuing affront to the normal. Here are
the wide range of reference and the habit of letting others speak for
her. Here she was, trading the present for past, her life for another's,
the facts for a personal fiction. Here was history as both an escape
and a dead end, since the choices she imagined were impossible (marrying someone who had lived almost two centuries earlier), mortal
(early death from smallpox), or self-abnegating (celibacy). Here she
was, too, fantasizing about proximity to Madame de Maintenon.
Here, despite the vivid fantasy and inflation, was a curiously banal-
ity ("no other destiny will be quite as suitable. Everything would
have been so completely satisfactory"), when she wrote about sexual and political union. And here was the mention of money, which
dogged her relationship with Gerald: "You are my nearest substi-
tute for the Duc de Bourgogne," she concluded, "and I long to see
you . . . Thank you so much for the [bank] deposit. It is *too* generous. My constitution is at last really quite robust."

But if history was a place for her imagination, it was also the
stuff of political analysis, six months before the United States de-
clared war on Germany, as President Wilson vacillated about the
role the country would play in the European conflict. Under Patrick
Murphy's influence, Esther grew up steeped in Democratic Party politics, while most of her peers—the gilded youth of the age—were
rich and Republican, the men landing on Wall Street, the women
landing husbands. Twenty years later, in the Hamptons for the weekend with the artist Betty Parsons, Esther ran into some of them,
"both men and women . . . pretty drunk and cursing Roosevelt and
praying that Landon would be elected. Very typical and pretty
dreary. They were all cordiality itself to me," she wrote, "made a terrific fuss over me, and accused me of 'deserting my old friends.' I
did not tell them how true it was and with what a light heart I had
done it." She quoted Browning's "A Toccata of Galuppi's": "Dust
and ashes, dead and done with, Venice spent what Venice earned /
The soul doubtless is immortal—where a soul can be discerned."

And she noted, "Hatred of Roosevelt is their theme song . . . It seems incredible that I once partly belonged to it [that milieu]." Partly: By the time she was eighteen, Esther knew that her politics was not theirs. Yet partly belonging made her privy to the hatred of Wilson and slanders against his second wife—Edith Galt Wilson, whom she knew and admired—that were part of the theme song of the Republican milieu in the teens and early twenties. It meant being invited to parties like the one on Long Island, a few months before the Armistice, at which a prominent lawyer told her that he had "incontrovertible" proof of Mrs. Wilson's treason, an assertion, she recalled, "accepted by everybody at the dinner table."

Partly belonging made it possible to understand history as a lesson about failure rather than triumph. In October 1920, after the Senate had twice defeated the Treaty of Versailles, *The New York Times* published Esther's letter to the editor comparing Wilson's work for the League of Nations to the stand of François Guizot, the nineteenth-century French statesman and historian, against a xenophobic foreign policy. Published as "The President's Appeal," her letter described how, as prime minister of France in the 1840s, Guizot had refused to be pushed to war with England. Like Wilson, Guizot had been accused by opponents "of seeking to sacrifice the ind[e]pendence of his country to foreign domination." Wilson's support of the League of Nations, she wrote, his "greatest contribution to the welfare of his own country and the world," was subjecting him similarly "to the most willful distortion and misinterpretation which partisanship or personal spite could dictate." But even if his opponents prevailed, "posterity will judge him not by what he failed to achieve but by the end to which he aspired." The next month, in November 1920, Esther voted in her first presidential election—the first in which American women could participate—for the losing Democratic ticket of James M. Cox and Franklin D. Roosevelt, against Warren G. Harding and his vision of a return to "normalcy." "Our supreme task is the resumption of our onward, normal way," Harding said in his inaugural address. Nothing was more inimical to Esther's way of thinking than Harding's incoherently progressive nostalgia. Twenty years later, campaigning for FDR, she referred to Harding's coinage of "normalcy" as his invention of "a nonexistent word for a nonexistent situation."

In her early twenties, she was still living alone with her mother much of the time, in Manhattan during the year and enduring "rather monotonous sojourn[s]" on Long Island during the summer. Unease had supplanted her childhood confidence: She knew that what had been charming to some in a child—her intellect and articulateness— was bizarre in a woman of marriageable age. But the unorthodox alliances of two of her Park Avenue friends soon gave her the kind of companionship she had otherwise known mostly with her father. In the spring of 1921 her parents allowed her to sail to Europe unchaperoned with a friend from Brearley, Margaret Grosvenor Hutchins, whose father was a banker and chairman of the New York, New Haven and Hartford Railroad. In London they stayed with Fred and Noel. In Paris they saw "nothing but other Americans." Back home Hutchins pursued the poet John Peale Bishop, Princeton-educated but middle-class and from the South. At the Bishops' wedding, their friend Alice (Amanda) Hall met the young critic Gilbert Seldes, who was Jewish and had grown up on a utopian farming community in New Jersey. Esther met Edmund Wilson, Bishop's college friend. She did not fall in love, but it was, she wrote him, "one of the best things that have ever happened to me." Over the next year, Wilson found himself "more and more devoted" to her. Their shared absorption in ideas, mutual admiration, and compatible lack of social skills made it a lasting and "unclouded" friendship.

She towered over him—he was just over five feet six inches— but as interlocutors they were a perfect fit. In the early 1920s he was working for *Vanity Fair* and writing for *The New Republic*. She struggled with a "'Victorian' article" for *The New Republic*, an assignment he had helped her get. This essay seems never to have been published, but she sent Wilson essay-length letters about her reading and his writing, long reports to someone who cared about books as much as she did. The quality she told him she appreciated in Shaw's preface to *St. Joan*—"the sheer intellectual passion which pervades the whole thing"—saturated her correspondence, which continued to be dense with citation. She urged him to be her guest in Southampton for a weekend: "We could discuss an infinitude of subjects and make 'many philosophical researches of every descrip-

Esther, full-length, during a "monotonous sojourn" in Southampton, 1923 (Esther Murphy's photo album, AFP)

tion of the advantage of human nature at large,—' as Lady Hester
Stanhope told the Duke of Wellington she had done." Thanking
him for lunch, she quoted *Love's Labour's Lost*: "the only complaint
that I can make is that . . . you listen to me with so much patience,
that I 'draw out the thread of my verbosity finer [than] the staple of
my argument,'—and talk instead of listening to you as much as I
should like to." This verbosity was shared: A colleague described
Wilson holding forth didactically, sometimes pausing in such a way
that you would think it an invitation to respond, then breaking
"ruthlessly in at the exact spot where he had left off." Esther was
one of the few people whose compulsive talking matched his and to
whom he listened. There were times, Wilson said, when she made it
hard for even him to get a word in edgewise.

In the 1950s, they met in Paris after an absence of several years.
"We fell on each other's neck," he wrote in his diary.

> It was wonderful to see her . . . Her explanations of the U.S.
> to the French ladies of her circle have long been a specialty
> of hers, and she and I performed admirably together, upset-
> ting the Europeans' preconceptions and astonishing them
> at every turn. I explained that the South had been an occu-
> pied country for ten years after the Civil War—thirteen,
> Esther corrected—and had never been reconciled to the
> Union . . . But the conversation may have been more enjoy-
> able for us than it was for the people we were talking at, for
> they very soon withdrew.

She also explained to him that the rue Gît-le-Coeur, which she
called "'the most beautiful street name in Paris,' commemorated
the grave, not of Louis XIV's mistress, as had once been supposed,
but merely of his favorite chef." On another visit to Paris, Wilson
contrasted the discreet "quietness and flatness and . . . conversational rhythm" he had fallen into recently in England with the mark-
edly American way that Esther and he were "soon walking up and
down the room and interrupting and shouting at one another."
Thinking back over her life, he was sensitive to how she had been

Edmund Wilson, 1922, photographed by Nickolas Muray (General Collection, Beinecke Rare Book and
Manuscript Library, Yale University, courtesy Estate of Edmund Wilson)

shaped by "her gawky girlhood, her dubious social position as an Irish girl in New York," and he wrote that he felt with her "the special characteristics of our race of the twenties: habit of leisure and at least enough money . . . freedom to travel and read, to indulge and exhaust curiosities, completely uninhibited talks, resistance to challenge of the right to play, to the idea of growing old, settling down to a steady maturity." It was a clear statement of how they had differed from their parents' generation. After one of these reunions in the 1950s, Esther was filled with affection for him, but amused by his new embrace of his own history: "I had always known that he was a Protestant—but he apparently had not and the discovery gives him the greatest pleasure. It is easy to see that he is descended from Cotton Mather and a long line of Protestant Divines."

In the 1920s, uninhibited talks about—or "at one another" about—literature and history superseded more intimate reflections. Esther wrote to Wilson about Hume, Nietzsche, Saint-Simon, and Metternich. She praised his admiring essay on H. L. Mencken, published in *The New Republic*, but argued that "the Philistines are flogged and the elect feasted by Mr. Mencken with no suspicion of the difficulty of distinguishing between them." Her embrace of irony was tempered by an expansive humanism, and she found herself increasingly drawn to the "redeemers of mankind . . . and away from the pure cynics who, particularly in their 18th century incarnation, used to delight me." The nineteenth-century philosopher Auguste Comte was one such figure, and she approached him with a biographer's eye:

> Perhaps he interests me more as a man than as a philosopher. He was a strange being . . . and he ended up by proclaiming a new religion of which he was the pontiff and his dead mistress, Clothilde de Vaux the tutelary divinity. (It was at this stage that George Eliot withdrew her adherence!) . . . His life has that something at once pathetic and impressive that clings about the men who believed they had found the faith in which humanity stands in need.

But at a time when American history and literature were not widely seen as worthy of serious critical thought, Esther also focused on America. In her generation of critics, Wilson and Gilbert

Seldes, who also became a close friend, championed what they saw as genuinely American forms of expression, paying attention to popular culture as well as to literature. Esther's instincts were of a piece with their work, with at least one difference: the feminism, although she did not use the word, that informed her thinking. Although she may not have finished the "Victorian" essay, she began writing occasionally for the *New York Tribune*, including shrewd reviews of Jane Austen's posthumously published juvenilia and of her final, uncompleted novel, *The Watsons*. Austen's dissections of character and social circumstance, like Wharton's, were a touchstone for Esther, who reread her novels all her life. She called Austen "among the greatest writers of the world" and "probably the keenest satirist and the most relentless opponent of the romantic school in all English literature." She also noted the "extraordinary frankness" with which Austen treated the marriage market. Her "recognition of the fact that matrimony was the only profession that a well-bred woman could enter," Esther wrote, "was always complete. And she was quite aware that it frequently presented itself in the shape of a painful necessity rather than as a matter of choice."

With an article Wilson was writing on Nathaniel Hawthorne in mind, she sent him an unpublished excerpt from Hawthorne's journal and her exegesis of it. Both concern Hawthorne's "obsession" with Margaret Fuller. Writing about Fuller, Esther was describing a frenetically scholarly American woman of letters and politics— another progenitor. Writing about Hawthorne, she was criticizing misreadings of such women's lives.

Hawthorne's animosity toward M. Fuller is most interesting to me. She appears to have disturbed him almost more than anyone he ever met. I've always thought it was due, not to any personal antagonism, for Margaret always appears to have tried to conciliate him; as to the fact that Margaret Fuller symbolized to Hawthorne, all the things he was afraid of and yet had obscure leanings to. I think Hawthorne had that malady, so characteristic of all the luminaries of the New England movement:—he was dreadfully afraid of life. Margaret Fuller was not, in fact she had a hunger and a capacity for living, unexampled in a woman of her day and her position.

Hawthorne's morbid fear of coming to grips with existence, and his hatred of the woman who had done so, are clearly displayed in the passages concerning Margaret's marriage being the result of Margaret's reprehensible desire "to try all things and fill up her knowledge in all directions." I think, (though it may seem a very obviously Freudian attempt at analysis,) that Hawthorne's fanatical preoccupation with ethical problems, his insistence on the ultimate judgment being a moral one, was due to the fact that all his life he was torn between his theories of conduct and his smothered but not extinct desires for things very incompatible with those theories. The bitter outcry against "Raphael's sensuality" which his son reports he gave vent to, when he was in Italy, (he was so unpleasantly affected by Raphael's treatment of the female anatomy that it almost overshadowed his trip) is on a par with his distrust of Margaret Fuller and her way of life. Both she and Raphael's women, were in different ways, a challenge to the part of his own nature, that he was always on guard against. The man was an artist and had a sense of beauty—when all is said and done, and in another age and milieu from 19th century New England might have been other than he was . . . I know this thing is not quite what you want for your "New Englander Abroad" theme. But it did seem to me to have a bearing on it and to be (at least so it struck me) a most astonishing document. The business about Margaret not leaving any "deep witness of her integrity and purity" is very precious. The judgment of her generation on her in short, was that she was not a nice woman or she would not have been quite as she was. I've always thought that Margaret's shrinking from facing that verdict with all its implications, was perhaps what made her so reluctant to desert a sinking ship in favour of her native land. The general, vague condemnation about her not being "a nice woman" is so curiously like the comments I hear all the time on Edith Wharton, from the women who were her contemporaries.

A childhood prodigy and a whirlwind of intellect whose so-called peculiar appearance and manner were remarked on as much as her learning; a writer, translator, journalist, editor, and feminist; a friend and colleague of Emerson and other "luminaries of the New England movement" in the 1830s and '40s; and a woman whose writings, her friends said, never measured up to her talk—Fuller was a woman Esther could appraise herself against and perhaps model herself on. Fuller's "Conversations," the structured, semipublic lecture-discussions she conducted in Boston to give women a place to debate the issues of the day, were a version of the sort of public discourse that Esther favored. When Fuller moved from the claustrophobia of Boston to New York, she went to work for Horace Greeley on the *New York Tribune*, becoming the first full-time book reviewer in American journalism. (Esther began reviewing for the *Tribune* in September 1922, the same month she wrote this letter to Wilson.) Fuller then reported for the *Tribune* in England and Italy, supported Giuseppe Mazzini's work for Italian unification, and had a child with an ally of his. She died on her return to New York when her ship ran aground and sank off Long Island.

Esther argued that both Fuller and Wharton encountered resistance that had nothing and everything to do with their work. "The comments I hear all the time on Edith Wharton" had been and were a burden for these women, as they were for an aspiring writer like Esther. With her half-joking suggestion that Fuller stayed on a sinking ship because American moralizing about women's sexuality was so difficult and endless, Esther turned Fuller's drowning from an accident into a judgment on such judgments. Which is to say that, reading Hawthorne's journal, Esther posited the past not as a difference to be repudiated but as a moment—at once distant and almost within living memory—that resonated in the present. And she saw failure as an attribute not of Fuller's and Wharton's persons or writing but of their critics.

Something like this view of American literature and sexual politics existed in the United States in the early 1920s, but it is now hardly remembered. Dorothy Parker, a friend of Esther's, is probably the only critic of her generation whose work is generally known, or at least known of, today. But she is seen more as a poet and fiction writer than a critic, and more as a wit than a writer. Katherine Anne Porter, reviewing regularly for the *Herald Tribune* and *The New Republic* in the 1920s, often focused on women's rights, but this interesting work is now virtually unread. Still, most critics of Esther's time—whether writing about aesthetics or politics, whether modernist, feminist, or both—proposed radical breaks with the past, while Esther posited affinities across half a century for Fuller and the woman she called "the Great and Only Mrs. Wharton."

That her view of these two writers was connected to her thinking about biography is clear from another letter to Wilson, also from 1922. To mark their shared appreciation of Wharton, Esther sent him a first edition of Wharton's 1901 short story "The Angel at the Grave." "I'm going to let 'The Angel at the Grave' speak for me," she wrote. This was all she wrote. But the story speaks for her. She speaks through it. Sending it to Wilson was a kind of massive act of citation.

"The Angel at the Grave" is a meditation on portraiture, reputation, and the gender of intellectual life in mid-nineteenth-century America. Wharton's protagonist grows up in the shadow of her philosopher grandfather's fame to become the keeper of his flame— "the custodian of th[e] historic dwelling" outside of Boston that was Orestes Anson's home—and his biographer. Toiling away on this book for years, Paulina gains "prominence as the chief 'authority' on the great man." She also, Wharton says, becomes her own biographer: "All her youth, all her dreams, all her renunciations lay in that neat bundle [her manuscript] on her knee. It was not so much her grandfather's life as her own that she had written." But the great work on the great man, when Paulina finally completes it, is no longer of interest—the man himself is no longer of interest—and her publisher rejects the book. Anson's own metaphysics and her biography, Wharton writes, were nothing but disuse, decay, death: "It was the sense of wasted labor that oppressed her . . . There was a dreary parallel between her grandfather's fruitless toil and her own unprofitable sacrifice. Each in turn had kept vigil by a corpse."

After the initial shock of rejection, Paulina tries to understand how she could have missed the signs of his diminishing reputation. "She passed from the heights on which he had been grouped with the sages of his day to the lower level where he had come to be 'the friend of Emerson,' 'the correspondent of Hawthorne,' or (later

Edith Wharton in Esther's photo album, later labeled by Chester Arthur (Esther Murphy's photo album, AFP)

Esther's ANIMA
Edith Wharton

still) 'the Dr. Anson' mentioned in their letters." Years go by. Then one day she is surprised by a visitor who is convinced of her grandfather's importance, an idea she has long since abandoned. The young man is interested in Orestes Anson not as a philosopher, however, but as a pioneering researcher in the natural sciences. Evolutionary biology has had nothing to do with Paulina's idea of her ancestor, but the story ends on a hopeful note as she unearths a document that supports her visitor's theory. She agrees to help him with his work, and is herself restored in some way. When he leaves, she "looked as though youth had touched her on the lips."

With Fuller, Esther had disentangled the writer from Hawthorne's and Emerson's views of her. With "The Angel at the Grave," she was giving Wilson an Edith Wharton whose stories about literary production, identification, and inheritance were equal to any of Henry James's work on these themes. As the title, with its play on "the angel in the house"—the nineteenth-century ideal of domestic womanhood—suggests, this is a story about women's intellectual work that both echoes and critiques that ideal of self-abnegating service, whether to the needs of a husband and family or to a laudatory text about a significant male progenitor. Writing about the bitterness of literary guardianship and the elusiveness of reputation, Wharton is of course thinking about different approaches to writing a life—and perhaps about the terror of living one's own. Paulina's aunts, Orestes Anson's daughters, are the archivists of his daily life and his fans. When pilgrims arrived at the "historic dwelling," these women pointed to his desk and dispensed facts about "what brand of tea he drank, and whether he took off his boots in the hall." But if Wharton is scathing about their devotion—"as pious scavengers of his wastepaper basket, the Misses Anson were unexcelled"—she is also skeptical about Anson's achievement and its commemoration. Paulina's years of dedication are a folly in which the "rock of her grand-father's celebrity" turns out to be something less than durable. "'It ruined my life!'" Paulina tells the young writer; "'I gave up everything,' she went on wildly, 'to keep *him* alive.'" Her encounter with this researcher is apparently a happy outcome, a turn of the screw in which the valuable, become worthless, regains value—albeit for reasons other than those that first established its importance.

Although it is not the case that Esther "gave up everything" for any of her biographical subjects, the ways that she was exceptional had everything to do with a similar readerly devotion. And her life and work, like Wharton's story and the genre of biography itself, continually beg the question of reputation. Djuna Barnes's barb notwithstanding, it was not "great Women in History" who caught Esther's imagination but women whose reputations were not at all secure. Or perhaps it makes more sense to say that in Esther's lifetime a biography of a "great woman" who was not a religious figure was necessarily a book about a woman whose reputation was not secure. Esther's first subject, Lady Blessington, rose from an impoverished Irish girlhood to a series of dubious liaisons with powerful Englishmen, socially advantageous marriage, and friendship with Lord Byron. She spent much of her life in a threesome with her husband and another man; weathered scandal and was shunned by society, but patronized by writers; wrote a book about Byron; and was the hostess of the most intellectual literary salon of mid-Victorian England. Although Esther referred to her in a 1922 letter to Wilson as "a dull enough person, I think. Really, a thoroughgoing mediocrity, save for her extraordinary personal beauty," she must have become intrigued, because in April 1928 the publisher Payson and Clarke announced " 'The Life of Lady Blessington,' by Esther Murphy" as "scheduled for future publication." Reading and writing about Madame de Pompadour and then about Madame de Maintenon, as Esther did for the second half of her life, she was focused on women whose status at the French court was uncertain, who were maligned by contemporaries and historians, and for whom judgments about their sexual conduct had long been part of even the scholarly work on their lives.

In "The Angel at the Grave," failure is overdetermined. There is Orestes Anson's early failure and the failure of perception about that work ("the specialists of the day jeered at him"). Paulina's biographical failure is steeped in a "sense of wasted labor" and "fruitless toil." Her inability to reconcile the two parts of Anson's career ("after a hurried perusal she had averted her thoughts from the [scientific] episode as from a revelation of failure"), Wharton suggests, was one reason her biography failed. Her guardianship was a success, however, because she kept the evidence of that episode from the flames. Her aunts had "said it was of no use," she tells the young man, "—that he'd always meant to destroy the whole edition and that I ought to respect his wishes. But . . . I wanted him to feel that I was always here, ready to listen, even when others hadn't thought it worth while." In this romantic view of biography, keeping vigil by a corpse is hardly "of no use." "Don't you see that it's your love that has kept him alive?" says the researcher.

Wharton is also thinking about the temporality of failure in this story—about what it means to make the right judgment at the wrong time, about the chasms in our ability to understand the present. She is thinking about discontinuity and anachronism, about misapprehension and missed opportunities, about occupying the wrong time in history, and about the possibility of rectifying the mistakes of the past—about how history itself fails and might yet be retrieved and revised. Everything that precedes the story's happy ending suggests that the final rescue, too, is provisional; that while Paulina may be restored in some way, assessments of Anson's work could change again; that there is no triumph over failure.

There was no way to know in 1922 that Esther Murphy, like Orestes Anson and Margaret Fuller—one of whose twentieth-century biographers described her as having been "demoted from a position of importance in her own right to one in which her only importance was in the company she kept"—would become known after her death chiefly as adjunct to others: the sister of Gerald Murphy, the friend of Edmund Wilson and Scott Fitzgerald. Nor was it possible to know then that Esther would spend her life steeped in someone else's, becoming prominent as the chief authority on Madame de Maintenon. When she read the biographies of contemporaries whom she outlived, Esther was interested in the problems of reappraisal, and of proximity or distance, temporal and personal, that marked such work, its writers, and its readers. She believed that some biographies could be written and read only at certain times, not because of censorship or some progress toward openness, but because of what it was possible to understand when. When critical interest in Fitzgerald resumed in 1951—ten years after his death and following a longer period of neglect and scorn—with the publication of Arthur Mizener's biography, *The Far Side of Paradise*, she wrote to Wilson, "I did not care for the biography of Scott but

I think the author did the best he could and tried to avoid being either sensational or vulgar. But it seems to me that writing a life of Scott at this time would be incredibly difficult. What a strange creature he was and Zelda too, for that matter, to anyone who knew them the book could never be convincing or satisfactory." Esther's interest in biography was not in making the forgotten or the trivialized great, but in making them live again, fail again. Visiting the past was not a bid to turn disaster into success, but a gesture of transmission. Her point was that history—stuff, story, memory, metaphor—links the elusive past to the equally elusive present. Lost and found and lost again, too far away and too close, groping its way forward to causes and backward to effects.

BACHELOR HEIRESS

The relentless party of the 1920s, in which Esther and Scott Fitzgerald were both strange creatures, ubiquitous and unavoidable, was inseparable from the great failure of social control that was Prohibition. When Prohibition became law, in January 1920, alcohol went underground—there were between thirty thousand and a hundred thousand speakeasies in New York City by 1925—and consumption increased dramatically. Drinking to excess was now indissoluble from social life, and the high cost of liquor made access to it a status symbol.

For a long time, Esther did not seem to suffer from hard drinking. In Europe on their own in 1921, away from all prohibitions, she and Margaret Hutchins had "decided to be daring enough to order liquor," but thought it "more decent and ladylike to confine themselves to Cointreau, of which they drank a whole bottle." At a house party for Fitzgerald's birthday several years later—Gilbert and Amanda Seldes were also there—"preliminary drinks" were followed by "pre-dinner drinks," and dinner, Edmund Wilson wrote, meant "floating divinely on good wine and gay conversation." Although "the aftermath of a Fitzgerald evening was notoriously a painful experience," Esther was the only person (other than Thornton Wilder, who was not drinking) not affected by the rigorous and desperate festivities. Decades of heavy drinking, however, were ruinous to her health and that of her friends: Wilson, Fitzgerald, John Peale Bishop, Dorothy Parker, Dawn Powell, to mention only a few. It is hard to think of an American writer of the first half of the century, iconic or less known, whose life was not bound up with alcohol.

Esther spent Christmas 1923 with Scott and Zelda Fitzgerald on

Long Island, along with the Seldeses, John Dos Passos, and Edmund Wilson. (A few months later, when the Fitzgeralds sailed for France, Esther gave them an introduction to Gerald and Sara Murphy. The complicated relationship between the couples has been well documented.) She was in the midst of all that literary machismo, not one of the wives, on the verge of being one of the writers. Their expectations for what she—for what they all—would accomplish were high, but the party never stopped. She was also in an element in which she was finally appreciated, one of many extravagant human oddities, men and women, observing and performing for one another, attracting and repelling others, as she did at one party at which the hostess "would occasionally bring up a strange gentleman or a beautiful blonde and present them, but they would soon disappear, frightened away by the incomparable but intolerant onslaught of Esther Murphy's eloquence." At an all-night party in her honor she "moved absent-mindedly about in a white dress trimmed with sequins," then went out to breakfast at dawn. In costume for the Beaux Arts Ball, she was "magnificent as the Abbess of a convent." She was often at the Algonquin hotel, where there was a waiter who said that he had learned to speak English by listening to her. She might stay home one evening, but only because she had been out every night the week before until five in the morning.

She was also part of the perpetual revels at the two town houses on East Nineteenth Street that the painter and muralist Robert Chanler had combined and named the House of Fantasy. Chanler's work was shown at the Julien Levy Gallery, the Armory Show of 1913, and the Hermitage; he painted Mercedes de Acosta, Carl Van Vechten, Jean Cocteau, Alfred Lunt, and others, and two portraits of Esther. A big man and a huge personality, he was emotional, generous, and violent. He would pound his fists on the table and bellow at his guests, and his parties went on for days, until he threw people out. One night, when he was Esther's guest, he "stormed and raged . . . while the Murphy servants looked on frightened to death." Esther called him that "indomitable, impetuous intransigent being" and she loved him deeply. "His friendship meant so much to me," she wrote when he died, in 1930. Two decades later she wrote, "Next to Muriel he was the most amazing human being I have ever known."

Muriel was Muriel Draper, another character of great kindness and eccentricity. Salonnière, supporter of young talent, "possessed of an almost cosmic gift of enthusiasm," she was Esther's most intimate friend from the mid-1920s through the '30s. She came from an old Massachusetts family, had married the singer Paul Draper, and in the first years of the century lived in Florence and London, where she presided over a salon that attracted Arthur Rubinstein, Pablo Casals, John Singer Sargent, and Henry James. She returned to the United States in 1915, divorced the alcoholic and gambling Draper, and supported herself and their two sons by working as an interior decorator, lecturer, and writer. With Carl Van Vechten, she was one of the white promoters of the Harlem Renaissance, and she was famous for orgiastic parties where anything went and for her "outrageous remarks and outrageous hats." "It was an imitation French salon, indiscriminate, but the nearest thing we had to that," recalled the photographer Walker Evans, who described Draper as "the great mother of all artists." In the 1920s, she was enmeshed with the guru Gurdjieff; by the mid-1930s, her enthusiasm had shifted to Soviet communism, where it remained for the rest of her life. ("Muriel Draper Dies; Organizer of Red Groups," ran the headline of an obituary in 1952, at the height of anticommunist hysteria.) For Esther, Draper's support was indispensable; she responded to Draper's excesses with her own effusiveness. "You were superb and magnificent last night as indeed you always are," Esther wrote early in their friendship; "what a particular and fortunate dispensation I think it is that I happen to be your contemporary."

Esther's own entertaining was also relentless. She had a string of soirées at home—the huge Park Avenue apartment—with guests to dinner every night, in the spring of 1927. Her father was in Bermuda; Anna Murphy sat by and watched it all. Scott and Zelda Fitzgerald, the composer and music critic Teddy Chanler (Margaret Chanler's son and Robert Chanler's nephew), and the young musician and writer Max Ewing, another protégé of Draper's, came to dinner, after which they all adjourned to Robert Chanler's and then to Teddy's. A big crowd came to tea one Sunday afternoon, and Robert Chanler "stood up & looked them all over & cried 'What a

Muriel Draper, "possessed of an almost cosmic gift of enthusiasm," photographed by Carl Van Vechten, n.d. (Muriel Draper Papers, Yale Collection of American Literature, Beinecke Rare Book and Manuscript Library, Yale University, courtesy Estate of Carl Van Vechten)

gang! What a gang!'" There was a dinner for the writer and translator Lewis Galantière; the journalist Louise Bryant, author of *Six Red
Months in Russia* and formerly married to John Reed; and the diplomat William Bullitt, Bryant's husband (he had been Woodrow
Wilson's envoy to the Paris Peace Conference and later was FDR's
ambassador to Russia and to France). Esther also entertained at
Ewing's apartment, using it to help her friend Emily Vanderbilt celebrate her divorce. Dozens attended (all of the women dressed in
black or white, except for one "in pink spangles, and Mercedes de
Acosta who wore red velvet trimmed with gold flowers"), stayed till
4:00 a.m., then went up to Harlem to dance.

Sometime in the mid-1920s, Esther and Teddy Chanler became
engaged, or flirted seriously with the idea. He was several years
younger than she, wealthy, committed to his music. He saw her
"wonderful vitality and unceasing activity of mind," but worried
that she was "a rather tormented dynamic sort of person, who
doesn't expect to live to be more than forty." He also watched her
struggle to focus her energy and saw how she met intimacy with
scholarly abstraction and quotation. At one point in their pas de
deux, he wrote:

> I'm so anxious to see you again that I don't really care what
> happens when we do meet. Will you repel my attempts at
> polite conversation with baleful looks and long passages
> from Jeremy Taylor [the seventeenth-century English theo-
> logian]? Will I be morose and unresponsive and abruptly
> leave you after ten minutes, giving you no further sign of
> life for a month or two? Anything may happen, but I don't
> really give a damn. May I come and spend next week-end
> with you?

"My boy friend had to postpone his visit," Esther wrote to Muriel
Draper. "I am at once keenly disappointed and obscurely but genuinely relieved to have any climax in our relations averted for a little
while longer.—So you see even our most sincere desires are paradoxical." The paradox of their desires was not only that Esther lived
at a pitch that Chanler could not, and that he, like those who followed him in her life, believed powerfully in her, but feared that her

intense but undisciplined work ethic might hurt his own. It was also that both of them more or less preferred their own sex. Perhaps this is what he was referring to when he wrote, "I have really tried to be honest with you . . . and it's the first time in my life I've ever done that with anyone without feeling betrayed afterwards . . . It's very difficult." They eventually disengaged themselves amicably— not "a very usual occurrence," he observed.

Esther had lived her whole life knowing that she was different, but there is no record of when her desire for other women became clear to her. By the mid-1920s, however, she was a visible presence in sapphic New York and Paris. Her close friends included the young journalists Janet Flanner and Solita Solano, who had settled in Paris in 1922; Katharine Cornell, an old friend of Noel Murphy's and a rising star on Broadway; Peggy Fears, a Ziegfeld Follies girl turned theater producer (and later Fire Island entrepreneur); the artist and future gallery owner Betty Parsons; and the heiress Alice De Lamar, whom Esther had known since they were children and who was now one of the richest women in the world. The socialite Hope Williams, a Brearley School friend who was beginning her career on Broadway, and Mercedes de Acosta, with whom Williams had an affair, were also part of this network of friends and lovers. In New York, after an evening of dissipated tourism in Harlem nightclubs, Esther would pass out at the home of Olivia Wyndham and her girlfriend, the actress Edna Thomas. Wyndham was the rebellious daughter of an upper-class English family. One of the Bright Young Things in London earlier in the decade, she had also worked as a photographer. She had fallen in love with Edna Thomas when the latter performed in London with the Blackbirds, the African American revue, then moved to New York to live with her.

Many of these women traveled regularly between New York, London, and Paris. Esther herself was perpetually sailing to France during the 1920s, and there was always an added flurry of parties on her departure and return. On "the long-roofed steamship piers," Fitzgerald writes in Tender Is the Night, "one is in a country that is no longer here and not yet there . . . One hurries through, even though there's time; the past, the continent, is behind; the future is the glowing mouth in the side of the ship." For Esther, as for many Americans, France and the future also meant sexual freedom. She often stayed at Alice De Lamar's Paris apartment (which Gerald and Sara had rented but were no longer occupying, having relocated to the South of France), and she spent time with Flanner and Solano, with Noel, and with other expatriates, including Gertrude Stein—for whom she had "long felt" a "profound admiration"—and Alice B. Toklas. But for several years much of the draw of Paris was Natalie Barney, the lesbian poet and salonnière.

Patrick Murphy may have been aware of this part of Esther's life, but there is no evidence that he ever tried to impose his will on her. Gerald, however, "upbraid[ed]" her for being one of the "un-attached young women who hob-nob with Natalie Barney." He had been her "outlet for sensibility" in her teens, but as she moved into the world on her own, her behavior became incompatible with his ideas about refined living, his need to protect himself solidified, and their long estrangement began. Gerald and Sara continued to distance themselves from Esther as the years went on, and she went virtually unmentioned in their family. Edmund Wilson observed that she "could not be accommodated to the little opalescent sphere in which they maintained themselves." Early on Gerald saw himself as her protector, especially after Fred's death and given their father's frequent absences. But worrying about Esther's association with Natalie Barney, he was also protecting himself. "Her behavior was a rebuke," observes his biographer, to a man who described his life as "a process of concealment of the personal realities."

When Natalie Barney was fifteen years old, she seduced her gov-erness—or so Esther told friends. She and the governess were then sent to Paris by her father, an Ohio railroad magnate, to get them out of the way of scandal. Instead, France allowed Barney's sexual and literary ambitions to flourish. When she printed a book of poems celebrating lesbian love, her father attempted to buy up every copy, but on his death she still inherited the equivalent of a billion dollars, which left her free to do what she pleased for the rest of her long life. She became known for her devotion to her libido, for her romantic ideas about literature, and for the salon she presided over on Friday afternoons at her home on the rue Jacob in the Sixth Arrondisse-ment. Her guests constituted a roll call of early-twentieth-century American and European cultural accomplishment. The painter Ro-maine Brooks, a longtime lover, mostly absented herself from the talk, readings, and music in the house and garden, but Colette, Stein and Toklas, Virgil Thomson, Ford Madox Ford, French academician Remy de Goncourt, and many others patronized these happenings. Ezra Pound was "full of homage." He brought William Carlos Williams, who called Barney "extremely gracious and no fool to be sure." Noel Murphy was another regular guest.

To other contemporaries, Barney was almost monstrous. Her friend Bettina Bergery said that "her strongest desire was to dominate." Sybille Bedford described her as "entirely selfish," with "no moral compass." In the last thirty years, she has been claimed as a model of sexual liberation and a catalyst for modernism. Esther saw her as a political throwback and a figure of fun whose conservatism and willful ignorance made her resemble a noxious nineteenth-century American industrialist and political operator. Barney's "vegetable-placid" manner, Esther wrote to Muriel Draper, was a "Mark Hanna certainty that nothing important happens really." Barney's self-serious, Lesbos-leaning literary affectations fed Esther's sense of the ridiculous—as did the cult Barney fostered around Renée Vivien, a poet and former lover who had died young. But Barney occupied a huge place in Esther's imagination and was inevitably a provocative literary subject for her. "Above all *don't* let the old Barney get any inkling that you intend to write about her," Teddy Chanler cautioned. "Don't let her see that lean and hungry look of the born novelist."

"Natalie Barney lay on her back in her bed clad only in a silk shirt and a rather dingy pink[?] kimono," began one of Esther's sketches.

It was about half past three on a hot afternoon towards the end of June and Miss Barney was enjoying a meal which it was rather hard to define since she was in the habit of eating it between her luncheon and her tea, but which consisted of cold ham, hard boiled eggs, pickles, chocolate éclairs and iced beer. As she ate Alice Robinson read aloud to her from a book entitled "Classical Erotology"—a modern compendium of ancient vices, containing some very curious footnotes in Latin, extracts from the original documents upon which the work was based, which it was Alice's duty to render into English for the benefit of Miss Barney whose many attainments did not include a knowledge of the dead languages . . . She had just paused after translating a note which gave a comprehensive account of the rather erratic sexual indulgences of a gentleman of the Roman decadence to observe, "there was a tribe in Paraguay where they did that."

"In Paraguay, you say," said Miss Barney taking a pickle from the tray beside her bed.

Esther enclosed this meandering satire—a twentieth-century tale of sexual manners composed in a Jane Austen mode—with a letter to Draper in 1926. In another letter to Draper she sent a parody of Barney's "Fridays," in which she quoted the salonnière giving a long, falsely modest peroration on the blessed memory of Renée Vivien that inspired Romaine Brooks to rush from the room and vomit "copiously" in the hall. Djuna Barnes's *Ladies Almanack* was a privately printed slap at Barney and her appetites, written in a vigorous, ambiguous combination of historical and modern prose, mixing neologism and farce. Esther's fascinated but biting stories predate Barnes's book by two years.

Yet Barney's blond allure and conviction about her own appeal were everything that Esther was not, and for two years Esther was also frantically in love. "We talked again for five solid hours about Miss Barney," wrote Max Ewing in March 1927. "The conversation becomes mad but always fascinating . . . After an hour or so the thought of Miss Barney sends her into an absolute extase like nothing on earth." Esther was crazy about Barney—"and by crazy I mean really almost *crazy*," Ewing noted; "Muriel is afraid that if it keeps going on like this Esther may eventually become really cuckoo." Esther was in love, perhaps for the first time in her life, but with someone who would never reciprocate: Although Barney was promiscuous to a fault, constantly juggling lovers, Esther was unattractive, too obviously smitten, and intelligent in a way that bored Barney and made her uncomfortable. " 'She is not for us!' " declares Dame Musset of Bounding Bess (Esther), in the *Ladies Almanack*, "and so saying, she cracked her Whip against her Boot, turning toward a Pasty Shop hard by."

In June 1927, however, Esther telegrammed Muriel Draper from France: "ON WAY TO CAPRICE," and that summer she accompanied

Barney to her villa at Santa Margherita, near Genoa. They met up with Max Ewing and drove—or were driven, in Barney's huge Packard—around northern Italy. When Romaine Brooks joined them, they proceeded with Barney and Brooks in one car and the lesser mortals in another, all of them stopping where and when Barney pleased. "Miss Barney directs this trip like a Roman general," wrote Ewing, "and Esther keeps maintaining that Napoleon would never have lost Waterloo if he had had Miss Barney to organize his troops." Dorothy Wilde, Oscar's witty niece and one of Barney's lovers, wrote to her, "Fancy Esther being with you . . . Does she sleep in my bed? I don't like that. Have you made listless love to her—out of charitable curiosity? *Tell* me if you have." Wilde's biographer says that "Natalie ended up in bed with the 'brilliant, didactic' Esther Murphy," but if she did, it was not for long. Years later Esther referred to her "strange stay with Natalie Barney" that summer. But she returned to Paris the following spring "in a state of frenzy," because she was again on her way to see Barney.

The appearance in New York of the young English writer and politician John Strachey interrupted her obsession. Evelyn John St. Loe Strachey was Eton- and Oxford-educated, from an old, upper-middle-class English family, second cousin of Lytton, and son of the editor of the conservative journal *The Spectator*. Although Strachey had left Oxford before getting his degree to help his father run *The Spectator*, his growing commitment to socialism meant that by the late 1920s he had withdrawn from the journal's day-to-day management. He was heavily involved in Labour Party politics, editing the magazines the *Socialist Review* and *The Miner*, and publishing books on economics. He had traveled to Russia, and his close friend Oswald Mosley, another well-off convert to left-wing politics—then a rising political star, not yet the face of fascism in England—encouraged him to go to the United States to study advanced capitalism. Strachey was in the middle of a steady affair with the young literary editor of *The Spectator*, Celia Simpson, who was part of his group of Labour-affiliated friends, but as he prepared to travel to New York in the autumn of 1928, a colleague remarked, "I suppose you're going to the U.S.A. to look for a rich wife." A few months later, in February 1929, Esther and he were engaged. "Bachelor Heiress to Wed Kin of Lord," announced a headline in the *New York American*.

In 1936, still working overtime as a spokesman for his moment, Scott Fitzgerald wrote, "It was characteristic of the Jazz Age that it had no interest in politics at all." This often-repeated dictum about the late teens and twenties may have described him, but it ignored the politics of the Harlem Renaissance, left-wing organizing and publishing, temperance and Prohibition, and feminist and anti-feminist activism during those years. Esther was not one of those American literary figures who first found a social conscience with the Great Depression, and in Strachey she responded to the offer of a life if not in politics, then as a partner in his promising career. Like her, he was an intellectual child of privilege who had embraced progressive politics. She had recently been commissioned to write the life of Lady Blessington, and her publisher, Joseph Brewer, was a young American who had studied at Oxford and worked on *The Spectator*; it was probably he who introduced her to Strachey. She may have thought that living in England would help her to write this book. She already felt her "inabilities to act," which she confided to Strachey, and she told him how much she needed his confidence in her. But joining forces with him also made it possible for her to avoid writing and to throw herself into work that was wholly different. It may be that it was only as a political wife that she could conceive of being in an intimate couple with a man. Certainly agreeing to marry him was an attempt to stop pining for a woman who kept in touch with but still disdained her: Barney countered the "startling and revelatory" news of her engagement with skeptical congratulations. "I must rejoice with you that you not only foresee but experience happiness," she wrote. "I am glad that you recall our meeting not too bitterly." And she asked, pointedly or obliquely, whether Esther had already slept with Strachey: "Just how your nature may sanction this nouveau régime is a thing already ascertained?" Esther's nature inclined mostly toward women, but she was also profoundly lonely. "She *dreamed* of being appreciated," said Sybille Bedford.

Strachey was motivated by a mixture of opportunism and genuine fondness. He was ambitious and wanted a career in politics, but did not have the money to finance it. His father had died in 1927, and he and his mother were not close. There was a real chance of a

Labour victory in the 1929 election—not just in the working-class, traditionally Tory district of Birmingham, in which he would run for Parliament, but in enough other parts of the country to bring in a left-of-center government—and he insisted on a large dowry from Patrick Murphy, to make his campaign possible. He admired Esther deeply and, knowing about her feelings for Barney, still convinced himself and was convinced by her that their marriage would work. He told her that he wanted to give her "a sort of keel . . . some heavy fixed centre against which your superb talents could get a purchase" and wrote with kind apprehension about her drinking and their shared tendency toward depression. He saw her strengths and faults clearly, yet he objectified her: "You are truly moving because you have lived and suffered," he wrote. "I need you very much Esther. You have very much that I lack. You have, for all that it is to some extent caught up and turned back upon yourself, an exuberance of spirit— you are one of your own examples of the . . . magnificent American Extravagance of type—that is to me immensely satisfying." He also expected to be able to continue his affair with Celia Simpson.

To an ex-girlfriend, the French journalist Yvette Fouque, he wrote,

I'm going to marry a girl called Esther Murphy—New Yorker, Irish descent, extremely intelligent, not pretty, 6 feet tall, 30 years old, with some money and a very, very good person indeed. She, I think, loves me very much. This, my dearest Yvette, is if you will believe me, not foolishness, not mere *lachété*, or resignation to the lure of the dollar, but a deeply felt, and absolutely necessary, development of my life. *Of course*, the fact that she has money is vitally important to me—ah, you know me well enough to know that— but please, please believe that I have not foolishly rushed at the money, sacrificing too much for it. She is a deeply civilized, deeply and passionately intellectual person, to whom the cultural heritage of man is life itself. She knows French literature and history, I really believe, as well as you do, and English literature and history far better than I do. She is the only other woman I have ever met whose intellectual equality I could never question. She knows England very little, but France very well. (She goes to France every year.) I know that this marriage will inevitably strengthen and help my life. It will give me the objective ability to go in wholly for politics and also a certain inner strength to do so.

He did not write to Celia Simpson, who learned of his engagement through a newspaper announcement. When he contacted her on his return to London, in late January 1929, as he began his run for Parliament, she told him she would never see him again.

In New York that spring, an epic series of parties preceded Esther's departure for London. "Last night . . . at James Leopold's," Max Ewing reported,

Esther Murphy was said farewell to by about fifty people for about five hours. Tonight she will be said farewell to in two places: (1) at dinner at Mary French's, where Mary, Esther, Muriel, Joseph Brewer, and probably Alice De La Mar and a few others will be at table and (2) later at a party at the Sheldons, to which forty are coming to bid farewell to Esther Murphy. Saturday night Esther Murphy is inviting hundreds of people to say farewell to her in her own quarters in Park Avenue. On the following nights it will be the same hundreds saying the same thing at Sarah King's, at Muriel Draper's, and elsewhere.

A week later, Ewing wrote, "You would think Esther Murphy were going to a nunnery in Siam and never to be seen again in this world. Whereas as a matter of fact everyone she knows will see her in Europe this summer and back here in New York next winter!" The engagement was announced and these parties duly noted in the columns of gossip writer Cholly Knickerbocker, and a hundred people saw Esther off at the pier when she and her father sailed on March 16.

On shipboard, and then from London, she telegraphed Muriel Draper: "THINKING OF YOU CONSTANTLY." The wedding, front-page news in New York, took place on April 24, 1929, at the Catholic church of St. Mary's, in Chelsea. Patrick and Anna Murphy were there, as were Noel and Gerald; Amy Strachey, John's mother; his sister Amabel Williams-Ellis with her family; and a couple of Esther's friends. (Draper and Mercedes de Acosta had planned to attend but were unable to.) Oswald Mosley was the best man. In a photograph taken outside the reception at the Carlton hotel, Esther is flanked by her husband, while her father looks on. Her face is largely obscured by her cloche hat, but she is smiling broadly—not at either man or at the photographer, but at one of the women in the group, who beams back at her.

Immediately afterward, she was "plunged into the General Election of 1929"—the first English election with universal adult suffrage. In addition to bringing money to Strachey's candidacy, she campaigned with him, appearing on the platform when he spoke and stumping for him at gatherings of women constituents and elsewhere. On a leaflet addressed "To the Woman Elector of Aston," there is a photograph of her looking distinctly pretty—fresh-faced, clear-eyed, Irish. "Dear Friend," the broadside reads, "I am writing to you, as a woman voter, in order to ask you to vote for my husband, John Strachey . . . I know his grasp of the problems which confront women, and his keen realisation of the urgent necessity of improving the living conditions of the people of Great Britain." The leaflet, which may not have been written by her, invited women voters to a series of meetings, where her speech—on American democratic traditions and the goals of the Labour Party—was certainly her own. She loved these appearances, and audiences responded to her commanding but matter-of-fact style.

Strachey defeated his Conservative opponent on May 30, 1929, and Esther and he moved into a house in Westminster, close to the House of Commons. He announced that he anticipated "the swift 'transformation of society into a Socialist Commonwealth,'" but there was little room for him and his colleagues to maneuver. While Labour had enough seats in the House of Commons to form a government, they had only a small majority over the Conservatives (the Liberal Party had the balance of the votes), and their prime minister, Ramsay MacDonald, began to undermine their aspirations for reform. In November 1930, as Labour's hold on government disintegrated, Esther wrote to a friend in New York describing it as "the most important failure since the Wall Street crash."

The fatuousness, and incompetence of MacDonald are almost incredible. There may be a general election any time—though no one knows when it will come . . . Mosley and John assure me that when the general election comes the present government will be snowed under. I don't doubt it for an instant. John says he is sure to lose his own seat in the debacle . . . He loathes MacDonald so that he will positively enjoy his own defeat, since it will contribute to Ramsay's discomfiture. Ramsay now frequents nobody but Duchesses, to whom he tells his troubles while [Chancellor of the Exchequer] Snowden carries on the government employing a financial policy that would have been deemed rather too conservative by Queen Victoria. Though Snowden's policy and his obstinacy are ruining the Labor party, one can still respect him as a human being . . . , while Ramsay is a pitiable figure, the mixture of his vanity, his Scotch sentimentality and his snobbery are atrocious. The aristocracy has him eating out of its hand.

But Esther's fascination with parliamentary politics was not enough to sustain the marriage, which was itself soon a debacle. Strachey had imagined a union of equals, but still expected his wife to run the household—plan meals, supervise the small domestic staff, make sure the house looked respectable—chores in which Esther had no interest and for which she had no aptitude. She cared about debate and policy, not domestic performance, felt isolated, and continued to drink to excess. She had her own money and had never answered to anyone, so often assuaged her unhappiness by spending weekends in France sitting in cafés drinking and talking with Dorothy Parker, Janet Flanner, and other friends; going to Barney's salon on Fridays; and visiting Noel, who was now living in the village of Orgeval, about twenty miles northwest of Paris. (Margaret Hutchins Bishop and John Peale Bishop lived in Orgeval for a time, too, and Esther saw them as well.) In the summers of their childhood, Esther and Noel had told other children ghost stories in

From left: unidentified woman, Lorna Lindsley, Patrick Murphy, John Strachey (sprinkled with rice), Oswald Mosley behind him, and Esther, after their wedding, April 24, 1929 (Muriel Draper Papers, Yale Collection of American Literature, Beinecke Rare Book and Manuscript Library, Yale University)

the Southampton cemetery. During the war, Esther had read her
Fred's eloquent letters from the front. Now Noel was rusticating in
a country house she had bought after Fred's death, but often host-
ing visitors from Paris (including Gertrude Stein and Alice Toklas)
and from New York. John Strachey did accompany Esther to France
occasionally, and even to Barney's salon, but it was his duty to be
available to his constituency in Birmingham on the weekends, and it
was customary for an MP's wife to provide support on these trips,
not flee to France. Their struggles included the question of children: He wanted a family—although her drinking eventually made
him reconsider; she did not. When she became pregnant, she felt
her whole body revolt against it, or so she said later. She eventually
had the miscarriage she hoped for.

The cultural collision was part of the problem. She was close to
one of her husband's colleagues, Aneurin Bevan, who had worked
his way up to a parliamentary career from a mining community in
South Wales, and she spent time with the novelists Richard Hughes
and Elizabeth Bowen. But most of Strachey's friends were baffled
by what they saw as his choice of an unattractive oddity for a wife.
They could not fathom Esther's intelligence, could not stand her
volubility, and considered American history a laughably trivial
subject. They also felt that Esther dominated Strachey. She talked
so much that he appeared to be in "second place," said George
Strauss, a Labour colleague, who described Esther as a "female po-
liceman." Strachey's childhood friend Robert Boothby, a Tory MP,
found her "hideous." Boothby recalled a gathering at Mosley's
country home during which "Esther was going on about" various
senators, and "Strachey said: 'if you go on about that any more, I
can't stand it.' Esther left the room in tears." When Strachey first
brought her to Mosley's country house, his biographer notes, "there
were many talkative Englishmen to lunch, and Esther, after being
silent a long time, wept. Strachey later told Mosley 'that was because, in America, everyone listens to her.'" These accounts, meant
to show Esther as self-absorbed and presumptuous, make the misogyny and insularity of the atmosphere she was moving in vivid.

Strachey's politics at this time were increasingly radical, but as
he wrote to Boothby: "Remember, every upper class socialist is a
neurotic, on edge, 'up against it' and so guilty." Esther's first taste of

this conflict, and of the differences between American and English versions of elite populism, had been during the election celebrations, when a working-class man had approached Strachey and said, "Congratulations, John!" clapping him on the shoulder. Strachey had recoiled and replied, "I'm Mr. Strachey to you." Stunned by his sense of affront, Esther later said that this was the moment when her trust in him evaporated. While they were driving through France in the summer of 1929—they stayed for a time with Gerald and Sara Murphy in Antibes—their car broke down, and so did the marriage. As they waited for the repairs, Strachey wrote to Yvette Fouque:

> It is not going well. I am still too young and foolish to have undertaken this . . . She is so *spoilt*—how could she be anything else? It is not her fault, of course, it is money, America, everything. But that doesn't make it any better for me. Isn't it *awful*, the poor people are the *only* possible ones—and they are, well, poor! . . . They [wealthy Americans] cannot even show enough decency, calmness, niceness to get over the tiny contretemps which the pursuit of their pleasure bring them. And yet we, the poor, are helpless, impotent, cringing before them. God forgive us, we go to the lengths of marrying them!

While he clung to distorted ideas about his own "poverty," Esther kept drinking and escaping to Paris and New York. It was not long before he was again seeing Celia Simpson.

"Darling, darling Muriel," Esther wrote, "I have missed you so much that nothing could ever convey it to you—at the same time feeling . . . that I only had to stretch out my hand to touch you . . . This year has been very strange." She was referring to the end of her marriage, to the growing economic crisis, and to her parents' decline. She and Strachey were together in New York in the winter of 1929–30. (Mary McCarthy remembered a gathering of leftist writers that included Esther and Strachey at which he had shocked McCarthy by adjourning to the toilet, leaving the door open, "unbutton[ing] his fly," and continuing the conversation.) But they spent more and more time apart. When he returned to London, she

stayed on with Anna and Patrick Murphy until spring. That summer, he traveled to Russia with Celia and several colleagues. The
following summer, Esther toured Germany with Noel and Janet
Flanner. Noel drove her old Ford; Esther and Flanner took turns in
the front seat. They stayed in country inns in the Black Forest and
went to the Jockey Club in Berlin. Noel and Flanner fell in love
during the trip—some happiness in the midst of increasing strain.
Until the end of Esther's life, these two women were her family. Back
in New York by herself in the late summer and autumn of 1931, Esther held "forth on the politics of all the world" and she had lunch
with Secretary of the Treasury Andrew Mellon in Southampton.
Her parents had fired most their household staff and put their automobile in storage, Mark Cross was operating at a great loss, and Patrick Murphy's bewilderment at the Depression was painful to see.

She sailed to England in early November 1931, but returned to
New York almost immediately. After years of immunity from illness, her father had contracted pneumonia, and he died on November 23, 1931. Esther and Gerald, both traveling from Europe, missed
his enormous funeral at St. Patrick's Cathedral. Several hundred
people, including seventy-five Mark Cross employees—the two
shops were closed for the day—attended the service, as did several
of Esther's friends, and Murphy was eulogized by a former U.S. secretary of state. As John Strachey prepared to accompany Esther to
New York, Celia told him that if he did not return to England within
ten days she would leave the country and never see him again.
Deeply unhappy, wanting to begin a life with her, but loath to hurt
Esther, he sailed to New York, delivered Esther to her parents'
home, and immediately returned to London, sending Esther a telegram to say that he wanted to end the marriage.

"The whole thing went to pieces *en grand*," said Sybille Bedford,
with Strachey "letting her down, her beloved father dying, then her
mother's illness, the Mark Cross company [in crisis], Gerald being
impossible, suddenly no money." Anna Murphy had collapsed and
been hospitalized when her husband died; within a month she had
a stroke and contracted pneumonia. Esther, in shock at her father's
death and deeply hurt by Strachey's failure to honor him—if not for
her sake then as the man who had helped make his career possible—kept vigil over her mother, who lay semiconscious for five

months, "a living corpse." She died that spring. Gerald, preoccupied with the illness of his eldest son, did not return to New York for her funeral. John Strachey moved with Celia to a house in rural Sussex, struggled with his ambivalence about divorcing Esther, "became ill with worry and guilt," and went into analysis. Muriel Draper's "sympathy and understanding" as Anna Murphy was dying were crucial. Draper and Joe Brewer also tried to broker a rapprochement. Esther "does love you," Draper wrote to John Strachey, "but . . . does not depend on you in any way—emotionally, intellectually, or actually; nor is she, as far as I can perceive, waiting for you as the one hope and solution of her life. She does believe that some sort of equality is possible between you, or that in any case some arrangement of your lives can be made which will prove less disastrous and ridiculous than this." Strachey's career was also in turmoil. Oswald Mosley had resigned dramatically from the Labour government, and in 1931 he, Strachey, and a few others founded the New Party, a short-lived experiment in opposition. But Strachey soon withdrew, seeing Mosley's turn to the right, and in the October election of that year he lost his seat in Parliament. Mosley went on to found the British Union of Fascists.

The women in John Strachey's family were not threatened or disgusted by Esther the way his male friends were. On the contrary: "She is a hero and a goddess," his sister Amabel wrote to him. "I have seen a good many great women, but never one to surpass Esther, and never one so vulnerable and inexperienced and exposed to the hard fate of being a human being." His mother could be forbidding—she was tall and thin and looked "like a Victorian coat stand," wrote Celia, "with scarves & chains and lace and shawls hanging from her"—but she adored Esther and emphatically took her side. Amy Strachey had encouraged her son's trip to the United States in 1928 as a way to separate him from Celia; she refused to see him when he was living with Celia in 1932; and she did not attend their wedding in the autumn of 1933, immediately after Esther and John divorced. "My heart quite literally bleeds when I think of" Esther, she wrote to Gerald. When Esther remarried, five years later, Amy Strachey told her that her new husband was "charming,—almost worthy of you, but you know my feelings that nobody is quite."

Within a few years, Esther and John Strachey had become friends. On her last trip to Europe before the war, in the spring of 1937, she visited him and Celia. Twice in the 1930s, on lecture tours of the United States, he was incarcerated at Ellis Island, accused of being a Communist advocating the violent overthrow of the U.S. government, a charge based on Hearst press pressure on the Department of Labor. In both cases, Esther pulled every string she could in Washington, even contacting FDR, and she wrote to Amy Strachey to reassure her. Strachey went on to have a long career as a leading theorist of the Labour Party and in world democratic socialism. *The Coming Struggle for Power*, his 1932 primer on the logics of capitalism and communism, is still seen as one of the most cogent expositions of the economic situation of the time. He helped found the Left Book Club, a populist publishing venture that produced millions of volumes (by George Orwell, Arthur Koestler, and others) and helped shift the British national consciousness to the left, enabling Labour's postwar ascendance. He was a member of Parliament and he continued to publish on economics and empire until his death in 1963. Esther liked and admired him.

But in New York in 1932, as she waited for him to come to a decision about whether to divorce, she was miserable. She faced and avoided her own failings, writing to him about eighteenth-century French history, not about their marriage, telling friends that it had not worked out because she belonged in New York, not London. She lived in a hotel and depended on Amanda and Gilbert Seldes. On Christmas Eve at their home, she pulled off her wedding ring and gave it to their young daughter, Marian. She had no real financial independence, because Patrick Murphy had made a "dotty . . . eccentric will" that appointed Gerald her trustee until she was fifty-five, meaning that she did not actually own the shares of Mark Cross her father had left her. Even if she had been capable of steady work, it would have been hard to find. Across the country, more than thirteen million people were unemployed. In New York, along Broadway and Fifth Avenue, shops were closed or empty, breadlines threaded through Times Square, and food was scarce and of poor quality even if one had money or a job. In June, Esther listened to the suspenseful Democratic convention with Draper, Max Ewing, the actress Kay Francis, and the lesbian nightclub singer

Spivy LeVoe. She and Draper outlasted everyone, glued to the radio. Finally the maneuvering for delegates ended, and Franklin Delano Roosevelt was nominated. Esther was relieved, but skeptical when he was elected by a huge majority, and the Democrats won both houses of Congress, on November 8, 1932. She saw in the new year at Draper's annual party, then returned to London to wait for her divorce. From Paris in the spring of 1933, she wrote to Draper:

> Never have I loved my country so much—and never have I been as despairing. Roosevelt seems to me to be applying homeopathic remedies that only lull the patient to sleep while the disease saps him.—I hope this is only a delusion, because I am over here and out of touch and don't grasp that great *wave* of enthusiasm and confidence which I am told Roosevelt has kindled in the country. But I *cannot* believe it.—Dearest Muriel, you are the only person I could write to . . . like this. Forgive me . . . My divorce was too squalid and depressing.

The year before, Strachey had written to Joseph Brewer, "I feel the frightful tragedy of our marriage as a heavy, heavy weight which I shall carry all the rest of my life. And I am more than willing to take all the blame . . . [T]he thought of Esther, and of her inestimable goodness, of the startling, beautiful and so overwhelmingly moving core of purest gold that lies beneath all surface irrelevancies haunts me."

THE RUMBLE OF THE TUMBRELS

One July 4 in the early 1920s, the drama critic Alec Wooll-cott had visited Esther in Southampton and watched as she responded to her father's drunkenness and mother's para-noia by reciting a litany about the English royal family, "saying, 'The Duke of York had three sons and two daughters,' etc., etc.," and gesticulating anxiously. In 1938, introducing an essay of hers on FDR, the editors of the progressive journal *Common Sense* described her as "celebrated for her mastery of American history." Dawn Pow-ell, after seeing her at Gerald and Sara's in 1945, portrayed her as

> tall, gaunt, in tweed suit with folded cravat, regretting the necessity of a body whose needs interrupt her conversation, studded with statistics on Third Empire, Economics, and European politics . . . her contact with the human race (she is concerned with only its major figures) is in shy revelations made to her that the great (in diadems of dates and robes of sparkling statistics) also were interrupted by body or mor-tal demands . . . Some alien hand might intrude or pry in silence, so barriers of statistics must be piled up like sand-bags to protect the small shy bird within.

Powell's brilliant portrait is, like Esther herself, at once precise, ex-aggerated, and inadequate. If Esther piled up facts and handled them like jewels—work that takes discipline and a delicate touch—she also played with facts and distorted them. She understood the present, including herself and her friends, as historical because she saw history as the medium in which we all live, the thing we are always making. Reading history, Esther wrote to Janet Flanner in April 1938, "or at any rate the tiny little bit of recorded history that has any semblance of authenticity, one realizes that the human race has survived in the last analysis not because of any of its qualities of virtue or intellect, but on account of that slavish pliant adaptability which has enabled it to survive even the mischief which it plots for its own self-destruction."

"To focus" Esther's "attention on [something] outside divorce and death" in the summer of 1932, Muriel Draper invited her to give a series of public lectures at her apartment. In the first talk, for which "quite a crowd for a hot night turned out to hear her," Esther compared the previous postwar period—the years following the Civil War—with their own moment in the wake of World War I. Two years later, she published an essay on Ulysses S. Grant and Reconstruction in H. L. Mencken's *American Mercury*, "Godfather to American Corruption," covering some of the same ground. "At the close of Grant's administration," she wrote,

> the pattern of the future had been fixed. On the ruins of that agrarian civilization which the Southern slave-holders had sought to keep, the most powerful industrial country in the world was being built . . . America was to be . . . conducted for profit by business men. Government was to be something that did not interfere while men made money. And in all of these decisions Grant had acquiesced without understanding any of them.

The statesmen and party bosses of President Grant's time "were actually more materialistic in their fundamental philosophy than most Marxians," she wrote in a review of a Marxist history several years later. The comparison was only partly tongue in cheek: Their "political talents [were] . . . great if ruthless," she argued, describing these politicians as "something more than the puppets" this writer "makes them out to be." "They discovered the necessity for unqualified party orthodoxy and the efficacy of the 'party purge' long before Moscow did. And they were all avowed believers in the dictum that all power is a permanent conspiracy." Esther's thinking about postbellum America was probably shaped by her reading of the historian Charles Beard, who argued in his *Economic Interpretation of the Constitution* that the framers were driven by financial interest. She was certainly influenced by the historian Henry Adams, a witness to Grant's administration, whom she described as incapable of understanding "Grant's particular kind of stupidity." Adams was "primarily concerned in attempting to discover a meaning or a logic in history" and she admired his "devastating" portrait of his "class and . . . caste in one of their most triumphant periods in America."

Esther was herself primarily concerned not with finding history's logic but with making it vivid and visible in the present. It was second nature to her to think about the crises and characters of her own time in terms of the European and American past—and anachronism and incongruity were as productive a way of thinking about that relationship as continuity. The Spanish Civil War, she told Flanner in 1938, was "like the religious wars in sixteenth century France and the Thirty Year War in Germany." She added: "Though I never idealized the Spanish government and disagreed with many of its policies, I think Franco's victory will be an unmitigated disaster both for Spain and for Europe." Writing to John Strachey that same year, she evoked both Roman decadence and the French Revolution and the Terror: "I have just been spending a few days in Santa Barbara, that Pompeii without a volcano." She added: "All the California millionaires and the Eastern plutocrats who inhabit the marble palaces in its hills are in a very strange state of mind . . . [and] are behaving as though they already heard the rumble of the tumbrels coming for them." "Well," she wrote to Amabel Williams-Ellis as the world careened toward war, "it is strange to live in a dissolving world . . . 'Toute la boutique s'en va au diable,' as Madame Pompadour observed to Louis XV on another occasion, which also turned out to have serious historical consequences." She planned to write a play about Louis Napoleon, because she saw that president turned emperor as "the great prototype of the present fascist leaders, since he was the first modern dictator." To her potential collaborator she noted, "It won't be easy to write as it is the sort of thing that has to come off absolutely or else be a complete failure."

At the same time, she articulated the European past in colloquial American terms. Years later, describing her frustration at trying to capture Madame de Maintenon's character, she announced
that she had decided to think of her as "The Slippery Sam of French
History." And she constantly traveled the border between history
and fiction, peopling her world not only with the living ("the uncertified lunatics amongst whom we live," as she wrote to Draper) and
the Great Dead but also with figures from literature and of her own
invention. It was a fluid vision. She had set pieces that could be re-
quested—or averted, since "when she got onto one of these stories,
it would take two or three hours to tell," as Sybille Bedford observed. One of these stories was about the Hanseatic League, a complex patch of Northern European history that Esther would declare
she was one of the few to understand—and would now explain. "I
used to say you had to steer her, like the *Queen Mary*," recalled
James Douglas, a friend of her later years, referring to the inexora-
bility of these long discourses. There were other personages and
events that Esther related as if they were true, and were believed to
be by many of her listeners, but were her own creation. One of
these was "The Reverend Mother," the corrupt abbess of a convent
in Louisiana who had the dirt on so many cardinals that she had
successfully thwarted the efforts of the Church hierarchy to expel
her. Esther retailed this woman's deeds as a report on the outrageous state of the Catholic Church in the American South, but "the
R.M.," as she also called her, was largely or wholly a fiction, a long-
running joke, and both a particular character and a malevolent
force whom she would pretend to blame for all manner of disasters,
personal and global.

Blending past and present, European and American, high and
low, Esther imagined contemporary politicians as literary characters, saw figures from literature as her friends, and posited her
friends as players in historical intrigues. She called FDR someone
out of a Philip Barry play—suave, upper-class, and too removed
from most Americans' experience of the Depression. She used *Pride
and Prejudice* to describe the way her old friend Peggy Fears "flirted
with me and threw me many a lewd glance" at a gathering in 1950:
"like Sir William Lucas at Lady Catherine de Bourgh's party." In

1958, at the height of the French atrocities in Algeria and with the end of the Fourth Republic imminent, she wrote to Gerald that the previous six months had "resembled nothing so much as the Queen's Croquet Party in Alice in Wonderland—but which nearly came to a denouement that would have been tragic and bloody." It was "eerie," she said, "to see the streets [of Paris] patrolled by the special police carrying machine guns." She had a theory about one long-time friend—a difficult woman who had fallen out with Noel Murphy but to whom Esther remained loyal—"that she traveled all over the world looking for the Boston Tea Party" (excitement, opposition, conflict). Edmund Wilson recalled that Esther's train of thought had to do with the fact that this mutual friend's "great-uncle (I think) was a renegade to the Republic in the War of 1812— he was an admiral who made an attempt to betray Boston Harbor to the British." When Wilson related Esther's idea to Janet Flanner, he "said something about Esther's theory not necessarily being reliable.—'But,' said Janet, 'I'm sure it's brilliantly illuminating.'" Esther's "talking, her devouring of history, is of course a release of energy," Wilson observed, "and the things she makes up, imagines, show that she has had partly to live in a fantasy not too close to reality." But as Flanner saw, Esther also transposed her friends and acquaintances to other centuries and locations and reinvented them as fictional characters to comment on their personalities in the present. History itself was about large political and social shifts, but it was also about character, in both the ethical and the fictional senses. And the constant literary allusions helped her to talk about the human repercussions of policy.

In another of Esther's stories about Natalie Barney, which she also sent to Muriel Draper around 1926, she cast Barney as the over-sexed abbess of a convent in thirteenth-century Italy. The hapless Alice Robinson appeared again, this time as a novice whom Barney hoped to deflower. Isabel Pell, another lesbian rake of their circle, haunted the convent, Esther wrote, taking the form of a dog to enter the cloister and debauch young nuns. "The Barney or 'Clotilde' as she was then called, but to avoid confusion we will speak of her under the name which she bears now," Esther wrote,

Esther and the news, February 16, 1934, photographed by Carl Van Vechten (Yale Collection of American Literature, Beinecke Rare Book and Manuscript Library, Yale University, courtesy Estate of Carl Van Vechten)

was the favorite child of that extraordinary man, [Emperor] Frederick II, and had inherited many of his gifts. She collaborated with her father in writing that celebrated work "De Tribus Impostoribus" in which the doctrines and revelations of Moses, Jesus and Mohammed are held up to ridicule . . . The Emperor had wished her to marry the King of Naples, but upon her expressing a great repugnance to matrimony and requesting she be made Abbess of the before-mentioned convent, he bowed to her wishes. She had ruled the convent for some ten years with an iron hand though on somewhat original principles, when Pell made her first appearance there . . . I hope to be able to give you an account of the very remarkable part which Miss Barney played in Constantinople during the last years of the Eastern Empire and of her amazing activities during the Crusades (in which she was very closely associated with Jane Heap,) but for the present this fragment drawn from the long history of her incarnation as an Abbess [an extremely long parenthetical comment follows] . . . is the only one which I can deal with here . . . Thus you see, dear Muriel, how all these events have their roots in the far past. How the Barney has always been a maleficent influence in the lives of our friends since the very dawn of history . . . The connection may seem very remote at a first glance—but according to the fundamental laws of Hegelian philosophy it is both self evident and menacing.

I submit this to your wisdom and judgment

And remain

Yours In Christ

A Portuguese Nun

The story was the fervid creation of someone not included in Barney's seductions, but it was also far more than clever sniping. As Djuna Barnes did in *Ladies Almanack* and Virginia Woolf did in *Orlando*, Esther used literary history to make excited and critical claims about anachronism and modernity; to link local and larger historical details; to suggest a relationship between lesbian sexuality and historical consciousness; and to argue that literary characters are themselves part of history, as are one's friends. Esther signed herself as the narrator and putative author of the seventeenth-century French novel the *Lettres Portugaises,* or *Letters of a Portuguese Nun.* Ostensibly and long believed to be five missives from a cloistered Franciscan nun to her lover, the text is now recognized as the fiction of a seventeenth-century Frenchman, the Comte de Guilleragues, and as one of the important precursors of the novel. The other text she refers to, *De Tribus Impostoribus* (*The Three Imposters*), one of the early manifestos of atheism (the "imposters" are Moses, Jesus, and Mohammed), is attributed variously to Frederick II, Boccaccio, Hobbes, and Spinoza; one version from the 1750s was published with the fictive date of 1598.

Esther considered Barney to be or to have a false character. Writing about Barney while citing and using the conventions of famous literary ruses, she satirized the intrigues of at least two subcultures, lesbian Paris and Catholic cloisters. She also skewered the belief in progress—the joke that is the logic of historical determinism, or "the fundamental laws of Hegelian philosophy"—and religious belief. Her reference to Jane Heap's involvement in the Crusades was a swipe at sexual and devotional heat: Heap was the charismatic former editor, with Margaret Anderson, of *The Little Review,* the first publisher of Joyce's *Ulysses.* She had been Anderson's lover, then became a disciple of the mystic Gurdjieff and disseminator of his "wisdom." Referring to the *Letters of a Portuguese Nun*—one of the exercises in ventriloquism that are the basis of the realist novel—Esther was also invoking the conversation between that emerging genre and the modern discipline of history. As the latter, with its emphasis on facts and evidence, rather than narrative, developed in relationship to the former in the eighteenth century, both emerged as separately gendered forms—history as the province of men, and fiction of women. In other words, Esther's satire was also returning the practice of historical writing to its own history as a literary form, and one that had had a more fluid relationship to documentation than was accepted in the twentieth century. Esther's own strangeness and novelty were partly to do with this paradoxical history of history—the fact that it was a male preserve that had worked to distinguish itself from its own past as a form "animated by rhetoric, not by evidence," as the historian Jill Lepore has put it.

From England in 1929, Esther had written to Draper about her encounter with a pleasurably contradictory figure: "a landed proprietor of Gloucestershire, who left England to assist Lenin in establishing the soviet republic . . . who still is a formal communist, but who is at present disquieted by the fact that the vicar who holds the living in his gift is in favor of 'the reservation of the sacrament' [setting aside some portion of the communion bread and wine for the ill or others absent from the service, rather than consuming it immediately after it has been blessed] which the squire feels is directly subversive of the Establishment." The ironies of this juxtaposition of communism and the traditional English sources of power (the Anglican church and the aristocracy) delighted Esther. "I walked across his acres with him," she went on, "while he told me the story of the storming of the Winter Palace in St. Petersburg at which he assisted—stopping only to point out with pride a great clump of trees, planted on top of a hill to commemorate Victoria's golden jubilee by his father, which is an object of his particular solicitude."

Esther saw something similar in FDR, who seemed to her "the liberal . . . 'born out of his due time' [here she is quoting the apostle Paul]—and his very appearance on the stage of history an anachronism." She also likened him to an impressive seductress, a gesture that allied him with Natalie Barney. He had, she wrote in 1936,

> that insidious charm which one is too apt to associate only with the great courtesans of history and which as a matter of fact every now and again a man is endowed with, and which by that being so rare an event, is twice as effective.— Franklin has taken his into politics instead of into the salon and the alcove, and it is such a novel element to be injected into the rough and tumble of the American political scene, that his "bonne fortunes" have been more striking than Lord Byron's own. He is the Mary Stuart–Cleopatra the Serpent of Old Nile of American politics and his seductions have certainly worked cruel ravages on the Grand Old Party's health and prospects. It is one of the minor ironies of history that the man who probably possesses more sheer charm . . . than any other figure in American history should

have had as his chief opponent the man [Herbert Hoover] who had the least. The spectacle of Roosevelt and Hoover mutually competing for the popular favor is rather like what it would be to see Madame de Pompadour opposed to Sairie Gamp [Sairey, the drunken nurse in Dickens's *Martin Chuzzlewit*].

This sort of analysis—at once historical, contemporary, and prescient; factual and literary; generous and incisive—saturates the hundreds of letters Esther sent and the several articles she published during the 1930s. In "Have You Heard About Roosevelt . . . ?" which appeared in *Common Sense* in 1938, she analyzed the hysterical "whispering campaign" against the president and argued, "Not since the great statesman Turgot worked to save the French monarchy from itself, has anybody worked as hard as Mr. Roosevelt has, to reform and to modify American capitalism so that it can survive." In "The Energists," for *Harper's Bazaar*, she wrote about the "incalculable influence" American women social reformers had had in the nineteenth and early twentieth centuries. She told John Strachey that she regretted

> that in dealing with the amazing Frances Willard I was not able to give an account of the part she played in the Labor movement of the seventies and eighties. She put the whole strength of the Women's Christian Temperance Union, one of the most powerful organizations this country has ever seen, back of the Knights of Labor, and came out for the forty-hour week. All that is a curious and little-known chapter in American social history. I wish to God we had a replica of Frances Willard on the Left today. She had a knowledge of American psychology and a grasp of the American political method as uncanny as Franklin Roosevelt's own.

Although it was not unusual for a liberal observer to be thinking about the history of reform in America during the Depression and New Deal, it was, once again, rare for such an observer to be focusing on women in that history. Esther was also unusual in her treatment of Willard as a serious political figure; following the re-

peal of Prohibition it was more ordinary to dismiss this temperance figure. Esther's use of the phrase *social history* is striking, too,
since it was not common among historians for several decades to
come.

Writing to the editor of *Harper's*, the great Carmel Snow, Esther
proposed another essay, which she envisioned as "a sort of pendent
to 'The Energists' "; she would discuss "critics and portrayers of the
American scene," including Henry James, Henry Adams, Edith
Wharton, and Margaret Chanler, and several lesser-known figures
who had written about Native American culture, such as Mary Austin, Gertrude Atherton, and Mabel Dodge Luhan. There is no trace
of that intriguing project (whether it was not assigned or not completed is not clear), but she did review, elsewhere, the "curious and
ambitious work" that was the final volume of Mabel Dodge Luhan's
memoirs, *Edge of Taos Desert*. Socialite, patroness of the arts, bohemian, and latter-day settler of New Mexico, Luhan had an "almost
unlimited capacity for making herself ridiculous," Esther wrote.
But even as she acknowledged Luhan's obliviousness to history,
penchant for melodrama, "bitter hostility to abstract ideas and . . .
deep fear of them," Esther still tried to give her book a place in history and called the "derision and indignation" Luhan had "provoked . . . almost everything except critical." Luhan may have been
"totally incapable of realizing the distortion of her own point of
view," but Esther read her as "an ardent and intransigent romantic
of the school of Rousseau . . . with its glorification of the man of
emotion and instinct as against the thinking man." Today, Esther
noted, "socialists, fascists and anarchists, the reformers and the
seekers after personal salvation, may all appeal to Rousseau's
doctrines for justification," but "Mrs. Luhan's . . . rebellion against
[society], though uncompromising, was essentially personal and always remained so."

Esther's own curious and ambitious work in the 1930s was
productive and thwarted. There were inevitable distortions in her
own point of view, the only ugly example of which is the evening in
1934 when she screamed drunkenly at a Jewish fellow guest at Muriel Draper's home, "You live on corruption! . . . you all ought to be
extirpated!" The recorder of this event was a young Lincoln Kirstein,
then Draper's lover, who said that Draper despaired at hearing such

virulence from an antifascist like Esther. Her outburst was at once plausible and out of sync. Malice of this sort was not unusual in the 1930s, even or especially among New Deal liberals, and there are two anti-Semitic remarks, about Jews taking over the Hamptons, in Esther's teenage correspondence to Gerald—ironic, given that the Irish-Catholic influx into the Hamptons took place in her lifetime. In general, she saw her time more lucidly than most and saw others with compassion. A few years after this incident, she wrote to John Strachey that she was moved to learn that Edith Wharton had returned an honorary degree from the University of Leipzig because "as far as she could see, culture and the freedom of the human mind had been banished from the Third Reich." Esther had seen Wharton in Paris not long before and considered her gesture "one of the very few decent things that a person who came from the upper strata of privileged society has exerted themselves to do in these last few disastrous years."

"As the late President Harding observed," she wrote to Draper in 1935, " 'the world is in a bad way.' " The news of the Munich Pact was so distressing that "one is forced to fall back on Talleyrand's famous comment on Napoleon's dull and dastardly murder of the Duc d'Enghien. 'It is worse than a crime it is a blunder.' . . . I wonder if that sly and stupid man [Neville Chamberlain] has any intuition of the enormity of what he has done." Quoting Jeremy Taylor's *Holy Dying* (but shifting his words into the first-person plural), she wrote, "As one grows older I think individual destinies take an added strangeness and sadness.—'We dream fair things all the way but our dreams prove contrary and become the hieroglyphics of an eternal sorrow.' "

ALL VERY QUEER
AND A LITTLE DEPRESSING

Few events in Esther's life lent themselves to the sort of historical imagining she favored, allowed her to engage so richly with
anachronism, and brought her so close both to her own failures
and to those of postbellum America as her marriage to Chester A.
Arthur III, grandson of the twenty-first president of the United
States. In 1935, she wrote to Draper announcing her engagement:

> You are too young to remember, (though I understand you
> are 65 years old,) [Draper was not yet 50] my awful dis-
> appointment in July 1882 when President Chester Alan Ar-
> thur failed to propose to me at Saratoga Springs. He was a
> widower, he had payed me marked attentions, I saw myself
> as mistress of the White House,—but he jilted me. I was not
> young in 1882—not in my first youth—it did not improve
> my matrimonial chances to be thrown over by President
> Arthur.—But I am marrying his grandson whose sense of
> chivalry had made him feel that it is the only right thing to
> do to repair the wrong his grandfather did me.

Here was another venture at being married to the past. It was also
something like her own history repeating itself as farce. If in her
first marriage she had aligned herself with a serious intellectual socialist, in her second she became involved with a character who
embodied "the man of emotion and instinct as against the thinking
man," whose belief in economic justice was tied to astrology and a
muddy utopianism, and whose privilege made plenty of room for
indolence.

Esther liked to tell people that "the only two things accomplished by [President] Arthur in his rather uninteresting administration had been civil service reform and taking the troops out of the South." (He also modernized the navy and was the first president to sign legislation restricting immigration.) Her boast about his ineffectual government was also a way to express her gratification at now being several steps closer to the Civil War and Reconstruction, at her newly intimate connection with this time. "It is curious to think," noted Edmund Wilson, "that, for Esther, to have married the grandson of Arthur means almost what it would have meant for Proust to have made an alliance with the Guermantes"— a suggestion that itself blurs history and fiction. Although she signed herself "Esther Murphy" on the title page of her Madame de Maintenon manuscript, elsewhere—in print and in private, and even after her long estrangement from the president's grandson—she was "Esther Arthur" for the rest of her life.

The first Chester Alan Arthur was "a man whose career was entirely in the Horatio Alger nineteenth century American tradition," Esther wrote to Draper, "up from the farm to riches and the presidency." Born in 1830, the son of a Baptist preacher, he grew up in Vermont and upstate New York, then trained as a lawyer. He was involved with several cases defending the rights of African Americans in New York, but spent most of his early career as part of the Republican Party machine in New York City and State, was a compromise candidate for vice president on the ticket with James Garfield in 1880, and became president after Garfield's assassination in 1881. He refused to move into the White House until it was redecorated, entertained lavishly once there, and took a great deal of the presidential wine cellar with him when he left.

This valuable purloined collection was the part of his inheritance that his son, Chester A. Arthur II, known as Alan, most treasured. Her father-in-law, Esther wrote, was "a marvelous character—very, very complete." She loved the way his conversation ranged "from the White House of the eighties through late Victorian and Edwardian society to the Saint Petersburg of the Grand Dukes. He discusses General Grant with the same sardonic objectivity as . . . [he does] Mrs. Stuyvesant Fish." He was "one of the most notable fornicators, and one of the greatest dandies . . . of his time," had divorced his first wife, Chester's mother ("Isabel Archer in 'The Portrait of a Lady' is her prototype"), and even at seventy-one was "utterly fascinating and entirely selfish." He reminded Esther of her own father.

Chester A. Arthur III was similarly preoccupied with his own pleasures, but his taste ran to working-class men rather than French actresses, and his politics diverged from his father's conservative Republicanism and toward a utopian socialism flavored with various precursors of New Age expression. Several years younger than Esther, he was handsome and self-dramatizing. In the early 1920s he had renamed himself Gavin, after a great-great-grandfather, dropped out of Columbia University, married a young dancer who had studied with Ruth St. Denis, and moved to Ireland, where he claimed to have spent four years as a member of the Irish Republican Army. Back in the United States at the end of the decade, he was commissioned by a newspaper to write about working his way around the world on a cargo ship, but after the first stage of the trip, from California to New York, he ended up in Bellevue Hospital with a strep infection, where, he wrote, he "almost died of acute arthritis" and was left "with a crippled wrist to add to my stammer and other spastic handicaps." Returning to Europe, he appeared in Kenneth Macpherson's 1930 film *Borderline*, an experimental melodrama about racial prejudice and sexual tension that starred Paul and Eslanda Robeson, the poet H.D., and Winifred Ellerman (Bryher), who was H.D.'s lover and Macpherson's wife.

Throughout the 1920s, Chester also practiced a sexual tourism that he conceived of as research. He made a pilgrimage to the English socialist, pacifist, and pioneer of homosexual rights, Edward Carpenter, talked to him about Walt Whitman, and spent an exciting night in bed with him. Carpenter gave him a letter of introduction to the sexologist Havelock Ellis, who then sent him on to Magnus Hirschfeld, the leader of the fight against the criminalization of homosexuality in Germany and founder of the world's first sexological institute. (The Institute for Sexual Science and Hirschfeld's archive were destroyed by the Nazis in 1933.) Chester was looking for an alternative patrilineage as well as sex, but his actual lineage remained important to him.

In the early 1930s, his wife "sued him for divorce for non support, citing the fact that 'he just wouldn't work,'" and he moved with another man to a shack in the dunes of Oceano, on California's central coast. There he and his trust fund became the driving forces of a small community of mystics, hermits, vegetarians, psychics, and nudists known as Dunites. He presented his vision for "a collective endeavor . . . that would lead the world into the Aquarian Age," threw all-night parties, welcomed the Indian mystic Meher Baba to the community, and founded *The Dune Forum*, of which he published five issues, running photographs by Ansel Adams and Edward Weston. The idea of the place was self-sufficiency, living off the land and sea, but the group collapsed when Chester left and his patronage ended. He then attached himself to the Utopian Society, an organization that was a brief force in California politics in conjunction with Upton Sinclair's 1934 gubernatorial campaign, during which Sinclair proposed reforms that included giving the state control of inoperative farms and factories to turn them into cooperatives. The goal of the Utopian Society was the abolition of the profit system and the education of "the masses" in modern economics, but the group was also inspired by the Masons, and membership involved pledges of fidelity and a requirement that the novitiate attend a sort of socialist morality play—"a series of pageants," in the words of one observer, "portraying the pilgrimage of the petty bourgeoisie through capitalist to Utopian society." At its height, the group had over half a million members.

Esther's politics and money made her a target for Chester's fund-raising when he arrived in New York to set up an East Coast branch of the society in September 1934. The Depression, the deaths of her parents, and the mismanagement of the Mark Cross Company, which Patrick Murphy had left in the control of a mistress, meant that Esther's income amounted more to the habit of having money and an inability to economize than actual wealth. But her name meant something to the moneyed radicals Chester wanted on his board of directors; both Harold Loeb, heir to a Wall Street fortune and founder of the literary magazine *Broom*, now writing on economics, and Alfred Bingham, the founder and editor of *Common Sense*, told Chester that they would not lend their names to the organization unless Esther was involved. Five years into the Depression, with fascism ascendant in Europe and capitalism failing there and in the United States, some form of socialist reform seemed like a solution to many Americans—from Republicans such as Bingham, to lifelong Democrats such as Esther, to those who had previously paid no attention to politics. Upton Sinclair's progressive candidacy and victory in the California Democratic gubernatorial primary was one sign of the times—as was the ferociousness of the campaign against him by Republicans and the Democratic establishment.

It is hard to believe that Esther found something to like in the Utopian Society's concoction of didacticism, spectacle, and inscrutability. Yet she allowed her name to be used, sold some of her family silver to donate to the cause, and even became the secretary of the organization for a short time. Her association lasted less than a year, and to some friends she always denied her involvement. Her attraction to Chester, whose anti-intellectualism was profound— Edmund Wilson described him as "full of a goofy kind of idealism," and Sybille Bedford saw him as a paragon of political naïveté—is at once easier and more difficult to fathom. Being the focus of his charm and libido flattered her, and his open bisexuality reassured her. They were often together—at the Dalí Ball, elsewhere around town, and in Walter Winchell's column—in the autumn and winter of 1934–35, and once again she became engaged within a few months.

She was thirty-seven years old when she married him, in April 1935, in a ceremony performed by a justice of the peace in a small town outside of New York City. The wedding party, at the home of Gilbert and Amanda Seldes, brought together "high-class old relics of the Chester Arthur family and Administration," Edmund Wilson observed, and "the usual Seldes cocktail crowd." Wilson recorded the uncertain tone of the event: "The bride and groom drove up, started to get out, then got back in again and drove away—it was said vaguely that Esther had to go to a drugstore. Then they finally arrived . . . It was all very queer and a little depressing: I got the impression that the bride and groom did not like to be congratulated and changed the subject as soon as anybody began to do so." Gerald and Sara had moved back to New York—he to rescue the Mark Cross Company—and the sudden death of their son Baoth, Esther's nephew, cast one pall on the party. (He died of a mastoid infection and meningitis after "ten days of hideous suspense and five operations on the brain entailing the cruelest suffer-ing," Esther wrote to Muriel Draper.)

Marrying Chester, Esther seems to have been guided by some combination of blindness, desire for intimacy, and the knowledge that he would leave her alone for much of the time. "They are ap-parently very sensible about it," Gerald wrote, "and realize that it is not a romantic match." Edmund Wilson thought that they had felt pressure from friends to marry. Chester recalled that she had pro-posed to him, that they had "promised to be true to each other heterosexually," and that they had both been "lonely, and . . . felt we could be happier with each other than we could be separately." In the beginning there seems to have been passionate feeling on both sides. "I feel that sense of a union of a oneness with you that I never felt with John Strachey," Esther wrote, "and knew . . . he never could feel for me . . . I miss you . . . in every way, emotionally mentally, physically." When they were apart, Chester wrote, "Are you disciplining yourself . . . ? Or are you just wasting all your mar-velous energy in talk? Well, whatever it is, I just can't help adoring you. My angel." And he reported to Havelock Ellis a "more inti-mate than . . . anticipated" sex life. It was queer for Esther, however, when she become pregnant again, although Chester assured her that he would take complete responsibility for the child. (Again she had a miscarriage.) And it was more than a little depressing for her when he brought home rough trade. There were frequent separations, some accompanied by long, loving letters, others by his vitriolic at-tacks and her remorse. "I know I am a very high strung and nerve ridden woman, with arbitrary instincts only too thinly veiled by an intellectual acceptance of the idea of tolerance," she wrote. "I have no illusions about how difficult and how wearing it must be to be with me day after day."

In the summer of 1935, they left New York and drove in "an enormous zig-zag across the country, six thousand miles in all," a trip that acquainted Esther with parts of the United States that she had never known. In New Mexico, she had what Chester called "a slight nervous breakdown," which a doctor "wrongly diagnos[ed] . . . as a cerebral hemorrage." She had no intention of moving to Cali-fornia, and he loathed New York City, so they agreed to spend half of each year on the other's coast. In New York they rented an apartment on East Fifty-first Street that, in Chester words, they envisioned using "as a meeting place for radicals of all kinds." One gathering, to help raise money for the Theatre Union, featured Clifford Odets, Elmer Rice, Irwin Shaw, and Thomas Wolfe. Dorothy Parker, John Dos Passos, Virgil Thomson, and Pavel Tchelichew also frequented the place. It was Esther's salon—her own, for the first time, just at the moment when political and literary life had self-consciously merged. Archibald MacLeish called it "the most brilliant in New York."

They also became involved in party politics. In 1936, Chester met privately with FDR at the White House, a visit that was more personal than anything else. Esther's respect for the president had grown and she asked Chester, "Do write me what you *felt* about the President as a human being . . . is he truly a historical minded man?" In Washington two years later, they both met with "various congressmen and other New Deal favorites," including Secretary of Agriculture Henry Wallace. They had lunch with the president at Hyde Park in the summer of 1938, and Esther, who deeply admired Eleanor Roosevelt, wrote a profile of her for *Harper's Bazaar*. In short, they were part of the fever in the air as the New Deal was set in motion that Dawn Powell described in her novel *A Time to Be Born*: "Everywhere people were whispering to each other, 'I've just got back from Washington,' with mysterious, significant looks as if now they knew the secrets of all nations . . . The mere name of the city, hitherto evoking only images of cherry blossoms and grisly state banquets, now invested whoever mentioned it with curious, enviable knowledge."

In 1938, they sublet the New York apartment and moved to a house in Oceano full-time. They had run through Chester's inheritances (his mother had died in 1935 and his father in 1937) and were living on the income from a small trust from Anna Murphy and on Esther's intermittent freelance journalism. She wrote a short profile of the American miser and financier Henrietta Green—"one of the great silent powers in American finance," who had had so much

---

"Chester & Esther ARTHUR Send their warmest greetings and wish you a Merry Christmas and a very Happy New Year," reads the printed text on the reverse of this image. Card sent to Edmund Wilson, December 17, 1940, from Oceano, California (General Collection, Beinecke Rare Book and Manuscript Library, Yale University, courtesy Estate of Edmund Wilson)

ready cash that she was "one of the six people whom J. P. Morgan sent for during the panic of 1893" as he prepared to bail out the Treasury. She began work on a biography of Madame de Pompadour. She agreed to collaborate with Chester on "a corrective biography" he wanted to write of his family—a triple portrait of his great-grandfather, grandfather, and father. She wrote a "scenario for Pompadour," which she recited one night, "taking all the parts in turn," Chester noted. "I never realized what a born actress she was!"

And she turned her attention to political organizing in California. She became the head of the Speakers Bureau of the Democratic State Central Committee (Chester was secretary of the committee), and wrote to John Strachey that the coming California election was "full of issues which will have great national repercussions" and that the "whole state is packed with political and economic dynamite, and has the most savage extremes of wealth and poverty, reaction and radicalism." She also worked on behalf of congressional candidates, for New Deal Democrats against conservative members of the party. "The Republican Party," she told an audience in June 1941, has won "again and again [even] when we have had a better cause and a better candidate, a more logical case to put before the voters of the country, because we failed on organization. But they have finally defeated themselves through a plethora of money and organization, and a bankruptcy of ideas." She lectured about the New Deal and foreign policy to party groups, women's clubs, and book clubs, and on the radio. Even in later years, when he most resented her, Chester still called her "a superb political speaker." And she was urged to run for national office. "You really might make us a hell of a representative in congress," wrote one observer of the local and national scene. "I've been fooled before—but at the present writing I think you have it all over the other potential candidates for the 11th District seat when it comes to understanding international affairs, an understanding which is woefully lacking in congress now, however imperative it is. If you are going to run, get in the race and tell the world you're in it."

She did not. She continued to write long analytical letters to her friends, saw clearly that appeasement was and would be a disaster. When Neville Chamberlain signed the Munich Pact, she wrote to Muriel Draper that the English prime minister had "betrayed far more than any man with his kind of a mind could ever envisage or estimate . . . nothing less than European civilization as we have known it." To Amy Strachey:

> the most charitable thing one can say about him is that he is consummately stupid. Heaven knows, I am as near to being a Pacifist as my sense of reality will permit me to be. I believe with Benjamin Franklin that "There never was a good war nor a bad peace." I absolutely agree that almost every conceivable compromise and sacrifice should have been made to avert the incalculable catastrophe of another general European war which, as we all know, would become a world war. But I simply cannot see that Chamberlain and poor intimidated Daladier . . . have done anything to prevent just such a war breaking out. In fact, I think they have done all in their power to make it almost inevitable by bowing to Hitler's bullying and blustering and thereby encouraging him in his mania for supreme power over Europe and all the rest of the world.

"Each new disaster comes over the radio to us as a fresh shock," she wrote in April 1939 to Janet Flanner, from whom she felt intolerably cut off. At the beginning of the 1930s, Esther's example had inspired Flanner to start research on a work that she believed would be taken more seriously than the journalism for which she was admired: "a book on the women of the seventeenth century . . . tentatively titled 'Without Men.'" And throughout the decade, Esther had parsed the American scene for Flanner. "The 'recession,'" she wrote,

> it is never referred to as a "depression," which is a metaphysical subtlety, was chiefly caused I am convinced by . . . the fact that the President listened to his more conservative advisors last spring and stopped the government spending too rapidly . . . Roosevelt is surrounded by counsellors of two diametrically opposing schools of thought . . . [T]he conservative or Old Guard senators and representatives who head the important congressional committees believed that the

1929–32 debacle was simply a normal if severe crisis in capitalism which needed some, but not too much government intervention to start the wheels going round again. The other school who might be called the real New Dealers . . . believe that if capitalism is to be saved . . . a great deal of government intervention and government control is absolutely indispensable. I, myself . . . do not believe that laissez faire can come back in any of the advanced and industrial countries during our lifetime nor for a great long while after it.

Now Flanner's *New Yorker* columns were keeping Esther and others informed about life in Europe on the verge of war. But "the incorrigible optimism of Americans," Esther wrote to her,

still leads them to feel that somehow everything must come out right in the end, in spite of the fact that there is very little chance of its doing so, and in consequence the country is very disconcerted when no sign of any amelioration in the European situation appears . . . I am abjectly pessimistic about the prospects of avoiding war. But I hope I am wrong. Chester and I lunched with Mr. Roosevelt at the end of June at Hyde Park, and, as I told you, he . . . said that if we managed to get through another year without a war it would be a miracle . . . the pattern the world seems doomed to follow is such a stupid and a tragic one. The one consolation is that human beings have lived through just as grim epochs in history as this one is before and have survived catastrophes as disastrous as the one now impending seems likely to be. It is a negative consolation, but, after all, it is something. I long to see you and to talk to you about all sorts of things for hours and hours. Whenever the new New Yorker comes I seize it to see if one of your letters is in it, so that I can read it and have the illusion that I am hearing the sound of your voice.

During the Spanish Civil War, Esther had called the Neutrality Act "one of the crassest blunders ever perpetrated," and when war

Chester Arthur, Janet Flanner, Esther, and Solita Solano, in Oceano, California, early 1940s
(Esther Murphy's photo album, AFP)

began in Europe, she campaigned energetically against American isolationism and for FDR. "We are not only confronted with an extraordinary situation in the world," she told one audience,

> we are faced with a state of affairs outside of our own borders that has never existed since we became an independent nation . . . The so-called Neutrality Act, which was a compromise born out of the isolationist doctrines, was one of those noble experiments like prohibition which was passed with the best intentions in order to keep us out of trouble; and just as the Prohibition Act, which was meant to bring about temperance, ended by bringing us into the worst orgy of drunkenness we had ever known, so the Neutrality Act which was mean to keep us at peace will probably get us into war under the most disadvantageous conditions unless we repeal it.

This work was the high point of her life in California. She continued to exist in conflict with herself, writing a little for the public—speeches, radio broadcasts, and a few published essays—while pouring her energy into correspondence, reading, and drinking. "On the side" of the Pompadour book, she was also "trying to write a short story about her, with a view to making some money—I hope I succeed."

Early in her marriage she had described Chester proudly to Muriel Draper as "that poltergeist . . . born into a solid republican family for its undoing," but he wreaked havoc in her already disorderly life as well. Neither of them was equipped for living with the other. He was drinking heavily, too, and there may have been physical violence between them. In late 1942 or early 1943, she wrote to him about "[a]ll the fights and rows and intrigues of the last three years" and said she had been "as close to a nervous collapse" during that time "as I have ever been in my life." For most of the four or five years she spent in California, she felt lonely and exiled. Early on she had appreciated Chester's "insatiable curiosity," through which she met "all sorts and kinds of people," and in California his hospitality and their location halfway between Los Angeles and San Francisco meant a constant flow of guests. There were her friends (Muriel

Draper and Langston Hughes from New York; Flanner and Solita
Solano, who had left France in 1939) and his (Robinson and Una
Jeffers, Lincoln Steffens and Ella Winter). But his "diversified circle
of acquaintances" was also distressing, since it included the sailors
and other men he brought home for sex.

Chester's strategy was to describe her flaws confidently, insult
her physical being, and suggest that they split. "The lonely eager little girl that I fell in love with," he wrote to her, "is turning into a
grim virago who seems to be trying to talk her way out of hysteria,
who talks thru Beethoven, talks thru sunsets and moonlight, talks &
talks & talks until I think I will go mad. And the fact that I know
this hysteria to be largely my fault does not help at all. But I also
know that no one could stand it, day after day, night after night."
She was "so bound by inertia," he said. She was "a huge & rather
clumsy tank or juggernaut car" on which was "mounted a loud-
speaker which blares forth brilliant ideas no one can refute and
which everyone wants to listen to for just so long." Addressing her
in the third person, he told her, "If she can't write or dictate or get
herself a lecture platform every night, she had better go back to
New York where she might inspire some real writer." He wanted
her to find "an outlet to the public for your ideas, & above all, a
sense of *work*." More kindly, he insisted, "You must really begin to
assume your rightful place in the world of letters, and not just be
known as a brilliant talker."

Instead of responding in kind, she exhorted him to "have confidence in yourself—I have always lacked it—it is a great handicap,"
and suggested that they "take heart and try to utilize our failures."
She interpreted the "fundamental trouble" between them as the
fact "that although neither of us are believers, you are a Baptist by
temperament and I am a Catholic . . . You have all the optimism and
the intense desire to see man perfect . . . which was the essential
spirit of the Reformation . . . You are amazed and outraged by men's
vices, I am astonished by their virtues and only amazed that they
are not infinitely more vicious than they are." She told him she
would rather be married to him "than to anyone else in the world
no matter what happens" and continued to treat him as one of her
interlocutors about the state of the union.

When he enlisted in the army in the fall of 1942, at age forty-one, she moved to Santa Barbara to live with his great-aunt, whose early proximity to President Arthur's White House made Esther exclaim, "She has seen so much of the dessous des cartes of the Seats of the Mighty—Arthur and Blaine and Conkling and Freling- huysen as a young girl, (do you realize that the year she was born was the year of Antietam, and of Napoleon III's invasion of Mex- ico!)." She forwarded a "very kind and gracious letter" she had re- ceived from Eleanor Roosevelt. She dissected the midterm elections of 1942, in which the Democrats lost many seats. "Some of the best and most disinterested democratic members of congress have been beaten and some of the worst of them triumphantly returned . . . A streamlined phoney like Claire [sic] Luce wins a large majority over a very decent, courageous and progressive democrat—and so forth." She predicted, with acumen,

> the republicans will join hands with the southern demo-
> crats to try and repeal or undermine every social reform the
> New Deal has put in. The hue and cry against labor has al-
> ready started! The republicans have not had an idea since
> Benjamin Harrison's time and the southern democrats have
> not had one since Appomattox—and I foresee an unofficial
> coalition of them running the country.

After Chester injured his foot in basic training (a long drama about his medical discharge ensued), they returned to New York, in the spring of 1943. That summer, he enlisted in the Merchant Ma- rine. He spent much of the rest of the war on a supply ship in the Mediterranean. Esther moved into an apartment at the Gladstone Hotel, on East Fifty-second Street, her home for the next several years, and regained her New York friends. She held court at the Gladstone's bar, which had a reputation as a hangout for gay women; at the nightclub and restaurant Tony's; at '21'; and at the Stork Club. She spent time with the actress June Walker, who also lived at the Gladstone, and she continued to be a resource for others— summarizing the history and significance of the French Third Re- public for the Time-Life journalist Rosalind Constable, for example. She became a regular panelist on the ABC radio program Listen— The Women!, a nationally broadcast weekly discussion of contemporary issues before a live audience that was moderated by Janet Flanner and featured Eleanor Roosevelt, Margaret Mead, and the popular novelist Fanny Hurst, among other guests. When they debated the role of memory, Esther's contribution was uncharacteristically brief: "A perfect memory is the enemy of thought," she said. Early in 1944, writing to a friend in California, she described herself as "very busy writing a book, which I expect will be published next year and doing some Red Cross work." A few months later she signed a contract with Harcourt Brace for her biography of Madame de Pompadour.

In debt to a number of friends and businesses, she sold more of her belongings at auction and waited for dividends from Mark Cross and for news about the company's sale or recapitalization. She assured Chester that if she died before she turned fifty-five (when her shares became hers), he would be her beneficiary, along with Gerald, and that if she did not, she would then "make a will leaving everything to you." She ended this letter, sent from Martha's Vineyard in the autumn of 1945, "It is terrible to think that I won't see you for another four months—but never never doubt how much I love you." Placating him this way was all very ambivalent, as well as fearful, since she was now living with the young European refugee and aspiring writer Sybille Bedford, with whom she had fallen in love.

As for her history repeating itself as farce in the person of Chester Arthur: From the late 1940s to his death in 1973, Chester's life was an amalgam of countercultural gestures and attempts at self-promotion. He counseled inmates at the state prison in Carson City, Nevada, and at San Quentin and appeared on *The $64,000 Question*. At San Quentin he met Alfred Kinsey (there studying male sexual behavior), and befriended Neal Cassady (there doing time). Through Cassady, he became close to Allen Ginsberg. ("Gavin Arthur smiled at me angry / for disbelieving Visionary sun / & Paradise we both believe in," wrote Ginsberg in the mid-1960s.) He sold newspapers on San Francisco street corners and made a reputation for himself as a gray eminence of gay bohemia. He appeared in *The Bed*, a short film by the gay poet and experimental filmmaker James Broughton; was a friend of the Zen philosopher Alan Watts;

became an astrologer; selected the date for the first Human Be-in; and never stopped bragging about his grandfather. His nutty New Year's forecasts appeared in Herb Caen's popular column in the San Francisco *Chronicle*: "Gavin Arthur predicts Martians will make contact with earthlings this year!"

Writing to Janet Flanner in 1967, he described himself as a creature free of financial concerns: "I have no bank account, no savings or insurance, no car to be attached. Yet I have everything. I go where I please & am lovingly taken care of by hippies." He protested too much: Along with a penchant for self-display he had a love of propriety and power. If in some contexts he styled himself a sexual activist, in his disputes with Esther he described "the social institution of marriage" as having "to do with something permanent rather than something ephemeral," and he was as obsessed with money as only someone who had grown up with wealth and lost it could be. He felt victimized because Esther and he had relied largely on his inheritance while they were married and he had never benefited from what he imagined were the Mark Cross millions. He saw himself as entitled to her money during their long separation; even after her death he demanded compensation from Gerald. In the 1950s, completing his college degree, he submitted a paper to one course that was, in fact, a thirty-eight-page letter to his lawyer in which he argued that his financial history with Esther "may prove an important legal case involving the new balance in the relationship of the sexes brought about by the new freedom and equality of women and their disproportionate share of the national wealth."

In 1966, he published *The Circle of Sex*, a book that combined his interests in sexology and astrology. Here he proposed a new vocabulary for sexual behavior—"*Homogenic, ambigenic,* and *heterogenic*" being "better in every way than *homosexual, bisexual,* and *heterosexual*"—and he outlined a twelve-point division of gender and sexual types along a continuum that corresponded to the clock, the seasons, and the phases of the zodiac. Twelve o'clock represented the "*paterfamilias,* completely heterogenic" type—"the ideal to which every male human must pretend to belong, whether he does or not." Six o'clock was the "female heterogenic category." In between, among others: the eight-o'clock type, which included "many business women," who were "very smart, very feminine in dress and toiletry, belonging definitely, in the alchemical sense, to the earth and water elements." He used friends and acquaintances as examples, outraging his first wife with his reference to her affairs with women, and classing Olivia Wyndham and Alice De Lamar—both unnamed but clearly described—in the "10 O'Clock, Homogenic, Late Morning" category, also termed the "Dyke Type."

Esther, who was no longer alive to object when this book was published, appears in several forms. He described the visit he and she ("my brilliant second wife") made to Havelock Ellis and quoted her conversation with Ellis. He invoked her without naming her, by calling Madame de Montespan, Madame de Maintenon, and Madame de Pompadour instances of the "Five O'clock hyperheterosexual female category" or "Courtesan" type. And he denounced her, in a thinly veiled, oddly prudish description of "a selfish Nine O'clock woman who has allowed her girlfriend [meaning Sybille Bedford] to poison her against her husband, to denounce him as a 'homo' and hold him up to the scorn of society, and who yet keeps his name for the prestige attached to it." There was something queer about this homosexual liberationist calling on the clichés of "predatory" lesbian behavior. "As Mrs. Arthur," he had written to Esther as early as 1947, "you have dragged a famous American name in the mud—by your open & ostentations liaison with an adventuress." The idea of Sybille Bedford using Esther for her money or social position is itself farcical. "I realized that this young woman," he wrote to his lawyer, "must be exerting an almost Svengali influence over her." And he invoked the notorious French play by Édouard Bourdet about a woman who leaves her husband for a woman—the Broadway production of which was shut down in 1927. "Memories of the play called 'The Captive' disturbed me greatly," he wrote.

While Esther's split with John Strachey had been painful, her separation from Chester Arthur was a strain and an embarrassment. But even ashamed of her former intimacy with him and upset by his periodic eruptions in her life, she could not help but see him as ridiculous. At the moment of their long-deferred divorce, in 1961, he was at once trying to extract money from her and attempting to marry a wealthy seventy-one-year-old woman. "What a pair they are," she wrote to Sybille. "Rather like characters in a very second rate Restoration comedy—Lady Maskwell and Mr. Plyant—who are both mutually deceived in each other when their manias collide."

Chester ended his days "in a crummy downtown apartment-turned-museum," its walls covered "with autographed photos of . . . Franklin and Eleanor Roosevelt, Walt Whitman, Havelock Ellis, Edward Carpenter, Robinson Jeffers, Alfred Kinsey, Woodrow Wilson, Henry Wallace, Aneurin Bevan, [and] Ernest Hemingway"— many of whom were Esther's friends. But his sense of his own historical importance did her at least one good turn. After his father's death, she had helped him organize President Arthur's private papers for donation to the Library of Congress. When she moved back to New York from California, she left behind hundreds of her own letters, some dating from the 1920s, a family photo album, miscellaneous papers, and many books. This material survived the Second World War, the occupation of the house in Oceano by the Coast Guard, and the almost three decades that followed. When Chester died, in 1973, much of it was donated, along with his archive, to the Library of Congress, where it now resides as part of the "Arthur Family Papers."

TOO LATE OR TOO SOON

I f Esther saw others as literary characters, she often struck others as one herself, and she figures in the fiction of the first half of the twentieth century more than once. In *This Circle of Flesh*, by the novelist and academic Lloyd Morris, Sheila Conway is "a strange girl" who "'substituted erudition for experience'" and proffered an "irresistible, if somewhat exhausting, hospitality."

> She was a trifle too tall and a trifle too heavy. She had the figure of a valkyrie, the broad and candid face of a plain boy, with a boy's brown hair, close cut. She had the warm, friendly, impersonal manners of a boy, likewise. But her eyes were those of a woman, and the puzzled eagerness that seemed to be their characteristic expression was, he thought, the look of a woman who has found no means of provoking desire in men.

This roman à clef did capture some of Esther's aura, even though Morris, whose own wish was to provoke desire in men, was also using her for this (somewhat exhausting) display of misogyny.

Her young friend Max Ewing put her in two stories, in one of which, an homage to Ronald Firbank, she was "Miss Bodicea Hangover, an appallingly erudite heiress . . . [who] declaimed excitedly, her voice resounding . . . On and on she went, Meditation after Expostulation, her memory never failing." But Ewing's close and constant observation of Esther, from the mid-1920s until his early death in 1935, suggests that the facts of her life were also broader than what was plausible for any fiction. "A very melodramatic incident

occurred" as Esther prepared to sail to London to marry John Strachey, he reported, describing what sounds like a bit of business
from a Marx Brothers movie:

> A girl whom Esther does not like very much . . . sent Esther
> a pair of [live] armadillos as a gift. The commotion on the
> boat was vast . . . They were delivered on the boat, crated,
> and wrapped in straw. Esther refused them. The steward
> said she had to take them because they were her property,
> and her responsibility on the voyage . . . She was furious and
> paced the deck, and ordered the animals away. They were
> carried away, only to [be] brought back by a ship official.
> The ship refused to take care of them. Esther refused to ac-
> cept them . . . When I left, the armadillos were still going up
> and down from deck to deck in the lift, being refused wher-
> ever they went.

"They are now," he concluded, "achieving almost international
importance."

Of all the writers who made use of Esther, Sybille Bedford best
captured her shyness and gregariousness, skepticism and naïveté,
gallantry and didacticism; the barrage of fact and fancy that made
up her train of thought; the hauteur and slanginess of her diction;
the fog of distraction about her; the physical authority and unease.
Writing to Sybille in 1953, Martha Gellhorn congratulated the
younger writer on her first book, *The Sudden View: A Mexican Journey* (now published as *A Visit to Don Otavio: A Traveller's Tale from
Mexico*), an account of the time Esther and Sybille spent in Mexico
after the Second World War. The figure called "E.," wrote Gellhorn, "is one of the finest characters you will ever invent." As
Sybille insisted, however, E. was not invented; she was a faithful
representation of Esther. "The wonderful thing is I never put words
in her mouth," she said. "She *was* like that." In *A Visit to Don Otavio*,
Esther is genuinely eccentric and is human—herself. In life, she
was the impetus for the book and the reason it almost never got
written.

Sybille Bedford had fled France in May 1940, just ahead of the
German occupation. Born in Germany, she had grown up in Italy,

England, and France. The most stable part of her peripatetic upbringing was in Sanary-sur-Mer, a town in the South of France
where a number of English writers, including Aldous Huxley and
D. H. Lawrence, had settled in the 1920s. Sybille's mother and step-
father ended up there as well, and Thomas Mann and other exiles
from the Third Reich later emigrated to the town. Befriended by
Aldous and Maria Huxley, Sybille also became close to Mann's
wild, brilliant children, Klaus and Erika. In the late 1930s, she
learned that she was on a Gestapo list—she was part Jewish and, living outside of Germany, had been "free to indulge in being an early
anti-fascist"—so when the Germans broke through the Maginot
Line, she and her friend Allanah Harper crossed the border to Italy.
One of the Bright Young Things in London in the 1920s, Harper
had moved to France in the 1930s and founded *Échanges*, a literary
review in which she presented the work of contemporary English
and French writers in translation. Sybille and she spent six anxious
days in Genoa until the Huxleys, in California since 1937, secured
them passage to the United States. Traveling on the last American
ship out of Italy, it took them twenty-one days to reach the United
States. They thought they would never see Europe again.

On her first day in New York, Sybille met Klaus Mann by pure
chance and was enlisted to drive his father's car, beloved dog, and
two African American servants from Princeton to Los Angeles, to
which the elder Mann was moving. This trip made it possible for
Sybille to reunite with the Huxleys, but she and Harper soon returned to New York. There she lived a precarious exile's existence,
teaching English to other refugees, doing occasional translations
for the art critic Clement Greenberg, keeping house for herself and
Harper, worrying constantly about friends and relations in Europe
and England. She had produced drafts of several novels, but nothing she or others yet deemed worth publishing. She spent time with
Greenberg, Mary McCarthy, and others in "the *Partisan Review*
crowd"; with Margaret Marshall, the literary editor of *The Nation*;
with Jane Bowles, with whom Harper was having an affair; with
Cyril Connolly's American wife, Jean, whom she had known in
Sanary, and her sister Anne, with whom she had a passionate affair;
and with members of what she called the "Trotskyite and Peggy
Guggenheim milieu."

Allanah Harper had written to Esther in Oceano when she and Sybille reached California in 1940, but Esther had been too ashamed of her life with Chester to reply. Harper had moved in the same circles as Olivia Wyndham in London in the twenties, and it was probably Wyndham who reconnected them after Esther returned to New York in 1943. A stream of historical references flowed from Esther when she joined Harper and Sybille Bedford at their apartment for cocktails one stormy winter night. In the elevator on their way out to dinner, she produced a discourse on the "Marseillaise" and the composer Lully. She took them to Tony's for the best meal they had had in years—the first of many evenings beyond her means to which she invited them. Harper went home after dinner, and Esther and Sybille adjourned to the Stork Club, two blocks from the Gladstone Hotel, where they talked for hours, until even the nightclub closed. Sybille, in her mid-thirties, was bowled over. Esther wrote, "I have never in my life felt about anyone the way I feel about you. I ask you to believe this." It was the kind of avowal she had made before, but it was the first time she had made it to a woman who was her intellectual equal, who admired her, and who wanted to be her lover. After they parted one evening, she sent Sybille a note describing her "elation, at the thought of your existence." As she was wont to do, she also made Sybille a character in her past, spinning a story of having met her some fourteen years earlier in France. She had been in Le Vigan, "that lost town in the Cévennes mountains," she wrote, sitting in a café "reading Albert Sorel's L'Europe et la Revolution Française," waiting for her car to be repaired, when a young Sybille appeared. With this story she also transplanted them both into a more distant past: The Cévennes were a stronghold of Protestant resistance during the religious wars that are part of Madame de Maintenon's story.

Falling in love with Sybille meant knowing much less than usual: "I know nothing," Esther ended this letter, "except that I love you and miss you much, much more than I can express or that I could have imagined missing anyone ever again. So I shall see you Monday night. Otherwise I shall send bailiffs after you so be careful." For Sybille, Esther—"super-naturally erudite"—was a way back to a seriousness she had been missing. Guilty about sitting out the war in New York, she also experienced Esther as a connection to

Europe. And Esther's "goodness of heart, her lovingness" moved
Sybille, who thought of her as having "the mind of [the] Founding
Fathers combined with a fragile and tender nature." She was also
baffled by her: Esther was shabby, even unkempt, yet she commanded respect wherever they went. The Stork Club operated on a
strict hierarchy, was one of the first nightclubs to use celebrities to
attract an exclusive public, and worked out its seating (whom one
could see and the extent to which one could be seen) almost scien-
tifically. But in clothes covered with cigarette burns—and wearing
slacks and an overcoat, not a dress or gown—Esther was shown to
a prime table on the floor that first night. "She just swept into the
Stork Club in old flannels and said to the maitre d', 'I *must* warn you
that Mrs. Bedford does *not* like ice in her highballs.'" Esther was
incapacitated by much of daily life and had "no aptitude whatsoever" for domesticity, but she was also fearless. When Sybille
moved into her room at the Gladstone, Esther would call down and
order breakfast for them both, not caring what the hotel management thought of her having a woman there.

Still, Esther—older, published, and at home in New York—put
herself in Sybille's hands. She was frightened before the broadcasts
of *Listen—The Women!* (Janet Flanner had returned to Europe and
the journalist Dorothy Thompson was the new host), so Sybille accompanied her to these performances, trying to calm her nerves.
The biography of Madame de Pompadour was due in eighteen
months; Esther was a mass of knowledge about seventeenth- and
eighteenth-century France; and Sybille did not doubt that Esther
would complete the book in time. But she also saw that Esther
would need support. "I thought I could make her work," she recalled. Despite or because of the time Sybille had spent in her
late adolescence tending her mother—another brilliant talker and
"writer manqué"—through a catastrophic addiction to morphine,
she believed that she could help Esther stop drinking.

When the war in Europe ended, Allanah Harper returned to
France. Her letters were full of warnings about the shortages of
food and every other necessity, and about the gulf between those
who had lived under occupation and those who had left. Booking
passage across the Atlantic was close to impossible, since service-
men had priority; getting train reservations across the United States

was difficult for the same reason. But Sybille wanted to travel before she returned to Europe, and Esther wanted to stay with her and not rejoin Chester in California, so when two tickets to Mexico City became available, they took them. On the eve of their departure for Mexico, in the summer of 1946, Edmund Wilson and Dorothy Parker joined them for farewell cocktails. When Wilson looked down at his glass and saw something floating in it, Sybille grabbed the glasses and retreated to the kitchen. She had been thinning the bourbon with tea, and a few tea leaves had made their way into the bottle. They left New York on the St. Louis Express of the Great Eastern and Missouri Railroad. They arrived in Mexico City knowing no one, knowing little of the country or language, carrying little money and "much too much luggage": too many clothes and "the bottom of [their] bags . . . falling out with books"; Esther also carried the notes for her study of Pompadour.

Esther is the first dedicatee and main character of A Visit to Don Otavio, and her influence permeates Sybille's book. She is a foil for the narrator's observations about travel in general and this journey in particular. "She hated to travel—God, she hated to travel," Sybille said half a century later. (Bouncing around Mexico was not like sitting on an ocean liner on the Atlantic, or in a café in Paris.) "She said, 'It took years out of my life.'" Esther's body was a problem: She was too tall for the spaces allotted her on buses, carts, and other vehicles; she got stuck in the trapdoors and secret passages of a clandestine convent built during the persecution of the Catholic Church in Mexico; she became "eloquent on the various phenomena of heat prostration." Her refusals of tourism have a life of their own in Don Otavio: "'I will not go to this volcano,' said E. in the manner of Edmund Burke addressing the House of Commons." And: "In my native country I successfully avoided seeing the Grand Canyon; I avoided the Painted Desert, my nurse did not manage to drag me to Niagara." Her characteristic gesture, in the face of every unnerving landscape, uncomfortable conveyance, or quotidian need, was to bury her head in Mansfield Park. "I laugh when I think of her in Mexico," said Sybille. "It was very, very funny—this tall Don Quixote figure, with a head like Jefferson, bowing to everybody and

saying, 'Viva Mexico,' with an American accent. It's the only Spanish she learned."

Sybille Bedford's style is her own—philosophical, hilarious, at
once lush and elliptical, viscerally precise—but Esther also inhabits
the texture of her prose. In Puebla, she writes, Esther "stalked past
it all, the way Dr Johnson must have stalked about the Hebrides."
The book's meditations on the vertigo of historical consciousness
also owe something to Esther: "In the spaces of the Plaza Mayor,
walking over the grave of a pyramid, one is assailed by infinity,
seized at the throat by an awful sense of the past stretching and
stretching backwards through tunnels of time . . . One is in a legend, one is walking in Troy." So does its mixture of fact and fiction;
Sybille acknowledged that she did invent parts of it. (Esther's cousin
"Anthony" is one fabrication.) The reading the two did in preparation for their trip also bears Esther's stamp. It included the diary of
Fanny Inglis, Madame Calderón de la Barca, an American who
married the first Spanish ambassador to Mexico in the 1830s, "became governess to one of the various children of Queen Isabella . . .
and . . . was created, like that other royal governess, Madame de
Maintenon, a marchioness."

Esther is the voice of history in the book. As their train navi-
gates a vertiginously steep "side of the Western Sierra Madre," she
muses, sanguine, to Sybille's terror: "I believe this is a very great
engineering feat . . . We had the same problem in the Rocky Mountains. No rail-bed can take that kind of stress long. You remember
the Colorado Pass Rail Wreck in '39?" During and after their trip,
she educated Sybille about Maximilian and Carlota, the perpetra-
tors and victims of one of the European maneuvers for Mexico,
who were made emperor and empress of the country in 1864. Esther stands for Northern liberalism, declaring to a Republican lady
from Virginia long resident in Mexico, "My father voted for Woodrow Wilson twice; I cast my first vote for James Cox against the
unfortunate Harding; I voted for John W. Davis against Coolidge . . .
Personally, Mrs Rawlston, I am a strong Roosevelt woman." She
represents North American impatience in the face of "Latin" modes
of life and work. She is the New World to Sybille's Old. " 'I am an
American,' said E. in an uncertain tone . . . 'I am an American. I will
not be pushed around.' " Yet her consciousness of European his-

tory never leaves her. At the miraculously peaceful establishment presided over by "Don Otavio," where they stayed for several months, she marveled at their host: "'Don Otavio,' said E., 'you must have seen great changes. Like a man born in France in 1770.'"

Getting stuck in the secret passage of a convent is an apt metaphor for Esther's writing impasse. But lodging with Don Otavio, she was transformed: She ate well, gained weight, drank in moderation, and at siesta time would pace "swinging a small stick, the single upright figure during the slow hours . . . composing step by step, clause by clause the periods of an exegesis of one of the more incomprehensible personages of seventeenth-century France." Here, although she was not writing, she was composing, in her head or out loud. The personage in question was Madame de Maintenon, however, not Pompadour. During their first summer in Mexico, their luggage had been stolen, and along with her suitcase and briefcase (both from Mark Cross), Esther lost her notes on Madame de Pompadour, as well as most of her clothes and a precious bundle of letters from her father. It was on one of those afternoons chez Don Otavio that Sybille was seized by the idea for a book that blended the history of Mexico, travelogue, memoir, and invention, a comedy about some of the tragedies of history.

They put off their return for months—at times because Sybille wanted to see more of the country, at others because they did not have the return fare or a place to live in New York—finally flew back in March 1947, and spent several difficult, impoverished months in the city while Esther tried to sort out her life. She negotiated with Gerald about Mark Cross and met with an insistent Chester, who had arrived from California wanting money and to reunite—or at least not to lose her to a woman. Sybille was under pressure to return to France before her visa expired, but she suspected that Esther was being treated unfairly by her family and felt that she could not leave her to manage her finances and Chester alone. Esther had at some point agreed to send Chester funds every month and, with Sybille's help, had mailed him several checks from Mexico. She wanted nothing to do with him, but was frightened of his vindictiveness in the event of a divorce and was used to ignoring what she hoped was not true. So she met with him almost daily, sometimes with Sybille and sometimes alone, at a bar on Sixth Avenue halfway between their apartment and his hotel. She and Sybille finally found passage to Europe on a converted troopship. Margaret Marshall "staged" a "mad farewell party" for them, and they sailed on June 9, 1947. Allanah Harper met them when they arrived at Le Havre ten days later. Sybille was thirty-six, Esther almost fifty years old.

During that first long, hot summer in France, which followed the coldest winter in Europe for years, Esther moved between the Hotel des Saints-Pères, an old Bloomsbury haunt near Saint-Germain-des-Prés, and Noel Murphy's house in Orgeval. Sybille was often with old friends from Sanary who were now living on a farm in the Touraine, who then invited Esther as well: "She came, she stayed, she spellbound her hosts," Sybille wrote, "with her broad evocations of French and American history delivered in an oratorical voice in near flawless French with a heavy not disagreeable accent, while she vaguely stirred about the *noisette de porc aux pruneaux* congealing on her plate." Meals continued for hours, while Esther talked and failed to eat. Janet Flanner and Noel— separated for most of the war and now involved in a complicated pas de trois with Flanner's new lover, Natalia Danesi Murray—also came to visit.

Sybille later described that homecoming to Europe as "part jubilant . . . part traumatic." Part of the trauma was that almost immediately on their arrival Esther became embroiled in romantic complications of her own, succumbing to the manipulative attentions of a woman who had once been entangled with Sybille and whose lover was now leaving her for Allanah Harper. Esther was "infatuated with her," she wrote when it was over, "and flattered by her infatuation for me." The result was two years of confusion, equivocating about her commitment to Sybille, and melodrama among the five of them: Esther, Sybille, Allanah, and the other two women. Neither Esther nor Sybille was writing. When Sybille left for Italy that autumn, Esther stayed behind, vacillating—her inability to follow Sybille, whom she loved, akin to her inability to focus on her book.

Over the next two years, she promised to join Sybille, and they spent stretches of time together in Rome, Florence, Ischia, and Capri. In 1949, she agreed to lecture at the Italian American Institute in Rome about "the twenty years preceding the Civil War, roughly from 1840 to 1861 (annexation of Texas, Missouri Compromise, 'Free Soil' policy, constitutional issue on slavery, Lincoln, birth of the Republican party). Tell them not to be alarmed, I can and *have* done it in an hour." But she always returned to France and romantic entanglement with a woman she did not particularly like or respect. "I have played fast and loose with our relationship," she wrote to Sybille, "and I would not blame you at all if you felt that my conduct has killed something in it that cannot be revived." Sybille, increasingly frustrated by Esther's "clouds of talk," began immersing herself in the book that became *Don Otavio*, working with the urgent knowledge that she had to commit herself to a writing life and accepting that Esther would never settle down to disciplined composition. From Ischia she wrote to an old friend, "E. is now an almost impossible person to live with because she is absolutely idle, and I fear will remain so . . . One must not put the blame on the other person. But I feel I cannot go on with this and must make myself another existence somehow."

"I love you really at last, the way I should have loved you always" Esther wrote in the spring of 1950. "But everything comes too late or too soon." By then, Sybille had decided to settle in Rome and had met someone else; Esther stayed on in Paris. Sybille remained her closest friend for the rest of her life and was the "*only* person," in Noel Murphy's view, whom Esther allowed to influence her behavior. "Next to my father and Muriel Draper," Esther wrote to Sybille in 1957, "I owe more to you than to any human being I have known."

Allanah Harper, walking into Esther's room at the Hotel des Saints-Pères in October 1950, found a "table . . . covered in notes on Madame de Pompadour or is it Maintenon, now?"

THE SUBLIME GOVERNESS

Sometime during the autumn of 1683—the exact date is uncertain—Louis XIV, King of France and Navarre, who was the most powerful man on earth, was married to a woman of doubtful antecedents who had been the governess of his illegitimate children. The marriage took place under circumstances of extraordinary secrecy. The ceremony was performed at night in the palace of Versailles by the king's confessor, Father La Chaise, assisted by the Archbishop of Paris, Harlay de Champvallon . . . No public or official announcement of the marriage was ever made, but in spite of this and of the elaborate precautions that were used to conceal the fact that it had occurred, the news of it spread throughout France and the rest of Europe with great rapidity.

Thus begins the principle exhibit in the case for Esther Murphy's failure: her unfinished study of Madame de Maintenon, born Françoise d'Aubigné.

There are several undated drafts of this project on which Esther spent at least the last fifteen years of her life. One version, probably the earliest, is written in an Italian notebook decorated with fleurs-de-lis. The rest are a collection of loose pages—type- and handwritten, incomplete, inconsistently paginated, now disordered. Although there are differences among the drafts, most revisit the same material, sometimes word for word. All are punctuated idiosyncratically. All are dense with citation. All begin with the secret wedding ceremony. The version written in the Italian notebook ends with the baptism of the infant Françoise d'Aubigné. The loose pages do not progress beyond her marriage at age sixteen to the writer Paul Scarron.

The material in the notebook is headed:

A Marriage of Conscience
by Esther Murphy
Louis XIV and Madame de Maintenon

She subtitled the first section "The Sublime Governess." She used three lines from T. S. Eliot's "Gerontion" as her first epigraph: "History has many cunning passages, contrived corridors / And issues, deceives with whispering ambitions, / Guides us by vanities." A second epigraph is from the eighteenth-century Huguenot writer Laurent Angliviel de La Beaumelle: "With respect to Madame de Maintenon who was regarded at Saint Cyr as a saint, at the court as a hypocrite, in Paris as a person of intellect and in all the rest of Europe as a woman without morals; I have let the facts speak for themself."

Esther focused first, as these lines from La Beaumelle suggest, on Maintenon's reputation. The eighteenth-century memoirist the Duc de Saint-Simon called her "'the famous and fatal Madame de Maintenon,'" she wrote, "and . . . pursues [her] with peculiar malevolence." She summarized the general low opinion of her subject by citing the writer Émile Henriot (her own contemporary): "Madame de Maintenon n'a pas bon[ne] presse." (Madame de Maintenon gets a bad rap.) She also focused on Maintenon's eventful, difficult childhood and on the extravagant reverses and advances of her life:

Françoise d'Aubigné, Madame Scarron and Madame de Maintenon, to give her the three names she bore during the course of her life, had been formed by an experience that was both harsh and wide and by a strange inheritance. The improbable fate that was reserved for her and that brought her at last, after so many vicissitudes and such a prolonged acquaintance with poverty, disaster and disgrace, to what she called "A Fortune that it is hard to imagine"; contained

some of the most extravagant elements of melodrama . . .
The second wife of Le Roi Soleil was born in a prison—the
fortress of Niort—where her father was incarcerated and
where her mother had been allowed to join him.

Maintenon's prehistory—her Huguenot forebears, the religious
wars of sixteenth- and seventeenth-century France, and the relationship of both to the dance of power during the reign of Louis
XIV and before—is another thread of Esther's narrative. This was
the bloody, irrational tale that fascinated her as much as Maintenon
herself did: the traumas of "a century that was almost as sinister as
our own." In 1534, shortly after Jean Calvin fled France for Geneva,
a third of the French population were Huguenots, and "there seemed
to be nothing that could stop the progress of Calvinism in France."
The Catholic attempt "to exterminate the Huguenots," Esther
wrote, turned into "a civil war of unparalleled ferocity, that was to
divide, devastate and exhaust France for thirty-six years; to leave
after it a fatal legacy of malice and hatred; and to prepare the way
for the absolute monarchy."

Françoise d'Aubigné's great-grandfather, Jean d'Aubigné, was
one of those converts to Protestantism. Her grandfather, Théodore-
Agrippa d'Aubigné, was a famous Huguenot soldier, poet, and
scholar, a leader during those civil wars. But her mother was a devout
Catholic, and Françoise was manipulated throughout her childhood
to fight small versions of the battles between the Catholic Church
and French Protestants. Her father, Constant d'Aubigné, was a gambler, rapist, murderer, forger, and counterfeiter who "changed his
religion whenever he thought it expedient to do so"; betrayed his
father to the French government; "was sentenced to death three
times"; spent much of his life in prison; and deserted his second
wife, Jeanne de Cardillhac, the daughter of one of his jailors, when
he was released from prison. Jeanne had Françoise baptized a Catholic, but the child was soon adopted by her Huguenot aunt Madame
de Villette, because of her parents' desperate circumstances. Growing up with this woman, Françoise "became a fervent protestant—a
fact," Esther wrote, "that some of her Catholic biographers have attempted to deny." However, "extremely precocious, she showed
great theological independence and she refused to subscribe to the

doctrine of eternal punishment, the cornerstone of Calvinism. 'You will see that God will change his mind, and that he will put out the flames of hell': she said when she [was] seven years old."

After then living with her mother for several unhappy years— including a time on the Caribbean island of Marie Galante— Françoise was adopted by a distant relation, Madame de Neuillant, who treated her as an unpaid servant and attempted to restore her to Catholicism. Madame de Neuillant's crusade was motivated by her desire to find favor with the monarchy and was part of the uneasy pre-Revolutionary negotiations between the aristocracy and the Crown. But "exposed to all the winds of doctrine," Françoise still refused to renounce her faith, so Madame de Neuillant sent her to an Ursuline convent, hoping that the nuns would be more persuasive. There, wrote Esther, the girl

> conceived a passionate attachment to one of the nuns, a certain Mother Celeste. That it was far more than a passing infatuation is shown by the way in which she spoke of it many years afterwards . . . "My dear Mother Celeste, I loved her to a point that I can never express. I thought that I would die when I had to leave that convent . . ." It was the most emotional confession that she ever made and it revealed a side of her nature that was deeply hidden . . . But in spite of her affection for Mother Celeste she remained implacably hostile to the Catholic religion.

By the time Madame de Neuillant sent her to another convent, this time in Paris, her case had become notorious: She was the granddaughter of the Huguenot hero Agrippa d'Aubigné and "was not an ordinary girl of fourteen," Esther wrote. "She had intellectual powers of a very uncommon kind and a will of iron." At this convent she met another special nun—humane, intelligent, and

> so persuasive that Françoise d'Aubigné asked that a catholic priest and a protestant minister should debate before her and that she should make her own decision on the merits of the two creeds . . . The debate continued for several days and throughout it Françoise d'Aubigné stood in the parlour

of the convent wearing a shabby dress that was much too short for her and holding a bible in her hand, in which she followed the texts which the priest and the minister were quoting with the closest attention . . . "Finally she perceived that the minister was garbling certain passages of the bible and . . . she determined to embrace the Catholic cause and made her abjuration:" we are told.

She based her decision, it seems, on the principle of correct citation. Noting her subject's later silence about the event and the few other sources on it, Esther asked, "Did she grow weary of the unequal struggle and decide at last that God was on the side of the heaviest battalions and that it was better to be a Catholic than a protestant in France? Did she realize that the French reformation was one of the greatest failures in history and did she dislike failure? We have no satisfactory answers to these questions."

Madame de Neuillant then married Françoise d'Aubigné to the comic writer Paul Scarron, who was an invalid many years her senior. She had been mistreated by Madame de Neuillant, and "the age was notoriously unsentimental about matrimony, nevertheless it was generally regarded at the time as a marriage that could only have been made by a young girl who was extremely cold-blooded and not very delicate," wrote Esther. "The opinion has persisted ever since." There is no record of the ceremony, which took place in April 1652, "and it is believed that it was destroyed after Madame de Maintenon married Louis XIV." She spent her wedding night nursing her husband, who was in excruciating pain "that could only be partially alleviated by doses of opium."

So ends the longest version of Esther's manuscript.

What she left out, in brief: That the poet, playwright, and novelist Scarron educated his young wife and introduced her to the brilliant company he kept, and Françoise, now Madame Scarron, became one of the attractions of his salon. Scarron died when Françoise was in her mid-twenties, leaving her with culture and connections but no money. After some years of struggle, friends at court helped her obtain a royal sinecure. Madame Scarron became close to salonnières and aristocrats, including Mademoiselle de Scudéry, Madame de Sévigné, and Madame de Montespan, and she did not succumb, or she did, to the advances of various admirers. In 1670, Madame de Montespan, then the king's favorite mistress, asked Madame Scarron to become the secret governess to Montespan's children with him. Madame Scarron's learning and discretion were admired, and several years later, when Louis XIV legitimized these royal bastards, she accompanied the children to court. She became indispensable, as they say, to the king and was involved in a long power struggle with Montespan. The king gave her the château of Maintenon (or the money to purchase it) and, as a further sign of favor, created her the "Marquise de Maintenon."

For the next several decades, Madame de Maintenon was a focus of political intrigue and questions about her access to policymaking. The extent of her influence on Louis XIV is still debated. She is generally held to have been powerful especially regarding religious matters—meaning both the politics of the day, from which religion was inseparable, and the king's own spirituality, including his late-in-life turn to God after decades of licentiousness. Her own increasingly fervent Catholicism included entanglement in offshoots of doctrine (such as Jansenism and Quietism), which endangered both her own position at court and the monarchy itself, because of Louis XIV's tenuous relationship with Rome. She urged conversion on her Huguenot relatives and essentially kidnapped a niece and raised her a Catholic. For many years she was loathed by Protestants and said to have been responsible for the revocation of the Edict of Nantes, the treaty of toleration of Protestants in France that her grandfather had helped broker—an accusation that has now been discredited. (Esther indicates in passing that Louis XIV made this decision with Maintenon's approval.) It is believed that Maintenon urged Louis XIV to renounce his mistresses and reconcile with his wife (which he did), even as she continued her intimacy with him. Her marriage to the king followed shortly after the queen's death in July 1683.

She was indisputably a powerful educator, making something of herself and of other women through self-instruction and teaching. In the early 1680s, she founded a school for the daughters of impoverished aristocrats as an alternative to the convent. The school was eventually established at Saint-Cyr, near Versailles, and the excellence of its curriculum was widely acknowledged: It served as a model for women's education in France, inspiring the founding of other secular institutions. From Racine, then Louis XIV's official historian, she commissioned two plays on biblical themes— *Esther* and *Athalie*—for the students. Their performances before the court were such successes, inviting courtiers' excessive attention to the students and dangerous rumors about the girls' chastity, that to save the students' reputations, the school's, and her own, Madame de Maintenon was forced to transform Saint-Cyr into a religious institution, subject to the relatively liberal Order of St. Augustine. She devoted enormous energy to the school, and her lectures to the faculty and students, the dramatic dialogues ("Conversations") and proverb plays she composed for the young women, and her correspondence (thousands of letters, first published in the nineteenth century and thought by some to rival those of Madame de Sévigné) are a remarkable and still underread part of French literature. After the king's death in 1715, she left Versailles and retreated to Saint-Cyr, where she died on April 15, 1719.

All of these cunning passages were part of Esther's monologues about the sublime governess. But they did not make it into print.

When Nancy Mitford, who had become a close friend of Esther's, decided to write about Madame de Pompadour, she asked and received Esther's permission to do so and borrowed many of Esther's books, carting them back and forth between their Paris apartments. It is probable that Esther had already abdicated the Pompadour project. It seems clear that she was not troubled by feelings of ownership of her subject, or by the paranoia about priority that often afflicts biographers. Several years earlier she had written that her work on Pompadour was foundering on her attempt to tell the story of that intensely political woman in the context of the world war of her day. "The writing is going well—better than I expected," she reported to Chester in 1943, "but I have tackled something . . . that was much bigger than I bargained for—the political implications of the Seven Years War and the whole change that took place on the face of the world are not going to be easy and I have had to revise my outline considerably."

Maintenon was different: a mark of Esther's engagement with the past almost from the beginning; a constant companion and burden for the last decade and a half of her life. She noted Maintenon's birth and death dates in her correspondence and quoted her constantly: "'My God, how sad life is, I cannot understand why we dread death.'—Mme. de Maintenon never spoke more wisely than that," she wrote to Sybille in the spring of 1949. A few months later she cited her to praise Eleanor Roosevelt:

> As Madame de Maintenon once wrote, "I know that God has his saints in every condition" but then went on to say that she was unable to recognize any of them among the denizens of the court of France—it is strange that one should turn up in this age in the U.S., in the most unlikely position of all,—the wife of a president. Mrs. R. and her life have the grandeur and simplicity of an integrity and a virtue that have proved insusceptible to corruption. At a time in history when it is not very reassuring to belong to the human race, I feel personally grateful to her, for having reasserted by simply being what she is, the moral dignity and stature of mankind.

Watching a play at the Comédie Française, she imagined "that ex-Huguenot, the Sublime Governess . . . nodd[ing] a qualified approval to some of" the swipes at the Catholic Church in the dramatization of André Gide's anticlericalist tale, *Les Caves du Vatican*. When she became close to Eileen Hennessy, of the Cognac-making family, and stayed at her house in the Charente, she wrote to Sybille that the area was associated with Maintenon's early life and that a local museum had "many relics . . . of her discreet and pious progress through the world."

These references, both mocking and admiring, were also a way for Esther to tell friends that she was at work on her book. Some of them were puzzled that the imagination of a committed American Democrat should be so fired by the environs of "monarchy incarnate." Maintenon's rags-to-riches story is different from but resonates with the American version of that trajectory. The extent to which her life seems to be the stuff of facts that speak for themselves, of facts that are irretrievable, and of improbable fictions also fed Esther's thinking about her. The extent to which all biography is autobiography, as Emerson wrote, meant that Françoise d'Aubigné's precociousness and scholarship, her mixed Protestant and Catholic parentage, her early, independent thinking about religion, her troubled relations with her mother and preference for her father, her political acumen and access to policymakers, and her deep affection for an older woman were all ways for Esther to tell, or not tell, her own story. Maintenon's written work, like Esther's, also had a complex relation to her speech, much of it originating in the hundreds of talks she gave to the students and faculty of Saint-Cyr, which they transcribed and she then reviewed and corrected.

Another way of thinking about Esther's attachment to this figure has to do with definitions of modernity, which historians sometimes date not from the Industrial Revolution, the turn of the twentieth century, or the First World War but from the Reformation. Here it is possible to see Esther's work on Madame de Maintenon not only as a fascination with a distant, monarchist—albeit personally resonant—history, but also as part of her attempt to think about the past in the political present. Living in Europe after the Second World War, in the wake and still the midst of destructive secular creeds that had been wielded with religious fervor, Esther was studying a woman whose life was shaped by an earlier moment of devastating violence over doctrine. The wars of religion had been followed by the rise of liberal democracies all over Europe—forms of government that were supposed to have prevented anything like fascism. Studying Maintenon in the postwar years, she was also remaining skeptical about creating the present either through clean breaks with the past or through a return to some mythically pure origin.

In her correspondence and in her manuscript, Esther often described a problem of documentation. "Nearly all the information we have about her," she wrote, "is contained in the autobiographical fragments in her letters, in her conversations with the nuns of Saint Cyr which they carefully noted down; and in the memoirs of her companion and secretary, Mademoiselle d'Aumale, and of her cousin Madame de Caylus." But Esther also called this problem of documentation a question of character. Maintenon was vexing because she left so few traces: Esther expressed this idea repeatedly, to the point that the most salient feature of Maintenon's character that

emerges from Esther's writing is her inaccessibility. "Like so many of her emotions, Madame de Maintenon kept it to herself," she wrote of Françoise's feelings about her father, Constant d'Aubigné. Maintenon's account of her conversion, "like many of [her] confidences . . . was extremely limited." When she married Louis XIV, "she confided" to her brother, "in her reticent way, her own feelings about her incredible elevation. 'It is a personal adventure that cannot be communicated to others'; she wrote . . . and as far as we know that was her last word on her [the] subject." The third epigraph Esther entered in the notebook draft announces Maintenon's refusal to be portrayed: "If I were to tell the story of my life I would not be believed." In another version, Esther quoted this statement as "I shall not write my life: I cannot tell everything; and what I could tell would not be believed."

Of course, her focus on Maintenon's reticence and "baffling character" was also a way to name her own frustration and ambivalence. In 1955, Nancy Mitford, "determined" that Esther complete this work, interested her publisher, Hamish Hamilton, in it. The prospect filled Esther with loathing for herself and for Maintenon. "I am really afraid now that I will have to finish the book about this unsympathetic and very important woman who as a whole disgusts me even more than I am disgusted by my self," she wrote to Sybille. When Mitford talked about her own plan to write the life of Voltaire, Esther told her that "it would not be more difficult than Madame de Maintenon & certainly less depressing." Yet Margaret Marshall's move from *The Nation* to an editorial position at Harcourt Brace, and Marshall's appreciation of a "fragment" of the book (probably forwarded by Sybille), "delighted" Esther. (The publisher had apparently agreed to a book on Maintenon instead of Pompadour.) "It will be a great help to me to have someone like Margaret at Harcourt Brace," she wrote to Sybille.

These mixed feelings thread through her correspondence, alongside allusions to illness, politics, reading, financial trouble, and social life. "The book is not going too badly as a whole," she wrote in the summer of 1956. The next month: "But the figure of Madame de M. is very perplexing. She was full of such evasive candour which

Esther, Sybille Bedford, and unidentified friend, circa 1950s (Private collection)

was obviously in no way insincere, because she believed it herself. One conclusion I have come to, whatever she was—she was not a hypocrite. But Saint Beuve was probably right when he said 'Françoise d'Aubigné est une protée insais[iss]able.' [Françoise d'Aubigné is protean and elusive.] Oh Dear!" In January 1959, after a visit from Sybille, she wrote, "I am so glad you liked what I read you about the Old Governess. She was quite a person. I find myself with a strange sympathy for her—though I started with none at all—only curiosity." Several weeks later she reported that "Madame de M. is going well" and that she found "her odder and odder, most unsympathetic, very extraordinary and absolutely fascinating. Do you know what she said when she was shown some filthy and obscene libels that were distributed about her[?] 'I am accustomed to live on poison.'" In the spring of 1962, six months before her death, Esther wrote to Sybille, "I am glad you liked my description of the Maintenon as the 'poor, crouching, human being.'"

Such swings of discouragement and hope are the usual, humiliating highs and lows of writing—focused, in the composition of a biography, on an actual historical human being. It is possible that the latter part of Maintenon's life eluded Esther because she was used to being able to learn what she wanted to know, say what she wanted to say, and—because she could not find the right mixture of irony and sympathy in this case—could not decide what she thought of her subject. Once Maintenon arrived at the court of Louis XIV, Esther would have had to contend with Maintenon's highly theatrical piety and with the conservative nature of her advice to young women: While the pedagogy she developed at Saint-Cyr was progressive, emphasizing dialogue between teacher and student and among students, the curriculum's focus on domesticity, conformity, and submission was not. The paradox of Maintenon preaching virtue to aristocratic girls when she was herself of uncertain reputation and low birth appealed to Esther. But there was no map to writing about a woman who, up to that time, had been the subject of either hagiography or attack, no clear precedent if one wanted to neither glorify nor slander. The most proximate attempt to tackle her subject is a resolute attempt at recovery. In *Madame de Maintenon*, published in London in 1929, the author, Maud Cruttwell, writes, "She, stigmatized as cruel, capricious, vindictive, fatal to

France, was in reality a paragon of honesty, loyalty and magnanimity; very simple, very straightforward, supremely charitable; a saint, whose sole ambitions were to convert her King and alleviate the misery caused by his wars."

Esther could not write for publication about why Maintenon mattered to and troubled her, even though such personal speculations had long been part of her letters and even essays. Today there are many self-reflexive works of biography. When Esther was thinking about Maintenon, there was one stunning example: A.J.A. Symons's 1934 *The Quest for Corvo: An Experiment in Biography*, a double portrait that tells the story of the difficult and prodigious Frederick Rolfe while tracing Symons's own "step[s] on a trail that led into very strange places" in pursuit of Rolfe's story. Symons himself wrote with the conviction that the entire genre of biography was a failure. In a 1929 lecture titled "Tradition in Biography," he argued that of all the literary forms, "biography alone has no convention save the sober one of truth, and yet biography alone has failed." Lytton Strachey's irreverent and condensed *Eminent Victorians*, published in 1918, is usually seen as having revolutionized English-language biography. But despite the book's impact, the Victorian biographical tradition (hagiographic, multivolume) still held sway in the late 1920s in England and the United States. The genre "has failed in beauty as it has in truth," Symons argued: "in beauty, for what biography could be re-read for the pleasure of its form alone? and in truth, for biography is still a form of panegyric. Its future is uncertainly hopeful; its past history is certainly bad; for so far as it has a tradition it has a *bad* tradition; and though of all forms of art it has perhaps most to say, it has certainly, in the way of accomplishment, least of all to show."

Symons's reinvention of the genre in *Corvo* notwithstanding, his own life has also been seen as one of thwarted achievement. Julian Symons, who edited a posthumous volume of his brother's published and unpublished work, described him as a man who lived at cross-purposes to his own goals as a writer and who was "absorbed . . . continually" by this contradiction and by his sense of failure. The men Symons wrote about "showed an imbalance between intention and achievement which fascinated him because it was echoed in his own nature," wrote Julian, and because he be-

lieved "that failure is almost always more interesting than success."
At his death, A.J.A. Symons also left an unfinished biography of
Oscar Wilde, about which Julian wrote, "He never really made a
final organization of the great mass of material he had collected,"
yet "enough remains, I think, to show that the book would really
have been a study that made others unnecessary and that it might
have been one of the high points of English biography." No one has
made this claim about Esther's Maintenon manuscript. Sybille Bedford referred to it as "thirty pages of Lytton Strachey's prose," but
it was not clear whether she was criticizing Strachey, or Esther for
not sounding more like herself. But Esther's unfinished book, like
Symons's, was made of long study and personal shortcomings; of
the challenges of producing a biography about a figure it was difficult to celebrate (Wilde in the 1920s and '30s was still a pariah); and
of the question of how and where a biographer's own story might fit
into such a work.

THE GRAVE'S INTERCOM

What if one cannot finish it? What if it is unreadable, impossible, undesirable, an embarrassment, when it is done? What if it is over, lost, when it is done? What if it is unclear why one began, when it is done? What if it never gets done?

She went on collecting material. In the spring of 1950 she described herself to Sybille as "sitting in triumph in an obscure tabac-café near the bookshop where I got for 200 francs, an unprocurable book on the Governess. Full of the royal low-down on her." She did "some research . . . in the Vatican library—which is very fruitful."

She went on writing, or saying that she was. Her travel plans, she wrote in the summer of 1956, were contingent on whether "work goes well this month."

She went on provoking questions: "Esther still believes herself to be working on her book on Mme. de Maintenon, and that she is coming back home when she has finished it," noted Edmund Wilson. "This must have been going on for twenty years. I wonder how much writing she does." Another friend wrote, after her death, "In the 10 or 12 years I knew her, the answer was always the same. 'Oh'—terrific arm sweep—'it's about a third done, you know'—quick pull on the cigarette—'yes, around a third done now.'"

In the last fifteen years of her life, she was frequently waiting for a dividend from Mark Cross. She still depended on the small income from her mother's trust, and on gifts from Gerald, Noel, Sybille, and Alice De Lamar. Her need for money was a constant refrain in her relations with Gerald: "I am sorry to be just another middle-aged failure," she wrote from Rome in 1949, "but things are pretty grim and worrying for me materially and I am not getting any youn-

ger. Will you find out if I can raise money on my stock, or sell part
or the whole of it. Otherwise I literally don't know what I will do in
the future." She wanted "a place of my own to live in, instead of always being in cheap hotels and pensions or in other people's houses
when they can have me . . . liv[ing] in terror of any accident or emergency, like another illness."

In 1935, Gerald had taken over the Mark Cross company, which
had fallen into debt and was on the verge of liquidation. He made it
a success again, running it for the next two decades, but felt that he
wasted years of his life doing so and called the company "that monument to the inessential." When he sold it, Esther's financial pressure eased for a time, and in 1951 she bought an apartment on the
rue de Lille, in the Seventh Arrondissement. She asked Sybille's half
sister—who was half-Jewish, had lived out the war in France in difficult and sometimes dubious circumstances, and was now at loose
ends—to move in with her and run her household. This woman's
stylish, spendthrift arrangements made it possible for Esther to live
in comfort and entertain, but quickly depleted her funds. Esther
was "so changed, gay, buying herself clothes," Sybille wrote to Allanah Harper, but "I'm afraid much too generous and spending most
of it on other people." There was a neighborhood joke that one
could never park in front of her building because the van from the
specialty food shop Prunier was invariably making a delivery. By the
late 1950s she was again in desperate straits: sustained by loans, eating in cheap restaurants or going hungry, still fielding "blackmailing
letters" from Chester, and talking about selling her apartment. "She
should go to New York & get a job as a reviewer," wrote Noel to
Gerald, "but that is assuming that she is capable of acting with some
normalcy.—Not the case." But Noel also believed that Esther had
been treated badly by her family, and she never stopped pressing
Gerald to send his sister more money. She reported to him that Esther had "*really* sent more pages to her publisher" and that the book
was "magnificent as far as it goes. That is all I know," she concluded.
"Esther is proud, generous & secretive."

Esther succumbed to and fought off depression, which she described as such, but also as "a strange spiritual and intellectual leth-

Esther, "gaunt as a shad," wrote Janet Flanner, and Noel Murphy, at Noel's home in Orgeval
(Private collection)

argy," "a tail spin," and "an attack of tedium vitae—which may be merely an excuse for indolence—but which is less enjoyable." Her drinking accelerated and abated. To Sybille, she wrote, "I am rigidly observing my diet and take no alcohol." But the next sentence—"I wish [miss] you terribly my darling"—looks like an orthographic version of a drunken slurring of words. Apologizing for having mistaken the date of Sybille's birthday, she quoted Jeremy Taylor's *Holy Dying* to describe herself as "'dishonoured and made unhappy by many sins' including procrastination, tobacco and indolence." She became ill—"skeleton thin, & her clothes hanging like old sheets," wrote Noel to Gerald—and in the summer of 1960 was diagnosed with epilepsy, "probably a pre-disposition activated by alcohol & a debilitated nervous system." There was a regime of "barbiturates to take every night of her life—no wine, beer or cigarettes, & if she shows undue excitement she should never be left alone."

Ashamed about her body, her writing, and her handling of money, Esther was now even more inclined to ignore her circumstances, physical as well as fiscal. Scattered, impractical, and "fatalistic" when it came to daily life, she was known for her bizarre handling of her body, including urinating when and where she felt like it and not eating. ("Her scrambled eggs got even more scrambled on her plate," said Sybille about Esther's habit of stirring her food endlessly while she talked.) Both behaviors were characteristic of her alcoholism and of her ability to lose herself in her ideas; both were forms of abandon that at once indulged and denied physical need. And she talked to the point that her friends wondered how she could take in what was going on around her. In fact, she took in everything. "Two things about *Esther* that puzzle me," wrote Wilson in the mid-1950s:

> She repeats [to others] at length what people have told her, yet I don't know how she can have heard them say anything, since she is always talking herself . . . Janet Flanner seems to think that she hears what people are saying when they are talking to other people, while she is talking about something else—says that she will read a book rapidly and be able to repeat passages from it, and at the same time listen to what is being said in the room. The second riddle: How

is it that she has lived in France so long and still speaks French so badly? It seems to me that she actually gets worse . . . I asked Janet whether she thought Esther did it on purpose, as some English people seem to do, and she said that she didn't think that Esther did anything on purpose.

But Esther could be intensely aware of her own "inertia and cowardice" and she was a keen analyst of the uses of inaction, of the ways that an impasse—the sort of "situation that no one concerned wants to solve," as she wrote to Sybille—could in fact be productive, "because it fits in perfectly with [a person's] own form of inertia and activity and it . . . would need a readjustment that no one is willing to make, to change it." She quoted "that wise seer Bob Chanler" about the paradoxical satisfaction people derived from such "impossible situations": " 'Everybody's just as pleased, my dear child,' " he would say, " 'but they won't admit it.'—I was too young then to know how right he was!"

"I have been a neurotic since birth God knows!" she wrote to Chester in 1943; "it simply is a thing you have to control as well as you can, in order that the dark waters of neurasthenia should not flood your mind and paralyze your will to live." But beginning in the mid-1950s, she also became—in the evocative phrase that Edmund Wilson used of his father—"at home with [her] own singularity." After a visit with her in 1954, Wilson wrote, "She is perhaps more comfortable, happier, now—freer and more at ease—than at any other time in her life. This life must have been full of frustrations, failures to find sympathy, alienation from persons she loved; but I have never seen a sign of self-pity." She did not retreat into anticommunism during the cold war, as many of her contemporaries did. Holding forth in Paris, "she would launch into a fantastically detailed, yet Olympian analysis of the character of . . . Senator McCarthy." Writing to Wilson in 1958, she concluded, "Dulles thinks Communism comes out of a bottle like the Genii in the Arabian Nights and that he can put it back in the bottle, and Eisenhower does not think at all." Unlike some of her male comrades, she was not invested in a romance of her own greatness or ruin, and she was never twisted by her incapacities into resenting what others accomplished.

Although she could not believe in herself, she did believe in Sybille. She encouraged Sybille, gave her concrete editorial criticism, answered historical questions, took enormous pride in her successes, and did all she could to promote *A Visit to Don Otavio* when it was published in New York in 1953, sending it to friends, many of them editors and reviewers. "I can't tell you how excited I am about your book," she wrote to Sybille in Rome, "much more excited than I am about my old Governess, however I am plodding away at her." At a flush moment, she gave Sybille a large loan or gift to allow her to finish her second book, the novel *A Legacy*, and she promoted it, too—notably giving Nancy Mitford a copy and asking her to pass it on to Evelyn Waugh, whose review saved the novel from obscurity in England and effectively launched Sybille's career. Over the years, Esther sent or recommended Sybille's work to Wilson, Carson McCullers, Lillian Hellman, Gilbert Seldes, and many others, and she told Sybille that it was one of her "very few satisfactions as well as one of the greatest . . . to be able to be of some help." Envy of the younger writer, who had begun to outstrip her, appears only once in their correspondence, and with more humor than bitterness. In the late 1950s, when Sybille began receiving praise for her legal reporting, Esther wrote:

I fear that to my great regret, I may be forced to break off all relations with you. Your connections are really becoming too high. First a Judge of the Pennsylvania Supreme Court— now the director of the Federal Bureau of Narcotics! My connections are too shady and too compromising. Many of my intimate friends have been drug-addicts and one at least died as the result of an overdose of morphine, others have been habitual drunkards, several of them have had communist and other subversive sympathies and one of them is a philosophic anarchist and believes in no form of government at all: none of them would be well regarded by the Federal or State Judiciary. I am myself a Conservative Christian Anarchist and a follower of Thomas Jefferson, whose ideas are no longer regarded as very respectable in the U.S. In view of all this, I feel that your connection with me may be highly compromising for you as you mount ever higher into these altitudes where the mighty and repressive of the earth, sit in judgment.

She went on socializing: With Nancy Mitford, disdainful of Americans but making an exception for Esther, who was "my learned friend Mrs Arthur" and "my dear Mrs Arthur"; with Natalie Barney, who still insulted and unnerved her; with "Alice De Lamar and her inevitable entourage"; with the poet and activist Nancy Cunard, brilliant and increasingly unstable, "passing through [Paris] like an uncharted comet whose movements defy the astronomers"; with other old friends such as Katharine Cornell, and new ones such as the young novelist Patricia Highsmith and the writer and composer Brion Gysin. John Strachey came to dinner when he was in France on business, as did the fashion editor Madge Garland, another friend from the 1920s. Mary McCarthy and Esther became closer friends; Esther was part of the small wedding party when McCarthy remarried in 1961. Janet Flanner and Noel Murphy were constant presences. "Noel brought me a recipe for cookies & Janet a crochet pattern," Esther joked to Sybille about her birthday one year; "(as a matter of fact they gave me 5,000 francs to buy books.)" "She had a great capacity for keeping friends," said De Lamar, "both old ones and new ones." And she mourned those she lost. "A whole part of my life is gone with her and with our mutual memories," Esther wrote to Sybille when Amanda Seldes died in 1954. Then she quoted Pascal.

She went on being a resource for and inspiration to others. Edmund Wilson, in Paris in the mid-1950s, began "under Esther's influence" to "almost imagine myself, as I had never done before, becoming a mellow old expatriate discussing world literature and history, and explaining America to Europeans, in some comfortable familiar café." A nostalgia for the canonical Paris of the twenties inspired some to approach her; when Hemingway died, she was interviewed on the radio. Others may have been looking for a link to the more open lesbian lives of the interwar years: "They came for stories of Djuna Barnes and Miss Alice Toklas," wrote a friend, "and got instead an up-to-date précis of, let us say, the politico-sexual anxieties of Monsieur Soustelle, delivered in enormous parentheses with elaborately cigarette-punctuated emphasis. It was all very confusing for them." (Jacques Soustelle was an anthropologist and member of the French Resistance, of postwar governments, and then of the anti–Algerian independence movement.)

She went on being a source of anxiety and frustration, a bore and a puzzle and an embarrassment to her friends. The mystery, felt one, was how she did the things she ascertainably did do. "She never woke up until 11 or later in the morning, and her days, even her later lonelier days, were always fairly full; so when did she manage to work on her book or read or write her letters or study seven daily newspapers and numberless political and learned reviews?" But many of her letters of this period are shadows of her earlier correspondence, vague and repetitive. "Esther worries a great deal, but is unable to face realities," observed Noel.

Once the sense of promise is gone, what is left? No more potential, only sour certainty—and the troubled conviction of those nearby that this foreclosure is transmissible, their terror of duplicating your failure. All of Esther's virtuosity and lack of tangible accomplishment intimidated and exhausted the writers who were her friends and chosen milieu, since if calling someone else a failure protects one from it, it also raises the specter of one's own vulnerability. She was a stimulant, irritant, and warning who made it easy to reassure oneself (*I am not that*), even as it made it impossible to avoid turning anxious questions on oneself (*Am I?*) and back on her (*What should she have done? Why couldn't she do it?*).

On November 23, 1962, she woke up late as usual. As she moved around her apartment preparing to take her habitual walk across the Seine to Galignani, the English-language bookstore on the Right Bank, she had a stroke and died instantly. She was sixty-five years old. The awkwardness of the next few days—her body had to be kept (packed in dry ice) in her home over a long weekend; a local priest insisted on blessing her body—was managed by Noel and Sybille. Her funeral was held at the Père-Lachaise Cemetery four days later. There was a funeral mass at the Église Saint-Germain-des-Prés organized by Eileen Hennessy, which some friends did not attend. Mary McCarthy confided to another mourner at this service that she planned to write about Esther. She never did, although she did mention her briefly in an autobiographical essay published at the end of her life. Sybille and Noel, executors and heirs, put Es-

ther's affairs in order and burned various papers. After that initial
work was done, Sybille found it impossible even to "put [her] foot
in the rue de Lille which was still permeated with Esther." Noel
shipped her ashes to Gerald, who buried the urn in the East Hamp-
ton cemetery, next to his sons' graves, and designed a headstone.
Noel tried to interest Farrar, Straus in the Maintenon manuscript,
in vain; apparently Harcourt, Brace had bowed out.

John Strachey, working in Africa, sank into "melancholy" when
he got the news. "Do you know she was my oldest friend?" wrote
Mercedes de Acosta, one of several who made this claim. Her intimates sent up a chorus of regret and compensatory effusions. "My
darling Sybille," wrote Allanah Harper, "I had no idea how fond of
her I was until I found myself calling out Esther, Esther. I cried all
the morning. One loved Esther not for her fine intelligence, but because . . . she was so generous, so kind. There was nothing small
about her, she had the mind and vision of a magnanimous man."
Janet Flanner: "The great tragedy is that her extraordinary intelligence, wit & historical comprehensions & interpretations will be
remembered only by us and in fragments: and alas never written
down in the really brilliant books she could have written whose
non-existence is a loss to literature of a special quality and dazzling
distinction." Dawn Powell: "I am sure that her brilliant monologues
on Madame Maintenon & Louis & Pompadour are stamped on her
friends' memories far more vividly than any written works which
we would have applauded but skipped. But how nice to have confounded her friends with Documents." Nancy Mitford, writing to
Evelyn Waugh, called her "a large sandy person like a bedroom
cupboard packed full of information, much of it useless, all of it
accurate." She added: "I was truly very fond of her."

Sybille Bedford was haunted by Esther until the end of her long
life. Esther had died four decades earlier, but Sybille's anguish at
what she felt to be Esther's failure remained alive. She talked about
Esther with a mixture of amazement and despair: "What's the use
of being brilliant," she asked, "if you sit at a café all day and are considered the greatest bore because you don't know when to stop talking and never write anything down?" She talked around what she
felt she could not talk about: The romantic tangle of the first two
years she and Esther spent in Europe after Mexico and New York

was still so painful that at first she tried describing it as an algebraic equation. She struggled with who Esther had been and what it would mean to make her visible again in all of her thwarted complexity— not just as the brilliant, comic, picaresque figure in *Don Otavio*— including the "sordidness" of her marriages. She still considered Esther an inspiration. She still missed her. When her last book, *Quicksands*, was published in 2005, she said that she wished Esther could know that her life had turned out well.

All we know: For thirty years or more Esther Murphy carried with her the idea of a book, or books, which she performed, over and over—to audiences small and large, to people who were moved, galvanized, worried, and frustrated by the performance. "Wellll," she would reply to almost any utterance, drawing out the word, preparing for a peroration. This preface, like "All we know," announced that she had seized on a subject and was about to be off, that her listener was in for much more. It was a sign of promise.

Her perfect memory never failed her, but as the years went by, her ability to speak distinctively about the past sounded more like deficiency than promise, looked more like the end and a commitment to the ephemeral than like a preamble to something more permanent.

Where, or what, was the impediment? Was it the ease that was the result of brilliance that made intellectual struggle unfamiliar and a certain kind of disciplined work seem unnecessary? The ease that was the result of relative wealth that did away with economic pressure and made such work less necessary? A vision of her success, her own and others', that she felt she could not live up to? "Finishing a book," she wrote to Sybille, who was in the last stages of *Don Otavio*, "is as lonely as beginning it—and brings other apprehensions." Was it fear, drunkenness, depression? All of these she carried with her, too. No single reason explains how someone so abundantly talented was unable to fulfill her ambitions.

The effortlessness: what she described as her "facile gift for verbalization," the fact that thinking sentences and paragraphs was

Sybille Bedford, London, 2005, photographed by Luciana Arrighi (Courtesy Luciana Arrighi)

like drawing breath to her. The comfort, for many years, of her material circumstances: not being required to apply herself to anything she found unpleasant or difficult, including the often lonely, chaotic task of writing. The widespread perception that she was exceptional—and her own sense that she was inadequate in almost every way: "I have never had much confidence in life," she wrote to Sybille soon after meeting her, "but I have tried and will continue to try to act as though I did. For some unknown reason that seems to be the thing to do unless one wants to succumb completely to cowardice and self pity." Her desperate need to communicate and equally powerful need to keep intimacy at bay: "She talks constantly," wrote Dawn Powell, "on nothing trivial, not as an exhibitionist but as a tireless defender of her own privacy." Her dependence on alcohol: She was "ruined by Prohibition," said Sybille, shattered like so many of her generation by the romance and necessity of forbidden alcohol. "She sat and talked and drank with John Peale Bishop and Wilson and Dorothy Parker, instead of writing." "She would talk about her eternal Mazarin, or Madame de Pompadour, while one was leaving for Europe and the ship was steaming out," Allanah Harper complained. "It is a form of selfishness and egomania, to speak as much as she does. Of course it is because she drinks too much and does not know how much or how long she is speaking, when she has not had four whiskies she is quite different." But if alcohol stimulated and hindered Esther, it did not wholly account for her verbosity, which dated from childhood.

Was it a fear of failure, or an unwillingness to risk it, that made her such a prodigious disappointment to herself and others? To fail: to make the mess one almost always has to make before a book achieves the form in which it appears to be inevitable. To fail: to expose oneself by producing the approximation of the book one had imagined. Or was failure just a way of holding on to hope?

In many ways, Esther could and did face the worst about herself. "I am not impressed by most human beings' stories about themselves," she told Chester in 1943; "(not that I suspect them of being liars,) but because I am so aware of the torturous self-deception of which I myself am capable." Perhaps the parallels between her own life and Maintenon's (as in her observation that "Madame de Maintenon had more sympathy for her unmentionable father than she had for her ill-used mother") were too difficult for her to reckon with. She herself had pronounced a damning verdict on the value of her own knowledge—and twenty years before Nancy Mitford's description of her mind as a useless but accurate storehouse—when she told the audience of *Listen—The Women!* that a perfect memory was the enemy of thought. "If any one faculty of our nature may be called more wonderful than the rest, I do think it is memory," Jane Austen writes in *Mansfield Park.* "There seems something more speakingly incomprehensible in the powers, the failures, the inequalities of memory, than in any other of our intelligences." Esther had used the word *failure* writing to Gerald in 1949. When Muriel Draper died in 1953, Esther wrote a bit more obliquely to Sybille about resigning herself to disappointment in herself. "For me, her irremediable absence from the world marks the end of a period of my life . . . still in the shadow of my youth," when it was still possible to expect some "kind of happiness . . . It is very salutary— if not very joyful." But she signed a letter the following year "ageing but hopeful."

What is it that allows some people to rescue themselves—to make something of what they know and have lived through—while others sink? What compels one person to set it down on paper, driven by the desire to get it right in writing, and keeps another from doing so? What is it that makes us recoil from that inability and call it waste or failure?

Her depression may have been a cause, or an effect. Or perhaps her failure, like her sense of history, confounds cause and effect. Certainly her life begs the question of why talking is seen as commensurate with failure, and why and how writing and publication mean success. Perhaps what Esther had to say could not be translated to print. Or to a book: Despite or because of her effusiveness, shorter forms suited her better; in her essays and letters she is a convincing, idiosyncratic critic. It may be (to quote her review of a Marxist study of Reconstruction politics and politicians) that it was "not historically possible" for her to complete those long works. Certainly her story is part of the dominance, during the first half of the twentieth century, of print culture. Her days and her world revolved around reading. She made of her life and the lives of her friends a kind of literary object. It was her belief and others' that accomplishment meant publication. Her orations were valued when it seemed that they would lead to a book. Still, had she not said that she was working on books—and convinced publishers that she would complete them—she might have been seen simply as that rare but known figure: salonnière, conversationalist, akin to some of the women she admired, including Margaret Fuller (in one of her incarnations) and Madame Scarron.

When Fitzgerald said, "There has never been an American trag-edy. There have only been great failures," did he mean that there were no American tragedies, or that when Americans look at trag-edy they see only failure? Esther was unable to write a biography, or to bend the genre to her uses, or the genre was incapable of express-ing what she wanted to say. She failed at the genre, or it failed her. But every biography is a disappointment of some kind, premised on unbearable impasses and opacities, on the impossibility of bringing someone back to life, and on the paradoxes of representing, inhabit-ing, and balancing the past and the present. All of these failures make history as we know it and as we refuse to know it. Esther's life seems to both call for a biography and suggest its futility, and to demon-strate the seductiveness of the facts and the necessity of fictions.

As she knew, failure has been a central subject of American lit-erature from at least the mid-nineteenth century. Ahab and Bartleby and Gatsby; James's protagonists in *The Beast in the Jungle*, *The Aspern Papers*, and more; Wharton's "The Angel at the Grave," Willa Cather's *The Professor's House*, Joseph Mitchell's Joe Gould, Truman Capote's *Answered Prayers*—these are only a few examples. All are characters or stories about ambition and its refusal; about grand, doomed, or nonexistent projects that their projectors could not relinquish; about a lust for knowledge that destroys oneself and others; about greatness imagined but never realized or be-stowed; about literary transmission and guardianship, successful and thwarted; about ruinous relationships to a subject or literary model; about enormous nonevents and misapprehensions and self-deceptions; about elaborate but never quite realized, or even real, lives and works, which their subjects or authors-to-be—fictional,

---

In the 1950s, Edmund Wilson wrote that "Esther's left eye is now partly closed all the time, and this gives her a perpetually waggish look—half of a jolly Irishwoman, half of an old New York clubman who is drinking with you and winking" (Private collection)

real, and somewhere in between—talk about until they collapse or the works evanesce, confounding themselves and their observers with a great, unachieved oeuvre. These are realist fictions and true accounts, but we experience many of them as horror stories. Some take up questions about aesthetics and representation; all testify to a terror about production that seems profoundly American.

Esther was herself a figure or character in this tradition. Still, literary as it is, her story is about not only her unfinished business, but American business. The epithet *failure* as we use it is a metaphor, writes the historian Scott Sandage, "the language of business applied to the soul." The term now "conjures such vivid pictures of lost souls that it is hard to imagine a time, before the Civil War, when the word commonly meant 'breaking in business'—going broke." Failure became a question of character and a condition of the American dream in the nineteenth century, Sandage argues, "when capitalism came of age and entrepreneurship became the primary model of American identity." One effect of this shift is that what Sandage calls "the constituency of failure" expanded: "Women, workers, and African Americans were put on notice: ruin was no longer just for white businessmen."

It is a commonplace of modern history that the emergence of women of Esther's generation into public life was one of the major shifts of the twentieth century. In the decades before, so the story goes, white women of means, energy, and intellect who were not interested in manipulating the social order were, with few exceptions, bereft of vocation or public pastime—unless, like Alice James, they took to their bed and enjoyed a long and productive marriage to their ailments. Now a brilliant career was conceivable; much professional, literary labor could be expected of a person such as Esther. Still, there was nothing simple about this shift in expectations and possibilities. As a young woman, Esther gravitated to Edith Wharton and other women whose ambitions and achievements became less exceptional in her lifetime. Yet she was always skeptical about conventional historicist assertions about a progressive relationship between past and present—about the idea that modernity was a promising improvement over the past—and her own story both followed and flew in the face of this logic. It was partly her inability to conform to a script of "onward" inevitability that made her failure so disturbing to her friends and observers. In the same way, it is possible to understand her life of unfulfilled promise as one that refutes the tired template of biographical writing, which asserts that what was in childhood will be.

As for the gender of failure: Edmund Wilson was obsessed with the collapses of his friends of the 1920s and had an idea for a novel that would consist "of a round of visits among 'the blasted young men'" of his youth. In his early sixties, he told two younger friends "that the twenties had in some ways been a dreadful wasteful time," and he meditated on the "casualties" of his generation, meaning the heroic, lost quality that he saw in many of his male friends. He was thinking of various Princeton contemporaries who lost their way or destroyed themselves, including John Peale Bishop, who published several books and worked for *The Nation*, but never seemed to come into his own. Most of all, he was thinking about Scott Fitzgerald, whose place in literary history is now secure but who, during his life, was constantly outrunning ruin and humiliation. In the essay "The Crack-Up," published in 1936, Fitzgerald wrote that he had seen his kind of breakdown everywhere: "My self-immolation was something sodden-dark," he wrote. "It was very distinctly not modern—yet I saw it in others, saw it in a dozen men of honor and industry since the war . . . And of those who had given up and passed on I could list a score." In his notebooks, referring to his competition with Ernest Hemingway, he wrote, "I talk with the authority of failure—Ernest with the authority of success. We could never sit across the same table again." When "The Crack-Up" and two subsequent essays appeared in *Esquire*, these revelations mortified Fitzgerald's friends, who felt that they would damage an already faltering career—and critics indeed attacked him. Wilson, however, paid tribute to him by publishing this essay and the notebooks after his death, and they are now seen as an important part of Fitzgerald's oeuvre.

Esther's stasis troubled Wilson, but it was Janet Flanner, Nancy Mitford, Sybille Bedford, and Dawn Powell who worried most ardently about her disappointed promise. Powell was a specialist in persistence—the will to keep writing despite financial and family trouble, insufficient recognition, and her own hard drinking—and literary failure was often her subject, as well her as quotidian fear. "After 21 years or more of writing novels steadily with inch-like progress," she wrote in her diary in 1944, "I am about where most of my contemporaries are who wrote one play, one book, of moderate success, and basked in increasing glory, prestige and (in some cases) affluence, ever since. They took care to nurse what fame came on their one outburst—they cultivated the rich, the publicity spotlight." In *A Time to Be Born*, set in wartime New York and populated by writers, editors, and publishers, one of Powell's characters lies in bed comparing himself with an ex-lover, composing an anxious rhapsody on failure:

> Failure frightened him, looming up all the sharper by Amanda's success. He seldom slept. He wondered if he was through. He was thirty-three. Sometimes people were through at thirty-three. Thirty even. They became old drunks. The world was full of old drunken failures. Has-beens. Warnings. Men who didn't realize they were never any good anyway . . . What did other men do . . . when fears, batted out the door like flies, left only to return by window? What did other men do, suspecting that what was for them had been served—no further helping, no more love, no more triumph; for them labor without joy or profit, for them a passport to nowhere, free ticket to the grim consolations of Age? Was it true, then, that this world was filled with men and women merely marking time before their cemetery? When did courage's lease expire, was there no renewal possible?

Esther was so unsettling to Powell that her death spurred an extraordinary consideration of Powell's own need to write and of the pressure she felt to conform to expectations about femininity. After noting that it would have been nice if Esther had "confounded her friends with Documents," leaving some written work after all, she wrote to Gerald, "But we read ourselves into those we love, and occasionally I catch a glimmer that some people don't want to *be* the action—they really *want* to be spectator. I daresay," she went on, "someone will sympathize with me for being obliged to write instead of breeding a big Xmas family on the range and I won't be able to use the grave's intercom to shout 'No No No! I had what I wanted!'"

The grave's intercom: Powell's startling image of the need to defend her ambition and speak to posterity is also a way to describe the work of a biography, a genre that can let someone who no longer speaks be heard. Her cry makes the intercom real while describing it as impossible, and it suggests the continuing need for an angel at the grave—someone who listens, keeping vigil by a corpse—even as it imagines doing away with that intermediary. But Powell was not quite right about Esther, who did want to "be the action," who loved and needed her own spectators, and wanted to instruct, amuse, distract, inform. Esther's need for an audience was so great that she could not isolate herself to write, so it was a lifelong performance rather than a document that she produced. The performance both kept her from writing and was a form of obsessive creation; it guaranteed her failure and immunized her from it. The performance was a way to create an intimacy with her subject and with her audience while distancing herself from both. Those who did not know Esther well, a friend wrote, could not see "the kindness that lay under that river of talk, or the loneliness, accepted and understood."

Esther alarmed Powell, but they shared a worry about the kind of American success that Powell criticized in *A Time to Be Born*. "Amanda" in that book is based on Clare Booth Luce. Married to a media magnate, like Booth Luce, this character achieves a bestselling romantic novel, which, ludicrously, leads the press to treat her as an expert on world politics. In the spring of 1953, as Booth Luce arrived in Rome as President Eisenhower's ambassador to Italy, Esther wrote to Sybille, "I don't know Mrs. L. and I have always considered her a terrifying kind of go-getting American woman with everything as grist to her mill, art, politics, religion.—undertaking everything without understanding anything—and then of course her blatantly reactionary politics and the vulgar publicity given to her conversion to Catholicism . . . Eisenhower blundered when he made that appointment."

Looking at the shipwrecked lives of her friends and associates, Esther herself focused on the women. She wrote about the wasted years and suicide of her friend Emily Vanderbilt Whitfield. She ruminated about the decline of Louise Bryant, another friend of the 1920s, whose bold journalism on the Russian Revolution had rivaled, but is now eclipsed by, John Reed's *Ten Days That Shook the*

World. Bryant married the wealthy diplomat William Bullitt after
Reed's early death, developed a rare and painful illness, drank to
alleviate it, and ended her days in poverty in Paris.

If American women's successes, in Esther's view, were often either phony or fatal, talking was perhaps a way around this conundrum. But it was also, she believed, an ethical stance, crucial to
democracy. In 1950 she sent Gerald a newspaper clipping headlined
"Our Tongue-Tied Democracy," a copy of a speech in which the author made a version of this argument. By talking, always talking,
Esther also kept her material alive, made sure that it never lost its
immediacy—or that she did not lose her access to it—as she could
not have had she finished her book. Her performance was a way to
keep the Sublime Governess herself alive. Not finishing her book,
she was also not finishing herself, sustaining the quality of attention she had received as a precocious child: praise, wonder, and interest. It may be that she also felt an obligation to her audience, to
compensate for what was not forthcoming—to live up to at least
one image of herself. It may have been a way to allay the fear that
people would forget her or lose interest if she disappeared for the
time it took to write a book. If so, she was at least partly right (as
Powell partly believed): It is unlikely that a book on Madame de
Maintenon would have been remembered and discussed as much as
its absence was.

In the meantime, Esther succeeded as a thinker and a friend, as
an original voice that was at once seemingly endless and bound to
disappear, and as one that, if it sometimes seemed to shut out conversation, nevertheless included and channeled the many other
voices she read and listened to. She thought of herself as inhabiting
a world of living and dead people who were worth quoting. The
habit was serious, sententious, ironic. "Winter is come and gone
but grief returns with the revolving year[s]," she wrote to Sybille,
quoting Shelley's "Adonais," on the reappearance of a slightly de-
ranged friend whose advent always seemed to bring "the usual disasters, inconveniences and misfortunes." She cited not only writers
and other known actors in history, but also living friends and acquaintances. "As Muriel Draper's Negro maid, Maude, used to say

The expatriate, circa mid-1950s (Private collection)

of many of Muriel's friends when she first saw them after a long absence 'She's disimproved, Mrs. Draper.'" Predicting de Gaulle's victory on the eve of the French elections in 1958, Esther wrote to Edmund Wilson, "As a workman who told me he had always voted socialist but said he was going to vote for de Gaulle, told me the other day, 'On votera pour de Gaulle par ce que la France est lasse.'" (We will vote for de Gaulle because France is exhausted.) She told Gerald that she had the impression that the French were "relieved to have someone in power who is midway between a President and King" and said she was "reminded of de Tocqueville's remark: 'Nous avons l'habitude de la Monarchie, mais on en a perdu le goût.'" (We are used to a monarchy, but have lost our taste for it.) Referring to the fierceness with which Sybille's half sister guarded a late-in-life love affair, she wrote, "As Jane Bowles once said to me, 'Life has more imagination than we have' so we must grab shamelessly what it throws us."

And then there were the whimsy and wild metaphor, the odd, epigrammatic utterance, itself quotable: "Joe Appiah wouldn't hurt an *apple!*" she said of the Ghanaian politician. She told Dawn Powell that she could drive a car but had no idea "what made it go or what made it stop beyond gas. What was under the hood that made trouble," Powell noted, "she never even guessed. 'For all I know,' [Esther] said dreamily, 'it might be a little cherub.'"

From Prague in the autumn of 1956, she sent Sybille a postcard: "We leave this city of strange contrasts—the Old City is a baroque marvel, the new could be anywhere in the U.S.—tomorrow. As Lady Mary Wortley Montague said on her death bed, 'It has all been interesting, very, very interesting.'" It may be an irony that Esther's own most "authentic" speech was constituted in part by citation. But this voice inhabited by others has precedents and contemporaries that include Madame de Sévigné, Emerson, Melville, and Walter Benjamin, many of whose works challenge the opposition between citation and originality. "She has a natural dwelling place in books," wrote Virginia Woolf about Madame de Sévigné, "so that Josephus or Pascal or the absurd long romances of the time were not read by her so much as embedded in her mind. Their verses, their stories rise to her lips along with her own thoughts." In *Representative Men*, his biographical essays on Plato, Montaigne,

Shakespeare, and others, Ralph Waldo Emerson writes, "Every book is a quotation; and every house is a quotation out of all forests, and mines, and stone-quarries; and every man is a quotation from all his ancestors." The poet Susan Howe, in her meditation on Emerson and scare quotes, cites his son Edward Waldo Emerson citing Oliver Wendell Holmes's biography of Emerson: Emerson *fils* writes that his father's essay "Quotation and Originality," in Holmes's view, "'furnishes a key to Emerson's workshop. He believed in quotation, and borrowed from everybody and every book. Not in any stealthy or shamefaced way, but proudly, as a king borrows from one of his attendants the coin that bears his own image and superscription.'" Howe's work with the labyrinthine processes of citation—these triply and quadruply embedded voices—is a comment on the literary practices called modernist and postmodernist that also animate earlier American writing. And this was how Esther worked: proudly, intentionally, productively, inclusively, haphazardly, distractedly, and obsessively; in the mode of *Moby Dick* and of the massive, unfinished accumulation of historical sources that was Benjamin's *Arcades Project*; by seeing the task of understanding history and character as a re-presentation of voices from the past; mingling the living and the dead, textual and spoken material, high and low.

Hers was the authority of failure. Writing to Sybille in 1953, she enclosed a line by the poet, priest, and missionary to the Huguenots, François Fénelon—a sentence that she spoke often and that Sybille was thinking of using as an epigraph. Like so much of what Esther read and retained, it was a kind of autobiographical utterance: "Here is the quotation—my memory is accurate," she wrote (she could not locate the book). "'C'était tout qui était possible, mais ce n'était pas assez.' 'It was all that was possible but it was not enough.' . . . I send this at once. All Love Esther." The line is from a letter Fénelon wrote to Madame de Maintenon in 1694.

Esther was the "poor, crouching, human being." She knew that we all are. Like Auguste Comte, her life had "that something at once pathetic and impressive." She was one of the people she might have included in the essay she wanted to write on those "critics and portrayers of the American scene." It was all that was possible. It was and was not enough.

FANTASIA ON A THEME BY MERCEDES DE ACOSTA

A little girl stands on a New York sidewalk, transfixed in front of a brownstone on West Forty-seventh Street—her own street. It is 1906. She sees licks of smoke float out of the house. She cries out: "Fire!"

The woman who lives in this building is a famous actress, great in the estimation of many and so significant to this child that she is filled with something unutterable, overpowering, and strange: love, the desire to be close to the extraordinary person, the desire to be of use to her—but also the need to be recognized herself, the rich feeling that would come from being seen to understand and honor greatness. She is the first to see the smoke as it billows from the basement and she wants to save the actress from the fire.

The actress is Maude Adams, the most loved player and greatest box office draw of the American theater in the first two decades of the century. Credited with a new naturalism in performance style, she attracts thousands of spectators—many of whom go to the theater only when she performs—and her photograph hangs in homes, restaurants, and saloons across the country, as well as in President Taft's study in the White House.

The little girl is Mercedes de Acosta, the youngest child of upper-class Spanish parents. She will grow up to be a writer, a feminist, and a devotee of various "Eastern" religions. She will grow up to be the friend or lover, and ardent admirer, of the most celebrated performers of her time: Eleonora Duse, Alla Nazimova, Isadora Duncan, Greta Garbo, Marlene Dietrich, and Adams herself.

Mercedes de Acosta, 1934, photographed by George Hoyningen-Huene (Courtesy Rosenbach Museum & Library)

Maude Adams was born in 1872, first appeared on stage at nine months old, became famous in 1892 as John Drew's leading woman, and became a star in 1897 in J. M. Barrie's *The Little Minister*. From then on, she was the leading American interpreter of Barrie's plays. Several of her most well-known parts were trousers roles: when she played Napoleon's son in *L'Aiglon*, *The New York Times* wrote, "One never thinks of her as a woman from the beginning of the play to its sad last scene." As the male lead in *Chantecler*, she received twenty-two curtain calls at the opening performance. Adams was also a brilliant theater technician. She spent seven years designing a three-ton, thirty-seven-foot piece of equipment that eliminated the need for footlights, "a structure unique in the history of stage lighting"; later, in the 1920s, she spent a year experimenting in General Electric's laboratory in Schenectady, New York.

But she was famous above all, to this electrified child and thousands of others, as Peter Pan.

The girl stands on the street, poised to save the day. She sees the first wisps of smoke emerge, then the flames leap around, and she raises the alarm.

Maude Adams's talents and James Barrie's sense of fantasy merged perfectly in *Peter Pan*, in which she performed more than 1,500 times in record-breaking runs in 1905–07, 1913, and 1918. Critics thought that the part "seemed almost like second nature" to her. Although she "had been technically a star for eight years," one noted, her performance as Peter marked the moment "that she actually came into her own." She had designed her own costume, which started a fashion for the rounded "Peter Pan" collar and peaked hat, and she encouraged the identification. After each performance, children would crowd the stage door waiting for her to emerge. But when she noticed the disappointment of one at seeing her out of costume, she stopped leaving the theater after matinees. She did not want to break the illusion, did not want them to see that she was a woman and not a magical flying boy.

The girl stands dreaming. She has sat in the dark of a Broadway theater watching the woman who lives in this house play a boy who will not grow up. She has waited with other girls and boys by the

Maude Adams as Peter Pan (From *Charles Frohman: Manager and Man*)

stage door after the show. She is herself a girl and a boy at once: Although her name is Mercedes, her mother calls her Rafael and dresses her in boys' clothes. When she grows up, she will become a woman whose striking personal style is distilled into costume. Greta Garbo nicknamed her Black and White. Others called her Countess Dracula, a name Tallulah Bankhead is supposed to have coined to fit Mercedes's pallor, her fondness for capes, her jet-black and slicked-back hair, and her reputation as a seductress.

"Peter Pan" made Maude Adams "a real personal friend of the American theater-going people," wrote one observer. And the moment in the play when Peter addressed the audience directly—asking, "Do you believe in fairies?"—is said to have "registered a whole new and intimate relation between actress and audience." Yet Adams was also famous for her desire for solitude and her efforts to keep her private life from public view. When she sailed back to New York in November 1902 after a retreat from the stage and a stay in a French convent, *The New York Times* reported that her name was kept off the passenger list, that she did not appear on board during the entire trip, and that she took all her meals in her stateroom. In the years that followed, she found solace in long stays at a convent in New York. The Pullman company designed a windowless private "theater car" to satisfy "Miss Adams's wish for absolutely private rehearsals while on tour"; it was "the only vehicle of its kind in existence." Her career is an early instance of whetting fans' appetites and feeding a star image by withholding publicity, since her need to be alone was based partly on advice she received from the powerful Charles Frohman, theater producer, actor's manager, early star maker, and her friend. "You are not to be interviewed," he is said to have instructed her. "You are not to be quoted. People will wonder at you, yearn for the details of your private life . . . Let them. It will only spur their interest and desire for you."

The girl stands on the street. She will become an immoderate personality who is most herself when flamboyantly appreciating someone else, a connoisseur of performance and performers. Her memoir, *Here Lies the Heart*, will achieve cult status for what she tells and withholds about her love affairs with famous friends.

After Charles Frohman's death on the *Lusitania* in 1915, Maude

Adams effectively retired from the stage. She gave her three-hundred-acre Long Island estate to a convent and at the end of her life "lived quietly with a companion, Margaret McKenna" in her home in the Catskills, where she died in 1953. She never married. "As long as she lived she was the particular idol of women and of young girls aspiring to the stage," *The New York Times* wrote on her death. "She did everything she could for them and for her own ideals of the theatre." The *Herald Tribune* was less decorous, describing "the almost hysterical acclaim that she was somehow able to inspire" and noting that "adolescent girls and single women were particularly susceptible to her charms." She was buried beside Louise Boynton, her secretary and friend for forty-five years.

The child stares at the actress's home. She sees the smoke and yells to alert those inside. They all rush out, confused, then thank her and thank her again for her bravery and selflessness.

She saves the actress.

She receives the grateful thanks of the great.

She gets as close as she can, then backs away.

But there is no fire.

The truth—of the star, of herself, and of her fantasy—is in the heat and light of her mind, in the heat and the lights of the theater and crowd, and in the radiance of this actress who is forever elusive yet bigger than life—strong enough to stand up to it all, but still, perhaps, in need of rescue.

Swoons of adulation, feats of seduction, acts of conservation—these were the gestures, the texture, of Mercedes de Acosta's life. From a young age she was both intimate with stars and ruled by starstruck fantasy. Imagine being rowed across a pristine mountain lake in the Sierra Nevada by Greta Garbo. Imagine watching Garbo strip off her clothes and dive happily into the freezing water, while you stand on the pier of the small private island to which she has just brought you. Imagine, when Garbo retreats from you and Hollywood to Sweden, having an admiring and aggressive Marlene Dietrich pounce

on you, cook for you, inundate your house with flowers, and then, when you mention that you have no place for so many roses, send over a collection of Lalique vases.

Mercedes de Acosta did not have to imagine these scenes. For her they were both fact and fantasy. Dietrich called her "mon grand amour." Isadora Duncan said that she would follow her to the ends of the earth. The young actress Eva Le Gallienne, at the height of their affair in the early 1920s, sighed in a letter that she felt she would die if Mercedes did not marry her. Some of Mercedes's lovers were later mortified by the association and their own emotion, and refused to have any contact. Janet Flanner wrote her an erotic tribute in verse in the late 1920s, then could not tolerate her. "I fear Janet will have to be affronted by the presence of Mercedes, who I understand will be there," wrote Esther Murphy of a gathering in Paris in 1950. Le Gallienne is later said to have called Mercedes's memoir "Here Lies the Heart—and Lies and Lies and Lies." But "Mercedes *never* lies," insisted another friend, the artist Eva Hermann. (Aldous and Maria Huxley agreed; to them she was a searching and sincere friend.)

There was nothing reasonable about Mercedes de Acosta. Generous, alluring, and witty, she was also self-consumed and suicidally depressive, her "undeniable gifts," as Esther put it, veiled in an "exasperating cloak of romantic egotism." A passionate fan, she was visually arresting and always aware of her own audience. Repudiating orthodox religion, she was caught up in a series of religious enthusiasms.

Nor has there ever been anything reasonable about others' responses to her. During her life, these tended toward romantic swoon or repudiation. Since her death, she has inspired either uncritical homage or lashings of vitriol—especially for her career as a seductress, particularly for her pursuit of Greta Garbo. She has been seen as a role model for sexual liberation, her erotic successes and lack of shame about her desires a cause for celebration. She has been called a fraud, a hysteric, and, despite her own charisma, "the first celebrity stalker." In death as in life, the question of Mercedes's lies and truthfulness still dominates the discussion of her character, with

Greta Garbo, Silver Lake, California, July 1931, snapshot by Mercedes de Acosta (Courtesy Rosenbach Museum & Library)

attackers and apologists treating her as a problem to be resolved or a side to be taken, in scholarly journals and star biographies, books about Hollywood's gay subculture, a full-length biography, and its reviews.

Obsessed with artistic "greatness"—"On Great Men Recognizing Greatness" is the title of one of her essays—Mercedes de Acosta wrote herself into history partly through her association with literary, theatrical, and religious greats. She saw these contacts as a way to make sense of her life and was both carried away by and savvy about her obsessions. She continued to pine masochistically for Garbo long after it became clear that the star enjoyed encouraging and deflating Mercedes's hopes, just as she enjoyed controlling others' access to her. But Mercedes could also be an astute analyst of celebrity and its appreciators, not only enduring and taking pleasure in, but also writing with irony and precision about, the continual, conflicting needs for intimacy and distance that direct the traffic between stars and fans.

She herself did not use the word *fan* when she wrote about her admiration of her celebrated friends, although she did refer to her "fanaticism" on various subjects. She described herself as overwhelmed by and subservient to the performers who inspired her. She also described herself as an expert on them. Every fan imagines him- or herself an expert on the star to whom he or she feels a special closeness, but Mercedes did so in ways that complicated her own cherished ideas about greatness. She knew that stars were often themselves fans. She knew that being a fan meant existing on a shifting ground that is also an epistemological problem: We want to get close to and know everything about the performers we admire; we want to stay distant and remain in awe. She knew that her feelings of adulation meant that she sometimes put herself on display in embarrassing ways. Describing her early, overheated adoration of Maude Adams, she mocked herself: "I often stood outside Miss Adams' house waiting to catch a glimpse of her," she wrote in a draft of her memoir. "One day I saw smoke coming out of the basement window. I decided at once that the house was on fire and I hoped it was. This was my moment to be heroic and save Miss Adams. I rushed up the front steps and rang the bell furiously," at which point "a rather annoyed maid opened the door" and said,

"Don't be a stupid child. The cook has merely singed the chicken." And so, she wrote, she "went home, humiliated and far from heroic."

She got as close as she could, then was sent away.

She was warmed by her adulation and by the transmutation of her shame.

As an adult, Mercedes de Acosta had a hard time holding on to people, but she was able to hold on to quantities of stuff associated with them. Over a lifetime of fantasies coming true and failing to, she built an archive that documented various artists' careers, traced her rapport with these figures, and described her own career. Saving the blank card that Greta Garbo sent her with flowers; saving photographs, playbills, manuscripts, and newspaper and magazine clippings; saving correspondence from famous and obscure friends and lovers; saving books, articles of clothing, dried flowers; saving a small metal canister holding two lengths of film of Garbo, each of about fifteen frames—delicate, stuttering celluloid evidence of Garbo's beauty and distance and of Mercedes's obsession and instinct for preservation. With all of this collecting, Mercedes was saving a famous actress from the flames. She was also saving less well-known figures and saving herself. Documenting the ephemeral and concrete impulses of a fan who was as willing to get lost in her adulation as she was to criticize it, Mercedes de Acosta preserved the time she lived through. She also styled herself a connoisseur of the fleeting pleasures of performance, with all of the exhilaration and need that such expertise implies. And she demonstrated that the concrete and fantastic postures of a dedicated fan have everything to do with the attitudes of a passionate reader, with the challenges of representing the past, and with the heightened feeling that hums around a particular style.

She was born in New York City in 1893. Her mother, Micaela Hernandez de Alba de Acosta, had arrived in the United States in the mid-nineteenth century and married at sixteen. A pious Catholic— she was one of the original pew owners at St. Patrick's Cathedral—

this woman spoke only Spanish with her children, raised her daughters in "the Spanish code of feminine behavior," and required them to marry a European or European-born American, with the result that not one did. Growing up in this "Spanish cloister," Mercedes and her seven older siblings nevertheless moved comfortably in upper-class New York. Her sisters were called "the most romantic girls in New York society," and their lives were chronicled regularly in the newspapers. All married into established American families: Aida to Oren Root (nephew of Elihu Root, the secretary of war and of state under William McKinley and Theodore Roosevelt); Maria to Andrew R. Sargent of Boston; the eldest, Rita, to the millionaire developer William Stokes, more than twenty years her senior, then to Captain Philip Lydig, both of whom she divorced.

Mercedes grew up in a world of privileges, which were also constraints. "Parents in the social world, " she wrote later, "considered it beneath their children to work professionally in almost any job." When her widowed mother bemoaned her disappeared fortune, Mercedes, by then in her twenties, was unable to help. "It would have been wiser to have discussed finances with a squirrel in those days than with me," she recalled. "I thought then that banks were a form of club to which one belonged and from which one could draw whatever sums of money one wanted to be refunded later when and if convenient."

She grew up in a Manhattan that was at once industrial and rural. Trains belched steam and smoke—Park Avenue was not yet covered, so the tracks running to and from Grand Central were open to the air—horse-drawn carriages paraded along Fifth Avenue, and "the country," a tree-filled estate belonging to friends of her parents, on acres of farmland abutting the East River, was just thirty blocks north of her home. She was sent to various Catholic schools in New York and Europe, including the Sacred Heart, where she first met Esther Murphy. Unlike Esther, Mercedes grew up with an intense Roman Catholic faith, to which she appended a habit of self-mortification. She put nails and stones inside her shoes and walked on them until her feet bled; she prostrated herself for hours with her arms outstretched in the form of a cross; she wrote "long religious essays and poems and very extraordinary love letters" to Jesus, Mary, Mary Magdalene, Saint Francis, and Joan of Arc. As this epistolary practice suggests, her ideas about love and her religious life were interdependent—just as, later, her religious life and her feelings about performance and performers would be intertwined.

She grew up troubled by dramatic, painful depressions and "a suicidal mania" that no psychiatrist could explain or help. When she was young, she often retreated to a corner of a room, "put [her] face to the wall and moaned." After her brother Enrique killed himself, when she was in her teens, a "craving for death" possessed her. She struggled so violently not to commit suicide, she wrote, "that blood often poured from my nose and weakened me so that I collapsed on to my bed in a semi-unconscious state." Keeping a loaded gun was the one thing that reassured her, and when she lived in Los Angeles in the 1930s and '40s, she would find release by going up into the hills and shooting at trees.

The injustices of her sex also weighed on her. She suffered constantly from "the frustration and indignity of being considered inferior to men"; she resented her mediocre education and wished she had been sent to a university, as her brothers had; and she came to believe, "without a shred of humor, in every form of independence for women." Yet for a long time she had not even known that she was a girl. As a child, "my hair was cut short," she wrote in a draft of her memoir, "I was dressed as a boy and no one ever referred to me as a girl." When a group of boys she was playing with told her otherwise, dropping their pants for extra emphasis, it precipitated a major crisis. She "raged in bed and ran a high temperature" for three days and suffered "a nervous collapse." She prayed to be made a boy and developed a theory to explain what made her different: "I am not a boy and I am not a girl, or maybe I am both," she recalled telling a nun. "And because I don't know, I will never fit in anywhere and I will be lonely all my life." By the time *Here Lies the Heart* was published in 1960, this material and her reference to these experiences as a "childhood tragedy" had been cut. Instead, she referred to herself at this age as the pet of the theater producer Augustin Daly, who wished to adopt a little girl. But boyishness endured as part of her sense of herself and her allure: Dietrich addressed letters to Rafael de Acosta; Garbo, who was fond of referring to herself with masculine appellations, called Mercedes her darling boy.

As this drama about gender identity disappeared from Mercedes's account of herself, what remained, in her memoir, were her love of the theater and her religiosity, both sanctioned arenas for women to display passionate emotion toward other women. Writing about her earliest obsession with a performer, Mercedes said of Maude Adams, "Every child was hysterical about her as the little boy who never grew up, and I was no exception. To me she *was* Peter Pan and when I saw her in the part I was thrown into a state of ecstasy." In her teens, she would meet a friend after school and together they would stalk Fifth Avenue, down to Washington Square and back up to West Forty-seventh Street, "like hunters out for game—we hunted our favorite actors and actresses." Her friend "very nearly swooned if she saw John Barrymore and I felt the same about Ethel." Confronted with Ethel Barrymore in person, a meeting her well-connected sister Rita arranged, Mercedes remembered herself as speechless. The actress took her to lunch, but she just sat there "too shy and excited to be anything but stupid, and praying all the while that I wouldn't suddenly turn peagreen and be overcome with a migraine." When, no longer a child, she finally met Maude Adams, she thought she "would actually die from shyness" and almost ran from her dressing room.

Yet Mercedes also grew up accustomed to celebrity, a result of Rita's influence. Nearly twenty years Mercedes's senior, Rita was a celebrated beauty, patroness of the arts, and voracious, talented collector who filled her homes in New York and Paris with the musicians, actors, and artists of the day—Sarah Bernhardt, the Barrymores, Rodin, Caruso, Eleonora Duse, Mary Garden, Toscanini, Paderewski, and others—and with rare books, paintings, and textiles. "Meeting these artists so often," Mercedes wrote, "I began to regard them as everyday people in my life." Rita also introduced her to "many celebrities other than artists—King Alfonso, Queen Marie of Roumanie, Count Boni de Castellane." All of her sisters were "persistently paragraphed and . . . photographed," but Rita was a star of the late Gilded Age and early twentieth century, a "magnetic personality" who was painted by Boldini and John Singer Sargent, photographed by Baron de Meyer, Edward Steichen, and Arnold

Rita de Acosta Lydig, "in her Persian trousers and one of her eighty-seven coats," 1925, photographed by Arnold Genthe (Library of Congress, Prints and Photographs Division, Arnold Genthe Collection)

Genthe, and sculpted by Rodin, whose marriages, divorces, romances, travels, purchases, bankruptcy, and illnesses were news
even after her death in 1929.

Rita was the woman who made the first and most lasting impression on Mercedes and for years she set a standard that others
could not reach. "I have known a number of extraordinary and
beautiful women the world over," Mercedes wrote in *Here Lies the
Heart*, "but Rita, considered objectively and without any prejudice
in her favor, seemed to me more striking, more unfailing in perfect
grace and beauty than any other woman." Rita was everywhere in
Society—she showed her Thoroughbreds at the National Horse
Show, where Patrick Murphy was often a featured speaker—but
"her presence raised the vibration of the most commonplace event."
Anatomizing her sister's celebrity, Mercedes wrote, "Without the
advance publicity of a movie star, without the recognition which
comes from films and photographs, she attracted people whenever
she appeared in public. She rarely went into stores and never into a
department store because crowds followed and surrounded her."

If Rita's glamorous femininity was a lifelong inspiration, so was
her collecting. For a time, she lived in an Italianate house on East
Fifty-second Street that Stanford White had designed for her. Her
friend Frank Crowninshield, the longtime editor of *Vanity Fair*,
described it as "a veritable museum," full of majolicas, Renaissance paintings, ecclesiastical vestments, and Queen Anne silver. In
1913 she auctioned the contents of this house. In 1927 she filed for
bankruptcy and again sold her collection. "The curators of the great
museums of Europe recognized her knowledge and her taste,"
wrote *The New Yorker* at the time of this second sale. She also collected clothes in abundance and designed most of her dresses herself, commissioning the couturières Callot Soeurs to make them.
And she never had one of anything: Her wardrobe was filled with
dozens of versions of every model, and when she died, she owned
150 pairs of shoes, all "really works of art." Handmade by Pietro
Yantorny, who called himself the "most expensive shoemaker in
the world," they had a Louis XV–style profile and were made of antique velvet, lace, damask, and embroidery. Rita also died owning
quantities of precious lace, her most profound obsession, some of it
dating from the Middle Ages. In 1940, Mercedes donated some of

these clothes, shoes, and laces to the Museum of Costume Art, the precursor of the Metropolitan Museum of Art's Costume Institute, and she helped organize a display of this material. In the early 1950s, she made an even larger gift to the Brooklyn Museum.

Mercedes saw Rita as a divided soul: serious and reckless; profoundly spiritual, but driven by a "mad extravagance"; idiosyncratic and "indifferen[t] to public opinion," yet forced to live as a society hostess. She was committed to woman suffrage, spent money on other people as quickly as on herself, and was careless about protecting what she had accumulated. Again inspired by her, Mercedes threw herself into "rebellion against the mediocre, the prudish" in the wake of the First World War. Now in her twenties, she worked for suffrage and other feminist causes "as if it were the only thing that mattered in my life," canvassing door-to-door, always leaving "a shower of leaflets and pamphlets strewn behind." She found like-minded friends in the Lucy Stone League, which fought for women's right to retain their own names after marriage, spoke on behalf of the League, and was quoted in the newspapers in response to the tirades of a businessman who wanted to burn all women's colleges to the ground. Like Esther Murphy, she began to move between the high society in which she was raised and the sexual subcultures that had such an extensive presence in New York City at the time, in nightclubs in Greenwich Village and Harlem and in friends' homes. She started to write, mostly poems and plays—aware that hers was a "minor" talent, but increasingly willing to show her work to others—and by the 1920s she had published three collections of poems and a novel.

She also continued to organize her life around the theater. Her mentor, to whom Rita introduced her, was the powerful theatrical agent Elisabeth (Bessie) Marbury, who represented J. M. Barrie, Oscar Wilde, H. G. Wells, and Somerset Maugham. Marbury lived for years with Elsie de Wolfe, for whom she devised an acting career, allowing Charles Frohman to produce her clients' work in exchange for casting de Wolfe. When de Wolfe's days onstage were over, she set her up in business as an interior designer, the career for which she is now known. Marbury encouraged and represented Mercedes's writing, and in the 1920s Mercedes had plays produced in New York, London, and Paris.

She also found lovers in the theater. She had a brief affair with Alla Nazimova, to whom Marbury introduced her, and fell in love with another intense young performer, Eva Le Gallienne, then rising to stardom. The web of performance, ambition, fandom, and passion among these women was complex: Le Gallienne was a former protégée and lover of Nazimova, who was then being compared with Eleonora Duse. Mercedes's first encounter with Le Gallienne was something like the meeting of a fan club. As she described it, it consisted entirely of a conversation in which the two of them "feverishly compared notes on everything we knew or had ever heard about Duse." (Their date was arranged by Betty Parsons.) Over the next several years, which coincided with Le Gallienne's tours of the Northeast and Midwest in Ferenc Molnár's *Liliom*, Mercedes and Le Gallienne sent each other yearning letters, arranged brief trysts, and continued to play out their romance through a love for Duse. They followed the actress in Paris and saw her perform when she came out of retirement in London and New York. After Duse's sudden death in 1924, on tour in the United States, they spent a night in vigil over her coffin in a New York church. Their affair coincided with, but seems never to have been impeded by, the beginning of Mercedes's marriage to the society painter Abram Poole in 1920. "I was in a strange turmoil," Mercedes wrote about her decision to marry Poole, "about world affairs, my own writing, suffrage, sex, and my inner spiritual development." Feeling pressure to please her mother, but convinced that matrimony was an archaic institution, she agreed to Poole's proposal only on the condition that she keep her own name. They divorced amicably in 1935.

Mercedes's sartorial predilections also tended to the theatrical and were so singular and sustained that she came to resemble an image of herself. As a child she had been overjoyed when Rita gave her a complete Russian boy's outfit, and in the early 1920s, she and Le Gallienne affected Russian folk tunics. By the end of the decade, she had made herself another sort of uniform. "She wears peculiarly characteristic clothes," a reporter observed, "and contends that she has succeeded in reducing the dress problem to a fine art. During the day she nearly always wears a black Directoire *redingote*—huge lapels, a tiny, tight waist, and enormously full skirt. Her

hats vary between a black tricorn and a little round black astrac-
khan Cossack cap." She had this coat, which was designed by Paul
Poiret, copied throughout her life. Her shoes were made by Yantorny, who designed Rita's footwear. One day in 1960, Greta Garbo
was standing in a health food store in New York City when she saw
a "long-toed, silver-buckled shoe" and the edge of "a black high-
wayman's cape." She knew immediately that it was Mercedes.

Although Mercedes can be said to have costumed herself, rather
than dressed fashionably, going out in costume was itself a fashion
in the 1920s—at masquerade parties held in private homes and in
public—and Mercedes got herself up as a Cossack, a Hussar, and a
Franciscan monk. At such parties, at drag balls, and at nightclubs,
men and women who violated gender norms were on display to insiders and outsiders. And their performances could be political
acts: Laws against wearing the clothing of the opposite sex were
among the restrictions used to police homosexuality. "These were
the days when the speak-easies were in full bloom," Mercedes wrote
in a draft of *Here Lies the Heart*.

> Everyone rushed up to Harlem at night to sit around places
> thick with smoke and the smell of bad gin, where Negroes ~~'in
> drag'~~ danced about with each other until the small hours of
> the morning. ~~This fad lasted all through the twenties and
> into the early thirties.~~ What we all saw in it is difficult to
> understand now. I suppose ~~it was the newly found excite-
> ment of homosexuality, which after the war was expressed
> openly in nightclubs and cabarets by boys dressed as women,
> and was, like drinking, forbidden and subject to police
> raids, which made it all the more enticing. Youth was in re-
> volt, and~~ outwitting the government and getting the better
> of the police lent a zest to our lives.

The lines struck through in this draft of *Here Lies the Heart* do not
appear in the published book, her memory and rumination on it
edited to replace sexual and gender transgression with the ordinary
misdeeds that were part of life under Prohibition.

If Mercedes had stood still on the street as a child—staring, waiting, longing—when she was a teenager and grown woman adulation

often meant being in motion. She "despised distance and belittled the world by moving about it quickly on large boats and small feet," wrote Janet Flanner of Mercedes's willingness to rush to a lover's side from across the Atlantic. (The line is from a 1928 concrete poem in the shape of a tulip in which Flanner also described Mercedes's lovemaking: "She ate flesh talking of flowers and flesh.") Mercedes's feelings for the actresses she loved were caught up in this disdain for distance, the attempt to erase the space between herself and the women she admired. Nowhere was she so persistent—and so bound to fail—as in her association with Greta Garbo.

With Bessie Marbury's help, after Rita's death in 1929, Mercedes moved to Los Angeles and found work as a screenwriter. In the kind of avowal of predestination that is typical of *Here Lies the Heart*, Mercedes writes there that at a party before she left New York, Tallulah Bankhead told her to pick a card out of a deck and make a secret wish. Bankhead examined the card and told her that she would get what she hoped for on the third day after her arrival in Hollywood. She had wished that she would meet Garbo. In Hollywood, she fell in with a group of displaced New Yorkers and European expatriates, including Igor Stravinsky, Aldous and Maria Huxley, and the screenwriter Salka Viertel, and on her third day in town she met Garbo at Viertel's home. The star of *The Temptress*, *Flesh and the Devil*, and *Anna Christie* was then at the peak of her popularity. Her reserve and desire for privacy were already legendary, and her character was dissected endlessly—in *Vanity Fair* and *The New Yorker* as well as in fan magazines. Most of her fans, called "Garbomaniacs," were women. Over the next several years, as Mercedes worked intermittently on screenplays for Paramount, RKO, and MGM, she became a minor celebrity herself: "The most talked-about woman in Hollywood is the woman no wife fears," proclaimed one gossip column, not naming her.

Mercedes's rapport with Garbo has been debated since it began, sometimes exaggerated by Mercedes, often diminished by those with a stake in keeping the star as free from intimacy as she kept herself. The two women were linked in fact: It seems clear that they were lovers briefly, that Garbo then withdrew, and that their friendship,

Greta Garbo and Mercedes, Hollywood, 1934. "It's no snap to snap Garbo" (Courtesy Rosenbach Museum & Library)

though vexed, continued on Garbo's alternately restrictive and affectionate terms until she severed ties just before Mercedes published *Here Lies the Heart* in 1960. They were linked in feeling: Both had been starstruck as children; both had lost their fathers when they were in their teens, and then siblings. "Both idolized their elder sisters," writes Karen Swenson, one of Garbo's more astute biographers. "Both were afflicted with an inner restlessness that was compounded by a chronic inability to sleep." Both felt foreign and alienated from others and "liv[ed] in a near-constant state of melancholia." They were linked in the media: from a much-reproduced paparazzo photograph of them wearing slacks and walking down Hollywood Boulevard in 1934 ("a cameraman who had waited for three hours on the running board of a car parked on Hollywood's main boulevard . . . just managed to snap the Garbo as she came out of her tailor's with her friend, Miss de Costa [*sic*]"), to the small tumult around the unsealing of Garbo's letters to Mercedes in April 2000.

But Mercedes did not focus on what they shared when she wrote about Garbo. Instead, she compared her friend to Rita. Greta and Rita, she felt, shared "a sort of despotic attitude" combined with "a certain tenderness and consideration," humor, and "tristesse." She also translated their celebrity into spiritual terms. Admonishing Cecil Beaton, who was writing about Rita in his book *The Glass of Fashion* (and who had his own vexed affair with Garbo), Mercedes advised him that "in depicting people who have stood for something in one walk of life or another, you should try and find the essence of their spirit—*their soul*, so to speak, and not concern yourself so much with the 'gossip column' aspect of their lives." But the gossip column aspect and the soul were always intertwined for Mercedes—and both were part of the language she found to articulate desire that could not be written about otherwise. The stars she admired condensed divinity and celebrity. Maude Adams had "a self-effacement rare in anyone but a saint," she wrote. The ballerina Tamara Karsavina projected "spiritual as well as physical beauty . . . across the footlights." Garbo had "a deeply spiritual hold" on her and "on the public." And Mercedes's spiritual awakenings, of which there were many, were invariably star-studded. In the 1920s, John Barrymore introduced her to Kahlil Gibran, who gave her a copy of the Bhagavad Gita and counseled her. In the 1930s, she studied "astrology, cosmic-astrology, mythology and yoga" with the dancer, set designer, and wife of Rudolf Valentino, Natacha Rambova, and was inspired by Rambova's interest in "ancient Eastern religions" and "psychic phenomena." The journalist and biographer Vincent Sheean wrote of *Here Lies the Heart* that Mercedes was "a worshipper—of artists and saints chiefly—and the quality of worship comes through."

Mercedes had often tried to integrate her religious and social consciousness with her love of the theater. One unproduced play, in which Duse expressed interest, was about the Virgin Mary. Another, staged in New York and London, concerned anti-Semitism. In 1925, Mercedes and Eva Le Gallienne collaborated on a spectacle about Joan of Arc, and in the 1930s, Irving Thalberg, head of production at MGM, hired Mercedes to write a screenplay about St. Joan for Garbo. Working on this script, Mercedes felt that it wasn't just the distance between herself and Garbo that expanded and contracted, but the distance between the saint and the actress, and the space between Mercedes's fantasy and the concrete facts around her. Although the two women would meet at the end of their workdays,

> Greta complained during these months that I was "not there." In a certain way I wasn't and yet . . . I was never for a second separated from her, as she and Jehanne D'Arc became inseparable in my consciousness. When I conjured up Jehanne in my imagination it was always Greta I saw. It was Greta who was the peasant girl. It was Greta who wore armour. It was Greta who saved France. So complete was this transference in my mind that when I actually walked with her in the hills or on the beach I often saw her in medieval costume or in armour. I arrived at a point when I could not tell which was Greta and which was Jehanne. Yet, curiously enough, I could not discuss the script with Greta. She was too much Jehanne to be able to talk it over with her . . . I suffered a strange shyness about the whole matter with her and if she ever mentioned it I changed the subject.

In later years, further mingling this fantasy with an idea about authenticity, Mercedes would insist that Garbo should have made a

movie in which she played a series of saints, "done as a sort of pilgrimage with the actual shooting done right on the scenes in Europe.
First, Jeanne d'Arc, then, St. Teresa, and maybe St. Francis."

When Garbo withdrew from daily contact with her, in the mid-
1930s, Mercedes wrote to Marlene Dietrich, "Until I was seventeen
I was a real religious fanatic. Then I met Duse and . . . gave her the
same fanaticism until I transferred it to Greta . . . You will see I
shall get over this 'insanity' and then perhaps you will love me a
little again. But if I do get over it, what then shall I pray to? And
what will then turn this gray life into starlight?" Mercedes's quest-
ing after spiritual support intensified at this time—but what is most
striking about her religious searching is the way that her guides
were excited by her affiliation with Garbo. Both the Franciscan nun
at whose remote convent in Umbria she stayed and the Indian guru
she consulted were eager to advise her on whether to maintain or
break ties with Garbo, wanted her to help them contact Garbo
themselves, and complained that they felt they were competing with
Garbo for her attention. The vow of silence taken by the Hindu
mystic Meher Baba did not keep him from sending Mercedes telegrams and letters in which he counseled her to calm down about
Garbo and pay attention, instead, to spreading his fame and working on a movie about him: "Greta will come to you. Go to Sweden
to see her, without fail. But at the present moment, my work is most
important . . . the work of writing [the] story for Baba's picture. Get
to work, immediately, with all the zeal, enthusiasm and love that
you could put in it." He needed her to be his fan, not Garbo's.

Yet it was partly as a kind of guru—but also as a performer and
even a director of sorts—that Mercedes was able to understand her
relation to Garbo. Writing to George Cukor in the late 1930s—she
now in Paris, he in Hollywood—she lingered on their elusive mutual
friend, from whose presence she was then excluded, and she appealed to Cukor to help her find work again in the film industry:

These past years I have given so much of my strength, and
brain, and vitality in teaching, inspiring, and taking care of
Greta, that I have had very little left for myself of any of
these things. It was perhaps stupid of me but I do not regret
it. I did a good job with Greta although she would never give

me any credit. In all the pictures she has done since I have known her, I have seen parts of myself and things that I have taught her. And I am glad that I have been able to influence her in her work and personal life—in spite of much handicap to myself, I would do it over again.

Portraying herself in noble but unsung service to Garbo, she described feeling erased by the star. But calling herself an inspiration to the younger woman shifted the balance of power. She had sacrificed, but Garbo emulated her. The star, in her proximity, had not rubbed off on the fan; instead, Mercedes had lent her language, gestures, and look to the star. She was not only a consumer and connoisseur of greatness, but a guide who had helped to mold it through careful tutelage, stylish example, and heightened appreciation. Of course, asserting her importance to the star is classic obsessive fan behavior, but Mercedes was also saying that it was possible to see herself when the actress performed. (And there is evidence that she in fact helped Garbo, with her English as well as with daily life.)

Part of Mercedes's plea to Cukor was that she had done a good deal of unpaid work on behalf of MGM. It was a labor of love, but labor nevertheless. Writing about the transitory and the transitive—what was lost, what she gave, what could be transferred—she was writing about her style. Asserting that there was something about her presence that Garbo had collected and incorporated, she was trying to avoid having her own reverence turn to resentment. If she was thereby rescuing herself from passivity, she nevertheless understood the relationship, as she did in most of her love affairs, as one in which she rescued the other. About Garbo she wrote, "Though there may be nothing particular to defend her against, I want to defend her, to protect her, to take her part." The accomplished women she fell in love with—later they included the actress Ona Munson; Maria Annunziata "Poppy" Sartori Kirk, who worked for Schiaparelli; and Claire Charles-Roux, the Marquise de Forbin, who had participated in the French Resistance—needed and welcomed her support initially, then chafed against it. When they asserted their independence, Mercedes could not tolerate it, became intolerable, and the objects of her affection backed away.

•

Mercedes spent the latter part of World War II in New York working for the magazine *Tomorrow*, which focused on mysticism and
parapsychology. After the war, she returned to France, where she
lived with Poppy Kirk. She more or less stopped writing, other than
occasional bits of freelance journalism and her memoir. She spent
time with her sister Maria, who had been a lover of the painter Mar-
garett Sargent and was now married to Teddy Chanler, Esther
Murphy's old friend. In the late 1950s, she kept company with Andy
Warhol, no less a devotee of celebrity than she; when *Here Lies the
Heart* was published, he drew the invitation to her book party. By
the end of her life, she was sending letters dated only "4 a.m.," and
entreating friends for professional or financial help with a tubercu-
lar aspiring actress she had befriended, a pale shadow of the women
she had once attracted. She was devoted to her pets and used them
as an excuse for her stasis. "Don't let a *cat* rule yr life," exhorted an
affectionate but frustrated Cecil Beaton. When she died in 1968,
Beaton paid tribute to her "gallantry" and was "relieved that her
long drawn out unhappiness has at last come to an end," but noted
that she'd "managed to make it [contact] difficult for friends, impossible for her lovers."

Mercedes wanted to worship and be intimate, at once. She
wanted it known that being a fan is itself a performance, individual
and collective, intensely personal and outrageously public. What
Garbo wanted was something else: "The German people are wonderful," she said early in her career. "They do not touch you, yet
they have their arms around you—always." It was a sort of oxymoron, in conflict with herself as well as with the desire of others to get
close to her. She provoked that desire in her friends as well as her
fans, and Mercedes thrived on and was debilitated by it. It was a
fantasy of control as potent as Mercedes's own.

Esther Murphy, who "always was fond of" Mercedes, reflected "that
even when she was in her most absurd incarnations . . . she was fundamentally an intelligent and subtle woman. But her mind seemed
to go in layers like Neapolitan ice, and some of the layers were pretty

trashy." In *Here Lies the Heart* and its drafts, Mercedes layers assertions about her "sexual reaction[s]" to flowers, her travels "out on the astral plane," and her ability to predict the future with precise social and historical observation. Many signs and wonders suggested that she was predestined to meet Garbo. Flowers, she notes, "affected and excited me as certain beautiful women have affected and excited me." (She also used them to deflower her lovers, but this she did not write.) She was able to halt the infestation by ants of her home in Los Angeles with meditation, "slow breathing exercises . . . call[ing] on all the Enlightened Ones" for help, and speaking "out loud to the ants . . . slowly, distinctly, and softly," telling "them that they were in great danger and would surely be killed if they did not go away," repeating, like a mantra, "Please leave the house."

But she also wrote about what it felt like to live in what was "a very different period for women. We had to battle every inch of the way for rights which are now taken for granted. Young women who vote today can never imagine the frustration and indignity of being considered inferior to men and not allowed to go to the polls. And today, when women can fill any job, it is impossible to realize what it meant to be completely dependent financially on a husband or family simply because jobs were closed to them because of their sex." She described the tenor of life in New York City in the years before the United States entered the Great War, when all of the young men she knew were in military training and most of the young women did volunteer work of some kind. First the men "disappeared one by one . . . to board ships painted gray and black which sailed secretly, surrounded by convoys, from unnamed ports." Then the city "was crowded with officers and soldiers of all the Allied Nations," including "wounded men who had been sent from the trenches to the United States for surgical care, some totally blind or lacking one eye, a leg or an arm, others with their heads bound in bandages. The tension in the atmosphere heightened from day to day" as everyone wondered whether and when the United States would enter the war.

These layers also characterize the portraits in the book. "While this is an autobiography," wrote one reviewer, "it reads like a book of many, many biographies woven through the life of Miss de Acosta." Some of her accounts of the other people in her life are simply lists, collections of famous names. In the winter of 1921–22, after her first two books of poems were accepted for publication, Mercedes began going to dinners given by Mrs. Simeon Ford, who fed writers, then asked them to recite their work. There she "met many of the most important poets in America: Edgar Lee Masters, Vachel Lindsay, Robert Frost, Sara Teasdale, Elinor Wylie and Leonora Speyer were often there, and also Charles Hanson Towne, Edna St. Vincent Millay, Dorothy Parker, Ezra Pound and Kahlil Gibran, all of whom I already knew." Even grief is an occasion for name-dropping. After Rita's death: "Friends were kind to me, especially my theatre friends including Noel Coward, Greta Cooper, John Wilson, Harold Ross, Alex Woollcott, Alfred Lunt, Lynn Fontanne, Margalo Gil[l]more, Clifton Webb, Kit Cornell and countless others." The party she gave in the 1920s for a star-studded collection of actresses who were her friends was another such catalogue: Helen Hayes, Mrs. Patrick Campbell, Laurette Taylor, Alla Nazimova, Jeanne Eagels, Katharine Cornell, among others, all came to dinner. But these women were unable or unwilling to converse with one another, and Mercedes said that she was forced to acknowledge that it was a mistake to bring together so many people used to having the spotlight on themselves alone.

Yet she also used *Here Lies the Heart* to portray people who had been prominent in cultural life but were no longer known by the time her book was published, and to document forgotten social networks. She writes about Cole Porter and Isadora Duncan, but also about the then-popular music hall performer Theodora (Teddie) Gerrard; about the collector Gabrielle Enthoven, who spent her life amassing approximately a hundred thousand playbills that document the history of the London theater from the early eighteenth century on; and about her friend and Esther's, Robert Chanler, that anarchic force and important "part of the social, artistic and Bohemian fabric of New York in the twenties." And she created in *Here Lies the Heart* a mildly coded history of a corner of twentieth-century gay and lesbian life. She writes that she was frequently at the apartment Enthoven and the writer and translator Cecile Sartoris shared on Washington Square in the interwar years. She notes that she and Le Gallienne shared a bed in the old farmhouse they stayed at during a vacation in Brittany. She describes Dietrich's extravagant generosity. She analyzes Marbury and de Wolfe's ménage, noting that many saw her mentor as ruthless, but "in her personal relationships the contrary was the case—other people were often ruthless to her," and when she lived with Elsie de Wolfe, "it was always Elsie who relentlessly got her way."

In her vivid short profile of Marbury, she describes her mentor as formidable in physique and reputation. She was short and "so fat that her feet, which were abnormally small, could not carry her weight" and she had to "wear steel braces on her legs" and use "two canes." But "seated, as she generally was, she gave the impression of being tall because of the heavy formation of her head and the bulkiness of her shoulders." Mercedes calls Marbury "an extraordinary mixture of worldliness and childishness; of shrewdness and Victorian innocence," and not only a powerful theatrical and literary agent but a canny Democratic Party operator. A convert to Catholicism and "a natural Jesuit," she "was thoroughly enmeshed with the powers of the Church from the Cardinal down. She was a sly and astute politician," Mercedes writes, "and, in the days when I knew her had a considerable influence in all the intrigues of Tammany Hall."

It was Marbury who first encouraged Mercedes to write *Here Lies the Heart*, telling her to keep notes when she was young so she could write an autobiography one day. Mercedes had not kept notes; she drew "from memory" to write the book. She did keep a collection—letters, clothes, clippings, and more—the tangible record of her engagement with the popular and high culture of the first half of the twentieth century. After the book was published, she sold and gave this material to the Rosenbach Museum & Library in Philadelphia, which she chose because of her friendship with its director, William McCarthy. Ailing, with her finances in disarray, she wrote to McCarthy in the summer of 1960, "Let me tell you again how happy I am that my little collection is at last with you. I have every confidence that you will treat it 'kindly' and do the right thing by it." Over the next several years, she continued to give and sell material to the Rosenbach. "Am sending you two pair of very beautiful evening slippers which *I wore* in the twenties," she wrote

McCarthy in 1961, "and which I prefer to give to you rather than the Metropolitan Museum who have asked for them." "Utterly broke," she wondered: "Do you think there is any chance of the Foundation paying me a little extra money for the continual new material I have been sending you and will continue to do over the years? . . . I have not even been able to pay my rent or telephone bill this month . . . I feel very humiliated to ask you this—it is not easy. With the world in the sad state it is in I feel very disgusting to be harassed by personal financial worries."

As she negotiated the transfer of her collection, which today consists of about five thousand items, she stipulated that the letters from people she identified as still living ex-lovers—Le Gallienne, Dietrich, Poppy Kirk, and Claire de Forbin—be sealed until both she and her correspondent were dead. To the Garbo correspondence she attached an additional waiting period of ten years. In 1964, she wrote to McCarthy, who was terminally ill:

> I never get over the feeling that one should never give away or show letters which, at the time, have meant much to one and are so very personal. And yet I would not have had the heart or the courage to have burned these letters. I mean, of course, Eva, Gretas and Marlenes [sic]—who were lovers. So it seemed a God-sent moment when you took them. I only hope, as the years go on, as you are no longer there that they will be *respected* and *protected* from the eyes of vulgar people.

And so the Rosenbach is the repository not only of typescripts of drafts of *Here Lies the Heart* and of Mercedes's other writing, published and not, of family photographs, and of an exercise book in which her mother practiced her English, but also of the remains, stockpiled for years, of this life fantastically intersected by celebrity:

> Eva Le Gallienne's breathless correspondence, out of which fall eighty-year-old, browned rose petals.
> Telegrams and telegraphic notes in green ink from Marlene Dietrich on rich green-and-silver monogrammed stationery.

A love poem in Isadora Duncan's hand that ends, "My kisses like a swarm / of Bees / Would find their way / between thy knees / and suck the honey / of thy lips / Embracing thy / too slender hips."

Longing scrawls from Ona Munson, which are also a window into lesbian flirtation and infighting in 1940s Hollywood. (Why has Dietrich been eyeing her? Munson asks. What are mutual friends saying about the director Dorothy Arzner?)

Intimate snapshots of Le Gallienne, Dietrich, Garbo, and others—and studio portraits of these women, in plush black velvet frames.

An incongruously homemade icon of Garbo: tiny, yellowed photographs of her face, cut from the newspaper and collaged on cardboard.

Pages and pages of Alice B. Toklas's spidery, minute writing, which seems, as Mercedes wrote, to have been penned "with the eyelash of a fly."

Letters from and an autographed score by Igor Stravinsky.

Clothing: "A single stocking" and "One yellow sock and one pink and black scarf in an envelope with a note"—gifts from Dietrich: the first two, metonyms of her famous legs; the last, lipstick-stained, of her mouth.

Shoes that belonged to Rita; shoes that belonged to Mercedes; shoes that Tamara Karsavina "wore during rehearsals when she took off her ballet slippers."

It is a body of work that makes it clear that the poetry for which Mercedes de Acosta should be remembered is made of the fugitive lines of a fan's devotion, and that this affect and activity have more than a little in common with an archivist's belief in the importance of preserving a material sense of history. It is also a collection that suggests how peculiar collecting, collections, and the idea of evidence are.

Imagine the power of a collection: to summon a world; to include and exclude; to define and protect the collector and her objects; to mark time as divisible and as infinite. Imagine the drive to save or acquire an object, in all of its permutations—a reiteration of ardor

imbued with tedium, for the object and for repetition itself. Imagine the endless interest and endless aspiration that collecting expresses. Imagine it as a form of pinning things down and turning them into property that also reveals their mobility and vulnerability, their endless need for protection.

And yet collecting and collections have been seen as antidotes to such feelings for the collector—as bulwarks against vulnerability, against loss, against the possibility of nothing. For Mercedes de Acosta, collecting was clearly a way to sustain a connection to her sister Rita. Having lost her father, a sibling, friends, and a lover to suicide, and being wracked by suicidal fantasies herself, she found collecting a way to hold on to life, a form of insurance, and a means to create a body of evidence. Whatever we may think of the blank card that came with flowers Garbo sent, Mercedes saw it as telling documentation. Employing clipping services, she documented the publication of her books and the production of her plays. Amassing material about her famous friends, she amassed proof that she had existed; proof that she had participated in worlds that she loved and admired; proof that she, too, had been loved and admired; proof that, although it was impossible to think of herself as great, it was possible to think of herself as someone who understood greatness and had inspired the great to be greater.

The Rosenbach Museum & Library was founded in 1954 to maintain and develop the collections of Abraham S. W. Rosenbach, a celebrated book dealer, and of his brother Philip, who specialized in the fine and decorative arts. It is now a house museum and archive that occupies two adjoining nineteenth-century town houses, one of them the brothers' former home, on an old residential street in downtown Philadelphia. The Rosenbach has holdings of about 350,000 items, including the manuscript of James Joyce's *Ulysses*; Marianne Moore's papers and a re-creation of her living room; collections of Judaica and early Americana; manuscripts and first editions by Conrad, Blake, Dickens, Wilde, and Lewis Carroll.

On April 15, 2000, forty years after Mercedes's initial transaction

Marlene Dietrich, Malibu, California, 1932, photographed by Mercedes de Acosta (Courtesy Rosenbach Museum & Library)

with McCarthy, more than thirty years after her death, and ten years to the day after Garbo's death, the Rosenbach opened Mercedes's Garbo material. Sitting in the reading room in the years and then the days leading up to this event, one heard museum docents come and go in the adjacent room, reciting a script about the Rosenbach brothers and their things. "This is the heart and soul of the museum," they said, over and over. They were talking about Joyce's death mask, Byron's card case, Whitman's manuscripts, and a model of the Globe Theatre, not about Mercedes or her collection. And yet: In the month before the end of the moratorium on the Garbo files, the Rosenbach—a place most accustomed to the eyes of scholars and school groups—sent out press releases announcing the imminent "unsealing" and it admitted reporters and cameramen. On April 15, its librarian tied two ribbons around the document boxes, representatives of the Rosenbach and the Garbo estate cut the ribbons, the material was quickly catalogued, and the curatorial staff mounted a small display.

Two days later, in a makeshift pressroom, they announced the contents. Relieved and dismayed, or imputing relief or dismay to others, they testified about a lack of evidence. "Anyone determined to classify Garbo as one of de Acosta's lesbian lovers will certainly be disappointed with the contents of these letters," said Grey Horan, Garbo's great-niece and executor. "There is no concrete evidence that any sexual relationship between these two women ever existed." Garbo's seminudity in some snapshots taken by Mercedes was a sign only of her Swedish lack of inhibition and love of the outdoors, not of her intimacy with the photographer. The museum director's more measured comment: "Garbo's letters do—the question on so many people's minds—reveal an intense friendship with Acosta, but one that waxed and waned before ending altogether about 1960." Journalists were then invited to view the exhibit, *Garbo Unsealed*. After seeing it, more than one returned to the pressroom muttering that there was "nothing there." Headlines across the country and around the world the next day read "Garbo Letters: Reveal Friendship Not Lesbianism" and (the off-rhymed) "No Hint

With Igor Stravinsky in Hollywood (From *Here Lies the Heart*)

of Love in Acosta Trove." Everyone had something to say about what they persistently identified as nothing.

Nothing: The document box contained five folders that held more than one hundred items dating between 1931 and 1959. There were letters and telegrams—playful, loving, aloof, annoyed, demanding—from Garbo. There was a short manuscript of adulatory verse by Mercedes: "When we climbed your hands so held / the rocks in their grasp / I felt they had the whole great / mountain in their clasp." And: "There is holiness in ploughed land. / Waves of black Earth being still— / Like a dark sea of barren dreams." There were the snapshots of Garbo from the vacation they took in the Sierra Madre. There was a tracing of her foot, and a small square of cardboard on which she had written Mercedes's address, apparently cut from a box she had sent Mercedes. Much of the correspondence is in pencil and unsigned. There are several letters that close with the initial G, a card signed "Greta," and a telegram signed "Harriet," for Harriet Brown, Garbo's favorite alias. One of the cards that accompanied the flowers Garbo sent Mercedes at Christmas and Easter over the years is marked with nothing but a large question mark, in blue ballpoint ink.

Much of the intense speculation about this material in the days before this event depended on the assumption, both desired and feared, that Mercedes de Acosta, with her reputation for flamboyantly expressed emotion, had been lying when she named Garbo as her lover. Still, that question—Had they been lovers?—posed repeatedly, seemed to have as much to do with a desire to ask it as to find an answer. It was a question that was both attracted to and dismayed by the elusiveness of evidence, and it was, like a collector's desire, incapable of being satisfied. It was also a question that depended on an understanding of identity as constituted largely by sexual behavior as well as on a belief that it was possible to gather positive evidence of desire. Only a few observers wondered publicly what such proof might consist of in the correspondence of a figure as demonstrably undemonstrative as Greta Garbo.

If it was all a kind of nonevent, nothing, it inspired a huge amount of publicity for Garbo and a palpable contempt for Mercedes. The story that circulated was about an elegant, elusive, beleaguered star besieged by a pathological, opportunistic, unreliable fan—a view of Mercedes and her collection that did nothing other than reiterate what we already think we know about stars and fans: the greatness and need for privacy of the one, the irrationality and presumption of the other. No one was asking: What does it mean to be a collector? What sort of biographical text is a collection? How do fans and stars need and desire each other, and what does the dance between them actually consist of? What is the relation between facts and feelings in an archive? How do you prove or disprove the presence of nothing?

She sets the fire. There is no fire.

A.S.W. Rosenbach ran the preeminent rare book and manuscript business in the United States in the first half of the twentieth century. He turned book collecting into a viable, valued form of investment and helped to build the collections of J. P. Morgan (now the basis of the Morgan Library), Henry Huntington (whose collection became the Huntington Library), Henry Folger (the Folger Shakespeare Library), and Harry Elkins Widener (in whose name Harvard's Widener Library was founded). Rosenbach had a reputation as an omnivorous, outrageous collector who saved some of his best acquisitions for himself. He was known, too, as "a lover of whisky and women" and as a man who habitually embroidered on his exploits and accomplishments, telling inflated and factually incorrect stories about his life. And he collected everything, notes his biographer, not just rare printed matter:

> It was almost as though Dr. Rosenbach had wanted a biography of himself written, to which unspoken wish his brother Philip had assented, for the brothers hoarded paper as misers do gold. In dozens of filing cabinets, cartons, ledgers, scrapbooks, salesbooks, and piles merely bound with string they kept the important with the inconsequential—high school notebooks and college examination papers, sheets covered

with doodles, personal and business letters sent and received, newspaper clippings, invoices of merchandise bought, and sales slips—a vast, unsorted accumulation of over fifty years.

Keeping the important with the inconsequential is one version of what it means to be a dedicated collector—the other being a relentless connoisseurship. A.S.W. and Philip Rosenbach seem to have engaged in both. The museum's educational material on collecting, directed at young visitors, puts it this way: "The brothers loved beautiful things, ugly things, old things, modern things, tiny things, gigantic things, weird things, rare things, expensive things, cheap things, fancy things, and plain things. They thought: 'As long as we love it, anything can be a collection!'"

Their vast, unsorted accumulation sounds distinctly like Mercedes's hoard. But while theirs has been seen as evidence of foresight and even an (auto)biographical impulse, hers has been viewed as the sign of typically trivial feminine need, of sexual derangement, and of arrested development. The catalogue of Mercedes's papers and the publicity for the exhibit *Garbo Unsealed* described her as "truly of the genus 'social butterfly'" and asserted that "it is as a 'confidante to the stars' that her papers have interest." Garbo's great-niece called Mercedes's Bible, in which she had pasted photographs of Garbo, reminiscent of her "11-year-old god-daughter's scrapbook devoted to Leonardo DiCaprio."

This Bible, on display in *Garbo Unsealed*, inspired much commentary and came to stand for the unsealing and for the idea that Mercedes and her collection were unserious and unstable. Placed at the entrance of the gallery, it was open to an early page on which Mercedes had mounted six small photographs of Garbo. On the facing page (where at least a decade earlier she had written, "The Bible of Mercedes de Acosta 1922" and transcribed a passage from the Book of Matthew), she had mounted another small image of Garbo. The Rosenbach distributed a photograph of those two pages as part of its press packet and mounted an enlargement of it on the wall behind the podium on April 17, 2000. As a result, the image was reproduced widely. During the press conference, the speakers gestured toward it repeatedly. "Acosta's fanatical devotion to Garbo is already well-known," said Derek Dreher, director of the Rosenbach. "The image behind me is further proof of this." "Case in point!" Horan, a lawyer, exclaimed, pointing to it.

The Bible was presented as though it, too, had been unsealed: released from a kind of bondage of necessary privacy, secrecy, and shame, and evidence of a singular obsession with Garbo. Yet it had never been restricted material, and Mercedes's decoration of it—the mingling of celebrity image and Christian devotional text—was not limited to Garbo. On subsequent pages she pasted photographs of Eva Le Gallienne and Eleonora Duse, two other actresses who inspired her—one her lover, one not. The association between Garbo and the spiritual, moreover, was not Mercedes's alone. This star had been "divine" since her appearance in *The Divine Woman*, in 1928. (Nor was it Garbo's alone: Sarah Bernhardt was "divine" before her.) As one reviewer wrote of Garbo's silent performances: "It was not so much what she did, or how she did it, but what she conveyed through some spiritual distinction of her own." Nor does Mercedes's obsession account wholly for her ability to save so many images of Garbo. Her papers include "a *great many* magazines . . . in which articles and photographs [of Garbo] appeared," as she wrote to William McCarthy, in part because there were so many to be had.

The Rosenbach had bought Mercedes's papers, remarked the museum's director that April, "because she insinuated herself into the centers of modernist thought and art." Garbo's writing was of a piece with the rest of the library's holdings, "round[ing] out a stunning collection that chronicles the great Modernists of the 20th century," noted the publicity for the unsealing. Mercedes's relationship to modernity, in this story, was that of an outsider who imposed on its legitimate centers. She was at once mocked and given no credit for her collection. As one critic has argued, she was "a pre-Enlightenment person in a post-Enlightenment age. She could never bring herself to give up on daydream or romance or superstition," and her plays were "almost entirely—as if obliviously—in the obsolete vein of 19th-century melodrama." While "Garbo was ruthlessly, corrosively modern, as thorough in her irony and disillusionment as Gibbon or Voltaire," de Acosta "was a throwback, a figment out of the Dark

The Bible
of

Mercedes de Acosta
1922.

"He that findeth his life shall
lose it: and he that loseth his
life shall find it......
Come unto me, all ye that labour
and are heavy laden, and I
will give you rest....
Take my yoke upon you, and
learn of me; for I am
meek and lowly in heart: and
ye shall find rest unto
your souls....
For my yoke is easy, and my
burden light". Matthew.

Ages, wedded to unrealities." It is true that her writing often eschewed the uses of distance, abstraction, and irony that were changing the literary landscape in the first part of the twentieth century and that have come down to us as the canonical version of modernism. Her plotting could be outlandish—"Probability is not a word that occurs in Miss de Acosta's dictionary," wrote one reviewer of her novel *Until the Day Break*. The book contains "purple passages that seem to belong to a past decade," noted another. Rereading this novel as she wrote in *Here Lies the Heart*, she was herself "amazed that the reviewers didn't throw it out of the window." The worst of her poetry reads like self-parody. Enthusiastically punctuated, it includes lines such as "Suddenly I thought of death!" and "reaching / out we extend our hands and lean far into the Vast / Space of the Infinite!" Yet her subject matter also struck a number of contemporary readers as modern, and her poems were appreciated by some critics for their directness of expression and for the way they conveyed her sense of being stifled by social convention. Her collection, *Moods*, had a second printing, and Harriet Monroe, a powerful arbiter of the new in verse and supporter of women writers, published Mercedes's work in *Poetry* magazine.

Separating Mercedes de Acosta from what we think of as modern not only flattens that category retrospectively. It also repeats a certain modernist formal orthodoxy by reproducing the attempts to purge nineteenth-century modes such as melodrama from its purview—attempts that have been so successful that it is still easy to think of overt and extravagant expressions of emotion as unserious. Elinor Wylie was the contemporary poet Mercedes said she most admired, but it is with the work of Sara Teasdale that she was most obviously in conversation. *Streets and Shadows*, the collection Mercedes published in 1922, echoes Teasdale's 1920 *Flame and Shadow*. Her poems to Garbo clearly owe something to Teasdale's first book, the 1907 *Sonnets to Duse and Other Poems*, which include "To Eleonora Duse," "To Eleonora Duse in 'The Dead City,'" and "To a Picture of Eleonora Duse as 'Francesca da Rimini.'" Amy Lowell, whom Mercedes also admired and met—and who was then considered part of the modern movement in poetry and is now too

The Bible of Mercedes de Acosta (Courtesy Rosenbach Museum & Library)

often ignored or dismissed—also commemorated Duse in verse. If Mercedes held on to much of what modernism repudiated (emotion, fantasy) as it established itself, her writing documents the links between those earlier aesthetic modes and celebrity culture—a connection that had to wait for Frank O'Hara and other gay male poets for it to be taken seriously.

And if her writing makes it possible to see modernism as part of what preceded it, her collection—her archiving of personal mementos and of mass-produced items of popular culture—suggests how disparate archival practices overlap. Like the Rosenbach brothers and the institution founded to memorialize them and their work, Mercedes was concerned with respecting and protecting the material she cared about. Yet her collecting—of Stravinsky's score, Dietrich's stocking, Alice B. Toklas's letters—proposes once more that there is a false distinction between a pop cultural and high-cultural way of understanding valued objects. Garbo's letters to Mercedes enrich the Rosenbach's holdings of modernist writing and artifacts not only because of the star's modernity, but also because the de Acosta Papers as a whole testify to the history of feminist activism and to the primacy of the individual ego, to spiritual search and to sexual adventure, to the feeling of being a fan and to the history of celebrity in the twentieth century, and to the material and emotional texture of all of these ventures.

In 1936, Esther Murphy wrote to Chester Arthur:

I have seen Mercedes be intelligent and discriminating in the past. But she . . . always flew off on a personal tangent, and I know of no one who could be more irritating than she could be when she was in one of her mood[s] of self pitying introspection. But either life, or the passage of time, or the influence of the Baba, or a combination of them all, seems to have worked a real transformation. She seems actually capable of getting outside of her own personal problems and seeing them in their relation to the larger problems that encompass all our lives . . . And this impersonality and sense of the true proportion of things, have given Mercedes a dignity and a conviction and a serenity she never had attained before . . . She seemed to me like a person released from a part of themselves that had always acted to diminish them.

While Esther grasped this complex, often annoying human amalgam, more recent observers, including her biographer, have tried to rescue Mercedes de Acosta, from herself and from others' scorn. It is a gesture that echoes Mercedes's relationship to her lovers and that ignores the fact that if we take her as she was, she needs no such help. She herself mocked her desire to rescue Maude Adams from a nonexistent fire. She also described herself, older, backstage with Adams, as "so absurdly and tragically intense that it's a small wonder I didn't blow up the whole dressing room." Aware that she used her feelings for Garbo to scuttle other intimacies, she wrote to Marlene Dietrich, "I do know that I have built up in my emotions a person that does not exist. My mind sees the real person—a Swedish servant girl with a face touched by God—only interested in money, her health, sex, food, and sleep. And yet her face tricks my mind and my spirit builds her up into something that fights with my brain. I do love her, but I only love the person I have created and not the person who is real." (Dietrich's response, according to her daughter: "Really! De Acosta is too vain for words!")

The correspondence from Garbo that Mercedes saved, which cannot be quoted without permission of the star's estate, illuminates Mercedes's romantic exaggerations. Her impromptu trip in the winter of 1935 to Sweden, for example, which in *Here Lies the Heart* she calls the result of Garbo's spur-of-the-moment invitation, was not Garbo's idea but hers. But these letters also make it clear that her connection with Garbo was not the delusion of a crazed fan. Garbo tells her to come closer and to go away; tells her how she has suffered from the film industry and describes her indecision about how to spend her life after Hollywood; describes her ailments, physical and emotional, and entreats Mercedes to take care of herself; sends her yoga mantras, sends her love, and sends her on household errands; bemoans her inability to settle, asks Mercedes to make her a hotel reservation, describes her plans in detail, refuses to be pinned down. She tells Mercedes not to bother her, tells her not to forget to write, writes that she dislikes writing, tells her

to ignore newspaper reports about her, apologizes for her odd behavior, tells her they are wholly different kinds of people, thanks her for buying her a pair of shoes, laments the waste of her life, chastises her for being too persistent, refers coyly to the jealousy of Mercedes's current girlfriend (Poppy Kirk), and hopes that Mercedes will take care of her, Garbo, should she decide to go to Paris. She is aloof, frustrated, demanding, loving, funny, and self-consciously evasive.

Garbo's star image, like that of Maude Adams, was produced (by Metro-Goldwyn-Mayer) to make publicity out of the difficulty of producing publicity about this idiosyncratic, solitary, gender-bending star. Today the books, photographs, magazine articles, and television documentaries that are part of the ongoing work of knowing Garbo almost always conclude that we can never know her. "Garbo Letters Leave Mystery Intact," explained USA Today in April 2000. Mercedes de Acosta, although unfamiliar to most, was assumed to be thoroughly known, in an epithet or two. Part of the lure of a collection of personal papers is that it offers the promise of answers about a life, simply by virtue of being grouped under one name. Yet the Mercedes de Acosta Papers have most often been used as a source for information about Mercedes's famous friends. The proof that her collection was asked to provide in the spring of 2000—that Garbo did or did not have a female lover—at once had everything to do with Mercedes and reduced her to next to nothing, creating a tremendously important cipher. To the extent that she and her collection were important, it was only as a proving ground for knowledge about Garbo, as an index of the star's desire. As such, she could have been anyone, or any woman.

Respecting and protecting Greta Garbo posthumously from Mercedes de Acosta meant denigrating the latter and her desires— even as Mercedes and her collection generated another wave of publicity for (and concomitant increase in value of everything to do with) the star. Respecting and protecting Garbo meant offering legalistic readings of the star's utterances rather than acknowledging that knowledge and desire can be as elusive as Garbo was. What was on display that spring, in addition to Garbo's letters,

Mercedes on the *Normandie*, 1935 (Courtesy Bettmann Archive, CORBIS)

Mercedes's Bible, and so on, was a form of guardianship that involved the familiar (and in this case familial), derogatory view of women's relationships to stars (trivial, unrestrained, juvenile). On view, too, was another attempt to assert the correct distance from this star, and a reminder that there is no arguing with the excitement of power. While Garbo's image and biography are monitored by constant family concern and litigation, de Acosta's are not. Garbo was born with nothing, but ended with enormous wealth: Her power today comes not just from her star image but from canny investments in real estate and stocks, which her family inherited. Mercedes, who began life with every financial and social advantage, ended with almost nothing: "One by one down to the end," she wrote to William McCarthy in 1964, "I seem to be selling everything."

Confronting a collection and a life like Mercedes de Acosta's means being forced to consider, over and over, the boundary between the important and the inconsequential, between intellect and emotion, between something and nothing. Which is to say, it means being forced to reflect on what we understand to be a biographical fact. Questions of evidence will always also be questions of access, yet there will always be something we cannot read, or see, or hear, even when it is right in front of us or spoken directly to us. And when it comes to a contest of wills and of power like this one, there will never be enough evidence. The trouble had to do with what Mercedes de Acosta did with her body, just how close she got to the star. Her body is gone. Fantasy and factuality, memory and material preservation, are all alive in her collection. This is how she is embodied now, in a place that is not simply a repository of paper and things but also a storehouse and producer of feeling. But how did she view her collection? It was, she wrote to McCarthy, "quite unique and certainly very human material."

VELVET IS
VERY IMPORTANT

There is a visibility so tenuous, so different, or so discomfited that it is easy to miss. And there is a visibility so simple, so precise, or so extreme that it, too, is obscure.

In a schoolroom in London at the turn of the twentieth century a young girl lies strapped to a sloping wooden board, a treatment ordered for her worsening curvature of the spine. During writing lessons, she is allowed to sit upright with the rest of the class, but then her arms are secured so tightly to the back of her chair that she cannot move her wrists normally, which forces her to develop a cramped and backward-sloping handwriting. There is also trouble with her throat and "graver trouble" with her feet and ankles, for which she wears lace-up orthopedic boots. In the summer, "when the world [is] at its prettiest," she suffers so acutely from allergies—to food, to flowers, to the air—that her temperature soars and she is forced to lie all day in a darkened room. To fatten her and restore her to health, she is fed strawberries and cream, but this therapy only exacerbates her ailments.

She is Madge Alma McHarg, a tall, thin, slightly bucktoothed girl with freckles and long, straight blond hair. Her eyes are a bit too close together, her clothes seldom flatter her, and her parents constantly remind her of her "deficiency both in looks and in manners." Her shyness is so devastating that it "amount[s] almost to paranoia," so acute that she experiences it as yet another physical distress. When she stands, she hunches her shoulders and drops her head, looking up from this bent and tentative posture.

Madge Garland, Londonderry House, London, 1949, photographed by Cecil Beaton (Cecil Beaton/ Vogue © The Condé Nast Publications Ltd.)

Despite or because of these aberrations, she is full of energy, desperate for learning, mad in pursuit of autonomy.

In the early evenings, she is occasionally required to present herself to her parents for inspection: to her beautiful mother, in her late twenties at the beginning of the century and always perfectly turned out, with flowers in her hats and feather boas around her neck; and to her father, not handsome but also impeccably dressed, with his taste for fine suits and shoes and his professional knowledge of textiles. Like other privileged girls of this place and time, Madge is dressed as she grows up "as a pale and meagre version of [her] mother." But at this young age, when her parents summon her to their drawing room, a nursemaid helps her slip a special pinafore over her ordinary day dress. It is made of white muslin, edged with Valenciennes lace, and threaded with blue ribbons that bubble up into voluptuous bows on her shoulders. For a moment, in this garment, she is transformed—suffused with pleasure and self-confidence.

This fragile, awkward, defective child, called "charmless" by her parents, grew into a woman who organized her life around such moments of transformation, around the experience and display of physical elegance. She became a woman of high polish and even, in Virginia Woolf's estimation, "rather excessive charm." In her twenties, she took her graceless figure and remade it, learning how to stand and move and dress, and she made a career in which flawless posture had meaning. She took her paucity of formal education and invented a life in style to compensate herself. And she renamed herself, at Gertrude Stein's suggestion. Discarding her family name and taking the floral, pretty surname of an ex-husband whose name she had refused when she married him, she became Madge Garland: a hyperfeminine but tough embodiment of the world of haute couture. She became a woman who rejected all training in docility, but outfitted herself to look as if she were no threat. She became an "intellectual devotee of *couture*," who was nevertheless often seen as the incarnation of trivial nothingness—a "meringue," as one colleague put it. "A bunch of froth," said another. She became a public figure whose organization of her life around self-display was bound up with a need to actively, continually conceal herself.

In her twenties, she ran away from home to become an apprentice journalist at British *Vogue*, then a magazine in which couture took a distant second place to flattery of the upper classes. She helped transform it into a forum for high fashion and high art, a mingling that seems self-evident now, but was a revelation to readers then and was resisted by Condé Nast and his managers as dangerously uncommercial. With her mentor and lover, Dorothy Todd, then the editor of British *Vogue*, Madge Garland helped make the magazine a place for writers and visual artists including Woolf, Edith Sitwell, Roger Fry, Duncan Grant, and Vanessa Bell, as well as Stein, Picasso, Proust, Cocteau, and Matisse. Coming into her own as a fashion journalist around the Bloomsbury group and with avant-garde writers and artists in Paris, Madge Garland made herself new in ways that had everything to do with the modernist valorization of novelty and mingling of art and the decorative arts. Knowledgeable about the history of costume, she often said that she had been "ideally cast" as a fashion editor because she invariably "thought that this year's clothes [were] prettier than last." To the end of her life, she was riveted by whatever was most contemporary: "I have always been a sucker for something new," she told an interviewer in the 1970s. She also made herself a trained observer whose professionalism, like her experience of fashion and of modernity, was inseparable from her feminism—her need to break away from her family, to repudiate a world of strictures about how she should live and of low expectations about what she could accomplish.

This was a woman who played a defining but still obscured role in almost every aspect of the English fashion industry in the interwar and postwar years. In the 1930s, as the fashion editor of other women's magazines in London, and then again at British *Vogue*, she promoted and dissected high fashion with intelligent wit. A symbol of effortless elegance, she also wrote about fashionable dress as a world of work, rather than as the natural exhalations of some enduring femininity. After the Second World War, she created the country's first school of fashion design, was a consultant to the textile industry, advised the government on schemes to coordinate art and industry, and wrote book after book on fashion and beauty.

Near the end of her life, however, she told a reporter, "I was never really that interested in fashion, but I wanted to be financially independent." Asserting that her work had been nothing more than a means to make a living was a way to express her anger that fashion had been one of the few fields in which a woman of her social class could find "respectable" work. It was a way to reiterate her sense of injury that her father had denied her the higher education she wanted and kept her unqualified for any other profession. It was an opportunity, too, to criticize her father's work as an importer of textiles and women's clothing. Yet Madge Garland was not shy about her expertise, nor about the idea that such a sphere of knowledge existed. "She believes in knowing things," wrote a journalist in the 1950s, "and the caprice and whimsies of some women of fashion have no place in her life or personality." Yet if she herself believed that she knew more than most about her field, she also held that what most women felt about clothes was important.

By dismissing her interest in fashion, she was both bowing to the idea of fashion as a trivial field of endeavor and preempting it. In fact, she was acknowledging that an argument about "importance" was at the heart of that industry and one of the engines of her own life. In her meticulous, unsentimental journalism, she grappled with this issue, grasped the world of haute couture as popular entertainment, and presented herself as a character in that story—a participant-observer, expert but amused, often self-mocking. Her denial, her investment, her constant refining of surfaces both sartorial and rhetorical—all have to do with how she looked: what she saw, what she looked like, what it meant to look like her, like someone to look at. Looking at her now means remembering modernism not just as the thrill of new ways of writing and painting but as a whole set of experiments in fields that are still understood as secondary: interior decoration, textiles, bookmaking and bookselling, magazine publishing, as well as fashion—so-called minor arts that provided a range of expression for and were significantly shaped by women who were breaking away from their families and attempting to create something new in their lives and in the culture. Madge Garland lived these experiments her whole life, well beyond the modernist moment, however it is defined.

"Fashion can be a mask to cover imaginative poverty, and is often the antithesis of individual taste," she wrote in the 1960s, "but it can also become a weapon to establish a distinctive personality." It is an assertion that says everything about her own battle to establish herself. "She really was a rebel," a friend observed, "but in many ways such an unlikely looking rebel." Like many of the women who shaped and were changed by the iconoclasm of the first decades of the twentieth century, Madge Garland also sought safety. She needed financial security, since she had no independent income and was never supported by a husband. The world she moved in demanded respectability, particularly for those who did not quite belong, but her social standing was always precarious. Conspicuously, wittily well dressed, she wanted to be admired by all, but desired by women, and she lived alone or with another woman for most of her life. Although she lived in London for nine decades, she was born in Australia and therefore seen as an outsider in England. Even after her death, the rumor or hint of someplace else about her persisted, and a sense that she had tried to hide her origins, along with an English scorn for un-English origins. She made sure that the facts were clear to almost no one: One old friend was sure that her family had moved to London from the Hebrides, or perhaps South Africa. Rumors of sexual scandal also persisted her whole life. In response to this pressure, she produced a style that was at once correct and distinctive, that played on correctness and was something more than correct: a bold performance. And she practiced an intense social discipline. Madge was a "kitten," said Mercedes de Acosta, who had "a dynamic drive hidden under all those blue bows and ruffles." Rebecca West, a friend for more than fifty years, called her "an exquisite piece of porcelain," but knew how strong she was.

An autodidact of the fiercest sort, Madge Garland was also perceived as someone of little substance or enduring interest: "She was undoubtedly a fascinating person—I mean really fascinating," said one of her closest friends, "but she has left no monument." He was trying to imagine both how she could be worthy of a biography and what materials one would use to tell her story. She herself did not believe that she had a legacy, but in old age, at the urging of friends, one of them an accomplished biographer, she tried to write a memoir. She wanted to tell a story of adversity surmounted, of professional success. She produced a number of antiseptic, jaunty, repetitive pages. She left out names, some of the most important parts of her life, huge stretches of time and feeling. She veiled or rewrote even the most apparently straightforward details about her birth and schooling. She could hardly get past the moment when she defied her father and left home to get a job—a huge wrench for a young woman of her background in 1920.

Clothes fade away and they are not easy to archive. "Fashion is both ephemeral and personal," she wrote in 1951, "it cannot be preserved. At most, the husk of a garment is left, a sloughed-off empty skin. Each dress may be said to die with its wearer, and the smart dress of to-day is only a crumpled curiosity to-morrow—soiled and worn." But Madge Garland knew how clothes—the experience of wearing them well or poorly, of looking at oneself and being looked at with rapture or scorn—could lodge in the memory and in the body, and in advanced old age she could recall the look and texture of clothes she had worn as a young child and the energy associated with them. Describing the outfit in which her nanny had dressed her when she was required to present herself to her parents, she wrote, "Never in all my life—and I have been privileged to be dressed by Chanel, Dior, Patou, Schiaparelli, Lanvin, Jacques Fath, etc—has any garment given me the feeling of absolute self confidence that . . . muslin, beribboned and lace frilled pinafore gave me as I put it on over my everyday dress."

Repudiating so much, she still inclined to optimism and desire. Strict with herself and others, she was stalwart in friendship and open to romance until the end. In a draft of her memoir, she wrote that she fell in love for the first time at age five, "a state in which I have remained all my life, only the objects have varied from time to time." Like the leaning, leaping people in the photographs of Jacques-Henri Lartigue, those figures who seem to be launching themselves into modernity, Madge Garland was always wanting more, wanting now, wanting what happens next.

So look at her. Look at her in a beige satin, drop-waist Chanel dress, around her neck a long rope of pearls and a multicolor, hand-block-printed silk scarf by Sonia Delaunay that she "cherished." It is the South of France in the late 1920s.

Look at her posing for the fledgling Cecil Beaton, her own modernity placed against his self-consciously modern backdrops (cellophane, props, faux-"futuristic" painting): her blond hair shingled, her eyebrows the thinnest pencil line, two strands of pearls around her neck, an enormous flower pinned to the metallic sheen of her outfit.

Look at her "beautifully dressed in logical suits and illogical blouses," circa August 1945. On her head, "an insane Hat." With her piercing blue eyes and "sophisticated pink and white make-up" she looks like a painting by her friend Marie Laurencin.

Look at her in her late seventies "wearing a Marimekko dress and yards of huge pearls," or wrapped in a knitted mohair coat of dusty but vivid aquamarine, still making people look up and the restaurant hum with interest as she pauses at its entrance.

And look at her well into her eighties out in the Kensington High Street, "looking absolutely marvelous" even on a bitter cold day. Or at lunch at the Reform Club in "the most beautiful mauve wool outfit." Or out at Harvey Nichols, where she is looking intently through the racks of clothes, studying them, said an acquaintance who watched her from afar, "as if she were a scholar in an archive."

I ABSOLUTELY REFUSED

At age two, Madge Alma McHarg moved with her family from Melbourne to London. She moved from the colonies to the metropolis, from a place of self-invention to a country obsessed with lineage. She attempted to discard her national and family origins as soon as she became conscious of them. Trying to make herself at home in her body, she cast off her orthopedic boots and the "horrid, thick . . . woolen dresses" and woolen underclothes she wore in winter. She thought of her life as a long struggle against the limitations of illness and of her family. She never entirely discarded her sense of imperfection.

"My family didn't enter into my life really at all," she said in old age. Alienated from her parents and siblings and desperate to erase her Australian middle-class antecedents, she was never nostalgic about her past. Refusal was the keynote when she described her childhood and adolescence. "I told them, 'No, no, *no*,'" she said; and: "I thought, 'No, I won't, I won't, and I won't!'" Refusal, and an inchoate but overwhelming desire for independence. Yet her father's business involved the stuff with which she composed her career: His company traded in "Millinery, Straws, Ready-to-Wears, Felts, Flowers, Ornaments, Paris Novelties, Ribbons, Neckwear, Veilings, Laces, Embroideries, Handkerchiefs, Silks, Velvets, Mantles, Blouses, Hosiery, Underwear, Gloves," and she remembered him as "very, very fond of clothes." If she gave him no positive credit for having influenced her professional life, it is not surprising, since he had done everything he could to keep her from having a profession.

For the record, she considered only three things about her coming-of-age significant: the brief but idyllic aesthetic education

she received at a finishing school in Paris before the First World
War, the time she spent in the United States just after the war, and
the extent to which her parents thwarted her and she rebelled
against them. The rejection and refusal to conform were real, but
the way she recalled them hid a story more complicated than she
was able to tell.

She was born in Melbourne on June 12, 1896. Both of her parents were first-generation Australians, the children of Scottish im-
migrants who had been part of the wave of voluntary migration
from England, Ireland, Scotland, and Canada during the boom created by the discovery of gold in 1851 in the newly founded state of
Victoria. In southeastern Australia, Victoria is roughly the size of
England, and its capital, Melbourne, has been the Australian city
most identified with England, especially with upper-class English
customs and assumptions. As people and capital poured into Victoria during the gold rush and through the second half of the nineteenth century, Melbourne became the financial and manufacturing
center of the country. By the mid-1890s, it was a busy city that
had already weathered a depression, the scene of enormous wealth
and poverty, and still a raw and sprawling frontier town.

Most of Madge's forebears were enterprising men of the type
referred to in Australian newspapers of the time as "just the stamp
of man to develop into a successful colonist." Coming from next to
nothing in Scotland, they did not doubt their right to remake themselves in Australia. There is almost no record of the women of those
generations. Her maternal grandfather, Thomas Aitken, immigrated
in 1842 and eventually founded the Victoria Brewery. Her mother,
Henrietta (Hettie) Maria Aitken, was raised in the mansion adjoining the brewery, on Victoria Parade in fashionable East Melbourne.
Her paternal grandfather immigrated the following decade and became an official in the colonial government. Her father, Andrew
Creighton McHarg, left school to work as a clerk in the garment
business, a trade his older brother James had already entered; a few
years later he joined James and two partners, who had founded
Brooks, McGlashan, and McHarg. They were "warehousemen" and
wholesalers of ladies' clothing and accessories who imported raw
and manufactured goods from Europe for distribution around Australia, catering to the growing colonial population and the Edwar-

dian vogue for elaborate, feminine trimmings. Brooks, McGlashan, and McHarg's warehouses were devastated by fires twice in the 1890s, but by the turn of the century the firm was one of the most successful businesses of its kind in Australia.

The business of fashion sent the McHarg brothers back in the direction from which the family had emigrated: They are said to have pioneered constant commercial travel between Australia and Europe in 1894, when Andrew McHarg first went to England and Europe for the firm; until then, Australian wholesalers had depended on supplies from English dealers. Andrew McHarg had married Hettie Aitken in 1892, and in 1898 he moved to London to position Brooks, McGlashan, and McHarg at the source, bringing with him Hettie and their two young children, Madge and her older brother, Gerald. The family settled first in Sydenham, in South London, and then in northwest London, in what Madge—alluding ironically to her mother's distress at its distance from the fashionable center of town—described as "the *wilds* of Hampstead." In the first part of the twentieth century, Hampstead was significantly Jewish, suburban in feeling, inhabited by businessmen and their families. In fact, it was fifteen years before the McHargs reached it; they lived first in even more remote areas of North London. If it was possible for Madge to allude to Hampstead as a disappointment to her mother's social aspirations (her longing for a good address in the West End, the apex of London social life and the place for pleasurable public consumptions such as shopping and the theater), the earlier addresses were so far out of the swim that Madge was careful never to mention them at all.

As white Australians, the McHargs were British subjects and could enter and leave England with ease. But despite their increasing wealth—there were holidays in Deauville, an expensive automobile, the best clothes for Hettie—they remained outsiders in London. Socially ambitious nevertheless, they made a kind of religion of respectability, and the proper conduct of their daughter was a key article of the faith. They expected Madge to become moderately educated (she wanted more), to socialize conventionally ("I won't!"), to learn to dance and do needlepoint (these she did with pleasure), and to participate in the rituals that would lead to a good marriage (she

Andrew McHarg (Madge Garland Papers)

refused). They would have nourished a sensitivity to the intricacies of status even if they had stayed in Australia, since their desire for respectability grew as much from the need to distance themselves from the idea of their country's convict past as it did from a desire to overcome their diminished social position in England.

Like many women of her generation and income, Hettie McHarg was a kind but remote figure to her children, and Madge was pained by her mother's inaccessibility even as she appreciated her style. She described Hettie as a wonderful dancer and needlewoman who "always smelled delicious" and was "beautifully dressed, always, always," never appearing until everything was in place—important, given the many minute fastenings and adornments on Edwardian women's clothing. Hettie told her daughter, "Never come out of your bedroom unless *every* button is buttoned." Madge called her "pretty-mama" and looked forward to wearing "blooms in my hat and feather boas around my neck," just as she did. Years later, Hettie's elaborate dresses and cool distance still signified: Madge told a story about being bathed by her nanny one evening when her mother came in to say goodnight before going out. Naked and wet, Madge ran to her, but was rebuffed, pushed away so she would not damage her mother's lovely clothes.

When she was not still feeling hurt, she referred to her mother airily and mockingly. "My *darling* Mama," she said, was pampered and not inclined to any kind of physical exertion. Cared for by her husband and servants (the household included a cook, a housemaid, and a nanny for the children not yet of school age, although not a separate ladies' maid), Hettie would not willingly walk farther than the distance between her front door and the Daimler waiting by the curb. Later, Madge understood that the constraints of Edwardian fashion—the close circumference of the dresses, the "many fringes, fish-tails, trailing sleeves, twinkling tassels, and elaborate hats"—required such limits on movement. But remembering her childhood, she was attuned to her difference from her mother and her own sense of confinement. One solution was to accompany her father when he golfed. There, she said, "at least I walked in the open air. Mother could stay home."

Henrietta McHarg at home on Fitzjohn's Avenue, 1919 (MGP)

Later she also understood how important it had been for her father to have a fashionable wife and the context in which her mother had been striving for clothed perfection. "It is hard for us with our expertly-cut crease-resistant clothes to imagine the amateurish and crumpled appearance most women presented in the past," she wrote in *Fashion*, the sophisticated primer on the industry that she published in 1962; "old family photographs give more than a hint." Between the mid-nineteenth and mid-twentieth centuries, the transformation of high fashion and the rise of ready-to-wear clothing meant that the two years it had taken "for a Paris fashion to become universally seen and worn in London gradually shrank to one, and [then to] a matter of weeks." Her mother was able to circumvent this long cycle and present a more polished appearance than many of her peers because she shopped in Paris while accompanying her husband on his constant business travels. As for Madge's clothes, she was dressed during what she called "my helpless youth" by "the now extinct species called the 'visiting dressmaker.'" These clothes were not fashionable, but they did fit, since they took "into consideration the peculiarities of my growing body."

If Madge considered her mother sensuously impressive but inadequately loving, she judged her father tyrannical. His crimes were to bring her up in affluence but ignorance, to presume to control her life, and to impede her desire for higher education. She grew up feeling deprived of ideas, of the open expression of emotion, of room for any aspiration other than the one that would have her reproduce her current circumstances. It was the claustrophobia of a conventional girlhood of means, conditions that can be difficult to conceive of now. For that atmosphere of censure and constraint, she also blamed her parents' faith. "If you want to put anybody off religion bring them up as Scotch Presbyterian," she said. Most of all, she expressed her deprivation as a question of aesthetics. "Art and literature didn't exist in our house *at all*," she said, offended that her father was concerned with money, not ideas, and describing him as Philistine in the extreme.

The house, which she described as "Victorian Gothic," was "entirely furnished by Maples," an emporium from which the wealthy ordered everything from the furniture to the carpets. "It had wonderful woodwork, and things built in, and Aubusson rugs specially woven for the room—things beyond price today," she said. "But it was nothing." She meant that this sort of taste had nothing to do with any real personal knowledge or feeling. The house was crammed, too, with the expensive, overembellished things that Andrew McHarg bought in his quest for status: Stinton porcelain, Sheffield plate, paintings by the "right" artists, the latest American gadgets. Much of his acquisition required visits to the luxurious showrooms of West End shops—the flattering experience of walking on thick pile carpets, being comfortably seated, and being brought wares to consider. The only personal touches in the home came from what Madge called her mother's "extremely bad copies" of paintings by Edwin Landseer, who specialized in what now look like perversely cruel, exoticized images of animals. Madge reacted against this atmosphere of sheer accumulation, of buying what one has been told is the best and what looks labor-intensive. Lingering, decades later, on her distress at her parents' environment, she was saying that her eye, both trained and instinctive, was her route to social mobility. Of the 1920s, she said, "the mass of people went on doing the same thing, but the few of us that didn't, we absolutely rejected everything our parents had and that our parents stood for." Rejecting their home, she rejected not only a stereotype of colonial crassness but also an older aristocratic model of taste, since what she wanted all her life was what was new and different—even if the new sometimes meant revaluing the old, as when, in the 1950s, she was among the connoisseurs who helped revive interest in the paintings and decorative art of the Victorian age.

To Andrew and Hettie McHarg, Madge was an awkward, willful, sickly girl who would not do as they asked, could not be appeased by their generosity, and was not frightened by their threats—the architect of her own unhappiness and of too much family conflict. They were often away for weeks and months on end, however, in Europe and Australia, and in her early childhood Madge was cared for by her nursemaid, May, who had come out with the family from Australia. May was a steady source of comfort and affection, and Madge, like many whose first bond was with their parents' employees, attributed the loss of her self-confidence to May's departure. In old age, she still longed for May, or for the feeling of having been loved so completely.

Her mother's usual response to a question was to say, "You wait till you grow up, then you'll find out," so being sent to school, the local kindergarten, was "a delight," because there the adults encouraged her curiosity. Describing her earliest schooldays, Madge wrote with surprising candor that she had first fallen in love there. The girl's name was Nina Brown; she was a year older, and Madge was so persistent in her demands to be close to this "idol" that her teachers finally broke the rules and allowed her to be accompanied by Nina at all ritual moments of the day: when they drank hot milk, or took their midday walk. Out one day with her new baby brother, Keith, and his nanny, Madge passed her friend's home and was startled to see "a small terraced house and not the palace" in which she "had expected so exquisite a person to exist." She transmuted her longing and disappointment by fixing on the purple clematis that grew over the porch: It was "like a beautiful star," she said, and it became one of her favorite flowers.

Throughout her childhood she suffered from her ailments— allergies, curvature of the spine, susceptibility to illness in the days before antibiotics—and their cures. She understood herself to be a problem in every way and felt as trapped in her body as she did in her family. A solitary, fastidious child in a home that held virtually no books, she escaped however she could and absorbed whatever was at hand. At twelve, she culled hundreds of images of beautiful women from her parents' magazines and illustrated papers. She lingered over these pictures and mounted them in a huge scrapbook. The only gesture toward learning in the McHarg house was the 1911 *Encyclopædia Britannica*, which came with its own special bookcase. She read every volume.

The 1911 *Britannica*, advertised as "The Sum of Human Knowledge," was published at the last moment when it was possible to imagine that such a sum could be contained in twenty-eight volumes. It is a repository of English thought at the height of empire. Many prominent scholars contributed articles. So did, for the first time, a significant number of women. From the entry "Women":

Though married life and its duties necessarily form a predominant element in the woman's sphere, they are not necessarily the whole of it . . . The whole idea of women's position in social life, and their ability to take their place, independently of any question of sex, in the work of the world, was radically changed . . . during the 19th century. This is due primarily to the movement for women's higher education . . . [I]n the English-speaking countries at all events the change is so complete that the only curious thing now is, not what spheres women may now enter, more or less equally with men, but the few from which they are still excluded . . . As the first half of the 19th century drew to a close . . . the conviction that it was neither good, nor politic, for women to remain intellectually in their former state of ignorance, was gradually accepted by every one.

The essay reads like the work of someone trying to will his or her hopes into fact. For Madge, it described a change that was by no means complete, presented as self-evident views that were accepted by no one around her. But its emphasis on education seemed to chart her way out.

And yet, when her parents decided to send her away to school, to Cheltenham Ladies' College, she refused. Hettie McHarg had become pregnant with a fourth child ("a very much unwanted menopause baby," Madge recalled), and "the problem" of "what to do with a teenaged daughter" in front of whom one could not "discuss or even admit such a condition" was acute. (Hettie was also forced to cancel a long-hoped-for move to Mayfair; she had even chosen a house in Hanover Square.) Madge had been given some "silly books" about schoolgirls ("illustrated by nauseating pictures of the horrible girls") and was convinced that she would be miserable at such a school. She objected to the communal living arrangements. She objected to the hearty athletic life. She objected, at least in retrospect, for sartorial reasons: "I discovered that you wore a navy blue, woolen, box pleated tunic over a white woolen flannel tucked blouse," she said. She told her parents, "I am not going."

She miscalculated. It was a badge of honor among the male writers and artists of her generation and beyond to have loathed their school days. Many were homosexual and most, no matter what their desires, affected a principled aestheticism as a way to rebel against the anti-intellectual quality of English public school life. This distaste was a prerogative of all sorts of privilege, which Madge did not have. Despite the dormitories, uniforms, and a residual emphasis on sports, Cheltenham Ladies' College was one of the few schools in England that took seriously the education, including the higher education, of young women. Whether her parents knew it—and she always described them as "totally unaware of and disapproving of higher education for girls"—this was an institution at which Madge would have been prepared and encouraged to go on to Oxford or Cambridge. But, presumably not knowing this, she continued to refuse and tried to discourage her father by reminding him that it would be very expensive and insisting that she would run away if sent there. And she was forever proud of her defiance. In the midst of this impasse, a friend of Hettie's remarked that her own "difficult and unruly daughter" had just returned "much improved" from a school in Paris run by a Mademoiselle Lacarrere. To this more romantic exile Madge agreed. She never acknowledged that her parents might have had her interests at heart, or that she could have ended up with no further education at all.

Like any "well-brought-up" girl in her milieu, Madge never went anywhere alone—she was well over eighteen when she first took a train unchaperoned—and during her year or two in Paris she was supervised carefully. To get to Mademoiselle Lacarrere's school each term, she traveled with her mother on the boat train to Paris, or her parents brought her to Victoria Station, where one of her teachers met her. At the school, "they always knew where you were, every minute." The place was nevertheless a revelation, a genuine education in art, architecture, and performance. It was essentially a finishing school, but unlike many, it was not filled with girls speaking English. Madge learned French well; one of her two best friends was Portuguese, the other Romanian Jewish. The students were given a reasonably good general education, and were given their own loge at the Opéra, the Comédie Française, the Opéra Comique, and various concert halls. They toured museums every Thursday and visited cathedrals, Versailles, and the châteaux of the Loire. Madge heard Chaliapin sing *Boris Godunov* and saw the Ballets

Russes, including Nijinsky's "jump through the window" (his celebrated exit in Michel Fokine's *Le Spectre de la Rose*). Sixty years later
she could still find her way to "remote churches all over Paris."
When she was required to exercise, she hid a book in her clothing,
pleaded illness, lay in the shade of a hedge by the tennis courts, and
read.

She recorded her time at Mademoiselle Lacarrere's lovingly in
photographs of her bedroom, classmates, and teachers, portraits of
the couple who took care of the school, and pictures of the places she
visited. Later, she sometimes suggested that the school had had the
fervid atmosphere of Dorothy Bussy's novel *Olivia*, whose English
protagonist falls in love with the beautiful teacher who is responsible for her intellectual and sexual awakening. Mostly she made it
clear that the place had given her the chance to see things she never
would have seen—the built and beautified world; artful thinking
about texture, light, and movement—and that she had grabbed it all
avidly, understanding for the first time what made her happy. Coming from the insularity and prejudices of England, she also found
something as elusive and enduring as this aesthetic awakening: an
instinct for the possibilities of friendship and an understanding
of the world as her home. She called it "freedom of thought."

The start of the First World War in August 1914 interrupted
the McHargs' plans to send her on to a school in Dresden for further refinement. The family had moved to an enormous house in
Hampstead, on Fitzjohns Avenue, but Madge found it "prison-like
after the freedom, excitement, and stimulation of Paris." She was
now eighteen years old, expected to pay calls with her mother, in a
mood of constant defiance, but unable to express her sense of the
inanity of her life in anything other than small rebellions. Even what
she could wear "was strictly limited." (Young unmarried women
were not supposed to wear furs, for example, or certain jewels.) "You
see my father had a *right* over me," she recalled; "it really was that
you were imprisoned in your home until you were 21." Looking for
ways to experience the pleasure she had known in France, she decided that "the most violent, wicked thing" she could do was visit
the Catholic extravagance of Westminster Cathedral, the interior
decoration of which was still being completed. She slipped off—"I

kept it a deadly secret"—drawn to the vast neo-Byzantine space and the intricate, multihued work of the craftsmen and women.

In a house with servants there was, in fact, little for her to do. She was not permitted to enter the kitchen other than for the annual ritual stirring of the Christmas pudding. She wanted to learn to sew, but after she used the machine once and broke it, her mother forbade her to touch it. She was told to occupy herself with the Kentia palms that sat in huge Japanese pots on the staircase landing. "You may polish their leaves with milk," she was told, "so that they glisten." Her brother Gerald had enlisted immediately—he was in one of the first groups of soldiers shipped to France that August— and was writing home about the horror of the battlefields. She knew that people were hungry and dying in London, not just in France and Flanders, and she could not stand to waste milk on plants. If she was aware of the young British women, a number of whom later became her close friends, banding together to nurse or drive ambulances at the front (moved to participate at least as much by the oppressiveness of their lives at home, Virginia Woolf later argued, as by patriotic feeling), she was still too tied to her family and without the money of her own she would have needed to make such a break. She was unsuited to nursing in any case and was still focused on education as the best route to independence. "After some months of sulking," she took herself to Bedford College, a pioneering women's college (mentioned in the *Encyclopædia Britannica* article) that had moved to new buildings in nearby Regent's Park. She secured the prospectus, "implored" her parents to let her attend, obtained Andrew McHarg's grudging permission, and enrolled for the following year in a course on English literature, which was then still a curriculum directed at women and colonial subjects.

The only other distraction in her life was Ewart Garland, the handsome, genial son of Melbourne friends, who arrived in London in 1915 at age eighteen, hoping to enlist in the newly formed Royal Flying Corps. Andrew and Hettie McHarg included him in the family and gave him his own set of rooms in their house. He received his commission in the spring of 1916, after basic training in the infantry, and on his days off from flight school at Oxford, Madge introduced him to London, and he took her to the theater and out dancing at the Savoy hotel. They became good friends, despite her embarrassment about all things Australian and her comment that Garland's father, who owned the Australian concession of the Dunlop Rubber Company, was "in trade." This expression of disdain for those who work is the product of culture organized around the idea (if not the actuality) of a distinction between a leisured aristocratic class and everyone else. In Madge it was a ridiculous affectation, given that her father, too, was "in trade," but if Ewart abhorred her snobbery, he admired her intelligence, appreciated the cultural education she gave him, and sympathized with her struggle against her parents.

Sailing back to England from Australia in March 1916, Andrew McHarg survived the torpedoing of his ship by a German submarine. Although travel was even more dangerous the following winter, he decided to return to Melbourne to supervise his business there. London was subject to zeppelin attacks, but with Gerald now stationed in Italy, Hettie McHarg wanted to stay in England, so she shut the house and moved to Cornwall with Madge's younger brother, Keith, and baby sister, Yvonne. Madge was told that she would take her mother's place and keep her father company in Melbourne. Once again, she refused. This time she was overruled. She spent the next two years with her father, in transit and in Australia. She spent these years, and many that followed, furious at this reminder that she belonged to the colonies and rightly convinced that this trip meant leaving behind her chance of a university education.

And she spent the rest of her life concealing these years. She said that she passed her qualifying exams at Bedford College with honors and won a place at Newnham College, Cambridge, but that her father refused to allow her to attend. She said that her father pulled her out of Bedford College before she could even take that exam. She said she had planned to go to St Hilda's, Oxford, but that he did not allow her to. She said that she lived in the United States for two years during the war. She let it be known that she attended Bedford College from 1916 to 1919, a claim that not only eliminated Australia and the fact of having left the country during the war from her résumé, but also subtracted at least two years from her age. She could not have attended a university without her father's support: There were no state subsidies for higher education at the time. She replayed this loss, her anger, her ambition, and the fantasy about where a degree might have taken her over and over. She felt so strongly about her lack of academic training, talking about it right up to her death, that some of her friends were convinced she would have been happiest as a university don. In her long life, she lost and destroyed many personal papers, but she never let go of several small notebooks she kept in the 1930s and '40s in which she recorded the books she had read and planned to read—the documentation of someone who does not take reading for granted.

She and her father left London on the long trip west in February 1917, weathering a treacherous Atlantic crossing on a ship under blackout to avoid German U-boat attacks. They arrived in New York in a bitter winter that Madge met "clad in silken underwear and a light woolen dress and coat," because on board she had handed "the astonished stewardess" her woolen long underwear, "a garment I had always wanted to eliminate from my wardrobe." The visual drama of New York City and then of the transcontinental train trip—the urban skyline, the vastness of the plains—bewildered but excited her. In California, they boarded another ship to cross the Pacific. There they met the Queeny family: John Francis Queeny; his wife, Olga Mendez Monsanto Queeny, of Spanish-German descent; and their daughter, Olguita. Queeny was the Irish American founder of the Monsanto Chemical Works, an upstart entrepreneur in the same mold as Andrew McHarg, on his way to spectacular success. Olga Queeny was decidedly not in the same mold as Hettie McHarg, and Madge was drawn to her warmth. She fell in love with Olguita.

Angular and beautiful, with long, dark, curly hair, Olguita had grown up a doted-on child in a newly prosperous St. Louis. Madge spent all her time with her, doing things she had spurned before (taking part in shipboard games, making costumes, dressing up) and again, as she had in Paris, finding a closeness with someone who seemed so different. The two families vacationed together in Hawaii, en route, and when they reached Australia, Andrew McHarg acted as host. In Sydney, they spent a day at Bondi Beach. In and around Melbourne, they met Madge's relatives, visited Ewart Garland's mother, took long walks through the Royal Botanical Gardens, and

---

In "fancy dress on board in the Pacific. Made hat out of cardboard!" (MGP)

toured the surrounding country in open cars, the women in long veils to protect them from the dust. Writing and talking later about her life, Madge seldom mentioned this friendship. Instead, she talked about "American girls" in general—their independence, openness, and sophistication—calling them "girls with just what I wanted." But her photo albums are full of images of Olguita. And when Olguita and her family returned to the United States, in the spring of 1917, Madge's sense of loss was acute. In her memoir, she expressed her unhappiness as aesthetic alienation. "I wanted to go to Italy to see the paintings," she wrote; "I wanted to see the cathedrals of Europe." From the moment the boat pulled into Sydney Harbor, she averred, "it was a disaster." The once-beautiful bay was "entirely encircled and overgrown with mediocre houses with no distinction whatsoever and its beautiful outline blurred with a suburban" ugliness. Melbourne "was worse. Trams clattered up and down the main streets where the buildings seemed to me mere shantytowns. Corrugated iron, surely the most hideous material yet invented by man, was everywhere." The land and vegetation were "alien and horrifying." The city was also full of impressive Victorian piles of brick and bluestone, but all she recalled or admitted seeing was that "there were no palaces, no great garden squares, no great cathedrals. There was nothing."

This idea of nothing was one part the emptiness perceived by the Europeans who had arrived on the continent and assumed the right to occupy it, one part distress transmuted and projected outward: disavowal, identification, frustration, and disgust in a complicated embrace. Invited to a hunting party in the country, Madge was sickened. She knew that this sort of sport took place in England and Scotland, but had not seen it there, so she held the brutality—"the piles of dead birds"—against the country of her birth. Writing about this time for a potential British reading public, years later, undoubtedly made her dramatize her revulsion at the expense of a more nuanced reality. But a young journalist she befriended late in life recalled her abiding racism about Australia and Australians: "She would talk to anybody about anything, whether it was about Jack the Ripper or fashion or politics, and she was fantasti-

Olguita Queeney, 1928, photographed by Madge (MGP)

cally uncensorious—you could have lived with six men and three dogs for all that she cared—but she would say the most shocking things about aborigines." In the 1950s, having survived the Second World War and looking for ways to escape winter in England, Madge toyed with the idea of spending time in Australia, but she never returned.

I WAS FREE

In 1920, in a letter to the *New Statesman* headlined, "The Intellectual Status of Women," Virginia Woolf argued that the resistance to women having professional lives was still so general and extreme that those who want such a thing "must make a dash for it and disregard a species of torture more exquisitely painful, I believe, than any that man can imagine. And this is in the twentieth century." Make a dash for it is what Madge did, but it took her several more years. After the Armistice was announced in November 1918, she and her father began the long return trip to London. There was a moment when they planned to travel by way of China, which Madge felt might have made up for "all the miseries and deprivations I had suffered," but her father changed his mind. The consolation was that in early December they reached St. Louis and Olguita, and when Andrew McHarg returned to England, Madge stayed on. "One of the prettiest affairs of the past week was the luncheon on Monday which Miss Olguita Queeny of Hawthorne boulevard gave in honor of Miss Madge McHarg," noted a newspaper social page. Such were the mannered conventions of society journalism. Then there was the way these women described their intimacy. Olguita later called it "rather special rather important and lacking in all artificiality. You were my dearest friend. I need say no more." Madge described "a relationship so precious, so unique."

The slaughter of Madge's generation of young men in the war suspended and changed some of the pressure of the marriage mar-

---

FOLLOWING TWO PAGES: Olguita, Mrs. Queeney, and Madge in St. Louis, circa 1918 (MGP); Madge (right) with Olguita, Richmond Hill Hotel, May 1919 (MGP)

ket, and in the postwar years many women set up households together, some out of economic necessity and some for companionship. For a few, sexual partnerships could be veiled by such arrangements. Madge and Olguita did not live together, independent of their families, but each was now the most important person in the other's life. In early February 1919 they sailed to London and found it in shock. Streetlights were on again, after four years of blackout, and food was less scarce, but the devastation of the war continued. There had been catastrophic casualties—from Britain alone, almost a million dead—and the flu pandemic of 1918–19 killed more people around the world than the war. Everyone knew someone who had died. Madge's generation in particular suffered from the feeling that they had been betrayed by a government that had orchestrated, prolonged, and lied about the conflict.

Against all odds, the two young men to whom she was closest had survived. Gerald had been wounded and returned to active duty several times. Ewart Garland had been sent to France and stationed near the Belgian border in July 1916, after only five hours of solo flight experience. As part of a reconnaissance squadron, he was immediately sent on photographic and observation sorties; soon he was going out on bombing raids. His bravery was mentioned in dispatches, and by the end of the war he was a commanding officer, publicized in a newspaper article as "the youngest Flight Commander in the whole Flying Corps." During the last several months of fighting, he was flying "to the limit of endurance, and beyond," being shot at and shot down, and engaging in dangerous reprisal bombing raids into Germany. "I can't shake off the feeling of being condemned to death or imprisonment," he wrote of these last assignments in his wartime diary; "it's not cowardice, only that . . . I know the danger only too well." He was unique in his cohort: Most of his squadron was killed, and every one of his classmates in Australia died at the Battle of Lone Pine, Gallipoli, in August 1915. He visited battlefields after the Armistice—"a nightmare of mud and unmentionable visions"—then returned to England in December 1918, fresh from the "general horror." He was

"Olguita, Ewart & I," London, 1919 (MGP)

appalled at the recklessness of what he had been told to do and had done, and he never again piloted a plane.

In the spring of 1919, Madge and Olguita visited Ewart, not yet demobilized, at the Hendon Aerodrome, in North London. They were rowed out on the Thames by Ewart and a fellow officer and had tea on Eel Pie Island. That June, on a boatful of North American soldiers going home, Madge returned to the United States with Olguita. When she returned to London by herself six months later, her old conflicts with her family intensified. Her parents sent her to cooking classes. She resisted by cooking badly and inviting them to sample her work. She took herself to a series of lectures on architecture at the Victoria and Albert Museum. At some point, Ewart proposed to her, and she turned him down. She was in a holding pattern, outraged by demands that were not seen as outrageous at the time, frantic to find a way to begin her own life, unsure of how to proceed. As a young woman of a "good family," she not only did not need to work to help support her family but also was part of a class and a culture in which the visible leisure of some women and the invisible labor of others was at once a fetish and accepted to the point of being common sense. Even if a young woman from such a family had parents who supported her choices, it was difficult for her to do what she wanted. One measure of Ewart's understanding of Madge's predicament was his alarm at Hettie McHarg's dedication to being waited on. He always remembered Hettie having stopped him when he tried to add a piece of coal to the fire in her drawing room—"Oh no, Ewart, we have servants to do that"— whereupon a young girl had walked up three flights of stairs to tend the fire.

Andrew McHarg's next move made Madge's choice clear: After more than twenty years in London, he decided to reestablish himself in Melbourne. Gerald would stay behind to run the London office of Brooks, McGlashan and McHarg; the rest of the family would return to Australia. This prospect, Madge felt, was "not a matter for discussion or rebellion. It was a question of life or death, and I said nothing." Sometimes, when she told this story—when she had lived long enough to see her part of the world change to the point

Madge and Ewart at 71 Fitzjohn's Avenue (MGP)

that her choices were no longer startling—she diminished the leap she made: "Well, it was really an awfully boring story. It was the usual thing in my time. I ran away from home, and I had no qualifications at all." Playing it down, she identified herself with a larger history. Talking to friends and acquaintances too young to have known her in the teens and twenties, many of them women beginning careers in journalism in the 1970s and '80s, she described herself as of "the suffragette generation, with Rebecca [West] of course as my idol." She said, "It was *quite* the usual thing, like in the sixties boys became hippies with long hair . . . there were many, many girls of my generation who did that." At other times, she told a story that had the archetypal quality of a fairy tale, but one in which she was both the heroine and the hero, saving herself from her own life.

She accepted that she would not go to a university and decided to find a job. She loved reading, "wanted somehow to be connected with literature," felt "vaguely" that she wanted to write, knew she didn't know how, and concluded that journalism seemed the place to start. When her father left on his next long business trip, on which Hettie McHarg once more accompanied him, there was no one at home to monitor her. She took the Underground from Hampstead to Chancery Lane every day and walked up and down Fleet Street, through buildings of newspaper and publishers' offices, stopping at each one and asking to see the editor. She was sent away from each office, having no experience. Finally, she presented herself at an organization called Rolls House Publishing, run by a man named William Wood. He knew that she had never worked in her life, but saw that she had good manners and dressed well. She was wearing the spoils of shopping excursions with Olguita and Mrs. Queeny in St. Louis and at Marshall Field's, Chicago, where she had had found ready-to-wear fashions of higher quality and better fit than what was available in England. She knew that she "had nothing to offer," but she was persistent. She said that she petitioned Wood three days in a row, and that at length he offered her a position at three pounds a week: "First of all he refused to consider my application," she said. "But I returned the next day. He refused to see me, so I returned the next day and sat on the stairs. And he stumbled over me as he came down the stairs. I stood up and said 'Mr. Wood you need never see me again, if only you will give me four pounds a week. I cannot manage on three.' He gave way and I had a job."

She had landed at the offices of the man who was editing *The Architect and Building News* and overseeing the English publication of British *Vogue*. Sometimes when she told this story it was an accident, as in this version. Sometimes she said that after visiting scores of offices, she finally remembered having confided her ambitions to Olga Queeny, who had introduced her to her friend Mrs. Nast, also of St. Louis, whose son Condé was in New York putting out a small society paper called *Vogue*. By 1916, when Nast had started to have some success selling his magazine in England, wartime shipping restrictions and paper shortages had made it difficult to export it across the Atlantic. His distributor, William Wood, persuaded him to publish an English edition, arguing that it would more easily get English advertising. Wood, wrote Edna Woolman Chase, the longtime editor of American *Vogue* and Condé Nast's right-hand woman, "became an organization in himself, for Nast appointed him his publisher, manager, and managing editor" in England. In 1920, when Madge met Wood, British *Vogue* (called "Brogue" by insiders) was a small, unglamorous business occupying four rooms "in a very dingy little office" off Chancery Lane. The entire staff consisted of seven people. Madge was the seventh.

The morning after her parents' return from Melbourne, she staged a cool exit, gathering her gloves after breakfast, saying, "I must go at once, because I have to be at my office at nine o'clock," and leaving before her father could stop her. When she returned that evening, he ordered her to behave, to stay home and help her mother prepare for their move. She went to work again the next day. Andrew McHarg then wrote to William Wood, man to man, explaining that he was capable of supporting his daughter and demanding that she be sent home. "You see, I wasn't yet 21," she recalled sixty years later; "legally until I was 21 the editor would have had to send me home, if Father had pressed." The truth was that she had long since come of age: She was almost twenty-four years old. When Wood showed her the letter, she asked him if she had let him down in any way, and he "replied that he had no reason for sacking me." She held her ground with her father, and he responded that he would no longer give her any money. "And that," she said, "was that."

She moved out of her parents' home and rented a small attic room in a boardinghouse in Earl's Court, a neighborhood whose down-market character was as far from the comfort in which she had been brought up as she could imagine. She saw her family off at Tilbury when they sailed for Australia in the summer of 1920. And then she was on her own. "I was free," she said, "but I was terribly, terribly poor for a long time." She had her minuscule salary. She pawned the few expensive possessions she had taken from home, including an elaborate silver brush set in a silk-lined, crocodile skin case that her father had given her. For a time, she still received a small allowance—"pin money"—from the clerk at Brooks, Mc-Glashan, and McHarg. She believed that her father had been too embarrassed by his inability to control his daughter to tell his clerk to stop these funds. "He never really forgave me," she said. "I didn't appear in his will at all." This was her sense of his shame. Her own—about being Australian, about being middle-class, about her body and its weaknesses—drove her from now on. "What I did," she said, "was work—all hours." She ate very little, often just a poached egg on toast and a meringue, which she had decided was the cheapest and most nutritious meal she could get, and she put all her energy into her job. She was the magazine's receptionist; she made tea on the gas ring on the landing and took it to the editor and the press-room; she ran down Chancery Lane to the delicatessen to get coffee and buns for the staff; she ran to the post office for stamps and to post the mail; she worked "as a messenger boy." She was at the office Monday through Saturday and, as time went on, was often needed at night. Out late trying "to get proofs passed by some actress," she might be kept waiting in a drafty corridor until eleven o'clock at night, but she was back in the office at nine the next morning. "I was very young and willing to do anything," she said, "and Vogue was very small beer in those days in England." She said, "I grew into it and grew up with it."

Most of the "so-called English edition" of Vogue "was taken straight from the American pages," she recalled, shipped from New York and reprinted in England. Production consisted "of inserting into the American magazine two photographs of ladies of title." These were the intricacies of status: "The frontispiece had to be a lady of title above a baronet's wife. The second photograph could be a baronet's wife, but had to be titled." Then there were "pages and pages of society snapshots." There were reports on Paris fashion, but these were still filed by employees of American *Vogue*. The English fashion contribution consisted of a couple of pages of drawings from what were called court dressmakers, such as Reville, Lucille, and Dove, who made clothes for upper-class women who attended functions of the court. But these firms tended to copy French fashions and were not always attributed in the magazine. *Vogue* did not list prices, and some of the designs shown were fictions: As Madge wrote later, magazines at this time were in the habit of showing fashions that were sometimes "dreamt up by their own artists," to be copied by the readers' home dressmakers (this practice began to change in the mid-to-late twenties). There were no professional models, so when photographs were used (instead of drawings), the woman "who wore the dress in the shop posed or the fashion editor's friends were persuaded to face the camera," Madge wrote, "with deplorably amateur results." As for the dresses themselves, "though the First World War did much to emancipate women and threw thousands into occupations hitherto reserved for men, it did not noticeably free their limbs. In 1921 the fashionable figure was still [almost as] encumbered . . . as her Edwardian predecessor."

The editor of British *Vogue*, Elspeth Champcommunal, known as Champco, was a forceful, sophisticated woman—"handsome," in the words of her friend Janet Flanner. The widow of a French painter killed in the First World War, she was also a friend of Roger Fry, Vanessa Bell, Cedric Morris, and other English artists. She was close to Nicole Groult, the couturière sister of the celebrated designer Paul Poiret, married to the artist-decorator André Groult. Adding photographs of upper-class Englishwomen to an American publication did not interest Champcommunal for long, and she eventually left to open her own couture house in Paris. But her friendship and her influence on Madge were "immense and far-reaching," as Madge wrote. "In fact, I should never have become Madge Garland without her." Champcommunal does not appear in Edna Woolman Chase's résumé of the early years of British *Vogue* (although a fiftieth-anniversary issue of the magazine, in the 1960s, credits her as the "first editor British *Vogue*, 1916–22"), but Madge always acknowledged her debt to Champcommunal, repeatedly paid public

tribute to her work, and corrected the factual record about her career. In a lecture on the influence of fashion on furniture design in 1979, she referred to Champco as "the only Englishwoman . . . to have had a couture house in Paris." Interviewed at this time, she credited Champco's designs as part of her own history, talking about evenings she spent with Man Ray and Lee Miller in Paris and describing being photographed by Man Ray in "a beautiful dress by Elspeth Champcommunal. A plaid *chiffon* . . . typical of the twenties in Paris."

When Champco quit the magazine, Ruth Anderson became the interim editor; she, too, became a mentor and longtime friend. Aldous Huxley was on the staff in the early 1920s, writing book and theater reviews; Madge's long friendship with him and Maria Huxley began at this time. Dorothy Wilde, Oscar's niece, was also working on British *Vogue*. Constantly trying to improve herself, Madge pestered colleagues to train her, took secretarial classes at night (she enrolled in a school in South London, not the West End, to save money), and gradually worked her way up. She became a typist, then a secretary, then assistant to the editor. She also learned that how she looked gave her entrée. Even though her material circumstances were precarious, her clothes were still better than what "a tea girl" was expected to wear, and her shoes were pretty because vanity had made her stop wearing "the hideous laced-up surgical . . . boots" prescribed by the doctors. Delivering the proofs of a portrait to Elizabeth Bowes-Lyon, whose engagement to Prince Albert was announced in 1923 and duly noted in *Vogue*, Madge was let in the front door, instead of at the tradesmen's entrance. To work in fashion in this way, it seemed, was not to be "in trade." One day Huxley passed her on the stairs and asked, "Are you dressed like that because you're on *Vogue*, or are you on *Vogue* because you're dressed like that?" It was a conundrum about clothing, work, and identity that she liked to cite to suggest the indissolubility of these two options—and to describe her suitability, at once natural and hard-won, for the job.

But after two years of "walking about and working all day, and

The staff of British *Vogue* in the January I, 1923, edition of *Vogue*. "Miss McHarg" is standing second from left, William Wood at center. Aldous Huxley is seated at left, Dorothy Wilde beside him. Ruth Anderson, interim editor, seated center (Courtesy Condé Nast Archive)

dancing most of the night, and eating very little," she collapsed, diagnosed with jaundice and other ailments. Her parents, with whom she had had little communication, happened to be in London, and appeared at her bedside to chastise her. They had often discouraged her ambitions by reminding her of her bad health. " 'Oh you won't be able to do this, that, and the other because you are so often ill,'" she said, mimicking them years later. Standing over her now, they told her this collapse was her reward for defying their wishes. Living on her own, too sick to work, with no income when she did not, she was frightened in a way that she had not been by relative penury and hunger. Ewart had remained in London after being demobilized and continued to be "on the outskirts" of her life during those years. He was perhaps in love with her, he certainly admired her, and he was inclined to be gallant. The family connection also created a sense of obligation. She cared for him, was not in love, was terrified of leaving the world to which she wanted to belong, and trusted that he would not thwart her. From her sickbed, she asked a nurse to send him a telegram. It read "COME AT ONCE AND MARRY ME."

WHO NEED NEVER BE MENTIONED

She was married in London on April 12, 1922, at the church of St. Martin-in-the-Fields, dressed not "in anything as conventional as white satin but in a very pretty dress and flower-laden hat." Her parents and just one other witness were present. It was not the ceremony Andrew and Hettie McHarg had hoped for, and as that telegram suggests, the negotiations that preceded it were intense and peremptory. Madge later said she would have preferred to live together unmarried, but that Ewart, with his "impeccable good manners, refused with horror such a suggestion." She told him that she would not wear a wedding band and chose a diamond eternity ring—a symbol of love, not bondage—from the jeweler Chaumet instead. She said that she would not be married in a church, but relented when a friend, probably Elspeth Champcommunal, arranged for her to be married by the pacifist minister Dick Sheppard, a hero of hers and the vicar of St. Martin. She told Ewart that she would not change her name to his, that she would continue to work, that she would not run the household, and that it would be "instant divorce" if she ever got pregnant. As she noted dryly years later, "Such a union, undertaken in such a spirit, would hardly become a great success, and within two years we had parted." Again, the story was more complicated than even this recital suggests.

One weekend in Paris in 1923 or '24, Madge sat in a movie theater watching the film and holding Ewart's hand. On her other side sat Dorothy (Dody) Todd, the new editor of British *Vogue*. Todd was strictly tailored and coiffed, shrewd, sophisticated, intimidating.

Back in London after a stint in New York, where she had been trained by Condé Nast and editor Edna Woolman Chase, she was at ease in Paris, had an American disregard for convention, and had apparently flawless English social credentials. Madge also held her hand.

Soon afterward, Madge left Ewart for Dody—moved with her to a small house in Chelsea that had been the home of Elspeth Champcommunal, who was now in France. "Madge has gone off with this woman," Ewart told his brother in despair. "Don't worry," his brother replied, "women are very peculiar. She'll come back. She'll come to her senses. Women usually do." Madge never did, and although Ewart's sympathy with her never diminished, his pride was injured to the end of his life, not by the considerable scandal of adultery, but by the more unthinkable conundrum of having been left for a woman. Still, Madge and he did not divorce until 1930, when Ewart, given the lack of no-fault divorce, did what was called "the honorable thing," allowing himself to be construed as the guilty party. The divorce may have been delayed because he was hoping that Madge would return, or he could have been protecting himself, or her. They had a number of mutual friends over the years, including the poet John Betjeman, the choreographer Frederick Ashton, and the dancer Billy Chappell, but they never met again.

Madge came to regret having hurt him, but at the time, all she knew was that Dody Todd was the key to the intellectual, aesthetic, and sentimental education she craved. Dody's seductiveness, her taste, her generosity, her sheer force—and her catastrophic problems—changed Madge's life. She desired Madge, took seriously her longing for art and books, dressed her in haute couture, convinced her of her value, and gave her entrée to a world of writers, performers, artists, designers, and gallery owners. She also gave her more responsibility at the magazine. She was "the absolute making of Madge," said Chloe Tyner, Elspeth Champcommunal's daughter, "and Madge lapped it up and absolutely fell in love." Madge once described this period as "the only two happy years of my life." Even right before her death, when she still found anything to do with Dorothy Todd "inexpressibly painful," she acknowledged her debt.

Madge, early 1920s (MGP)

"I owe her everything," she told her friend, the biographer Hilary Spurling. *"Everything.* She had this gift for finding and sponsoring young people. I was one." It was not easy: "You can imagine how tongues wagged. You can imagine what was said." And when the affair ended, Madge was ruined, "financially and socially. A lot of people never would—and never have—known me, because I was associated with her. But I would have left my husband in any case."

Early in *A Novel of Thank You*, written in 1926, Gertrude Stein names Dorothy Todd and reflects on the act of naming her:

> When Miss Todd came to see, us, when Miss Todd came to see, us, when Miss Todd came to see, us.
> When Miss Todd came to see us.
> Who need never be mentioned.

In this perverse introduction, the etiquette- and celebrity-conscious Stein also ostentatiously introduces, though does not name, "us": herself and Alice Toklas. Stein loved proper names and knew how to drop them; her love of making meaning from repetition had something to do with her understanding of fame and advertising and the excessive reference they involve. Like everyone who was anyone in the arts in the first few decades of the twentieth century, in England, Europe, and the United States, Dorothy Todd "came to see, us," that couple set apart by genius, love, sex, artistic dependency, and idiosyncratic punctuation.

In the mid-1920s, in several of the circles in which modernism is said to have been formed, everyone also came to see Dody Todd. Her name was repeatedly, admiringly, jealously, and scathingly bruited about—linked to everything fashionably avant-garde, commercial, and sexual in London and Paris. She was someone to reckon with or to please: a source of interest, irritation, and income to Virginia Woolf, Duncan Grant, and other Bloomsbury figures; fearsome and encouraging to an admiring younger generation of

Dorothy Todd in Haute Savoie, mid-1920s, photographed by Madge (MGP)

writers and artists; respected by and troubling to colleagues at *Vogue.* By the end of the 1920s her name was seldom mentioned (although Stein did so, in 1933, in *The Autobiography of Alice B. Toklas*), nor was it particularly desirable to see or be seen by her. In debt, drinking heavily, shunned socially, unable to find work, she fled to New York. It was the moment of the prosecution of Radclyffe Hall's *The Well of Loneliness* for obscenity, and at a Manhattan party Mercedes de Acosta made a splash by calling Dody "the bucket in the well of loneliness."

But in her prime, Dody radiated ambition and a tough self-assurance. She had a "tremendous mind," remembered Chloe Tyner, and was "very quick . . . very amusing." Virginia Woolf described her as having "a shimmer of dash & 'chic' even. She stands on her two feet, as she expresses it." She was small and heavy and had dark hair, which she kept short and slicked back in an Eton crop. She wore a uniform of a suit—the jacket with a velvet collar, the skirt a fashionable length—with a fresh flower in her buttonhole every day. She moved in an aura of expensive perfume and had a commanding, pleasing voice and a plummy accent.

Her family history, however, was "a wasp's nest of the most unpleasant character," as Madge put it—a story of debility and lies that reverberated through generations. Her father, Christopher Todd, trained as a carpenter, then followed his father (who had originally made his living as a bricklayer) in the profitable business of constructing and managing property in an expanding mid-Victorian London. By the 1880s, Christopher Todd was a wealthy developer who owned real estate all over London, much of it utilitarian, cheaply built housing in Chelsea. Her mother, Ruthella Hetherington, the daughter of a Carlisle butcher, twenty-five years younger than her husband, was his second wife. Dody was born in London on May 1, 1883. On the birth certificate of her brother, Alfred Guy Eric Todd, born two years later, her father listed his occupation as "Gentleman." The family lived in one of his grander properties, a large house on the newly developed Cromwell Road (which was not yet the main route west from Knightsbridge), where Ruthella enjoyed the life of a pampered Edwardian lady. According to one source, they spent six months of every year on a yacht in the South of France. In her impoverished old age, Dody would gesture at the area around the Cromwell Road and say, "All that belonged to us, once upon a time." She would say that "Ruthella had known Winston Churchill's mother very well."

Christopher Todd died suddenly of a heart attack when Dody was nine, and in the years that followed, Ruthella squandered the vast sum he left—over £33,000, plus stocks, property, and other assets—which by the terms of his will she was to hold in trust for his children from both marriages. She had become, or perhaps had always been, an alcoholic and a gambler, and she periodically found herself broke and stranded at casinos around Europe, requiring rescue "by friends or the family solicitor, who would travel out to Monte Carlo to pay her debts and bring her back." Eric was sent to Eton, but appears to have been pulled out after only a year or two. Unlike Madge, Dody was well educated by the standards of the day for a girl. She said that she had run away from home as a child and returned only on the condition that she be allowed a tutor in Latin and Greek, and she learned at least enough of the classics to be able to quote some of these texts in later life. But she also spent much of her childhood accompanying her mother to those exclusive gaming places. In the process, she learned to speak French and to love the South of France. She also learned to gamble—to take huge risks, Madge said, "not only at the baize table, but in life."

A "Dorothy Todd, artist" appears in the New York City directory at a Greenwich Village address from 1917 to 1919. She may have been living in London in 1920 and 1921, when the telephone at the Cromwell Road house was listed in her name. She and Ruthella were both in New York in June of 1922, at which time Ruthella transferred the title of the house to her. By then Dody was working in the New York office of *Vogue*. Edna Woolman Chase called Dody one of the first editors of British *Vogue*, but does not say when or how she came to her, or Nast's, or William Wood's attention—or what sort of work, if any, Dody did before being hired by *Vogue*. Some of the details of her life in her twenties and thirties are hard to know because of the absence of a masthead on the magazine during its early years, and because of the way Condé Nast managed his employees, sending them back and forth across the Atlantic on what often felt to them like a whim. Her progress is hard to track, too, because the British *Vogue* offices were bombed during the

Blitz, which destroyed whatever records might have been saved until then. The contentious end of Todd's employment at *Vogue* plays a part in these gaps. But much of what is unknown about her early adulthood has to do with her attempts to cover a family secret, the exposure of which would have ruined her and everyone around her.

Soon after she met Dody, Madge learned that she was the guardian of a teenage girl called Helen, her niece, the orphan child of her brother Eric, who had been killed in the April 1917 Arras offensive of the Great War. In fact, Helen was Dody's own illegitimate daughter, born in Paris in 1905, when Dody was twenty-two. The child's origins were hidden from almost everyone—even, and most disastrously, from Helen herself: Although she grew up with Dody, she always believed her to be her aunt. It is unclear how Dody explained her responsibility for Helen in the twelve years before her brother's death. The secret of the girl's parentage was sometimes implied but never discussed, even among Dody's closest friends. "I never heard who her father was," said Chloe Tyner; "I never heard who her *mother* was. We didn't talk about such things." For a long time, Madge could not understand why Dody took so much trouble with Helen, who lived with them when she was not away at school and then university. Nine years older, but still running away from her charmless childhood self, Madge resented not just the girl's presence but the fact that when she was absent she was getting the education Madge had wanted for herself. To Helen, Madge was just another of "the innumerable young ladies"—Dody's girlfriends—"who stayed with us."

In Paris in October 1905, Ruthella Todd and a man named Harry Lukach had registered Helen's birth at the *mairie* of the Sixteenth Arrondissement, testifying that they had been witnesses to the birth of "Dorothy Thompson," the child of an unnamed father and mother (*"fille de père et mère non dénommés"*). As a result of her place of birth and unspecified parentage, Helen was considered a French citizen. Six months later, she was baptized in London. On this document she was identified as Dorothy Helen Todd, and her mother as Dorothy Todd; Eric Todd stood as one of her godparents. Dody was able to procure her daughter an English passport and citizenship by claiming that she had been born in Toronto—another fiction Helen grew up believing. The other half of Helen's parentage is unknown. In 1915 a public trust was set up for her and Dody; money from this fund materialized at odd intervals for years, almost until Dody's death. Helen later believed that it had been provided by Lukach, an American businessman resident in London who was almost certainly Ruthella's lover. The Todd and Lukach families had known each other well for years. They were neighbors in London and in Brighton, and Eric Todd and Lukach's son were at Eton together. After Christopher Todd's death, Ruthella left the Cromwell Road house and lived either at or adjacent to various addresses in Piccadilly at which Lukach also lived.

As an adult, Helen's interpretation of her origins was informed by her bitterness toward Dody, her experience of Dody's interference in her life, and her belief that Dody made it a habit to disrupt couples; she had watched her mother's lovers regularly move in with them and then return to their husbands as she was growing up. She believed that Dody had enticed Lukach away from Ruthella, and that he was her father. But Helen also left a record of Ruthella's incapacity and dissipation that suggests another version of the story. As a child of nine, she had been left with Ruthella while Dody was in the United States, and she wrote that she became "accustomed to drunkenness from an early age." She knew about her grandmother's gambling habit and saw her lie in bed shaken by delirium tremens. (The gambling and the drinking continued until Ruthella's death in January 1924, when she was hit by a car at the entrance to Hyde Park.) Helen's son, the writer Olivier Todd, knowing this history, less resentful of Dody, and finding it impossible to imagine Dody inviting a man's advances, believes that Lukach may have molested her. Certainly a woman as out of control as Ruthella Todd would have been incapable of protecting her daughter from Lukach or anyone else. She may have allowed Lukach to use her daughter, or tried to hold on to him by making him a gift of Dody. A distorted concern that Dody was a lesbian may have made it easier for her to sanction such a liaison. None of these possibilities particularly rules out the others.

Dody's rapport with Helen was fraught at best, an impossible mixture of repudiation and commitment. For a woman in her social position—from a family once monied and respectable, now tenuously so because of Ruthella's excesses—the stigma of bearing an illegitimate child and the difficulty of raising her alone was immense, even in the more open milieu in which she moved in the 1920s. Rebecca West, who lived openly with H. G. Wells and had Wells's child; who did not hide the circumstances of her son's birth (some ten years after Helen's); and who, like Dody, refused to compromise with convention in all sorts of ways, nevertheless suffered acutely: "People disapproved of H.G. so much less than they did of me," she said; "they were very horrible to me, and it was very hard." The resolutely bohemian Vanessa Bell, still married to Clive Bell, but living with the mostly homosexual Duncan Grant, was incapable of honesty with the daughter she had with Grant, not telling her that he was her father until she was forced to. Dody never went out of her way to lie when it came to her desire for women—she never married to make herself more acceptable socially, unlike many contemporaries who preferred their own sex—but she found it almost impossible to acknowledge that she had a child and she treated her daughter in private as the liability she was in her public life. She cared about Helen, never gave her up, always provided for her, but faulted everything about her, holding on to a place at the center of Helen's life while keeping her at a distance. Helen's illegitimacy would always have meant that she was a vexed part of Dody's life, but Dody's charged ambivalence—love, disgust, neglect, frantic overinvolvement—make it plausible that her daughter was conceived in a violence and betrayal that were unresolved and irresolvable.

Helen was predictably angry and insecure, wanted a "normal" family life, and couldn't understand why "Dodo," as she called her, "who didn't particularly like children, [would] have adopted a niece." As a student at Somerville College, Oxford, in the late 1920s, she fled Dody, her education, and England for Paris, where she promptly had her own child out of wedlock. In 1929 or '30, Madge and Janet Flanner, sitting at the café Les Deux Magots, saw Helen walk by with her infant son. "I see Dody's niece has had a niece," Flanner quipped. It was not until the 1930s or '40s that Dody told Helen that she was her mother, saying roughly that she "should have felt" it all along. It was not until 1946 that Dody officially acknowledged her, registering her as her legitimate offspring at the French consulate in London, thus making it possible for the document that had recorded Helen's birth in Paris to be amended. But this legal recognition changed little privately; the two women were bound in mutual incomprehension and dependence their whole lives. Dody was proud of her grandson, Olivier, in a way that she never could be of her daughter, but she still introduced him to friends as her grand-nephew.

It was with this complex person that Madge fell in love, with this household that she allied herself when she left Ewart Garland. But for a long time, preoccupied with her own progress, she saw only Dody's allure, not her instability. As far as Madge was concerned, she had finally found her place. Of the troubled end of their affair, she said, "Other people will say she ruined my life, she ruined my marriage, she gave me a terrible time. To hell. I have no regrets at all. She fostered me and helped me. She opened many doors. I repaid that debt in full, because I supported her in later life. But I owed her more than I could ever repay."

Edna Woolman Chase, the keeper of the *Vogue* flame, later insisted that Dody's tenure as editor was marked by too little care about the place of fashion in the magazine. But Dorothy Todd, working with Madge, was the first person in England to combine high fashion, high art, and journalism. "It was entirely Dody Todd who put *Vogue* on the map in London," Madge said, making it "for about four years the mouthpiece of literary and artistic London." Madge herself was a key ingredient—inspiration, labor, support, collaborator, incarnation of the idea. There had been other young women in Dody's life, but Madge was her equal. Together they made a fashion magazine that invested in, explained, and created the English and French avant-garde as a fashionable world, representing haute couture, painting, photography, literature, theater, modern design, and good food as part of the same excitement, and treating all as elements of celebrity. As a recipe for a magazine, these ingredients are now commonplace. At the time, it was unprecedented. In the early 1970s, Rebecca West called Madge and Dody "two very remarkable women" who "changed *Vogue* from just another fashion paper to being the best of fashion papers and a guide to the modern movement in the arts." Transforming British *Vogue*, they were arbiters of a new kind of taste, mixing the outré with the respectable, bohemia and "Soci-

ety." Their rendering of the magazine also made it clear that both high fashion and the high art with which they were surrounding it depended on the idea of novelty.

Chase and Nast had brought Dody to New York to groom her, but when they sent her back to London to take charge of the magazine, it was "not only [to] London, as it turned out," Chase sniffed, "but a very specialized district thereof. Naturally of a literary and artistic bent she soon became at home in the coterie of English intellectuals and artists known as the Bloomsbury Group." In fact, Dody had been influenced by Frank Crowninshield's *Vanity Fair* in New York as well, but Bloomsbury, broadly speaking, was a key to and a beneficiary of her editorship. Clive Bell now wrote art criticism for British *Vogue*; the poet Richard Aldington and the young critic Raymond Mortimer reviewed books (replacing Aldous Huxley); Woolf published several essays, as did Vita Sackville-West and Mary Hutchinson (writing as "Polly Flinders"); Vanessa Bell and Duncan Grant's interior decorations were on display, as was the work of the painter and graphic artist Edward McKnight Kauffer and of his companion, the artist and textile designer Marion Dorn. The magazine published Edith Sitwell's poems. The focus was also newly international. Fashion had always looked to Paris, but British *Vogue* now showed Man Ray's "rayographs" and "helped Roger Fry in firmly planting the Post-Impressionists in English soil," as Rebecca West wrote. Madge and Dody "brought us all the good news about Picasso and Matisse and Derain and Bonnard and Proust and . . . Raymond Radiguet and Louis Jouvet and Arletty and the gorgeous young Jean Marais." They were the first in England to publish Cocteau's painting, Gertrude Stein's writing, and photographs of Le Corbusier's architecture, as even Chase acknowledged. The feature "We Nominate for the Hall of Fame" (borrowed from *Vanity Fair*) was a way to applaud people as diverse as Sigmund Freud, Marianne Moore, and Bertrand Russell, conferring celebrity status on high art and intellectual work.

This inclusiveness and productive juxtaposition—presenting a range of work in the magazine and making connections among people—opened and improved the insular, segmented worlds of

Madge and Dody (MGP)

English art and fashion. What Dody did for Madge—instructing her and lifting her into public view—the two of them and *Vogue* did for others, established and fledgling. For already recognized artists, it was a new kind of fame. "Vogue," Woolf wrote in her diary, "is going to take up Mrs Woolf, to boom her." Gertrude Stein credited Dody with arranging her 1925 introduction to Edith Sitwell, who had written an "enthusiastic" article about Stein's *Geography and Plays* for the magazine. Sitwell then became the emissary who persuaded Stein to lecture at Cambridge and Oxford in the summer of 1926. After Stein delivered her talk, "Composition as Explanation," Leonard and Virginia Woolf and the Hogarth Press published it. *Vogue* also gave many young English writers and artists their initial exposure. Cecil Beaton credited Dody with first encouraging him. Madge was his entrée and one of his earliest photographic subjects.

Where Madge had been faulted she was now accepted, and she acquired a poised and even thrilling presence. Her thinness, previously a mark of ill health, was de rigueur by the mid-1920s. She attended the Paris collections and was able to buy couture clothing because she had access to the more affordable designers' samples, which fit her. "She . . . could have been a model," said Rebecca West, "had she not" been "a connoisseur of the first water." British *Vogue* did not yet have its own photography studio and most often used the team of Maurice Beck and Helen Macgregor. Watching them work in their mews studio, Madge learned how to hold herself and how to face a camera. She began directing the shoots of models and clothing, and of the actors, writers, and artists now being featured in the magazine. Visiting other artists' studios, she became friends with the people she met—in London with Ted McKnight Kauffer and Marion Dorn, and with the young painter, decorator, and textile designer Allan Walton; in Paris, with Man Ray and Lee Miller, with Nicole and André Groult, and with their friend Marie Laurencin, whose book illustrations, theater costumes, and textile, carpet, and wallpaper designs were as admired as her paintings.

She was studying. In Paris, she sat and watched Brancusi at work; on breaks, he made them omelets on his studio stove. In Lon-

Her thinness was now de rigueur (MGP)

don, at tea parties at Edith Sitwell's "perfectly repellent Bayswater flat . . . very unlike the elegancies of the brothers' [Osbert and Sacheverell Sitwell's] house in Carlyle Square," she made the tea and passed the cakes and bread and butter (so did a young John Rothenstein, later head of the Tate Gallery), taking in the conversation while her elders spoke. Her eye for art impressed the directors of the Leicester Galleries and Agnew's, who introduced her to the work they owned and represented, gave her lists of paintings to look at in London and abroad, and quizzed her on what she had seen when she returned. When Miss McHarg went to see Gertrude Stein, the writer in her "downright forthright manner" told Madge that her surname was unappealing and asked if she had another. There was her husband's, Madge replied, but they were separated and she had never used it. *Do*, Stein counseled. From then on, she was Madge Garland.

Some of Madge's work at this time—organizing, coordinating, advising, and making connections among people—integral then, is difficult to pinpoint now. The fact that she was professionally subordinate to Dody means that a number of contemporary references to Dody refer to her as well. (Again, the lack of a masthead on the magazine is part of this problem of attribution.) But at some point in the mid-1920s she was made the fashion editor of British *Vogue*. She became known for dressing others—the anonymous women who read the magazine pages she produced, but also her friends in haute bohemia: the writer Violet Powell, wife of novelist Anthony Powell; Clive Bell's mistress Benita Jaeger, who did her hair and dressed according to Madge's prescription, "her curly hair cut short . . . and wearing a Lanvin evening dress which plunged daringly low at the back"; and Virginia Woolf.

To up-and-coming young gay men such as Cecil Beaton, George "Dadie" Rylands, and Steven Runciman, how Madge looked and what she thought mattered. She was more experienced and sophisticated than they, despite her lack of a university education. They were cowed by Dody, who was, in Raymond Mortimer's words, "a very forcible lady," but Madge encouraged them and was in a position to help with access to a world that was now hers. She brought Runciman, later a leading historian of Byzantium, to parties. When

Madge, one of Cecil Beaton's first subjects, in 1926 (Courtesy of the Cecil Beaton Studio Archive at Sotheby's)

Rylands, then knocking about Bloomsbury, needed money, she got him a job as a model; for a time this future Cambridge don was visible on the sides of buses in a cigarette advertisement. To Beaton, who never tired of pronouncing on women's beauty, Madge invariably "looked charming—extremely chic. She's so thin and wears her dresses wonderfully well." As an undergraduate at Cambridge, Beaton and other aspiring sophisticates had waited eagerly for each new issue of *Vogue*, which "was received as an event of importance." Back in London, desperate to extricate himself from his middle-class family and increasingly savvy about how to use publicity and his nascent photographic skills to do so, he was highly attuned to the doings of what he called "the Vogue gang" and always hoping to find a way to impress Madge and Dody so they would publish his photographs. To foster his anxious social advance, "he concentrated," notes his biographer Hugo Vickers, "on Allanah Harper . . . and Madge Garland." It was a coup when Madge and Dody attended his parties and lunches, when he was invited to theirs, when he danced with Madge, and when she suggested that she might be able to use his sisters as models. It was a thrill when Madge told him "one or two rather indecent stories, typical of Bloomsbury." A young Anne Scott-James, who joined *Vogue* in the 1930s after an Oxford education and went on to a long career in journalism, first saw Madge at a party in the 1920s: "She absolutely knocked me out. I'd never seen someone so extraordinary . . . I kept saying, 'Who is that? Who is that?' She was a star."

Treating the magazine as a kind of salon over which they presided, Madge and Dody courted contributors and entertained friends at home and at their favorite restaurant. It was the beginning of Madge's lifelong practice of connecting people she admired with one another—a habit she pursued to the point that she was "almost like an agency" for bringing people together. She introduced the interior decorator J. Duncan Miller to the photographer, painter, and interior designer Curtis Moffat; the latter had worked with Man Ray in Paris, and in 1925 opened a photography studio with Olivia Wyndham. She introduced the designers Eyre de Lanux and Eve Wyld to Moffat when he opened a gallery in 1929. For a lunch to present a young Sylvia Townsend Warner to Virginia Woolf, both of whom were known to be shy, they asked the restaurateur Marcel Boulestin to prepare the food but serve it at their home on the Royal Hospital Road. Townsend Warner had just published her first novel, *Lolly Willowes*, whose protagonist is a witch. When Woolf asked how she knew so much about witches, Townsend Warner startled her by answering, "Because I am one."

Boulestin had first run an adventurous interior decoration business in London, selling Paul Poiret's textiles and wallpapers. His restaurants helped to popularize authentic French food and they made the same point that British *Vogue* was trying to make: They were vehicles for modern design, combining English and French sensibilities. The architect of the first, the Restaurant Français, was Clough Williams-Ellis, John Strachey's brother-in-law; its decorator was Allan Walton. The murals at the second, the Restaurant Boulestin, were painted by Marie Laurencin and Jean-Emile Laboureur; the curtains were from a fabric designed by Raoul Dufy; André Groult, who ordinarily concentrated on making austere but sensuous objects in opulent materials (furniture covered in shagreen, lacquered screens), supervised the work. Dody commissioned Boulestin to write about food for *Vogue*, and his restaurants became their clubhouse; "You'd never go there and not know somebody," said Madge.

Their own flat, which Madge called "a beautiful house for parties," was furnished sparely, but was "charming & very cleverly thought out," said Beaton. There, at "impromptu wild parties," were writers, actors, designers, photographers, painters, dancers, and composers. When the revue *Blackbirds of 1926* played in London after its run in Harlem, Madge invited its star, Florence Mills, and felt that "it was like having somebody from the Royal family" in her home. "Several ultra smart young women came in," wrote Beaton of another occasion, "wearing lovely clothes & lots of false pearls." There was Olivia Wyndham, from an old aristocratic family, wild, but something more than a party girl; the socialite and drug addict Brenda Dean Paul; Allanah Harper; Dorothy Wilde. And there was Madge, "the thinnest person I'd ever seen," recalled Anne Scott-James, "wearing these incredibly graceful twenties clothes with a very long waist."

Madge was one of "the people one always saw at these mad bacchanals" around London in the 1920s, wrote the composer Vernon

Duke, author of "April in Paris." But she was not one of the Bright Young People, upper-middle- and upper-class youths such as Wynd- ham, Harper, and Dean Paul, who had money and time to burn. Out all night in London or Paris, or up late at home at her own parties, she still had to go to work the next morning. Attending the couture collections in Paris, she understood the spectacle to be as chal- lenging, in its own way, as studying paintings in galleries and museums—perhaps even more so, since the work was constantly in motion and journalists were not allowed to sketch or take photo- graphs during a showing (they could, discreetly, take notes) and em- bargoes enforced by the Chambre Syndicale de la Couture, the industry's governing body, meant that members of the press had to wait for six weeks to publish what they had seen. These demands created lifelong habits for Madge. Decades later, Hilary Spurling commented on the intensity and speed with which she moved through art exhibits; Madge replied that it was an effect of having learned how to look quickly and deeply at the collections.

It was the work of a party, the dance of work. It was the way the clothes worked and how they danced. "The 'twenties in Paris," said Madge, "was a moment when you went out every night . . . and one's clothes were very light, because one danced all the time." The truth of the cliché of that decade as a time hell-bent on fun is that the ex- hilaration of that dancing, the mobility, was meaningful to people who had lived with physical restraint and diminishment. She was out dancing at hotels and nightclubs; out at a dance hall in Notting Hill Gate, where she met Frederick Ashton, then an aspiring dancer; out dancing with Olivia Wyndham, then back in the middle of the night to the impressive Wyndham family home to make scrambled eggs and try not to wake up Wyndham's elderly and daunting fa- ther. If she stayed in, she would push back the furniture, roll up the rugs, wind up the Victrola, and dance. "And if one wasn't dancing one watched people dancing," Madge said. Out at the ballet with the actress Viola Tree, daughter of the actor-manager Herbert Beer- bohm Tree, and afterward to the Eiffel Tower restaurant, where they were joined by Vita Sackville-West and Virginia Woolf for cof- fee. Out with Dody at the London premiere in 1924 of Bronislava

Nicole Groult, seated, at home, with Marie Laurencin (Courtesy Colombe Pringle)

Nijinska's *Les Biches*, for which Marie Laurencin did the décor and costumes, Madge was struck by "the vein of poetry" that ran alongside the austerity of much modern design. Out by herself one morning, having breakfast at an ABC restaurant, she was still wearing evening clothes from the night before, returning from an assignation, possibly with Wyndham.

Wearing those incredibly graceful twenties clothes, including Chanel's simple chemise dress, which appeared in 1924, Madge was participating in a fashion that "eventually swept every other type of dress off the fashion map," she wrote later, "and put women as nearly into uniform as anything short of a Government department has ever done." Yet it was in these clothes that she established a distinctive personality. Her clothes were also a way to be adorned in a whole series of relationships: the exchange between high fashion and interior decoration in the 1920s, the artistic and commercial traffic between London and Paris, the sexual fluidity of the time. Cecil Beaton saw these connections when he looked at Madge in early 1926 "look[ing] perfect in a most lovely costume by Nicole Groult. Very influenced by Marie Laurencin—in pale blue and pink." The outfit Beaton referred to was a "patterned jumper [sweater] and skirt, and a long silk coat of a plain color, lined with the pattern, and beautifully bordered," as Madge described it, with "a hat to match, and so forth." Teddy Wolfe, a protégé of Roger Fry and a member of the London Group of artists, loved Madge in this ensemble so much that he painted her in it, in 1927. But he left one eye in the portrait unfinished, Madge said, because toward the end of the sitting they "put the gramophone on and danced."

Nicole Groult was charismatic and driven, the creative and financial force in her household. Laurencin was her intimate friend, and Maria Huxley and Sara Murphy were among her clients. Nicole and André Groult's circle of friends also included Dorothy Parker, the photographer Henri Lartigue, the illustrator Georges Lepape, the sculptor Ossip Zadkine, and the designer Eileen Gray. The Groults profoundly shaped Madge's taste and they introduced her to that "whole school of Paris *artistes-decorateurs*." Laurencin and the illustrator Charles Martin painted the murals on the walls and ceiling of the Groults' apartment. Madge described Laurencin, to whom Groult introduced her in 1924, as "both Bohemian and *bour-*

geoise," at once "the independent New Woman [and] . . . the most enclosed, most feminine" person. Laurencin was associated with Cubism and Dada, but her paintings are curvilinear and whimsical, the forms willowy, the palette pale. Her "costumes for 'Les Biches' were momentarily as influential on fashion as any of Chanel's designs," notes the historian of art and design Charlotte Gere. Laurencin frequented Natalie Barney's salon and, Madge recalled, disliked painting men, rarely did, and asked a higher fee to do so. Although many of her figures have a kind of typological sameness, she created vivid portraits of Nicole Groult and of Madge. After she asked Madge to sit for her in 1937, she gave her the painting, telling her it had been a labor of love. Wherever Madge lived, this work was the centerpiece of her rooms. A Laurencin still life was another of her prized possessions; it, too, was a kind of portrait of Madge, a friend of hers noted, because it was "both modern and exquisite." In a profile of the painter published in 1963 (several years after Laurencin's death), Madge wrote about a long summer holiday in the Basque country that she took with Laurencin, Marcel Boulestin, and his boyfriend Robin Adair in the 1930s, and recalled Laurencin's physicality, the pleasure she took in walking in the woods, biking, swimming, and dancing "in her espadrilles to the *piano-mécanique* in the local bistro."

For Madge, being dressed well by Groult and others meant the sensual pleasure of living and moving in strong designs, made to measure, in lush fabrics. It meant the experience, fleeting yet profound, of being shaped, included, and transformed. It meant feeling the division between how she saw herself and how others saw her, and feeling that difference disappear. It meant all of these combined with her technical understanding of the garment. That mixture of emotion and expertise, and of the simultaneous fluidity and painfulness of borders, is the complex experience that Virginia Woolf, in the orbit of Madge and Dody and thinking about fashion and narration in the mid-1920s, called "frock consciousness." Woolf understood that it was impossible to separate having clothes on one's mind and on one's body. Her writing, from adolescence on, documents her fascination with the relationship between clothing and consciousness, and records her frequent despair at having to get dressed to appear in the world. Her diaries, letters, and stories of the mid-to-late 1920s record the effects Madge and Dody and *Vogue* had on her and her circle of friends.

In the spring of 1925, Woolf noted that she had just been photographed by Beck and MacGregor for the magazine:

> I have been sitting to Vogue, the Becks that is, in their mews . . . But my present reflection is that people have any number of states of consciousness: & I should like to investigate the party consciousness, the frock consciousness &c. The fashion world at the Becks—Mrs Garland was there superintending a display—is certainly one; where people secrete an envelope which connects them and protects them from others, like myself, who am outside the envelope, foreign bodies. These states are very difficult (obviously I grope for words) but I'm always coming back to it.

Frock consciousness is apparently an oxymoron: The first word refers to a winsome sheath, something for the outside, while the second describes the quality of mind we imagine inhabits our insides. But clothes, as Madge knew from a young age, both constitute a boundary to the self and suggest its permeability. Lying between what we understand to be public space (the social world at large) and what we consider private (the body of an individual), they depend on and challenge this distinction. Frock consciousness, a state of dress and of mind, also issues an invitation and presents an obstacle to vision and visibility. As an articulation of the modernist conundrum of how to represent character—another person's life and mind—it is a key to Woolf's understanding of consciousness as a social phenomenon, not simply a rarified vessel for private concerns. In the same way, although biographies tend to focus on a single life, that life owes everything to milieux and influences—in Madge's case, ineffable and concrete networks of artists and of women.

"My love of clothes interests me profoundly," Woolf wrote in her diary in 1926, "only it is not love; & what it is I must discover." After the success of *Mrs. Dalloway*, Madge said, Woolf "knew that she didn't look right" and she told Madge "that she would not be afraid to enter any restaurant if she was as beautifully dressed as I was." Woolf particularly admired the ensemble by Nicole Groult, so Madge procured a version of it for her, in blue rather than pink, taking her measurements, consulting with Groult, and arranging for fittings in London. "So there is a real history attached to that outfit," Madge said. To Woolf, Madge was someone "there superintending a display," but she was also a brain to pick, a personal shopper, a provocation, and a conundrum. To Madge, Woolf was a venerated writer who was scared of and moved by clothes. Both women were fascinated by how we wear what we wear, by the effects of clothes on the body and mind, and by the effects of corporality and consciousness on clothes. They shared an appreciation of the awkward details to do with dress and character—a sense of elegance spiked with glee—and an understanding of fashion's powers of humiliation and conversion. When the fashion expert who was never really that interested in fashion and who made of herself a kind of resistant modernist text first glimpsed Woolf, at a lecture by Roger Fry, she saw "a very beautiful woman . . . But what also attracted my attention was that she appeared to be wearing an upturned wastepaper basket on her head"—a comically unflattering hat. One night at a party, Woolf was interrogating Madge and they ended up in a "hilarious conversation about corsets," the clothing convention of their mothers' generations, trying to fathom how people who had always worn them managed in the mid-1920s, when dresses were meant to be moved in, slouched in, danced in.

As sympathetic, provocative representatives of the fashionable world and of a certain kind of journalism, and as a visible couple, Madge and Dody not only excited Woolf's thinking about and through clothes but also incited her thinking about the relationship between her fiction and her journalism, about fame and literary reputation, and about intimacy between women, including "sapphism." The two of them stand in Woolf's writing of that period for the knot of art, commerce, and sexuality that haunts and defines both modernism and fashion. The making and marketing of British modernism is often understood as emerging from intimate ventures: little magazines, small presses, personal relationships. But it also depended on commercial enterprises such as British *Vogue*. The contact between British *Vogue* and Bloomsbury was an exchange that provoked and benefited all sides: editors, writers, and those written about. The conversation between the art now called modernist and the equally vital products of popular and consumer culture of the time includes the fact that the latter were often the stuff of the former: The advertising and shop windows that Woolf uses to represent consciousness in *Mrs. Dalloway* are just one such example.

Woolf agreed to be photographed for "We Nominate for the Hall of Fame" and to write several essays for *Vogue*, was excited about the high fees the magazine paid, and was intrigued by the thought of greater exposure: "I asked Todd £10 for 1,000 words: she orders 4 articles at that fee." At the same time, Woolf worried about "the ethics of writing articles at high rates for fashion papers like *Vogue*." When Raymond Mortimer invited Woolf to a party, she despaired at her desire to go and equally strong wish to stay away: "Why," she wrote to Vanessa Bell, "do these young men all run to vulgarity, snobbery, shoddery, Toddery?" When a friend told her she was demeaning herself and cheapening her work by writing for *Vogue*, she did not take the accusation lightly, but concluded that the censorship a young writer of her acquaintance had encountered at the hands of *The Times Literary Supplement* was "perhaps worse than the vulgarity, which is open and shameless, of Vogue . . . Todd lets you write what you like, and its [sic] your own fault if you conform to the stays and the petticoats." To Vita Sackville-West she wrote: "And whats [sic] the objection to whoring after Todd? Better whore, I think, than honestly and timidly and coolly and respectably copulate with the Times Lit. Sup." The stays and the petticoats are a metaphor for rhetorical constraint and for a kind of "feminine" writing supposedly practiced in such magazines. But as Woolf's conversation with Madge about corsets suggests, the phrase also refers to an interest in the actual objects, their effects, and their meanings.

Complaining about demands made on her time and attention, Woolf wrote, "I want as usual to dig deep down into my new stories, without having a looking glass flashed in my eyes—Todd, to wit." The irony of this grievance about *Vogue* as a mirror, annoyance, and social demand is that the stories Woolf refers to are precisely those in which she explores "the party consciousness, the frock consciousness," which, if they were impeded by Dody and Madge, were also stimulated by them. In "The New Dress," written in 1924 and first published in 1927, the protagonist, Mabel Waring, commissions a new frock based on an old design, watches her dress-maker produce it, and tries it on in the squalid intimacy of this woman's workroom, where "an extraordinary bliss shot through her heart. Suffused with light, she sprang into existence." But when she wears it out to a party, she is humiliated. The story shows how easy it is to think of certain clothes, like certain behaviors, as inevitably belonging to certain people; it exposes how the ineffabilities of taste are a function of class, but are often passed off as part of the natural order. "It seemed to her [Mabel] that the yellow dress was a penance which she had deserved, and if she had been dressed like Rose Shaw, in lovely, clinging green with a ruffle of swansdown, she would have deserved that." Mabel is both transparent to the other guests, who always "saw through" her, and able to see "through [them] instantly." Woolf also makes Mabel and her dress hypervisible by putting her experience of being watched on display—which experience, ironically, has a great deal to do with what other people look like. We don't see Mabel so much as see her being seen: someone else's "marked" gestures, "their eyelids flickering as they came up and then their lids shutting rather tight." The dress's crime seems to be that it is long out of fashion, but if Mabel is marginalized because of her frock, her predicament suggests graver social dislocations. Woolf describes Mabel feeling "like a dressmaker's dummy standing there, for young people to stick pins into"; she writes of "the misery which she always tried to hide"; she makes us privy to her sense "that she was condemned, despised."

"The New Dress" is a story about clothing, class, social aberration, and the visual paradox of discretion: the way in which all concerned pretend not to see what is perfectly apparent. It was exactly this set of problems that Madge confronted in her professional life. While British *Vogue* represented commerce to Woolf and others, Condé Nast believed that Dody and Madge had produced something excessively bohemian. In the beginning, the New York office seems to have supported the changes they made. "Vogue is going to be altered considerably," noted Harry Yoxall, the young business manager of British *Vogue*, in 1923; "the percentage of fashion pages is to be cut down, the fashions shown are to be more in keeping with the

present economic stress of this country, and the rest of the magazine is to be considerably broadened and humanised and brought
into keeping with the apparent taste of the British public." But by
1926, Nast, Yoxall, and Chase were arguing that Dody's preferences—
aesthetic and, it was implied, sexual—had perverted the magazine.
Chase's description of Dody as "naturally of a literary and artistic
bent" (like the epithets *bookish* and *highbrow* that she and other
chroniclers of Condé Nast use to describe Dody's editorial stance)
always seems to stand for less mentionable terms. "Fashion Miss
Todd all but eschewed," wrote Chase, incorrectly. "The British edition was not intended to be the advanced literary and artistic review she was turning out." (Decades later, the magazine's hierarchy
was appalled by another, very different visionary editor, Diana
Vreeland.) Woolf and Nast were each wary of being tainted by the
other, whereas Dody and Madge were interested in—and Madge
herself was made of—the mixture. Madge's wearing, unlike Mabel
Waring's, was resolutely of the present, a way of *being* what writers
and artists were investigating in their media.

If *Vogue* succeeded in the United States by targeting an elite de-
mographic and pioneered using marketing that limited appeal rather
than trying to reach everyone, it nevertheless, as Nast knew, could
work only by a double standard. On the one hand, he wrote, "the
publisher, the editor, the advertising manager and circulation man
must conspire not only to get all their readers from the one particular class to which the magazine is dedicated, *but rigorously to exclude
all others.*" On the other, the magazine must "attract readers *who did
not yet belong to the class which he had chosen, but who aspired to it.*" He
and Chase thought that British *Vogue* had neglected the service elements of the magazine ("Seen in the Shops, Smart Fashions for
Limited Incomes, and the Hostess and Beauty articles"), which were
attempts to attract this second group of readers. Dody and Madge,
however, interpreted the "apparent taste of the British public" as
what they should like and what they did not yet know they wanted
(as Vreeland did in the 1960s at American *Vogue*). Still, the idea that
made *Vogue* a success in the United States (we shall cater to those
with money while presenting the high life for the aspirations of the
middle class) may not have been viable yet in England, with its more
rigid understanding of social class.

Nast and Chase also accused Dody of failing to turn a profit. But the magazine had lost money for years before her tenure, and Nast had often been on the verge of abandoning the whole venture. Most recently, British *Vogue* had struggled through the crisis of the General Strike of 1926, when production and transportation were shut down all over England. Still, if Dody was a brilliant editor she was probably not a good manager. Edna Chase had appeared in London more than once during her tenure, trying to whip the staff into shape. Harry Yoxall, who found Dody stimulating if difficult, was startled by her swings of temper in the office and described her borrowing money from him in order to invite someone else to lunch. Madge suggested at the end of her life that Dody had mishandled Nast's money. But she also said, "The world was changing and he [Nast] wanted much more space given to commerce. In those days, I'd never been inside a store. It was quite another world. We went only to court dressmakers."

In September 1926, Yoxall fired Dody, on instructions from Nast, who was himself invariably "difficult to find" when "situations became too fraught," as Madge later observed. Several days later, Yoxall dismissed Madge; he referred to her in his diary as "Miss McHarg (Mrs. Garland), the *maîtresse en titre*" (favorite or official mistress). Yoxall had written to Nast, annoyed at Todd's "prolonged absence at a crucial time, with all her fashion staff too" (a reference to Madge), and he had long been troubled by the difficult "play of personalities" in the office, but he had never expected "such drastic consequences" to follow his complaint. Yet he also said he believed that both firings "should have been done long ago, and would have been but for Nast's fatal procrastination when any unpleasant doing or thinking is required." Musing on Dody's personality, he predicted that she would "end on the Embankment [i.e., in the gutter] one of these days, or in some similar situation." Dody consulted a lawyer, who advised her to threaten a suit to obtain a settlement for breach of contract. Nast and Yoxall responded by threatening to publicly attack her "morals." Trying to protect herself, her daughter, and Madge, she backed off. "For details of the Todd developments see files of my private correspondence with Nast," Yoxall noted in his diary in November 1926—but we cannot see; these files have not survived.

"This affair has assumed in Bloomsbury the proportions of a political rupture," Vita Sackville-West wrote to her husband, Harold Nicolson. "It is said," Virginia Woolf wrote to Vanessa Bell, "that Condé Nast threatened to reveal Todds [sic] private sins, if she sued them, so she is taking £1000, and does not bring an action." "So poor Todd is silenced," wrote Sackville-West, "since her morals are of the classic rather than the conventional order." Other *Vogue* staff resigned in protest; contributors threatened to stop writing for the magazine; and Chase got to work hiring a new editor, Alison Settle, and "immediately . . . transforming her into the correct image of a *Vogue* representative." Chase recalled the firing and its aftereffects in inflated, sexual terms: "The lady [Dody] had a forceful personality and the sound of the wrench, when it came, reverberated from London to New York and back again. When the long, shuddering roar finally subsided we were weak, Toddless, but headed for the Nast formula." Contemporaries, such as Sackville-West, who shared Dody's "classic" proclivities understood Nast's threat as referring to her lesbianism, which implicated Madge. Reviewing Carolyn Seebohm's biography of Condé Nast in 1982, Madge wrote that "in the days when homosexuality was a criminal offence he was not above using the threat of disclosure to avoid paying up for a broken contract." But describing this period to Hilary Spurling several years later, she said that Nast had been aware of Helen—perhaps guarding her own privacy by attributing Nast's intimidation to a potential revelation about Dody's illegitimate child. Homosexuality was never a criminal offense for women in England, but the threat— I will bring your private life into public view—was real. These are the vicious mechanics of discretion: the extent to which it is possible to be disgraced by the "exposure" of facts that are already evident.

Dody and Madge had not only orchestrated the publicity of people whose work they admired, but had also become public figures who provoked sexual gossip on Fleet Street, London's grubby, male newspaper world. Their cachet as a powerful couple, the visibility of their ménage, and the contrast of their styles—one young, thin, and blond; the other older, heavier, and dark—impressed some and distressed others, but always incited comment. "A Garden is a lovesome thing, God wot [knows]," wrote the nineteenth-century poet Thomas Brown, and in the 1920s someone rang a change on

the line: "A Garland is a lovesome thing, Todd wot." Dody was referred to as "Das Tod das Maedchens" (The Death of the Maidens).
And there was a "joke": " 'What is a Sapphist?' 'A Doderast who
practices Todomy.' " The question of what a Sapphist might be troubled the air in England between the 1918 libel suit the dancer Maud
Allan brought against a newspaper that alleged she was a lesbian
and the 1928 obscenity trial against Radclyffe Hall's *The Well of
Loneliness*. The question was part of a relatively new way of thinking
about sex—the idea that a lesbian was a particular type of person—
that was making certain women newly visible, or visible in new
ways.

Madge and Dody's own crowd mixed an exhilarating sexual
openness with fear of exposure, excelled at innuendo, and took the
kind of pleasure at in-jokes that can only be had when a simultaneous vigilance about and disdain for appearances is the rule. Cecil
Beaton's diaries capture the catty tone of their milieu and the extent
to which the two were sources of fascination and revulsion. Sometimes Dody is "that filthy Editor of Vogue" who "has got an objec-
tionable face . . . like a sea lion," and Madge is "her bit" on the side.
At others they are "Miss Todd the Vogue Queen with that nice little Madge Garland." Frederick Ashton was so dazzled by Madge
and Dody that he included two characters based on them in his first
ballet, the 1926 *A Tragedy of Fashion*. Madge called this dance "a
brilliant evocation of the period" that reflected "not only the physical appearance, but the whole tonality of my youth." The pair in
this dance—one figure outrageously butch, the other sinuously
feminine: no more stylized than Madge and Dody themselves—was
a bold answer to what a Sapphist was. But while the term clearly
attached to Dody and her "mannish" style, it applied to Madge,
whose self-presentation conformed to her gender, in more elusive
ways. Her visibility was the unspoken part of what concerned Nast
and Chase.

The firing devastated both women. They had occupied positions of
cultural power; now they were unemployed, tainted by scandal, and
so virtually unemployable. Bloomsbury did not shun them, but they
were ostentatiously avoided by many other former colleagues and

friends, some of whom were afraid of having their own homosexuality exposed. When Madge walked down the street, people crossed
away from her. But she did not retreat. She and Dody held on to the
flat on the Royal Hospital Road, and Yoxall was stunned to see
them out at the ballet a month or two after the firing, "both looking
very full of life, and both very gaily dressed." They made plans to
start a magazine of their own. "Fashion Miss Todd all but eschewed,"
Chase had argued, as if *Vogue* were simply the vehicle for Dody's
"real" interests in art and literature. Yet the plan for the new magazine—it was "to be Vogue, only quarterly," with Dody as editor and
Madge second in command—suggests that fashion was important
to both of them, and not only for advertising revenue. Beaton was
upset about the turn British *Vogue* had taken under Alison Settle
(and Chase's firm hand). They were "trying hard to make the magazine like a woman's pictorial," and he did his best to be affiliated
with Madge and Dody's new venture, to which Raymond Mortimer
and others had already been recruited. He had them to lunch several times, along with Edith Sitwell (who wore "a black toque from
which fell masses of black lace, and a tweed dress") and several of
the other queer young men who supported them: Dadie Rylands,
Steven Runciman, the poet Brian Howard. "I wanted to impress her
[Madge] with some of my photos," Beaton wrote, but "she talked
hard—hard without ceasing—about Brancusi and Vogue—& how
badly they'd been treated . . . She, of course, was smarting with the
injustice . . . She says she was given the sack by Condé Nast for making Vogue too highbrow too Bloomsbury. They published pictures
of obscure actors and actresses." Madge's talk was "all very smart &
intellectual & terrifically Vogue." After lunch, he photographed
her in her "coat & claret-coloured skirt & hat & flower."

While Madge scrambled for freelance journalism, Dody worked
on a survey of modernist design in England, Europe, and the United
States, *The New Interior Decoration*, which she eventually asked Raymond Mortimer to write with her. They still entertained. At a
crowded cocktail party at the Royal Hospital Road flat in the autumn of 1926, Beaton noted that "Todd was a little nervous & shaky
at first but later became normal." But by early 1928 they still did not
have funding for the new magazine, and the strain was starting to
show. Friends saw them bicker, having "rows in front of everybody

and Dody really behaving like a sort of Victorian father—you know, 'Do this, do that,' 'I won't do this, I won't do that,'—and poor Madge . . . dissolving into tears and crying for hours." Elspeth Champcommunal, who showed her collections with Nicole Groult in London in the late 1920s, became a refuge. Madge arrived at a party at Champco's country house in Provence one afternoon "in a state of devastation" about Dody, "dressed in a scarlet dress with pearl buttons all the way down the front, and an Eton collar, bright gold hair, and very tearful."

Woolf was hyperbolically critical at this time, describing Todd as grotesque: "like some primeval animal emerging from the swamp, muddy, hirsute." After Dody and Madge had Woolf to lunch to introduce her to Rebecca West in the spring of 1928, she wrote, "The Todd ménage is incredibly louche: Todd in sponge bag trousers; Garland in pearls and silk; both rather raddled and on their beam ends." This description is for Vanessa Bell's entertainment. In her diary, Woolf wrote, "Todd's room; rather to her credit, workmanlike; Garland pear[l] hung & silken; Todd as buxom as a badger. Rebecca a hardened old reprobate I daresay, but no fool; & the whole atmosphere professional; no charm, except the rather excessive charm of Garland." Rebecca West, however, remembered the lunch lasting till nearly five o'clock.

If Madge had been unprepared for the firing, she was completely unmoored by what happened next. Increasingly, she came home to find Dody passed out with an empty whiskey bottle beside her. Then the bills started coming in from businesses all over London—florists, dressmakers, galleries, restaurants—and she was confronted with Dody's catastrophic handling of money. "She had been running up bills" for years "on a scale that was almost lunatic," Madge said. "She begged and borrowed from her friends." A painting by Vuillard that she had given Madge for her birthday was reclaimed by the gallery, as was a Duncan Grant portrait. Madge learned that Dody had used her name at a number of establishments, including when buying clothes for Helen, so that some of this debt was literally hers. The deception was terrible; the fact that Dody had committed it at "stores"—middle-class establishments—that Madge had never even entered made it even more baffling and humiliating. In this way, Ruthella Todd's destructive legacy became real to Madge, and she began to think of Dody's character as an inheritance from her "gambling mother." She said, "Condé Nast didn't realize it in time—he saw the brilliance—he didn't see the instability. It was awful." She did not say that she herself had not seen it in time.

Forced to settle the bills in her own name, Madge also cleared Dody's debts over the next four years, feeling that she owed it to her. In the meantime, nearly everything they owned, and those things they had merely appeared to own, was seized by bailiffs. In a draft of her memoir, not identifying Dody, Madge wrote, "I had never thought of keeping a record of the things I had paid for myself and so in the bankruptcy of my friend the entire contents of the house, which was in her name, vanished." A kind daily servant hid some of Madge's books, keeping them safe for the next several years. Her dresses were all that was left: "So now once again I was homeless, penniless," she wrote; "only a few lovely and rather inappropriate clothes remained."

TO REMAKE MY CAREER

Long after her separation from Dody and even decades after Dody's death, Madge was haunted by her. Yet it was her ability to distance herself from Dody that made it possible to get by. "Dody went downhill, you might say," recalled Chloe Tyner. "And Madge, she soared uphill. She had to fight very, very hard. But she was able to do it because her manners were better and she managed to always look charming." For the rest of her life, there were people who would not acknowledge Madge, because the two had been lovers and because of Dody's disgrace. As the student outstripped the teacher, there were also those who thought ill of Madge because they believed she had used Dody to get ahead. As she retreated from London, reemerged, and continually refashioned herself, her ability to wear clothes well and her understanding of what she and others wore were signs of her debt to Dody and of her own distinctiveness.

Escaping the end of their life together, Madge went with Ted McKnight Kauffer and Marion Dorn to stay at Vanessa Bell's house in Cassis; she treasured a painting Kauffer made of the place during that stay, which he gave her. Soon afterward, she moved to France, where "it was much cheaper and easier to be poor than in London." She occasionally found work reporting for provincial English papers about the collections at the couture houses where she still had contacts. She lived "almost anywhere," subsisted on yogurt and vegetables, and often shared these "miserable meals" with the painter and theater designer Sophie Fedorovitch, who had done the set and costumes for A Tragedy of Fashion. A "remarkable small woman with short fair hair and very keen blue eyes," Fedorovitch was the

daughter of Polish gentry, had studied painting in Russia, survived the Revolution, then escaped to London after almost starving to death. Madge and she shared an instinct for textiles and clothes; they may have shared a bed. ("One night we slept on the floor in somebody's flat," Madge recalled.) Despite Fedorovitch's own "sober habit," wrote a friend, "she loved . . . beautiful clothes on other women" and she had a real "feeling for ethereal fabrics on the stage." When Fedorovitch moved back to London, she continued to work closely with Ashton over several decades; he called her "my greatest artistic collaborator and adviser." In Paris she sometimes worked as a taxi driver—which many Russian émigrés did, but not many women did—and she memorialized this pinched time with Madge in a still life of a carafe and a glass of water—a joke, since they could seldom afford to drink wine. Madge and she often spent evenings in some basement boîte, "drinking tea and singing Russian songs till all hours." Madge would meet Janet Flanner at Les Deux Magots and sometimes accompanied Flanner when she filed her copy for *The New Yorker*, putting it on the last, late-night train to the coast to meet a boat to New York. Virgil Thomson brought her to meet Gertrude Stein and Alice Toklas; she heard him play "the early beginnings" of *Four Saints in Three Acts* at another friend's house.

She spent a summer in Cannes, where her flat, in the rue d'Antibes, was devoid of furniture other than a bed. She had no money to furnish the place, so she asked the artist John Banting to paint images of tables and chairs on the walls. It was still a relative novelty to spend the summer in the South of France, and the Cap d'Antibes, as she said, offered a new "way of life and dress." She wore sailor pants, a striped top, and espadrilles. She wore these trousers with a white singlet, tennis shoes, and a sailor cap at a jaunty angle. Or she was in a Chanel dress, and well shod. That new way of life had to do with being part of a critical mass of independent women, the first generation that was moneyed and had left home without marrying. In one series of snapshots taken in her flat, Madge and a group of friends lounge theatrically on her bed. What is pictured, the feeling arrested there: the ease with which they are tumbled together, the looks among them and at the camera, the sense of shared leisure and pleasure.

Summer in Cannes (MGP)

Madge never found steady work—unlike these friends, she did not have family money—again became ill, and eventually returned to London. But once there, she was approached by the Illustrated Newspapers Group and offered a job editing the women's section of their two recently amalgamated magazines, *Britannia* and *Eve*. It was a coup, given the dire state of the economy and the disgrace she had lived through. It was another thing to reconcile it with the kind of work she had been used to. Rebecca West told her she could not possibly be associated with such a lowbrow publication, especially one with a name as absurd as *Britannia and Eve*. (They had kept the titles of both papers.) "I can and I will," Madge said, citing the salary. West continued to tease her, referring to the magazine as "Madge's two old girls" and calling the night she closed her section "putting [her] two old girls to bed."

Hired as the "Woman Editor," Madge told the editor in chief that she was qualified to produce the fashion pages but had no knowledge of "what are called women's interests": "knitting, and babies, and cooking." She had Elspeth Champcommunal's old nanny check the knitting patterns, managed the pages on child rearing with the help of friends and their nurses and governesses, and paid the cook of wealthy friends (Lord and Lady Sainsbury) to test recipes. She published an early article on flower arrangement by horticulture and household design guru Constance Spry, which began a friendship that lasted until Spry's death. The editor congratulated her on her knowledge of knitting ("I said nothing") and cooking ("In those days I don't think I'd seen a saucepan"), then asked her to edit the fashion pages of another of the company's magazines, *The Bystander*. She began producing five pages a week for *The Bystander* along with twenty pages a month for *Britannia and Eve*. She had a minuscule staff, but loved that the work was "such a challenge"—and that in the worst years of the Depression she had two salaries and two expense accounts. She lived in Mayfair—her mother's dream, achieved in her own way—surrounded by the luxury goods about which she was writing. In one flat, on Bruton Street, she was flanked by the couturiers Norman Hartnell and Victor Stiebel. She had a favorite table at the Ritz, bought a country house in Sussex, and resumed her

Sailor style in the South of France (MCP)

life in Paris, in style. The Illustrated Newspapers' offices were close
enough to Victoria Station that she could catch a 4:30 train to Paris
on a Friday afternoon, arrive by midnight—the fashionable hour
for art openings—spend the weekend in Paris, and return home in
time to be at work on Monday. She made longer visits for the collections at least twice a year.

It was not just the money. The November 1929 issue of *Britannia
and Eve*, her first, carried the headline "Fashions Feminine and Otherwise by Madge Garland" along with her photograph—one of the
portraits Beaton had taken several years before. "What I Saw in Paris,
by Madge Garland" was another early headline. Beginning in January 1932, her name was also splashed across the pages of *The Bystander* every week: "Madge Garland writes a Forecast of Fashion";
"A Portfolio of Spring Fashions Compiled by Madge Garland";
"Madge Garland Brings Back News from Paris." The 1930s, she recalled, was when "I lived the fullest life." Her medium was her self-
presentation. She began appearing on television, talking about
women's clothes for the BBC. Able to buy couture clothing again,
she wore Lanvin and Schiaparelli—the wit and conceptual flair of the
latter especially pleasurable to her. She was "always very elegant,
slightly affected, willowy, soignée." She was "always in a hat." She was
in a black wool coat with sleeves of leopard skin, designed by Victor
Stiebel.

Her medium was also the mixture of technical vocabulary, rap-
turous hyperbole, and didacticism that was the language of fashion.
She was working at a time when fashion was a set of demanding
but always changing rules handed down from above. As she said
later, "I thought I should inform people, be absolutely clear and exact—whether they like[d] it or not!" As in: "Dark brown is excellent
when accompanied by brilliant sapphire blue." "Pink and brown
is good, provided that both colours approximate to mushroom
shades." The logic is sometimes elusive: "Sports clothes favour colour contrasts, but skirts are often divided." At times, the more
she rendered the clothing, piling detail on detail, the more the object seemed at once to escape and reward her—and the reader: "For
evening wraps nothing is so satisfying to the eye, nor so practical
to wear since it does not easily crease, as a good lamé, particularly when it is shot with multi-colored flower colours which per-

mit it being worn with several different coloured satin or velvet gowns."

Emphatic and effusive, this rhetoric also careened toward the telegraphic. Madge's report from the spring 1930 collections, described in *Britannia and Eve* as a "copy of a telegram received from our Woman Editor in Paris," reproduced not just the syntax but the look of an urgent, condensed communiqué: "SHINY STRAW HATS FEATURED FOR SUMMER STOP BIZARRE JEWELS CRYSTAL ENAMEL ETC WORN WITH SIMPLE EVENING GOWNS WOOD AND METAL NECKLACES FOR SPORTS WEAR STOP." And: "LATEST SHOES FROM BUNTING MADE OF FISH-SKIN RESEMBLING SHAGREEN BUT FINER AND SOFT STOP." Then there is the question that is not a question: "Don't you think a spotted handkerchief knotted closely around the throat is a practical and becoming fashion?" she wrote in late 1931, as if searching for another way to be didactic. "Does your new winter hat reveal one side of your waved hair and dip abruptly over the other side?" "Are you one of the enthusiasts who are delighted at the so-called return of the bustle?" And: "Which Would You Choose—Pink Velvet or Black Tulle?"

Writing on fashion, the physical, and the electricity of the present in the section of *Tender Buttons* called "A long dress," Gertrude Stein uses a version of this form:

What is the current that makes machinery, that makes it crackle, what is the current that presents a long line and a necessary waist. What is this current.

. . .

Where is the serene length, it is there and a dark place is not a dark place, only a white and red are black, only a yellow and green are blue, a pink is scarlet, a bow is every color. A line distinguishes it. A line just distinguishes it.

These, too, are questions that preempt themselves, doing what they ask. Writing about the space of waists and of necessity, the relationships among colors, and the crackle of technology, Stein is concerned with the way lines of text and the lines of a dress—"long lines," "the serene length"—intersect. "Practice measurement, practice the sign that means that really means a necessary betrayal, in showing that

there is wearing," she writes, in the section of *Tender Buttons* titled "A chair." And: "Actually not aching, actually not aching, a stubborn bloom is so artificial and even more than that, it is a spectacle, it is a binding accident, it is animosity and accentuation."

Both the fashion journalism and the modernist writing are practices of expressing and caressing objects that rely on oracular utterance: "Looking is not vanishing. Laughing is not evaporating. There can be the climax. There can be the same dress. There can be an old dress," writes Stein in her "Portrait of Mabel Dodge at Villa Curiona." And: "There can be pleasing classing clothing." In both forms, the language is almost furiously static: full of emphatic, precise pronouncements. (As Stein writes elsewhere: "For this is so. Because.") In both, descriptive energy and precision blend with a euphoric proliferation of sense. Both involve addressing oneself to nouns while celebrating verbs: "showing that there is wearing." Both concern accentuation, pattern, regular arrangement; the practice of measurement; the artificial or accidental quality of the natural; resemblance that is not resemblance; the spectacle that is emotion and the emotion (animosity, crackle, betrayal) circulating around these items meant for display—more and more garments.

Writing about couture clothing has, until recently in the Anglo-American context, been termed trivial—ephemeral and apparently inconsequential, appearing most often in trade papers, magazines, and newspapers. Yet, or perhaps as a result, the language of fashion itself continually stresses significance. (Which is another message of the urgent "telegram.") "Velvet is Very Important," Madge wrote in *The Bystander* in 1932. "The ANGLE of one's BRIM is important." The detailed focus on surfaces in this writing also implies that these objects and the work that goes into producing and consuming them deserve respect. The emphasis on significance is direct and unashamed: "This insistence on a smooth and tight-fitting hip-line is another universal characteristic of the spring fashions, and one of the utmost importance," she wrote in *Britannia and Eve*. And: "Importance is given to the shoulders of this black camel's hair coat by appliqués of satin gaillac." Importance is the question begged by fashion at least since its more exclusive association with

With friends in the South of France, late 1920s; Madge is second from right (MGP)

femininity, following what is called the Great Masculine Renunciation—the abandonment of surface adornment and the adoption of
sober similarity in men's clothing with the ascendance of the suit in
the nineteenth century.

It is characteristic of fashion—historically the premier public
arena for women—that it has been relentlessly characterized as trivial even in the face of its economic, aesthetic, and psychological
importance, made a receptacle for concern about the meaning of
our surfaces. Madge addressed this cordoning off and willful ignorance candidly in *Britannia and Eve* in 1930: "There is a tendency in
England to regard everything which concerns the lighter moments
of men (sport, for instance) as important, while the more mundane
occupations of women are universally condemned as frivolous."
She is echoing and expanding on a point that Virginia Woolf made
the year before in *A Room of Her Own*: "it is the masculine values
that prevail. Speaking crudely, football and sport are 'important';
the worship of fashion, the buying of clothes 'trivial.'" But, as Madge
wrote, "the desire to dress up is too deeply rooted an instinct to be
treated lightly, nor may it be thwarted without detriment to the
character of the individual."

To make this point, Madge also put herself and the rituals of
haute couture on display. "It is a rule that that no one is allowed to
leave until the collection is over," she wrote in "This Fashion Business," also in 1930.

> The other day when I had seen about three hundred models
> at a certain house, I discovered that if I were not to be late
> for an important appointment I must leave at once. I was in
> Paris for a few days only with much to do, and having seen
> about three hundred of the five hundred models presented
> by this house, I considered, rightly or wrongly, that I had a
> fairly good impression of the style and line of their clothes,
> and that I must go. I got up to leave, but at the door a charm-
> ing but very firm young lady begged me to be reseated. I
> explained my dilemma. She scolded me, the assumption be-
> ing that on the day when I had the honour to be admitted to
> such a house I should have made no other appointment. I
> explained my brief visit to Paris, conditioned by such and

such circumstances. She demurred. I begged that my case should at least be referred to the higher courts of the publicity manager, whom I happened to know well. Reluctantly she consented to dispatch a mission to him. Time passed. Eventually he arrived, but I could see by his expression that I had committed a grave misdemeanour. He treated me to a long homily about how to attend a serious collection of the importance of So-and-So's; I heartily agreed to everything he said, pleaded extenuating circumstances, and, promising never to do it again, I fled. I shall probably not be allowed to re-enter that house.

She also made the physical atmosphere of the couture showings vivid for her readers. "A huge modern entrance in the Champs Elysées, vast salons in the everlasting grey, an incredibly large number of extremely uncomfortable cane chairs," she wrote in *Britannia and Eve* in 1933. "A mannequin enters in the unassuming two piece woolen suit which convention ordains shall begin even the most sensational collection." At another show: "A magnificent Hotel of the Empire period. Huge salons decorated in the authentic early Empire manner, slender gold bas-reliefs on cream walls, sand colour taffeta curtains draped in the window embrasures. Small tables with bouquets of tea roses are arranged around the vast room which has a stage at one end and slightly raised rows of seats at the other. A slight, very discreet murmur—then silence and against the velvet curtains the first mannequin appears." Later: "Enormous applause breaks out—a mannequin has just appeared wearing a magnificent black velvet evening wrap cut on Florentine cinquecento lines . . . The previous mannequin . . . turns round to give an envious glance to her admired successor." In "yet another series of salons," she sees "a new colour which resembles stewed blackberries and a lot of lamé."

Madge was now a success. But the question of importance still preyed on her. She continued to immerse herself in modern design, and when she was not regretting her missed academic career, she sometimes said she wished she had been an architect, a more respected form of containing bodies than the one from which she made a living. She had traveled to the Bauhaus in the late 1920s, probably to assist Dody with *The New Interior Decoration*. She later lived in one of the London houses designed by Halsey Ricardo and wrote several articles about these buildings—rich subjects for her, with their emphasis on color and decoration. She met Charlotte Perriand, Le Corbusier's collaborator, and was "madly jealous of her, because there she was working with Le Corbusier, and there was I sweating it out in the fashion world, about which I didn't care a hoot in hell." In the 1920s, walking into Jean Désert, the decoration business and showroom on the Faubourg Saint-Honoré of the designer Eileen Gray and her collaborator Evelyn Wyld, Madge had fallen in love with the rich simplicity of Gray's work and the stark geometry of Wyld's rugs, and she became close to both women.

Wyld had formed the French War Emergency Fund during the First World War with a group of friends, including Gray; she received the Medaille de la Reconnaissance Française—a decoration given to volunteers who helped the wounded and refugees—for this work. She remained in France after the Armistice, able to live more openly as a lesbian in France than at home, and eventually settled in an old house in the South of France, in the hills between Cannes and Grasse. A tough Scotswoman with bright orange hair, she came from a family of committed suffragists and "always set her own style, dressing in beautifully cut trousers, Byronic silk shirts and wide embroidered belts." She had no formal education in art (she had studied music), but Gray—who had moved to France in 1907 and worked first in lacquer, then in wood and metal, making screens, chairs, tables, and lamps—invited her to produce textiles with her. After travels with Gray in North Africa and research on her own into weaving in England and Scotland, Wyld began running the weaving studio and designing rugs for Jean Desért. When Gray began to focus on architecture rather than interior décor, their partnership ended, and Wyld collaborated with the American Elizabeth Eyre de Lanux. Madge described one apartment designed by de Lanux as combining "the most austere lines . . . with most precious materials." Wyld and de Lanux exhibited at the Salon des Artistes Décorateurs in 1928 and 1929, the Salon d'Automne, and the Union des Artistes Modernes, then in the early 1930s moved their operation south, opening a studio in Cannes and working out of Wyld's house.

The work of all three women "was radical in its stress on surface qualities, bareness and elegant comfort," notes Isabelle Anscombe in her pioneering study of women and the decorative arts. They created interiors that "were among the most sophisticated but practical of their day," entirely distinct from the homes they had been raised in, modern yet attuned to physical ease. Madge, writing in 1930, noted how the unusual color schemes, "the grain of the wood, the smooth surface of leather, the roughness of hand-knotted rugs, are all employed to give interest to what otherwise might be banal." In 1930 she organized an exhibition of rugs by Wyld and furniture by de Lanux at the Curtis Moffat gallery in London. (Rugs by Marion Dorn and Ted McKnight Kauffer were also on display.) For Madge, becoming friends with Gray, Wyld, and de Lanux meant that she "grew up in" their work, and for forty years she spent most of her holidays at Wyld's house in Provence. But they "were all completely independent, all had their own money, then lived their own lives the way they wanted to," she said. "They accepted me as being an exception; it couldn't be helped. I was *literally* the only person they knew who had ever earned her living."

After working for *Britannia and Eve* and *The Bystander* for several years, Madge found her health again deteriorating. Her solution, which she kept secret from her employers, was to check into a clinic. She went to work every day, but lived under a doctor's supervision until she recovered. Then, in the spring of 1934, Condé Nast and Harry Yoxall asked her to return to British *Vogue* as fashion editor. It was a vindication on every level: the personal satisfaction of being recognized by them; the fact that no other glossy magazine had the prestige of *Vogue* (and daily papers still did not cover fashion). Still, she bargained hard. Nast finally agreed to match her two salaries, cabling the London office from shipboard on his way back to New York: "Give Madge what she wants."

She found *Vogue* a wholly different place from the magazine she had been forced out of in 1926. By 1934 many aspects of the magazine and fashion industries had been professionalized, and the alliances between editorial, manufacturing, and retail solidified. It was now standard practice for wholesale copyists and retailers to get credit for designs. The advent of photographer's models and modeling agencies, long resisted, was another shift. The industry still revolved around Paris and haute couture—although ready-to-wear was becoming more prevalent, it still imitated couture—and twice a year, buyers and journalists converged on the city, and the showings went on from early morning until late at night. Most designers showed at least two hundred models, and a journalist would see four or five collections a day—nearly a thousand dresses. Select wholesalers of ready-to-wear clothing could attend the couture showings by paying a high entrance fee, called a "caution," which they would forfeit if their firm did not go on to buy or pay the patent on the toile, the garment from which the pattern and then copies could be made. These buyers were "toadied to in no uncertain manner," Madge wrote later, "and the more influential American ones treated like princesses." She was not treated badly herself: When she arrived in her room at the Ritz, she invariably found a new hat from the milliner Suzy.

She had a great deal of power. Half a century later, Hardy Amies, who became the official dressmaker to Queen Elizabeth II, remembered exactly the moment in 1935 when Madge encouraged him to open his own *maison de couture* and told him, "You will go far." She influenced which dresses would be mass-produced, since by the early 1930s it was accepted that being a fashion journalist at a glossy magazine was not entirely distinct from "the rôle of merchandise-stylist." This merging was initially "looked on with equal disfavor by both sides," Madge recalled. "The fashion editor, who had never dealt with firms other than *couture* houses and court dressmakers, turned up her nose at the ready-made clothes, which in the main were quite dreadful, and the wholesaler, who had not yet realized what a power the press could be, was annoyed by her criticism." But the new level of coordination with manufacturers and stores also meant that a good fashion editor could "be the pivot around which revolves the whole complicated apparatus of launching a new idea." Madge made "deals with the heads of wholesale companies, such as Olive O'Neill at Dorville, whereby *Vogue* would feature a particular couture gown, mention the manufacturer who bought the toile or pattern," and even help "distribut[e] copies of the gown to the most important stores." She had a contact at one firm, a talented copyist, who would tell her which models her company was buying from which Paris houses and which department stores—"Selfridges or Harrods or a place in Newcastle or wherever"—would retail them.

Alison Settle was still the magazine's editor. The staff included Anne Scott-James, the travel writer and memoirist Lesley Blanch, the society writer Johnny McMullin, and a young Audrey Withers. As fashion editor, Madge had a staff of seven. She worked closely with Cecil Beaton, who now did much of the magazine's photography, and she set up *Vogue*'s photography studio. To one subordinate, she "was the chicest and most terrifying woman"—impatient with bureaucracy, exacting, delicate, haughty—but also someone who made you "laugh a lot." Scott-James saw her as someone who had "antennae" for what was new and good, but was high-strung and an egotist, the kind of person who blamed others when things went wrong. When Settle was forced out in 1935 (Nast et al. using tactics that, again, did not reflect well on them—indeed, that damaged their reputation in the fashion and magazine businesses in England), Madge lobbied hard for the job. But more than competence was at stake. Edna Chase and another manager were "bitterly anti-Garland on the morality issue," wrote Harry Yoxall in his diary. "Can't see why, myself, her editorship should cause such a scandal," he noted, "when her appointment as fashion editor did not do so." A lesbian at the head of the magazine was not acceptable, and Condé Nast and his executives eventually chose the American Betty Penrose, whom Scott-James called "much more boring and solid and reliable."

Madge had become romantically involved with Frances (Fay) Blacket Gill, one of the first woman solicitors in England, and she was not hiding it. Blacket Gill specialized in representing designers (Victor Stiebel, Norman Hartnell, Hardy Amies, and the milliner Aage Thaarup were among her clients), actors (the Redgraves), artists, and writers. Her clients were also her friends and were mostly "people who happened to be homosexual." When Madge and Fay entertained at their home near Grosvenor Square, Harry Yoxall was often a guest. (Drinks one evening featured "Claire [*sic*] Luce and a German film star.") Yoxall also visited them several times at Madge's country house on the Kent-Sussex border, once to see the house and garden "and have cocktails with her and 'girl' friend," on another occasion to bring Chase and her husband to the cottage for sightseeing, lunch, and dinner. "Good food and talk," wrote Yoxall, and Fay "acted as host."

From an upper-middle-class family in Newcastle (her father was a solicitor who had encouraged her to study law), Fay was about nine years younger than Madge and had something in common with Dody—and with Andrew McHarg—with her butch style, small stature, and domineering personality. She dressed in beautifully cut suits—"straight skirt, nice jacket, roomy pockets, shirts with double cuffs, and a huge pair of cameo-style cufflinks"—wore her hair short but well coiffed, always had three chunky gold chain bracelets on one arm, three strings of pearls round her neck, pearl studs in her ears, a huge cameo brooch with diamonds, and a large diamond ring on her right little finger, "hideous, but spectacular." She loved cars and never let anyone else drive her Jaguar.

Madge and she were a combustible pair. Fay was a divorce lawyer who was good at "sorting out everyone's problems but her own," said her last girlfriend, the actress Patricia Laffan. "She had no sense of irony," recalled Patrick Woodcock, a London physician whose patients were actors, designers, and artists—the same crowd as Fay's clients. She was "a very complex and not very kind person," said Sybille Bedford, "Philistine and difficult"—but she also recalled that Madge always "quarreled . . . bitterly" with her lovers. (Sybille knew Blacket Gill well, because Allanah Harper later lived with her.) "In a match between her and Madge, I don't know who I'd bet on winning," said the novelist Francis King, a friend of both. At the end of the affair, Madge is said to have thrown Fay's belongings out the window. Decades later, at a fashion show, Fay turned to Patricia Laffan and muttered, "Here comes that bitch Madge Garland." There are no photographs of Fay in Madge's albums. One has a number of missing pages, ripped out—black stubs sticking out of the binding—that may mark her presence in and expulsion from Madge's life.

When the Munich Pact was signed in November 1938, British *Vogue*, like other businesses, began preparing for war: provisioning itself with fire extinguishers, first aid kits, and gas masks; determining the chain of command in the event that staff members were killed;

carrying out air raid drills. There was the threat of bombing, and for a time it was unclear whether it would be possible to conduct nonessential businesses such as *Vogue* if England were under attack. Facing confusion at home and the New York office's failure to understand their situation, the editorial board in London decided to continue publishing provisionally, at least "until we see some daylight in the fog of war." Of the Paris collections in August 1939, Madge wrote later: "The clothes were the most fantastically beautiful ever seen. The influence of Surrealism, which had been dominant in art . . . and had inspired Schiaparelli's most original models, was now visible in picturesque clothes suitable only for a fancy-dress existence remote from reality, and which showed all too clearly that no one cared to consider the present or dared look into the future."

In the months of the "phony war"—from the German invasion of Poland and England's declaration of war on September 3, 1939, until Germany attacked France, Belgium, Holland, and Britain the following spring—food rationing and price restrictions were instituted, paper rationing was imminent, London was under blackout, and friends and colleagues on the *Vogue* staff were killed in the accidents resulting from the completely dark nights. Harry Yoxall tried to communicate all of this to Condé Nast: "The cost of living is beginning to rise substantially. Employés are experiencing difficulty and discomfort in getting to and from their work. At any moment they may have to face grave danger of life and limb in doing so." Tax increases were also making salaries inadequate, and distribution problems were considerable, since the railways were moving troops and munitions, and road transport was impossible because of petrol rationing. At night, most members of the staff did some kind of volunteer duty: as fire wardens, as ambulance drivers, and at air raid centers. In October 1939 the magazine began publishing one issue a month instead of two.

Madge was a pacifist; she supported the Peace Movement—later called the Peace Pledge Union—organized by Dick Sheppard, the minister who had married her and Ewart Garland. He was a man "reckless in the expenditure of himself, orator, organizer, legend in his own life-time," Sybille Bedford wrote, someone "who could make contact with every human being he met." Madge had venerated him since the early 1920s and she signed the group's pledge: "We renounce

war and never again, directly or indirectly, will we support or sanction another." Aldous Huxley had thrown himself into lecturing
and working for the cause before he left England, and other early
members included Bertrand Russell, the writer Siegfried Sassoon,
and the journalist and peace activist Vera Brittain. Madge's beliefs
did not mean that she was less affected by the run-up to war, but it
complicated her position on the magazine. She first refused to attend air raid drills with the rest of the British *Vogue* staff, and in
October 1939, Yoxall wrote to Nast that in the event of Betty Penrose's death he had placed Madge "low in the table of succession for
the acting editorship," because Penrose believed "that in the circumstances contemplated—i.e. presumably serious and continuous
bombing—Garland would not operate well." He added: "In any
event she is a bad organizer of editorial assignments, and is too
much of an individualist to make a successful director of a team in
times of stress." He was a conflicted observer: He respected and
liked Madge, wanted Nast to acknowledge the extra work she had
assumed when Penrose was ill for an extended period in 1936, and
eventually felt that she "turned up trumps," able to "make things
brighter," during the "phoney war," despite his earlier misgivings.

But in late December 1939, he fired her, largely at Penrose's insistence. "It was a beastly job," Yoxall wrote in his diary, adding
that "Madge took it well." Penrose set down her desire "to get rid of
Madge" in a scathing, thirteen-page, single-spaced document detail-
ing Madge's flaws, among them her "fundamentally artificial approach to life"; her poor "capacity for executive work"; her "lack of
clarity of thought" and of a "journalistic instinct"; her "uneven . . .
taste with its distinct leaning toward the chi chi" and its absence of
"what one might call for lack of a better word 'breeding'—it has no
sympathy with the traditions of elegance and conservatism." (One
example of Madge's poor taste included her championing of a Picasso painting to accompany a feature; Penrose suggested a Renoir).
Nast himself seemed to value Madge more for her "contact with the
artistic, literary, theatrical crowd in London" than for "any flair for
clothes." It was a "difficult situation," wrote Yoxall. "I think Betty
is fundamentally right, but . . ." His gratitude at how well Madge
took it inspired him to send her to Paris one last time: "There are to
be Spring collections & it's necessary to keep the Brogue flag fly-

ing—and give her a bit of a holiday first. So that's a nice outcome of a messy business which has caused me much mental anguish." He called the trip her "swansong" and described her report:

> Says the collections were quite good in the circumstances. Chanel, Vionnet and Rochas have all closed and Mainbocher beat it to New York. Others all showing. Only 5 British buyers there & 45 Americans. Carmel Snow came for Harpers and Emmy Ives for Vogue. Paris has an early curfew and taxis very difficult; otherwise not more warlike than London. Showed me a clever and persuasive anti-British booklet dropped by a German plane near Paris. Great difficulties in getting back as no planes left for a week on account of the weather, and eventually, since we had to have the illustrations, she came back on an incredibly inconvenient boat trip.

"Then once again I was out of a job," Madge wrote, "but so were most of my friends." She was forty-four years old, grateful that she had not been called up to do war work, but aware that her professional future looked bleak. Recalling this time in interviews, she did not admit to having been fired. Instead, she said that the German occupation, the fall of Paris, and the closure of so many couture houses meant that a fashion editor was no longer required. She left the magazine in February 1940, however, and Paris fell in June. The industry was eviscerated but not shut down during the occupation; it kept itself going through a mixture of collaboration, resourcefulness, resistance, and infusions of foreign capital.

When one of her contacts in the wholesale dress business recommended her to Stafford Bourne, of Bourne and Hollingsworth, a middle-class department store on Oxford Street, she began to remake herself again, shifting her focus, if not her preferences, to mass-produced clothing and new textiles, and becoming involved with the politics of fashion as the industry was recruited in the service of the nation. She was in no position to be choosy, but at first she refused the job Bourne offered, as merchandise manager, telling him that she knew nothing about his stock. It was both an honest assessment and a way to distance herself from his world of "chil-

dren's socks, or grandma's underclothes, and that sort of thing."
Telling the story later, it was a way to say that her success at Bourne
and Hollingsworth had not been inevitable but was the result of hard
work. The salary was small, but she was grateful to be employed. and
the job gave her power over every section of the store. She ended up
staying until the end of the war and became committed to creating
and marketing good ready-to-wear clothing at affordable prices.

She found the place in chaos and deeply old-fashioned. Most of
the buyers were men, and many of them had been called up for military service; those who remained were either much older than she
or completely inexperienced. She began by asking the board of directors for a number of changes to make the staff more comfortable, allowing them to smoke during their lunch break and buying
a gramophone so that they could listen to music. The board was
annoyed that she would emphasize "such trivial matters at such a
serious moment," she said, but her championing of the employees,
her enthusiasm, and her attention to the minutiae of sales technique
gained her the support of the staff and allowed her to make more
substantial changes. She reorganized the links between wholesale
and retail and reconfigured the store's displays. Her most important reform was a new way of sizing the stock. Britain was far
behind the United States in manufacturing quality ready-to-wear
clothing and in adopting a consistent numbering system; the two
were related. Different manufacturers used different scales, which
were based not on body measurement but clothing measurement.
The most common designations were, in Madge's words, "a series
of unintelligible and mysterious letters (w x, etc.)," unrelated to human dimensions. Taboos against coming in unseemly contact with
the body, which made it impossible to take accurate body measurements, accounted for part of this confusion. Many size charts were
also made by tailors, who each had their own methods; even the
parts of the body they measured differed, depending on their theories of cutting. Remembering the well-made ready-to-wear copies of
French designs she had bought with Olguita in St. Louis and Chicago, and how easy it had been to find "the right type of dress in the
right size," Madge instituted a rational sizing system for Bourne and
Hollingsworth's clothing. She "began to dabble in design" herself
and had these pieces made up in the store's factory.

For much of the war, she was without a home of her own: bombed out, always moving around, camping in empty flats or staying with friends in London and in the country. She could not get to her house in Sussex, because it was in a restricted area and fuel rationing made regular travel there impossible. In May 1940, the phony war ended; the London Blitz began in earnest that September. Four hundred Londoners died on the night of September 7, 1940, and the docks were set on fire. The Germans bombed London steadily for the next three months—they began dropping incendiary bombs in late December—and these raids continued until May 1941. Many people and businesses left town; thousands of homes were destroyed; thousands were killed; fires burned everywhere. One walked "through shattered streets ankle-deep in glass," wrote Vera Brittain, and when bombs damaged the water mains, through streets running with water. The whole physical pattern of the city changed. Everyone was living in a combination of fear, defiance, and dailyness—getting up in the morning, going to work, returning home, changing clothes, and going into shelters. Madge stayed with friends at their country house near Windsor, then rented a small house of her own nearby, taking the train to work as often as possible. On the worst night of the Blitz, May 10, 1941, German planes dropped hundreds of tons of bombs on London, destroying the House of Commons and tens of thousands of homes, killing thousands. Three weeks later, from her friends' home, Madge wrote to her brother Gerald, who was now running Brooks, McGlashan and McHarg in Melbourne:

> I don't know what to write about conditions here, at the moment we are all overwhelmed by the tragedy of [the German invasion of] Crete . . . I feel too deeply about the general situation to worry much about my own affairs—which is perhaps all to the good! The news of the clothes rationing yesterday came as a complete shock, I can see no hope of retaining my job and am not exactly looking forward to going to the office tomorrow. If the worst happens it will be the third time I've joined the unemployed ranks since the outbreak of war. However it is no good worrying. Everyone is in more or less a similar situation . . . The petrol rationing

is severe and all we can manage is to get to the station and back three times a week . . . Travel in London is fantastically difficult but remarkably simple when you consider the conditions under which any travel is made possible. The dust from the ruined buildings was appalling this spring but the rainy weather has made things easier . . . To work in London this last year has been a Herculean task . . . but on the other hand I have been so lucky . . . Several of my friends have been wounded and maimed or have lost all their belongings. It is unbelievably horrible. I am afraid this is a very unsatisfactory letter but I find it utterly impossible to write. Either I must write a six volume novel or not write at all.

Madge had been in little contact with her family for ten years after she left home, but sometime in the 1930s the relationship had thawed. Andrew McHarg had given her a loan to help her buy her country house; he considered it a good investment. She had chaperoned her sister, Yvonne, around London and helped her find work. And when Hettie McHarg was diagnosed with cancer on a visit to London, Madge had cared for her until the end. Hettie died in 1938, and Madge buried her at Golders Green cemetery in North London. Now her father was failing: "One can only hope that the end will be peaceful and painless," Madge wrote to Gerald, still troubled by "the horror" of her mother's death. She thanked Gerald for contriving with their father to send her about twenty pounds a month, without which, she said, "I don't know what I would have done."

The effect of the war on clothing was not only, as she wrote to Gerald, that "nowadays one only wears plain suits & sensible shoes & pretty clothes are unnecessary & never seen." It was also that fashion became the subject of policy discussions at the highest levels of government. "The news of the clothes rationing" was announced by the Board of Trade on June 1, 1941. The "Utility" cloth and clothing scheme and the subsequent "austerity" regulations were designed to use scarce raw materials carefully and to free labor for enlisted and civilian war work. ("Utility" clothes were those made from so-called Utility fabric; *austerity* referred to style restrictions on both Utility and non-Utility clothes.) The government was also concerned with ensuring a decent standard of living, to

boost morale and prevent resentment in a deprived civilian population—a calculated response to the profiteering that had marred
the home front during World War I. The various regulations "to
restrict the amount of material used in each garment, to limit the
number of models any one firm could create in a year, and to forbid
absolutely the manufacture or import of all trimmings" (no more
than two pockets and five buttons; no superfluous decoration),
seemed to Madge likely to limit trade to such an extent that she
would be out of work. Instead, they led to more work, both at Bourne
and Hollingsworth and, a year later, for the Board of Trade itself,
which asked her to consult on "coupons, clothes, style restrictions,"
and more, when it introduced the austerity guidelines. "No salary
attached," she wrote to Gerald, "but interesting & I am quite keen
to do it because I really do know so much more about the whole
set-up than most of those dear old chaps in the B. o. T."

With Paris cut off during the war, so the story goes, countries
that had depended on French fashion were forced to design their
own clothes. "I never thought of buying a hat in London" in the
1930s, Madge said, "which is very odd when you think of it." It is
hardly an overstatement. Charles James's genius—his passionately
sculptural approach to dressing women—moved her. "He had more
knowledge of fashion in his little finger than the whole world of
couture put together," she said. But he was unusual and was in any
case an American working in London. She supported Hardy Amies,
but did not love his clothes. She occasionally wore the designs of
Victor Stiebel, who was a friend, and of Digby Morton, who worked
to translate men's tailoring standards to women's clothing and was
known for his adventurous color sense. Otherwise, the perfection-
ism that characterized men's tailoring and outfitting in England was
absent from women's dress: "It was always hit and miss," Madge
said. "You bought a pretty dress and perhaps you had your shoes
dyed to match." As for wholesalers, until the war most of them
"were backward in styling," she wrote, "had not sufficiently studied
proper methods of sizing, and had relied on showy details to conceal their poverty of cut and fashion." Now only cut mattered. At
first, wartime restrictions required manufacturers only to adhere to
certain fabrics; they could make their own choices of pattern and
design. But in 1942, the Board of Trade went further and commis-

sioned the Incorporated Society of London Fashion Designers to design stylish sample models that met the new austerity regulations and were simple to produce. The Board selected the samples most suitable for mass production and had them manufactured. The result was that during the war many ordinary Englishwomen were able to wear well-made clothes for the first time in their lives.

In the 1930s, Madge had helped found and chaired the London Fashion Group (an offshoot of the American Fashion Group), organized to promote English couture by bringing together designers, journalists, and manufacturers. The group also scheduled showings in London the week before the Paris shows—an attempt to make it easier for the powerful American buyers, en route to Paris, to see the work of English designers. It "died a quick death, of course, with the war," she said, but its work was revived in 1942 by the Incorporated Society of London Fashion Designers, whose member firms included Stiebel, Amies, Morton, Edward Molyneux, Norman Hartnell, Peter Russell, Bianca Mosca, and Worth of London, for which Elspeth Champcommunal was now head designer. The Board of Trade granted the members of the group various exemptions so they could obtain scarce material to complete couture orders for export to North and South America. Madge worked on some of these export collections, which earned funds for the wartime economy, helped advertise English materials, built prestige for these firms, and kept them going when the luxuries they produced could not be sold in England.

In November 1941, in a letter that took four months to reach Melbourne, she wrote to Gerald: "Uncertainty with regard to all matters, especially one's job, is a characteristic of all our lives at the moment. My job, thank goodness, continues & I love it for it takes one's mind off the horrors of the war & keeps one occupied all day . . . In the meantime the problem of where & how to live is acute." She was able to sell her country house and in 1942 bought another, in the village of Shoreham, in Kent, on a train line close enough to the city to commute to work. She was proud of this place, a Queen Anne house on the Darent River that was associated with the artist Samuel Palmer in the early nineteenth century, and she cultivated its extensive garden to feed herself and others. Fay Blacket Gill was still in the picture, but Violet Powell, who also lived in

Shoreham during the war, remembered Madge complaining about Fay "in the abstract," saying, "The person I want to come and live with me won't do it." Powell also remembered Madge being aggrieved that Fay had a new silk pajama case with her initials embroidered on it, upset both that Fay had made a black market purchase and that she herself could not have these things.

In June 1944, German V-1 bombs began hitting London, flying over Kent on the way, and the skies over Shoreham were nicknamed Bomb Alley. Also known as fly bombs, buzz bombs, and doodle-bugs, these forerunners of the cruise missile were frightening especially because of the way they cut out unexpectedly and went into a steep dive. Madge's house was "very badly blitzed" that summer. "The fly-bomb fell only 50 yards away," she wrote to Gerald,

> just the other side of the garden wall. That and the river end of the garden are a complete shambles and all the garden side of the house badly damaged and the top floor practically non-existent, roof blown off, walls only skeletons, ceilings down, no windows left, doors blown off etc. All the (to us) all too-familiar damage. Luckily I was not there when it happened and no one was killed so the damage is only material, but what damage! . . . You know (or more probably you don't know) what a maniac I am for order and cleanliness . . . One could do absolutely nothing amid the piles of plaster, glass, torn curtains, smashed china etc. etc. and I had to abandon it and stay in London. A friend who was away lent me a flat and there I had to stay, alone, during the raids, until another friend arranged for me to be a p.g. [paying guest] in Surrey, where the raids were less severe tho' still noisy sometimes. I finally arranged for removal men to come and take away all removable objects and all curtains and carpets to be cleaned and stored, and I rescued some of my personal belongings . . . The chaos of my daily life is unbelievable. You see I have clothes in about five different places, (most in my office) have had all my private papers mislaid and a lot lost, so I have no references or addresses, my stores [of food] are still in the bombed house (or I hope they are for they are beyond price in this rationed country

and the result of two years of hard work, growing, pickling, bottling, making preserves etc. etc.) my personal odds and ends are god knows where, one trunk is left at an hotel, another at a friend's and so forth. Every item of clothing I had in the house had to go to the cleaners . . . All my work in the garden has gone, the wall blown all over the place, and glass fragments everywhere. The greenhouse and frames ruined, and my crop of tomatoes was really beautiful, all ruined, hundreds of pounds of them—also the melon and eggplant which I was growing for the first time. All the spring planting was ruined, not a leaf left of the bush fruits, apple trees blown away and those left with their apples blown off them. Total disaster.

Through it all, Madge took only two days off from the office, but eventually she became so exhausted that she took sick leave from Bourne and Hollingsworth and went to recuperate in Elspeth Champcommunal's childhood home on the Isle of Wight. In London, as in Paris, Champco lived with Jane Heap, whose life after she stopped editing *The Little Review* was devoted to teaching Gurdjieff's brand of self-improvement. Champcommunal and Heap had been on vacation with Janet Flanner and Solita Solano in the Bavarian Alps when the war broke out. During the Blitz, they left London for the Isle of Wight, then moved to a farm outside London. But in the autumn of 1944, Madge and Champco were lodging together in a club in Grosvenor Street, so as to be able to reach their jobs. Janet Flanner saw them when she returned to Europe for *The New Yorker* that November. Madge, she reported to Solano, had procured her a pair of warm boots from Bourne and Hollingsworth, and Champco's fashion sensibility had survived the Blitz: No German "planes in hundreds," nor the "pyrotechnics" of anti-aircraft fire, nor "incendiaries like Catherine wheels" had dimmed her ardor for clothes. But the scene was grim. In Jane Heap's words, "The streets were lined with broken glass, like snow swept up in piles . . . It is as if something came out of hell and blasted and blighted. One wonders where things go—an apartment building is hit and lies on the ground like a small mound of bricks and kindling, no furniture, no bedding, no carpets, nothing, nothing."

The continued bombing meant that business at Bourne and Hollingsworth was slow. All of Madge's money—sums that would have been "enough to live in luxury in a pre-war world"—was going toward "living in hotels, friends' houses and incidental expenses, all in the utmost discomfort and confusion." The end of the war seemed to be in sight, but thousands of people were in the same position. When friends offered her a room in an unfurnished flat on the top floor of an empty building, she did not relish it. "I never *was* brave," she wrote to Gerald, "but four years of raids have considerably diminished my physical resources." She lived for the last few months of the war in that room, "with rockets and sirens around." She did not find a home of her own until December 1945.

As manufacturers began thinking about how to reestablish themselves in a postwar world, Madge started consulting for the charismatic owner of the West Cumberland Silk Mills, Miki Sekers, a Hungarian-Jewish immigrant who had made material for parachutes during the war and wanted to move back into fashion. Madge was his entrée, and he went on to commission designs from artists and was one of the first English manufacturers to produce artificial fabrics for high fashion. Madge had kept up with innovations in textiles in the United States, through a friend who had been the London correspondent for *Women's Wear Daily*, and she decided that it would be valuable to the English fashion industry if she could learn about the new uses of synthetics and about ready-to-wear manufacturing and marketing in the United States. The Board of Trade agreed, seeing fashion as a way to help pay the country's immense war debts, and arranged for her get the permits to take enough money out of the country to make a long stay in the United States possible. (Such sums were strictly limited then and for many years after the war.) Bourne and Hollingsworth gave her three months' leave and underwrote her trip, a generous gesture, since her research would be shared with its competitors. The Board of Trade granted her extra clothing coupons as well, "so that I could appear well dressed and not shabby," and Digby Morton made her a "splendid black suit, most beautifully cut, and suitable for most occasions."

She left "the greyness of London" with one small suitcase, traveling on an American Clipper Flying Boat that stopped first in Ireland, Morocco, and the Gambia, then took off across the ocean, landing in Trinidad (where she drank her first orange juice in four years), flying on to Puerto Rico, and arriving in New York on the day Roosevelt died, April 12, 1945. She spent four months in the United States, staying in New York with Ted McKnight Kauffer and Marion Dorn and often seeing Mercedes de Acosta, then traveled to Boston, Chicago, St. Louis, Dallas, and Los Angeles to interview manufacturers. In California, she was excited by the sports clothes and leather clothing, completely new to her, and by the use of traditional Latin American motifs. She was happy to see Aldous and Maria Huxley, who were now living on a forty-acre ranch in the Mojave Desert. She was their first postwar visitor from England and seemed to them "pretty and gay but so serious," with "none of that malicious wit and brilliance" of their milieu of the twenties and thirties. ("She thought Aldous was wonderfully 'transformed,'" wrote Maria, his sight was so much improved.) Hedda Hopper devoted a large part of a column—otherwise full of news about Clark Gable, James Cagney, and Jane Russell—to Madge: "Talked with Madge Garland, who's in this country making a fashion survey for a big British firm . . . The plane trip over cost $800. She traveled 10,000 miles getting here. She was pretty proud of her traveling suit and topcoat, both made from rugs."

Back in London, Madge submitted her report to the Board of Trade ("where I expect it lingers to this very day," she wrote thirty years later) and became an even more vocal advocate for English fashion. In a culture where quality was reserved historically for men's clothing and where feminine chic was elusive, and at a time, given the devastation of the country, when anything to do with fashionable dress was even more easily dismissed as trivial, Madge insisted on the importance of women being well dressed and on the possibility that good clothes did not have to be the province of an elite. As postwar governments across Europe pushed exports to help pay off debts, many found ways to support new designers, provided that their fashions emphasized their country's materials. Madge touted English textiles and argued for improved standards of design. One newspaper article on her return from New York, headlined "Dress Reformer," described her as a "colorful, impudently gay, yet shrewdly practical, working woman," who "says, and

proves, that being well-dressed has nothing to do with being rich"
and who is trying to get "pretty, well-designed, low-priced clothes
made here to equal those in America." The parallels between her
work and Elizabeth David's postwar education of the English palate
are unmistakable.

And the demand was real. Life in England—"this poverty stricken
island"—was difficult, dark, and meager long after the war was over.
One waited hours in queues to buy meat (John Strachey, Minister
of Food from 1946 to 1950, was responsible for postwar rationing);
returning factories to civilian manufacture was a slow process; there
were strict limits on the movement of money and goods in and out
of Britain; the fuel shortage was acute. At Bourne and Hollingsworth, consumer need was so intense after years of wartime deprivation, and goods still so scarce, that Madge's most difficult task
was to keep merchandise on the shelves. Like many civilians and
everyone she knew, she was constantly ill from malnutrition and
stress. Her childhood back problems also returned. "I have a good
job here & work for people I like & respect," she wrote to Gerald.
It "is really too big & exacting for my strength, still I have made it
myself & it has much to recommend it." The winter of 1947 was
one of the coldest on record, and she kept warm at home by shutting up most of her flat, but her office at Bourne and Hollingsworth
was "*icy* . . . With the temperature well below freezing this is no fun
at all. Then the store is in partial darkness & absolutely deserted,
the factory closed etc. a most gloomy outlook—we are all desper-
ately depressed—& the blackout at night doesn't add to the ease of
getting about in frozen streets with treacherous mounds of frozen
snow everywhere."

When the postwar trade pacts were signed, in March 1946, she
traveled to France to look at materials and styles that might be copied. The trip was "epic: fourteen hours from London to Paris—about
as long as it took by packet in Victorian days. Hours of standing in
queues, masses of papers and visas and permits and customs." In
Paris there were "no buses or taxis on the streets and only a handful
of private cars. No one talks of anything but food and the situation
is awful. The rations just are not sufficient, those who cannot afford
the Black Market starve: it is quite horrible." To get a seat on a train
south she had to offer a bribe of 500 francs. She did business at the

Syndicat de la Soie in Lyons, then went on to Cannes, where she was reunited with Evelyn Wyld, who had spent part of the war in an internment camp in the Vaucluse. Madge was her first visitor after the war, as she had been to the Huxleys, bringing news from England, butter from the black market in Paris, and coffee.

In spite of it all, she wrote to Gerald, "the clothes in Paris are heaven, it is unbelievable that they should have so much taste and flair even in such conditions—a real pleasure for me to see good hats." She bought one at Legroux, which she intended to use as a model. The artificial silks she saw in Lyons "you would have to see and above all to feel . . . to believe—and the maisons de couture say they handle and make up better than real silk. All very interesting." Prices were still too high to do business with France during that trip, but she was back at the end of the year to supervise hat buying when Bourne and Hollingsworth was granted its first import license. In the autumn of 1947 the Council of Industrial Design, founded in the last years of the war to improve design across British industry, appointed her "to set up a prototype design center" covering all types of clothing, fabrics, and accessories. As part of this job, she returned to Paris with £1,000 of government money to acquire the accessories of the New Look for British manufacturers to copy, buying gloves, shoes, and underwear to accompany the fitted jacket and long, full skirt that Christian Dior had introduced to such acclaim (and censure) that year. On this trip she also found Marie Laurencin and other friends; in a gallery on the rue des Saint-Pères, she found Laurencin's still life *The Lemon and the Rose* and was able to buy it. Several times in the past fifteen years she had had, as she wrote to Gerald, "to remake my career from top to bottom (or rather the other way up)." Now she was "in the thick of the export drive . . . only a temporary civil servant & have joined the Council just to put on this demonstration—& after I don't know what I shall do."

PROFESSOR OF FASHION

Look at her again: It is London in the early 1950s. She is teetering down the street on enormously high Ferragamo shoes ("as soft and easy to wear as a pair of gloves," she said), draped in a broad-shouldered coat of skunk pelts, drenched in Worth's Je Reviens. Her students at the Fashion School of the Royal College of Art peer out the window, watching her. "Madge is coming!" they cry. They laugh but are also afraid. She is in her early fifties, but owning up to her forties. They are young queer men with a feeling for fabric and drape; talented, driven young women; and good girls from good families who are there to raise the tone of the school, many of whom will end up casualties of what Madge called its "high marriage wastage." Madge is coming—and she seems to have appeared from nowhere. Has a taxi dropped her around the corner? Is she taking a bus but not using the stop closest to the College, so as not to be seen descending from something so plebeian? She is preceded by these questions; by this mixture of respect, anxiety, and scorn; by her perfume; and by the vision of her outrageous coat and precarious-looking, cantilever-heeled shoes. She is "London's most unusual professor." She is "The First Professor of Fashion."

When she left Bourne and Hollingsworth, she turned her experience in the United States into a way to earn a living, working as a freelance representative of five English textile and fashion firms, promoting their products in the United States and reporting to them on the American market. She continued to appear on television, to give radio talks, and to lecture on textiles and fashion to industry associations all over England and Ireland. She imagined that she would do this kind of freelance work for the rest of her career. But in June 1948 she began work at the Royal College of Art. During the war, the College, founded in 1837, had evacuated to Cumberland and scaled back. Now, led by Robin Darwin, a painter and descendant of the scientist, its mission was to produce graduates in design who could revitalize devastated peacetime manufacturing. When Darwin realized that the College did not train students for the fashion industry, he consulted Victor Stiebel; Audrey Withers, who had become the editor of British *Vogue* during the war; and Allan Walton, who had his own textile business and had directed the Glasgow School of Art, and whom Darwin had just appointed head of the Royal College's textiles program. Walton recommended Madge and persuaded her to take the job. Darwin made her Professor of Fashion and Principal of the School of Fashion, which she then created. She took one more long trip to New York, where she did her usual consulting, but also studied the curriculum at the Parsons School of Design. Walton's sudden death in September 1948 was a blow that almost deterred her, she said later, but she did not give up the chance for this new sort of legitimacy.

What did it mean to profess fashion? For Madge, it meant, first, being what she had been denied: a woman associated with higher education. In 1949 the Royal College of Art gave her an honorary degree. Proud, self-deprecating, and still angry, she wrote to her brother:

> My dear Gerald, I enclose a cutting from yesterday's Times which may interest you and which will I hope, give you pleasure. I must say I do wish Mama had lived until now. I know she would have been so pleased. In 1917 I gave up the prospect of a degree at Cambridge in order to accompany Father to Australia because Mother could not go while you were at the front. It was the most bitter renunciation of my life. I think Mama knew this and now, 30 years later, I have got what I wanted. It isn't really of importance but I must admit it is pleasant. I think you get English Vogue regularly so I am not sending you the June copy which has two photographs

of me by Cecil Beaton and a blurb about my work as I expect
you have already seen them. So enough of my egotism.

It isn't really of importance: The Fashion School was "not only the
first thing of its kind" in England, noted *Harper's Bazaar* in a profile
of Madge, but also "the first official recognition of fashion as a serious industry." Designing the school, Madge Garland was creating a
program that would produce a crop of native English designers. She
did not teach courses, but she invented the curriculum, critiqued
students' work, ran the school, promoted it, and sat on the College's governing board. Her knowledge, contacts in the industry,
and style made it a success. The only competition was a program at
Central Saint Martins College of Art and Design, started by Muriel
Pemberton at around the same time, which focused more on art
training than on training for the fashion industry.

Like many passionate autodidacts, Madge had strong views
about education. The College was under government supervision,
and she began her tenure by fighting with "the civil servant stuffed
shirts": the Ministry of Education and Sir Stafford Cripps (former
president of the Board of Trade, then minister for economic affairs
and chancellor of the exchequer). The dispute took place because
she insisted on hiring professionals in the field, not teachers of art:
Digby Morton's tailor gave the instruction in tailoring; a cutter from
Berketex taught designing wholesale clothing to scale; Victor Stiebel's
dressmaker trained students in pattern making; a representative
from Wolsey taught knitwear. She also hired a number of refugees,
Jews who had worked in textiles or design in Europe and were starting over in England. "I wanted people from the trade," she said, but
"trade was a dreadful word to use in connection with art." It was, in
many ways, a revolution in her own thinking. But it was also another
version of the sort of mixing she had worked on early in her career.
"I tried so hard to marry art and industry," she said. The curriculum
included "costume history, cutting, designing with a price limit, millinery, accessories, embroidery," toile making, children's clothing,
and lingerie. Madge studied fashion magazines with the students.
She arranged for them to sit in on editorial conferences at magazines
and in business meetings at manufacturers. She required them to

work for a designer, in a textile mill, or in a factory for at least two months. To help place graduates, she appointed a committee that included representatives of the top wholesalers. The year-end student fashion show, first presented in July 1949, became an annual tradition—in high style and including royal guests.

Along with these intensely practical requirements and goals, she wanted the students—who had grown up during wartime and postwar austerity and had often completed degrees at their local art colleges, but hardly knew London, let alone the rest of the world—to learn things that may not have been teachable. She wanted to create for them something like what she had experienced at school in Paris, to impart not only "facts and technique," noted *Harper's Bazaar*, "but . . . that rare, undefinable but essential quality—sophistication." She arranged for them to see plays as well as fashion shows, clothing factories, milliners' workrooms, and beauty demonstrations. She invited them to her home, "to train you how to behave in society," noted Joanne Brogden, an early graduate who went on to direct the school from 1971 to 1989, and who found these occasions "frightening . . . awful." Every year, she took two students with her to the Paris collections. (She would see Esther Murphy on these trips.) "She was an entrée to anywhere you wanted to go," recalls the couturier David Sassoon, who matriculated in 1955. David Watts, a student of the early 1950s who designed for Jaeger for forty years, concurred:

> You had visits to the collections in London—in the ready-to-wear, such as it was in those days, like Dorville, Susan Small, Frederick Stark, Brenner Sports, Matita, and to a few couture houses, like Hardy Amies, Digby Morton, Victor Stiebel. And they all did such great clothes in those days. In the coronation year we went to Victor Stiebel's collection. Of course all the peeresses who had to go to the coronation had to have gorgeous gowns underneath their robes, and there were about twenty of those at the collection, like you couldn't imagine these days . . . We learned about quality, which just didn't exist at the time.

Madge's own look and taste were also a lesson. "She wears clothes with an easy authority," British *Vogue* noted, in the article to which she referred Gerald, and "educates with intelligent wit." In one of Beaton's photographs for this feature she wears a wasp-waisted "late-day suit of blue-black brocade" by Bianca Mosca, a version of the New Look. There are multiple strands of pearls around her neck and wrist. A straw cartwheel hat by the milliner Rose Vernier frames her face, and there is an eruption of blond curls on her forehead. With her hands in her pockets, her shoulders thrown back, her gaze calmly meeting the camera, she is the image of cool, intelligent, feminine postwar style. Set against the intact, ornate moldings and marble mantel of Londonderry House, the image is also one of personal and architectural endurance in the face of the ravaged reality of London in the 1940s. Another profile from this period described her "original approach to fashion" as the "easy elegance of the woman who seizes instantly upon each new trend and stamps it with her individuality." When she had students to her house for dinner, David Watts recalled, she would appear in "a very glamorous house coat"—evening wear, not something in which to do housework— "with an enormous black satin skirt and a fitted blouse . . . buttoned all the way up the front with long tight sleeves." "She was what fashion was about," said David Sassoon. "There was a woman actually walking around in couture clothes . . . That to me was heaven." It was "the way she was, not just her clothes," said the designer Gina Fratini; she "epitomized everything to do with fashion, with style . . . and I sat in awe."

Because of Madge's predilections, the Fashion School was referred to as "Paris, Kensington." It was set apart from the main College buildings—in a town house in Ennismore Gardens, behind the Brompton Oratory, on a square where lamplighters still illuminated gas streetlamps every evening—and was separate in other ways, too. "We were a very precious little society of our own," recalled the designer Anne Tyrrell. The building contributed to this atmosphere: Students worked in a huge L-shaped space, a Victorian reception room that had two fireplaces and extended the length of the building. This room was also the setting for parties to which Madge "would invite all sorts of amazing people." And then there was her own setting: "Madge's office I can never forget," said Watts. "I've never seen anything like it. It was like a drawing room; it wasn't like an office at all." The walls were pale pink and covered

with paintings and sketches, including the work of Marie Laurencin. The curtains were thick hangings of pink glazed chintz, lined
and interlined. The cornices were ornate, and the space was lit theatrically. Her desk was placed on the bias. She sat there in front of a
bay window, often playing with fabric samples from Miki Sekers's
factory with her "immaculate scarlet varnished nails—this fair, well-
coiffed person with astonishing blue eyes," said Joanne Brogden.
"If you came from the suburbs of London," this mise-en-scène was
"frightfully impressive and grand . . . I really was so bowled over."

She had continued to consult about experimental textiles for
Sekers (rayon) and Imperial Chemical Industries (their polyester
was called Terylene), helping to develop these fabrics for women's
clothing and interior decoration. On breaks between terms, she
traveled all over Europe to promote Sekers's and ICI's materials and
to learn about innovations in French textiles. She also represented
a French textile company in England. She traveled regularly to the
North of England and at one visit to the mills "addressed 600 locals," showing them the clothes that had been made from their materials and exported. Writing later about the history of these fabrics,
she noted bluntly, "The early attempts to create synthetic materials
date back to the last century, but for a long time 'art silk' was as re-
pellant as its title was vulgar; it was harsh to handle, had a sleazy
surface, and creased abominably . . . the rude forebear of the delicious materials which have transformed women's clothes today."
Edward Molyneux and Bianca Mosca in London, and Dior, Pierre
Cardin, Givenchy, Pierre Balmain, Jacques Fath, Jean Patou, and
Balenciaga in Paris were among the houses supplied by Sekers. Some
of these fabrics were "staggeringly beautiful," notes Brogden, and
favored students were allowed to use samples. There was a sense in
which it "was never a favor, because no one really knew how to use
them, but they were exciting because you didn't see them anywhere
else except at couture houses."

A newspaper article from the period noted "the rigorous self-
discipline which Mrs. Garland has displayed in allowing her
students freedom of experiment," which produced "twenty personalities, instead of twenty reflections of Mrs. Garland's personal,

Professor Garland and Lady Ashton, photographed by Paul Tanqueray (MGP, courtesy Estate of Paul
Tanqueray / NPG)

powerful and professional taste." Still, if some students found her inspiring and supportive, to others she was terrifying and autocratic. The school was run like a couture house, and dicta about hair and clothes and makeup were part of the program. Madge's secretary told the students when to arrive and leave and had them sign in to a book opposite her desk and door. Joanne Brogden remembered "walking in one day with what I thought was this wonderful new color of lipstick on, and Madge came wafting down the carpeted stone stairway: 'My child, go and take that terrible lipstick off.'" The place had the air of a finishing school, said one student from the early years:

> We were "her girls," and there was the feeling that it was important how you conducted yourself. Sometimes she would swan into a studio and say, "My dear child, your hair is perfectly atrocious." Or, "What a lovely color your legs are. Where did you get those tights?" She was very critical of how we looked. I remember showing up in trousers one day and a third-year girl said to me, "If Madge sees you she'll be furious," so I had to go home and change. I was twenty-two at the time; I'd done five years of art school already and worn trousers practically all the time. We were terribly fifties *Vogue*.

The Professor of Fashion was tough, she was a snob, and she was sometimes intimidated by her students. Some were clear favorites, which demoralized those who were not. "I definitely would say that I was one," said Sassoon, "and that's why people laughed at me. Because she was terribly cruel to some people. She came into the room one day, and I said, 'Oh Mrs. Garland, what a wonderful hat!' And she said, 'Do you like it? It's by Aage Thaarup.' And when she'd gone out of the room the others said, 'You jammy bugger, fancy telling her she looked good in that hat.' . . . A lot of students were frightened of her and therefore didn't like her." "She was really very mean to some people that she took against," said Brogden, and was disconnected from the reality of students' lives—she "thought that she wouldn't intimidate." It was that "she thought she had to play that grande dame part," said Sassoon. "When I left college she was much nicer and warmer."

However they felt, the effect of this visionary program was that by the end of the 1950s, and with shifts in social life and improvements in the economy (rationing was in effect until 1956), the College had become recognized for its training in fashion, and companies began to conceive of "employing a designer, and a young designer," as Tyrrell put it. As a result, men and women could now plan careers in fashion, and many of those who had studied under Madge began to make their mark. The excitement of the London fashion scene in the late twentieth and early twenty-first centuries is in part a result of her work. By the end of the 1950s, however, she had resigned from the College, saying that she was ready to move on to other projects. "In 1948, when I took over," Robin Darwin wrote to her, "I believed that a School of Fashion Design here might eventually make a real contribution to industry, but I knew it would be a tremendously uphill task, and if Allan had not told me all about you and I had not met you . . . I very much doubt whether we would have gone ahead with the project at the time. In the event, your success and that of the School far outstripped my most optimistic dreams and everything has been due to your vision and energy." This was his gracious goodbye, on paper. But they had argued, or she had, and she was privately unhappy to leave. Certainly she was combative, or not afraid to stand up for herself. She also seems to have taken offense at decisions he made, some seemingly minor, to do with protocol concerning the Queen Mother's visit to the Royal College. He may have pressured her to go, wanting to appoint Janey Ironside—formerly Madge's assistant, with whom he was having an affair—in her place. As soon as Madge resigned, he made Ironside the new principal of the school.

Still, for many years, Madge was invited back to speak to students. "She'd arrive staggeringly dressed, usually in black, and was quite riveting about her experiences, the people she knew, her life on *Vogue* and at College," said Tyrrell, who remembered her as "immaculately turned out, with wonderful hair and pearls, looking stunning, sitting on a large settee, the students crowded around." Her influence also continued, as many of the designers hired to teach in the program were her ex-students. She made a point of buying from their collections and directing friends to their work; Ernestine Carter, the most powerful fashion journalist in England during those years and a close friend of Madge's, helped publicize their accomplishments. Carter was an American trained in art and design who had worked at the Museum of Modern Art as curator of architecture and industrial art in the 1930s. She was the fashion editor of *Harper's Bazaar* in London after the war, then a writer and editor at the *Times* in the 1950s and '60s. Like Madge, she was an intelligent advocate for fashion who was attuned to its connections to other forms of design.

The School of Fashion was a novelty. It was dedicated to the idea of fashion's significance. And it was invented in an atmosphere that verged on disdain. In 1951, in a lecture at the Royal Society of Arts, when the school was still viewed skeptically by many, Madge attempted to explain the school and to present a theory of English fashion. During the postwar years, a period broadly characterized by both aggressive investment in the future and nostalgic glances backward, she also continued to focus on the creation of the present. In this lecture, she linked the School of Fashion, the complex attention to the current moment that is the fashion designer's purview, and the grammar of modernism: "The proper function of this School," she said, "is not the dissection of motives, not the study of the past. Rather is it concerned with the translation of the immediate past into what Gertrude Stein called 'The continuous present.'" Citing Stein, she was gesturing to a more respected art form, but she was also invoking an artist whose radical rethinking of representation affirmed the quotidian.

Madge also argued that the endemic English "lack of professional expertize, brought about by our tendency to consider fashion as a frivolous subject suitable only for female amateurs, totally ignored the knowledge of the designer and the craftsmanship of the worker (let alone the number of people employed in the fashion industries)." Together, these issues did "much to account for the slow development of a national style." Part of the problem was that "most people think they know something about fashion," she said, and because they are *clothed*, are tricked into thinking they understand *clothes*. Yet eating an elaborate dinner does not confer the knowledge of a Brillat-Savarin . . . Habitual responsiveness of the eye in daily life is rare . . . Few of us have trained eyes . . . Few people can observe objectively the lines and colour of a new fashion . . . A trained *fashion* eye can translate: "She had on a loose sort of brown coat with rumpled sleeves" into "A snuff coloured three-quarter length facecloth coat with the folded sleeves from Balenciaga's last collection."

Establishing an atmosphere of intelligent analysis was crucial: "The fashion writer is usually only a reporter; an informed critic is rare," she wrote in 1962. "This creates a very different climate from the bracing cut and thrust of ordinary journalism and is largely responsible for the vast amount of nonsense written about fashion."

In Paris, in contrast, fashion was "based on a solid foundation of skilled workers, surrounded by artists, critics, and beautiful women, fed by a magnificent fabric industry, with a large home market and a big export trade, the inheritor of a long tradition of culture." She had dramatized this seriousness in another description of a visit to a *maison de couture* in *Britannia and Eve* in 1930:

> I went—not on my official business—to see a certain collection with a rich and frivolous friend. She was a client of the house, and therefore "had" a *vendeuse*, who consented to our entry, although it was still early in the season and the collection was being shown to buyers rather than private clients. We laughed and chatted and carelessly watched the mannequins drift by, but my friend saw nothing which took her fancy. As we got up to leave the *vendeuse* reproved us and said: "No wonder you have seen nothing you like: you were not attending properly. How can you expect to know whether or not our collection pleases you if you laugh and talk while it is being shown?"

The English ethos of antiprofessionalism influenced every aspect of the arts, Madge believed, and could result in work of real integrity.

"The English have always been inspired amateurs," she said, citing Beaton's approach to his craft: "Cecil would come [to the *Vogue* photography studio] . . . and he'd arrange everything too beautifully and then he'd say to the boy underneath the velvet cape, 'Well, now take it!' He never was a technician," and yet he was an example of "this English amateurism which has great quality." Some of the "decorations done by Vanessa [Bell] and Duncan [Grant]," however, lacked that quality. And of the products of Roger Fry's Omega Workshop, she said, it's not "enough to paint a kitchen table, you've got to make the kitchen table first, and they hadn't got the knowledge."

But her commitment was not only to a field of knowledge; it was to a way of being and feeling. Pleasure was as important as professionalism, and both were as powerful as her occasional dismissals of her work. Clothes were a place where emotion and expertise collided. Janey Ironside recalled "how sensually she adored colour and texture. She did all but eat her little [textile] samples" on her desk at the Royal College. "What woman does not know that comforting feeling of 'looking her best,' and the immense self-confidence imparted by a really becoming new gown?" Madge asked in *Britannia and Eve* in 1930. Much "serious" writing about the field—whether it described fashion as a reflection of social and political forces or as itself constituting them—was inadequate, she believed, because it did not account for the expressive experience of shopping for and wearing wonderful clothes: "There is a considerable body of work concerned with the history of fashion, and there is also what is known as the psychological approach to fashion," she said in her lecture to the Royal Society. "But no amount of reading Veblen and Flügel has managed to give me that appalling sense of guilt which can be conferred by a mere gusset, or even allowed me that spark of excitement derived from a glimpse of vice discreetly indulged in." She concluded her talk: "I can, with truth, say with Mme de Sévigné, 'Dieu, comme j'aime la mode.'"

If being the Professor of Fashion meant believing in and articulating, over and over, the importance of what she and others knew, and made, and wore, it also involved making visible as work what was seen as natural. "We admire a faultlessly dressed woman," she argued, "without realizing that this deceptive simplicity hides a world of calculation." Far from trafficking in clichés about women's duplicitous surfaces, Madge was describing the work and affective experience of fashionable dress—acknowledging that pleasurable self-transformation involves physical, psychic, and intellectual labor. "Apart from money, the two chief requirements are time and attention," she wrote in "How to Dress on Nothing a Year," in the midst of the Depression. "Good dressing takes up a lot of time, and it also requires much concentrated thought." In other words, style is thinking.

In the late 1920s, she had assisted a friend who was a *mannequin de ville*, a socially prominent woman who was given an expensive wardrobe by a *maison de couture* that gained prestige and publicity when she wore its clothes to every opening and ball. Madge described the routine as "really hard *work*" for her friend. Each season, this woman received between twenty and thirty new models and returned the previous collection (which was then sold at a discount by the designer). "The selection of the shoes, coats, bags, gloves, and underwear to match the bi-annual new wardrobe was a work of patience and application which required two or three weeks in Paris," she wrote, because everything was made to measure. Her friend had appointments all day long, going from one accessory firm to another, bringing the patterns "pinned to a sheet of paper, and standing for hours under the arc lights of the salons," so that everything "match[ed] perfectly" and "every line fitted." Her point in describing this little-known practice was that all of these preparations for dressing perfectly in "three outfits a day, every day"—a morning suit, something for five o'clock to eight o'clock, and evening wear—were "done in a professional way." Even being dressed "at no cost" by a couturier was not what it sounded like, she noted, since a *mannequin de ville* had to have a husband or lover with a ready reserve to pay for furs, jewels, and so on. In other words, at a time when it was neither ordinary nor politic to do so, Madge Garland wanted to make visible the time, effort, and money that went into creating public femininity—and to acknowledge the expert standard that was achieved. "In those days," she wrote in 1962, "the job of being a fashionable beauty was a full-time one and entailed the wearer's complete subjection to her appearance—everything else

came second . . . There are few women today who would be prepared to undertake such an existence even if they had the necessary
money."

As for herself: Being a woman who personified fashion at its
highest levels and who also labored in the industry was a kind of
oxymoron, since couture is all about the look of leisure. "To consume without producing has always been the prerogative of the
privileged," she observed in British *Vogue* in the 1960s; "to appear
to do so was until lately the ambition of the middle classes whose
women wished to ape the leisured lady." Writing in the mid-1970s
about the interplay of fashion, architecture, art, and the decorative
arts in the first part of the twentieth century, she called the simplicity of
twenties couture—the sweater suits and straight chemise dresses—
"as deceptive as the [decade's] plain furnishings. Chanel's little car-
digan suits were of the finest wool lined with the same rich silk as
the accompanying blouse, belts had jeweled buckles with matching
clips for neckline and the 'cloche' hat. It was a rich woman's whim
of pretending to dress like a poor one and demanded expensive perfection in every detail."

Even before the top-down model of fashion began to shift in the
1960s—when street fashion began to influence high fashion—
imitation and exchange had been fundamental to the industry, in
part because many of its practitioners were middle-class adepts who
aspired to, and made careers promulgating, the image and actuality
of haute couture, and the elite world on which it depended. Madge
was one of those outsiders who moved up in what is called "the fashionable world." She understood the industry's dependence on the
invisibility of labor and the visibility of leisure, but she was proud
that she had worked all her life. She believed that the period between
the wars had made possible "the best life for women," but acknowledged that her freedom, by which she meant her ability to have a
career, had depended on the availability of cheap domestic labor by
working-class and immigrant women. As a fashion icon, she modeled aspects of femininity while distancing herself from others (domestic labor). And if her talents and lifetime of work made her an
authority in the field, her position was also emblematic of many
women's relationships to femininity, in which distinctions between
production and consumption, labor and leisure, often blur.

Madge Garland dressed correctly, beautifully, professionally, and imaginatively for her own pleasure and others', to set an example, and to achieve a certain social mobility. She did so balancing a deep ambivalence about the way she spent her life. In the process, she became one of the most interesting writers on fashion in the twentieth century. The trained eye, and how she trained it, and how she trained herself to be seen—none of these can be disentangled from the eternal English questions of class and status, and from the ways these impinge on desire. Which is to say that professing fashion for Madge was also about the habit, the advantages, and the costs of discretion.

NOTES ON DISCRETION

Madge Garland had a mesmerizing voice, "a vibrant voice, which woke everybody up and held your attention. Her whole personality was very flamboyant." She camped it up, vocally, while maintaining her carefully wrought appearance of propriety. She leaned into her words: flirtatious and commanding, censorious and self-mocking, confiding and bemused, impatient and languid. When asked how she kept a circular planting of ivy in her garden so perfectly round and neat, she replied, "*Darling.* I get down every morning and *trim* it with a nail scissors and *tuck* it with hairpins." Comparing sexual reproduction to the form of cultural production she knew best, she opined, more than once, "I like my children ready-made, and my clothes made to order." She referred to Ewart Garland's second wife as her "wife-in-law." (They had met and liked each other.) Athletic activity, especially anything to do with throwing or hitting a ball, was idiocy she wanted to be spared: "Sport is absolutely—ça n'existe pas. Ça n'existe pas," she said. "If you want the damn ball, keep it, don't throw it away."

Soignée and proper in her continental Britishness, she also used colloquial Americanisms to achieve the campy thrill of contrast. "She used to say—it came from a film—'You can say that again, honey bun!'" recalled Patrick Woodcock, "and it was so strange coming from this frail little lady, who was a different kind of creature." David Sassoon's family connection to Siegfried Sassoon impressed her, and when he entered the Fashion School she asked him if he had read the poet's *Memoirs of a Fox-Hunting Man*. "My child, you *should*," she said, when he told her he had not. "She always said 'my child,'" he recalled. "And if she looked at a sketch she didn't

like, she'd say, 'It's so déjà-vu.'" When Sassoon was in a college production of *Uncle Vanya*, he powdered his hair, then came in the next
day still wearing it. Madge sent for him and said, "'Now, my child,
you're not in a circus.' And I said, 'Oh Mrs. Garland I can't wash my
hair every night.' And she said, 'Why *not? Stars do!*' She was divine."

She also depended, for dramatic and comic effect, on expansive
descriptions of her own inadequacies, including her encounters
with voluminous female form. When she talked about her travels
in Greece between the wars, she described herself becoming "hysterical" when confronted by an infestation of fleas and sleeping buried under every article of her clothing—coat, dress, underclothes,
and hat all piled on the bed—in an attempt to keep the bugs away.
She told a story about a postwar trip to Constantinople, where she
attended a conference on Byzantine art and where, in the spirit of
adventure and economy, she rented a room from mutual friends of
the writer Theodora Benson, rather than staying with the rest of the
group at a hotel: "It was interesting alright," she said. She woke in
the small hours to see

> an army, a small army of termites, coming up the bed, dear . . .
> I had leaped out of the bed and screamed of course, and my
> hostess came out of her room, and I was sobbing—I always
> sobbed—and I said *"Awful* things in my *bed!"* And she said—
> she was half-naked and very fat, and she put her arms round
> me and pressed me to her pneumatic bosom—very *large*
> pneumatic bosom—and said *"Come* and sleep with *me."* Oh,
> I cried and I cried, louder and louder! I spent the night sitting
> up on a hard chair in the middle of the room.

This, too, is camp, a way of creating a scene: the highly competent
professional woman making a spectacle of her helplessness—and of
the supposed awfulness of another woman's body.

Insisting that fashion had been nothing more than a way to
make a living was another sort of performance. As was her sense of
humor about her field: Despite her commitment to its rules, despite
her belief in her expertise, despite the fact that it was her armor,
livelihood, and pleasure, Madge wanted to send it up. Writing in
Britannia and Eve about the autumn 1933 Paris showings, she noted,

"The atmosphere is suffocating and there is an indescribable babel of noise; dozens of pretty and well-groomed young women are running about, apparently without any reason, and occasionally over the hubbub comes an agonized scream for Marguerite, Hélène or Renée. One never knows whether the cry, obviously that of a person in great distress—and, if you are new to the game, you think of someone about to be murdered—is answered." In the 1940s, when she made regular appearances on BBC radio and television, she proposed a number of program ideas that were meant to be instructive but that she seemed to enjoy most for their comedy, including one about what it was like to watch Parisian women wearing the New Look, with its volumes of fabric, trying to get into the tiny cars of the postwar period. This distancing irony was another way that her practice was allied to modernist aesthetics.

But along with a flamboyant wit she had a profound commitment to discretion, which made her life a complicated dance of concealment and display, honesty and dissimulation. Her professional and personal being was made of her intimacy with and enjoyment of women, and she spoke fearlessly about her appreciation of female beauty. *Four Thousand Years of Beautiful Women* is the delicious, immodest subtitle of her first book, *The Changing Face of Beauty*. Describing her postwar travels in the United States, she would say that the girls in Texas were the most gorgeous she had ever seen. When Hugo Vickers interviewed her for his biography of Cecil Beaton, when she was in her eighties, this enthusiasm, "the way she spoke of other women—beauty in women and so on"—made him wonder whether she "might be a lesbian." Having met a frail woman covered in a shawl, about halfway through their conversation he saw her toughness and passion emerge.

Yet Madge said little directly about what it meant to work in fashion and to love her own sex. Her silence is no surprise: "She lived very much in society," said Francis King, and had to be accepted in that milieu, "so she wouldn't want to appear to be a rebel, which she was." This caution was especially necessary for someone who had no money of her own and no family or social position to shelter her from opprobrium. Some complied with her reticence, hoping to protect her. When Anne Olivier Bell was editing Virginia Woolf's diaries for publication, she deleted the phrase "Going to bed with Garland" from a sentence of Woolf's about Dorothy Todd, feeling that "revelations or insinuations about her private life could have been both distressing and damaging at that time." King, a generation younger than Madge, said, "People of that era, they learned discretion. You didn't talk freely about your private life because it was often dangerous to do so." Such constraint may seem obvious: Being perceived as a lesbian had damaged her career more than once and was incompatible with the higher echelons of social life, on which the fashion industry depends, so of course it was necessary for Madge to conceal her private life. But discretion depends on the distinction between public and private, a distinction in the name of which much violence is still done. It is a particularly white male vehicle for veiling power: where one's money comes from, how one happens to have the job one has. Its successful practice requires being in a position to say, *You can't get to me.*

Discretion is composed of power and of fear. It is power that masquerades as politeness—what "we" don't discuss, what "we" don't believe it suitable to call attention to, what "we" call private: money, and everything to do with the messy thing that is the body. Which means that not everyone can benefit from it. When one is Australian, a woman, desiring other women, and middle-class, and one uses discretion to avert danger or not cause offense, then the tactic is invariably a double bind: an advertisement of vulnerability, an invitation to be "exposed" or "disgraced," a shabby agreement that will never be honored, a shield that fails at the least insinuation. Less: at the threat of an insinuation. Discretion has been the only way to protect oneself when exposure would lead to social and professional disaster. But since it never delivers what it promises, since it is so easily turned against one, it would seem to take a wild optimism or presumption to depend on it. In fact, the idea of presumptuousness is often invoked against the person who is in jeopardy when discretion fails: *What made her think she could keep this from view?*

But discretion is not simply the opposite of the artful, arch, apparently public, fearless stance of camp. Madge was an iconoclast and perfectly correct, at once; she wanted to be seen for who she was and she feared it. Describing the way women like herself and Madge lived, Sybille Bedford said, "It was in one way very open and in one way very discreet." Both camp and discretion, like fashion, require a strict discipline, rigorous standards imposed on oneself and others. Both stances are a performance, extravagant and invented. Camp is clearly understood as such, but the proprieties of discretion involve a show, too. Both involve the truth of artful lying, whether of exaggeration or omission—those "gestures full of duplicity" observed by Susan Sontag in her essay "Notes on 'Camp.'" This duplicity affects all concerned: actor and audience. Of course, social life demands practiced prevarication. To be outrageous and to tell a story well you must be convinced that you are fascinating; you must also be selective, must monitor what you show and what you hide. To wit, the fact that Madge was highly eccentric but did much to avoid the appearance of oddness. That she gave "the impression of being extremely fragile," as one observer put it, and yet it was also clear that "underneath it all she was as tough as old boots." "She was so typical of her period: terribly thin, frail," said Patrick Woodcock, "but in fact that was a double act, wasn't it?" Her thinness was itself double—both natural and produced, a legacy of her illnesses and a way to control her body. To one friend, Madge used to say, "I wish I could take a pill, darling," instead of eating. Sybille Bedford thought she would have been considered anorexic in another age; she recorded a dinner in the 1950s chez Esther at which Madge "ate next to nothing." Sybille felt that she "would have preferred one important or chic person to us and all the food."

The authoritative verbal and visual pronouncements of the fashion world are a pivot point between flamboyance and discretion. In fashion, the person who feels or is seen to be aberrant may be perfect, even for a moment, with the help of a perfect carapace. Both camp and discretion, in other words, partake of certain paradoxes of visibility. Madge's flamboyance was inseparable from her discretion, and vice versa. If discretion is a way to remain invisible and inoffensive, its perfect, faithful execution can also produce the effect of camp. If camp is a way of making a scene so as to be seen, it is also a way to remain invisible, a kind of cloak of visibility. Madge's exaggerated horror at the proximity of another woman's undeniably female body is a form of camp flamboyance that is also a gesture of discretion: a way of using the extravagance of the former to repudiate her own desires.

Discussing hairstyles (MCP)

Camp has been seen as a male preserve, yet one of the untold stories of style has to do with how gay men and women have copied and inspired each other—learned poise and polish and how to pose. How he crosses his legs, how she smokes her cigarette, the way he holds his drink, how she speaks, what he likes to look at, even the contours of one's body—*I can do that.* Of the willowy physique shared by many of their friends in the 1920s, Mercedes de Acosta wrote, "It was the vogue for young men of artistic pursuits to appear to be falling apart. And this resemblance to a swaying reed or willow tree gave an impression of fragility, although actually many of them proved unusually durable." Many of those on whom Madge modeled herself and many of those she inspired were gay men. "It was the era when many young women wanted to look masculine and many young men wanted to look feminine," wrote de Acosta. Exchanging verbal and visual styles with gay men was also a way for Madge to distinguish herself from women whose butch gender style was, from the 1920s on, increasingly understood to signify their sexual choices—and for her to be attractive to just those women.

To Patrick Woodcock, Madge "represented . . . a particular kind of forceful lesbian who had a terrific influence on other people but was a rather wispy figure." To Madge, Allan Walton "had this flair, this eye . . . I always wanted everything that Allan had. In fact, if I have any taste at all you could say it was formed by Allan." When she first visited this young artist's studio in the 1920s, preparing it to be photographed for *Vogue*, she was "staggered." She remembered the space, on Cheyne Walk in Chelsea, as "something completely new": filled with things that were "quite simple. Some early Staffordshire, a marble-topped table, all things that became the vernacular later," and nothing was of great value, but Walton had assembled everything with an eye to color, to the point that the place looked "like a painting." She described Walton as "equally staggered," because being anxious to arrive early and not empty-handed—"I was a very *serious* young lady," she said, laughing at herself—but not thinking it correct to bring a man flowers, she had bought a fruit that was still rare in England, so he woke up to find "a strange girl carrying a grapefruit" in his room. They became close "friends from that day on."

Like many of these men, Madge worked herself into more acceptable social standing by becoming knowledgeable about art and design, a kind of literacy that is particularly useful currency in "Society." Which is to say that if "seeing the world as an aesthetic phenomenon" is characteristic of camp sensibility, as Sontag observed, it is also a technique of discretion—in part because taste-making has for the past century been viewed as a tolerable form of expression for those seen as sexually aberrant. (As Sontag writes elsewhere, "taste is not free, and its judgments are never merely 'natural.'") Madge was proud of having decorated fourteen flats and two country houses—several of which appeared in magazines, either on their own or as the settings for fashion shoots. Her homes were "like stage sets," said Hilary Spurling—and every time she moved, she created a new one. Her bedroom in the Royal Hospital Road flat was "painted elaborately by Douglas Davidson in Marie Laurencin colours," observed Beaton, who also thought her bathroom "chic, ingenious, uncommon & daring." She remembered it "in pink and green, obviously very [influenced by the] Ballets Russes." A flat of the 1930s, she recalled, "was all white—white curtains and built-in white furniture," except for the rug, in pale blue, which was designed by Ted McKnight Kauffer. She later donated this rug to the Victoria and Albert Museum. "You had to have things actually made for you," she said, "because you couldn't find what you wanted and you wouldn't have what your mother had." She wanted to furnish another flat with a glass table on a metal stand, an item uncommon enough then that she had to design it and have it fabricated. She chose the glass— so thick and green that "it looked like a piece of solidified sea"—and designed the base of cast aluminum. "I was very proud of it," she said, "then I changed and wanted something completely different."

Her last flat, on Melbury Road, "was like going into a sort of treasure trove, Aladdin's cave," recalled Gina Fratini, because her things "were so beautiful and yet sometimes very strange, not conventionally beautiful." The accent everywhere was on a duck-egg blue, a pale greenish blue, she had a collection of Bristol blue glass, and the walls were covered with Victorian paintings of "dead birds, surrounded by flowers, on rocks with water lapping at their feet, in lovely oval frames," said Chloe Tyner. In fact, Madge was one of the collectors responsible for the revival of interest in Victorian art and design in the second half of the twentieth century; she owned a ta-

ble that had appeared in the 1851 Great Exhibition, which the V&A
bought from her in the 1970s. She recognized an undervalued painting by the eighteenth-century artist Thomas Jones, before his work
was rediscovered, and bought it. When Isabelle Anscombe, a young
writer on the history of design, interviewed her in the late 1970s,
she was struck both by Madge's connoisseurship and by the inclusiveness of her taste: "She was the first person I met who said, 'It's
all good; you can mix this with that.'"

Among her comrades in connoisseurship were George Furlong,
who had run the National Gallery of Ireland; the painters Geoffrey
Houghton-Brown and Edward Wolfe; the interior decorator Herman Schrijver, who "held that all men were essentially homosexual";
and Neil "Bunny" Roger, who ran his own couture house, then designed for Hardy Amies and for Fortnum and Mason. Roger wore
rouge during active service in Italy and North Africa in the Second
World War. He dressed in high Edwardian style in the mid-twentieth
century, "with a grey top hat, or a bowler, and a stock [a white cra-
vat], and a morning coat, a swallowtail coat." Or he wore patent-
leather hip boots and rode a motorcycle. Or he appeared in full
drag at his notorious parties, such as the "Purple Party," to which
he wore a purple sequined gown. (There was also a Fetish Party,
scandalous in 1956.) In the 1950s, Madge spent many weekends at
the Oxfordshire home of Gavin Henderson, Lord Faringdon, a
friend since the 1920s, who had transformed himself from a Bright
Young Thing (fictionalized by Evelyn Waugh and Aldous Huxley)
into a committed pacifist and progressive politician. He used Buscot
Park for political conferences and weekend parties that mixed people in the arts with leading socialist figures, and he and Madge also
celebrated "non-Christian Christmases" there. One room at Buscot
was devoted to pre-Raphaelite art—Burne Jones's Briar Rose and
paintings by Rossetti and Watts. These had been acquired by his
father, but Gavin was a collector, too, and a trustee of the Wallace
Collection. He was also known to have—in a moment of camp glee
or absentmindedness—begun a speech in the House of Lords by
addressing his colleagues as "my dears," instead of "my Peers."

In April 1952, Madge married Leigh Ashton, another queer
friend from the 1920s. It was an attempt at discretion that created a

spectacle and a scandal instead. Ashton had joined the Victoria and Albert Museum in 1922, working first in the Department of Architecture and Sculpture, then as curator of textiles and of ceramics. He quickly became a "very bright star in the museum world," noted for "his flair for the aesthetic arrangement of objects," a reputation cemented by his work on influential shows of Persian art in 1931 and Chinese art in 1935–36. He was appointed director of the V&A in 1945, but by then it was not an enviable job: The collection had been dispersed for safekeeping during the war, and the building was dilapidated. But he reconstituted the museum assertively, reorganizing the holdings to present a view of the development of style. Doing away with the previous divisions according to crafts and materials, he produced a series of "Primary Galleries," in which the best work in all media from a particular period was shown together—an idea about display that is "now commonplace, but . . . was quite revolutionary at the time," notes the art historian Graham Reynolds, who joined the museum in 1937. Ashton's redesign made the museum's collections more accessible and was the basis for the V&A's self-presentation until the 1980s. In the competitive, close-knit London art world, he is still considered one of the most creative curatorial figures of the twentieth century.

Madge and he were often out together at art openings, the opera, or dinner, and when she joined the Royal College of Art, her professional world overlapped with his even more. Still, "it was a very strange thing," said Reynolds; "she was fundamentally lesbian and he was fundamentally queer . . . There was a general cry of mirth and 'whatever do you think?' It wasn't regarded very seriously." Allanah Harper, herself married, wrote to Sybille Bedford: "Just read the announcement in the Times of the forthcoming marriage of Mrs. Madge Garland to Sir Leigh Ashton . . . Isn't it a scream. The papers are full of it." "Fashion Professor to Marry Museum Director," read one of these headlines: "London's most unusual professor is soon to marry Sir Leigh Ashton, director of the Victoria and Albert Museum." Madge invited her students to the engagement party.

The marriage was a bid for social and financial safety for both, but most observers focused on Madge's ulterior motives. The fact that Ashton had been knighted in 1948—the director of the Victoria and Albert Museum was always honored this way within a few years of his appointment—made Madge "Lady Ashton," an incentive and another element of what was both "a scream" and part of her carefully conceived armamentarium. "A title draws a line in the sand in this country," notes Isabelle Anscombe. "You can't even begin to describe England without describing the status fabric," observes Patrick Woodcock. "She loved to be Lady Ashton," said Madge's goddaughter, the French journalist Colombe Pringle. But her title also demonstrates how discretion works as both a cover and a signpost, since the implausibility of the arrangement was evident even to much of its intended audience. Gerald McHarg had met Ashton on a trip to London and, back in Melbourne, made a show of mocking Ashton's homosexuality. And when he received Madge's telegram—"DEAR GERALD MARRIED YESTERDAY NOW LADY ASHTON LOVE MADGE"—he said to his son, "Well, someone's finally made a lady out of Madge."

Few acknowledged how Ashton benefited from the alliance. Madge and he were both in their fifties, imagining a sexless but warm companionship. If the increasingly conservative social atmosphere in the 1950s made it hard for Madge to imagine living with someone with whom she was in love, and if she hoped for greater social success—"an ambition which was apparently not furthered by Leigh," said Graham Reynolds—Ashton needed protection from the ferocious policing of homosexuality in postwar England, which did not respect status or celebrity. After the relative openness of the interwar period, harassment and prosecution of even accomplished or socially prominent men for homosexual acts was constant. The arrests and convictions of John Gielgud and of the writer Rupert Croft-Cooke in 1953; the arrest of Michael Pitt-Rivers, Edward Montagu, and Peter Wildeblood in 1953, and their very public trials the following year; and the arrest of the mathematician and computer scientist Alan Turing for homosexual offences in 1952, his acceptance of a hormonal "therapy" of estrogen injections to avoid a prison sentence, and his suicide in 1954 are just a few examples of the climate for men like Ashton in those years. For Madge, the danger was not criminal prosecution but social ostracism.

Ashton also imagined "a nice cosy home," a change from the "austerity" of his bachelor flat, and so they planned to pool their resources and occupy separate rooms in her house in Priory Walk in South Kensington. They envisioned a household like that of many of their friends: Vita Sackville-West and Harold Nicholson, or Willie King of the British Museum and his wife, Viva, whom Ashton had introduced to each other and at whose wedding he had been best man. (Madge and Viva were old friends, and Madge had lodged with them in Chelsea during the war.) Then there were the architectural historian James Lees-Milne and his wife, Alvilde, and the collectors of Victoriana Charles and Lavinia Handley-Read. All were alliances in which one or both parties preferred his or her own sex, needed the protection of marriage, and believed that the institution could be a rational, businesslike "agreement." "Don't marry," Madge told Isabelle Anscombe in the late 1970s. "Or if you do, make very strict rules and regulations." But none of her own rules and regulations helped her in this case, in part because Ashton's "drinking career" turned out to be as "spectacular" as his museum career. On one "notorious occasion" he had to be carried from the club White's, passed out. He also collapsed at a reception at the Polish consulate that marked a collaboration between the V&A and the Polish government.

Madge had suffered from Dody's alcoholism, had no understanding of the problem, and could not tolerate it. She saw it as a question of self-control and respect for appearances, and when Ashton fell down drunk next to her in public shortly before the marriage, she sent him a letter calling everything off. "Dear Leigh," she wrote, "When we became engaged you agreed that you would give up drinking. Last night again you were disgustingly drunk. In view of this I cannot proceed with our agreement." Ashton's response was to sit a protégé (the young curator and art historian Peter Ward-Jackson) on his knee, read him the letter, and ask the young man for advice— a scene that is emblematic of the whole arrangement. Madge put away her misgivings, they went ahead with the ceremony, and he moved in, but she threw him out of the house before the end of the year. "So the performance only lasted for about nine months," Reynolds said. Soon after, when Ashton's alcoholism became too much of a liability, he was forced to resign from the museum, officially stepping down "for reasons of failing health." He spent the rest of his life, almost thirty years, at St. Andrew's Hospital in Northampton, his memory for everything but games of bridge gone.

As Lady Ashton, Madge had a dignified if tenuous position to which to retreat: Although she remained Madge Garland in professional life, she continued to use the title. Yet discretion remained the rule when it came to this interlude. She became close to the novelist Ivy Compton-Burnett around this time, and describing her friendship with Ivy said that it worked "because nothing was said. *Nothing.* We didn't have to say anything. There was complete trust on both sides." After her break with Ashton, "Ivy came to tea and, as she entered, went directly to the glass doors which opened onto the garden, turned to me and said, 'You have the garden, you have the house, there are worse things than loneliness.' And never spoke of the matter again." Compton-Burnett had known Ashton for decades, too—he was part of the coterie of museum men who had gathered around Margaret Jourdain, the pioneering historian of English furniture design with whom she had lived for over thirty years—but her allegiance was to Madge. The Jourdain–Compton-Burnett ménage was one that their friends constantly tried to parse: Were they lovers? How did Jourdain dominate the fearsome Compton-Burnett? Madge's own deep bond with Ivy, which developed after Jourdain's death in 1951 and which Madge described as "one of the happiest things in a long and troubled life," also mystified observers. Ivy was acerbic and exacting, yet she felt that "Madge could do no wrong," said Sybille Bedford. "She was besotted with Madge," said Francis King, "dazzled by this woman who moved in the fashionable world." Ivy loved food; Madge did not care what she ate. Ivy did not care about the look of her surroundings and dressed like a fierce, elegant governess. But Madge believed that Ivy, "although she belonged to an epoch when women of her age habitually wore black . . . appreciated other people's plumage," and "when I wore something new she invariably commented on it."

Madge thought that Ivy cared about her because "she knew that I was wholly dependable." She accompanied Ivy to Leeds when she received an honorary doctorate from the university. She went with her to the theater, where Ivy, who attended only matinees, was known

to talk back to the play and actors. Madge was an accomplished gar-
dener, and Ivy "had strong feelings about flowers, as about all matters." Together they visited Kew Gardens, the shows of the Royal
Horticultural Society, and—at a different month every year to see it
in its various incarnations—Vita Sackville-West's garden at Sissing-
hurst. Sackville-West would give them the substantial afternoon
tea that Ivy liked and, "in her mannish clothes," tall riding boots,
and "dark, cropped head," Madge wrote, "was the antithesis of the
small Ivy, dressed in brown tweed, matching brimmed hat, and
brown lace-up shoes and gloves to tone." Together Madge and Ivy
took annual summer holidays in Kent, going on long country walks.
They never discussed their work, but Madge noted that on these
walks Ivy sometimes seemed to be rehearsing out loud lines of dialogue from the novel she was writing at the time. When Madge left
the Royal College of Art and started spending the winters in warm
climates, it displeased Ivy, who took her friends' absences from England as personal defections. "Madge is in Spain"—she was in Cór-
doba with Rebecca West—she told a mutual friend one year; "I think
that's very selfish of her."

Ivy was established as a brilliant, idiosyncratic writer by the
time Madge met her, but her early novels had been dismissed by
Jourdain and some reviewers in much the same terms that Madge
herself was. These books are populated by languid men and resil-
ient women—characters with a "passion for clothes and parties and
gossip," her biographer Hilary Spurling has noted—and the books
themselves were seen as "silly" and trivial, code to some extent
for *homosexual*. Most of them describe toxically constricting families. They are set in a moment that is at once modern, Victorian,
and indeterminate, and seem to create a new kind of time. They
also create their own rhetorical universe, being largely composed of
conversation—apparently polite speech that shows off the aggressive behavior of intimates. Compton-Burnett is interested in the
emotional heat that rises from the icy surfaces of talk. Her characters utter and ring changes on conventional verbal expressions; they
argue about the meaning of idioms to the point that the possibility
of meaning is often unhinged. This emphasis on rhetorical surfaces
has a corollary in Madge's attention to sartorial surfaces. The constant analysis of speech and silence—a style that is at once playful

and deeply serious, and that stresses implication and deniability—also reads as both campy and discreet.

More Women Than Men, published in 1933, has been called the most "clothes-conscious" of her novels: Its characters dissect their own and others' outfits as well as speech. "Oh, pray let us drop this subject of clothes," says Josephine Napier, the toxically benevolent headmistress of the girls' school in which the novel is set, interrupting one such discussion. At the end of the book, "as she unfastened her bonnet and cast it on a chair, she saw it with a new sense of its significance." The novel is equally striking for its description of the sorts of passionate attachments to women—mentors, rivals, colleagues, friends, lovers—and violent reactions against such intimacies, that marked Madge's life. "Are you interested in different human relationships?" one teacher asks another, with knowing indirection, near the beginning of the book. The pressing analysis of the artifices of language and of dress in *More Women Than Men* is also, pointedly, an inquiry into the idea of "naturalness." Felix Bacon, the drawing instructor at Josephine Napier's school, who constantly interprets his clothing to others, says, "It is little, unnatural corners of the world that appeal to me. I am very over-civilised." And yet there is no fixed identity, sexual or otherwise, in this world: Felix Bacon seems reliably "unnatural," but turns out to be wedded to convention. He sits happily on the knee of the older man with whom he has lived for years and, equally blithely, gets married. Compton-Burnett's pleasure is often to show how sibling or same-sex intimacy is sacrificed to make way for a marriageable couple, and that plot is one strain of this novel. But conventional couples are also in danger in *More Women Than Men* as irritating partners of the opposite sex are eliminated by sudden accident or fatal illness.

At the end of the novel, one of the teachers, Miss Rosetti, accepts Josephine Napier's offer of partnership in her school and life. "I have said that there is nothing to tell of my life," she says, "but there is one thing that I will tell . . . I have cared in my way for the women whom one by one I have tried to care for; and I have come without trying and almost without knowing to care the most for you." This is not euphemism, yet the allusion to not speaking and the circularity of the avowal seem to make it at once more emphatic and less direct. "Miss Rosetti knew that on some things there would be silence," the narrator tells us. "We begin our new life from this moment," says Josephine Napier. And Miss Rosetti replies, "It will easily cease to be new to me; it is my natural life; my happiness depends on women."

"Different" human relationships; autocratic but self-pitying parents; children whose power is tenuous, absent, or emerging; the thorny obliquity of a radically new style—it is clear why Madge would find Ivy's work meaningful. As for the woman herself: "Ivy educated me," Madge said. Madge had always been attracted to powerfully intellectual women (Rebecca West was another). She was often a guest at Ivy's large teas—a kind of exclusive open house and local institution, mostly populated by art historians and writers—and she knew that Ivy was not above terrorizing people socially. ("The whole thing was that you went to tea at Ivy's and she never introduced anyone," said Sybille Bedford.) The first time that Madge offered a reciprocal invitation, Ivy listened to the other guest chat about modern literature, then cut her off to ask about her butcher's bill. When Madge invited Ivy to a Christmas party—"a wildly mixed gathering" to which she had also asked her old friend Nancy Cunard—she found "the sight of Nancy Cunard decked out in all her corals, with spit-curls on her cheeks," sitting on the sofa next to "Ivy in black velvet," stunning, but she was made so anxious by the fact that Compton-Burnett and Cunard did not acknowledge each other all evening that "in the end the only thing I could do was go into the kitchen & get drunk."

Madge herself inspired and valued Ivy's sympathy and "deep tenderness." "She might flay an equal—but she would never wound a friend," Madge wrote. "To be inside her charmed circle was to be safe." When Madge fell and broke her hip and wrist in June 1968, Ivy arranged for her to be cared for at home by a private nurse and despaired about being too unwell herself to do more to help. "I felt I had had my third accident," Ivy wrote, "I minded so much . . . I have never been so angry at my own helplessness." When Ivy died, at age eighty-five, in 1969, she left Madge a Chinese glass painting that had hung over her desk and a sixth of her estate. Her funeral was so banal, Madge wrote to a mutual friend, "that it prevented my tears, so furious was I that Ivy should be connected with anything so dreary. But as you know she had no belief in an after-world. Nor have I. So there it was."

Although Madge needed Ivy's silence, she was distressed when she came up against areas of intentional opacity in Ivy's life, calling them "submerged stones against which one stubbed one's toe." Once, when she mentioned a person from Ivy's past, "Ivy said nothing. But I knew . . . I must never, never, mention that name again. The temperature dropped to freezing point." At other times, Ivy's conversational style could be hilariously blunt. "He's getting married," she said of someone in their milieu, "like so many homos one knows." The comment could have referred to any number of their friends—perhaps the actor and embroiderer Ernest Thesiger, whose wife, Janette, had been an intimate friend of Margaret Jourdain's. "Will you come to tea on Saturday?" she once said to Madge, "*my lesbians* are coming." She was referring to the writers Kay Dick and Kathleen Farrell. Citing this comment to Hilary Spurling as an example of the way Ivy played with her image as a prim governess, Madge took advantage of its apparent exclusion of herself: She was invited, but she was not one of Ivy's lesbians.

When it came to broaching the silence that Madge herself required, the penalty could be harsh. The decorator Herman Schrijver, also part of Ivy's circle, was known for the relish, assurance, and only occasional accuracy with which he dispensed wild stories about his friends. One evening, after a small dinner party at his flat, he escorted Madge downstairs in the elevator. "Come on Madge," he said, pressing her about Ashton, "you know you married him for the title." Francis King, also at this dinner, waited for him to return: "And then he came upstairs, after putting her in a taxi, and he was very shocked, and he said, 'Madge spat on me.' He said that she was absolutely furious and spat, and that was the end of their friendship. Then he laughed and said, 'For a Lady it's a very unladylike thing to do!'" King went on: "The extraordinary thing was this very elegant woman—at dinner she looked so beautiful, and behaved impeccably—and then this sort of vulgarity coming out. But I think that was the rather crude Australian side. And that great toughness of hers."

Schrijver's story is a foray into the twisted workings of discretion. There was Madge, allegedly infuriated at a statement by someone who knew the compromises and losses in her life and his own: He was a gay man and a Dutch Jew whose family had suffered under the Nazis and who was himself "discreet to the point of obsession." There he was, betraying her. There it is: the way the story makes the audience visible, too—the question of whom "the whole performance" is for, of why she persisted in what King called "this great façade," often with people with whom one would think she did not have to. With King, for example, "she never, as it were, came clean. I realized that her interest was not in men but in women. But she would never broach that any more than Ivy Compton-Burnett would. I wouldn't have dared to say anything to question her about that side of her life." Yet with women like herself, as Sybille Bedford said, Madge "didn't make any bones about it." A visibility so tenuous, so different, or so discomfited that it is easy to miss. A visibility so simple, precise, or extreme that it, too, is obscure. In 1927, Cecil Beaton, perhaps naïve about his new friend Allanah Harper, wrote in his diary that he wanted to warn her, "tell her a few home truths about what people think about her going about with Madge Garland, Dorothy Ireland & other Lesbians." That the fear of homosexuality that is part of discretion can be mobilized by homosexuals is nothing new, and in fact is part of what Madge internalized and was up against.

Part of the story is simply that, unlike Ashton, Madge lived on in the world, was there to be scrutinized and criticized. It is easier to vilify those who survive than those who fade away. A number of Ashton's colleagues blamed her for his downfall, saying that the marriage and its demise had made him an alcoholic, although it is clear that drinking was already a way of life for him. "It wasn't Madge who drove poor Leigh to drinking," said Peter Ward-Jackson; "he was already drinking badly before they got married." That great toughness of hers also inspired its share of misogyny. "She was always very nice to me, but you knew that she was a bitch like all women," said Hardy Amies—who credited her with giving him early confidence in his abilities, described her as "a wonderful bridge between London and Paris," and saw her as someone who "had no patience with the second-rate." That Madge spat, and at a friend, was in fact one of the worst things one could say about her: a perfectly condensed yet expansive way to insult her, as Schrijver knew. Spitting was animal, aggressive, inappropriate to her gender, the inverse of discreet—a messy bodily act that sent what was properly inside out. But spitting also has a place in the history of fashion: Rose Bertin, the eighteenth-century couturière known as the Minister of Fashion, was reputed to have done so when her *première*, Mademoiselle Picot, left and set up business on her own. In 1968, Madge published a profile of Bertin in which she wrote that the Minister of Fashion "was so furious [at this betrayal by Picot] that when she met Mademoiselle Picot in the Grande Galerie a very unpleasant incident took place. Mademoiselle Picot asserted that Mademoiselle Bertin had spat in her face. She took the matter to court, where Mademoiselle Bertin was found guilty and made to pay damages, but again the Queen intervened and the decision was quashed."

To say that Madge spat when confronted with her marriage to Ashton was to say that her manners hid a lack of manners; that her perfect surface at once shielded and indicated class deficiency (it being impossible to imagine anyone not wanting an English title); that her social failure was also attributable to non-Englishness (that difference always being a failure); that her attempt to be something other than what she was born to "be" was a form of effrontery. Madge would have been furious at Schrijver about these messages and more, including the implication by a friend that she was nothing more than a social-climbing female, since if she loved the title, she cared about Ashton and was devastated by his decline. Rebecca West, writing to Janet Flanner in 1958, noted, "Madge came down for the week-end, and I am firmly keeping her an extra day. She has had . . . bronchitis, and is thin and pale and wheezy, and I wish she had not to cope with a half-finished house. She is deeply distressed by Leigh's final relegation to a lunatic asylum. I will keep her longer if she will consent to stay, as the house is warm, but I fear she will go off to keep appointments with builders and get on with her work."

"What Camp taste responds to," Susan Sontag observes, "is 'instant character' . . . and, conversely, what it is not stirred by is the sense of the development of character. Character is understood as a state of continual incandescence—a person being one, very intense thing." Biographical writing is generally understood to be concerned with the steady development of character rather than incandescent performances of the self. But Madge Garland's life of progress also depended on moments of theatricality, excess, artifice, and lying, and on the effulgence of fashion. There is the story of self-transformation and struggle, and then there is this woman with her "great amount of dazzling personality" that you felt "as she came into the room," a continual, perfectly clothed presence.

In a 1932 photograph in *The Bystander* in which she used herself as a model, Madge stands with her back to the camera next to another woman who faces front; both wear "parchment velvet . . . informal dinner gowns." A slip of blue typing paper on which she wrote, "Margaret and me" (it was the actress Margaret Rawlings), marks this page in her copy of the magazine. It is the only way to tell that she is there.

Madge was literally, psychologically, and aesthetically both, or all: highly visible and hidden; fearless and terrified; of the colonies and of the metropolis; "terribly tough, with herself and other people" and also "just fantastic fun." Her charm—mannered, an exaltation of "manners," and a style that seemed inimical to intimacy—was so successful that it convinced, even alienated, all but what she called "the most percipient of friends." This was the paradox of the level of polish and chic she achieved: attempting to be seen, she obscured herself; obscuring herself, she made herself visible. Hilary Spurling, who met her when researching her biography of Ivy Compton-Burnett, first assumed that Madge embodied Compton-Burnett's "smug, self-assured and profoundly conservative South Kensington circle"—then "realized the opposite was true": Madge was "brave, shrewd," and "indifferen[t] to received opinion on all fronts. Nothing shocked or startled her. She never passed up an opportunity or turned down a risk, and she felt nothing but contempt for those who did."

And her charm, both genuine and mannered, never did away with her need for love. In one draft of her memoir, describing the end of her marriage to Ewart Garland, Madge wrote, "within two years we had parted; I to live as what is now called a loner for most of my life." Dody Todd is not the only person elided in this summary. Madge's life was filled with extreme and ragged behavior as well as smooth surfaces, and there were always more women on whom her happiness and her unhappiness depended. "Everybody was one of Madge's old flames," said Sybille Bedford, referring to

F. J. Gutmann

Compiled Weekl

for "The Bystande

by Madge Garla

PARCHMENT velvet is news, and good
H. J. Nicoll make it into the most cha
informal dinner-gowns; they also ma
selection in black: they also copy
of these models in any colour you
Posed by Miss Margaret Rawlings, whe
shortly play opposite Leslie Howard in
Side Idolatry," a new Gilbert Miller prod

Eve Wyld and others. Olivia Wyndham's 1939 photograph of a plaster cast of Madge's hand, part of Madge's papers, is a reminder that Wyndham's American girlfriend was so jealous that when they returned to London for visits, Wyndham had to scheme elaborately to see Madge. The collector Gabrielle Enthoven told Madge that if only she, Enthoven, were a little younger she would pursue her. Mercedes de Acosta, Madge said, was "one of the women I have loved most in my life." The women she loved and who loved her were friends, colleagues, and lovers, and it is not always possible, or necessarily useful, to define them as one or the other. The point was that she cared in her way for those whom, one by one, she tried to care for.

Writing in her eighties about her nanny, May, and recalling her distress when she learned that May "was leaving me and going to marry a man," Madge noted that this memory had been precipitated by a more recent betrayal. Hurtling through her long life after May's departure in just a few sentences, she wrote:

> The years passed, lovers came and went with the usual amount of drama and pain. Hard work, increased financial security and a passionate interest in the world and its artifacts helped me to present a reasonably confidant appearance—a thin veneer with many cracks, many papered over by pretty clothes, but one which was adequate for all but the most percipient of friends. Then, as I was approaching my eightieth year, almost simultaneously, two disasters broke the façade, ~~the death of a~~ a great sorrow and an agonising physical illness. I put out my hand to clasp that of a much-loved and (I thought) utterly trustworthy friend—but there was nothing there. Only the dust of a trivial fascination. I was utterly alone. ~~betrayed and abandoned~~. It was then, 75 years later, that I thought of May.

Olguita Queeny, the first real love of Madge's life, committed a series of betrayals and remained a charged subject. In old age, Madge spoke openly about her unhappiness when she learned that

Madge, back to camera, with Margaret Rawlings, in *The Bystander*, September 1933 (MGP)

Olguita had married: "I cried and I cried and I cried, for days on end," she told Peter Ward-Jackson; "I couldn't stop crying." She said that she had locked herself in her room in the Queenys' home in St. Louis and stopped weeping only when she was taken to see the Grand Canyon. It is a moving confession, but a confusing one, since Olguita did not marry until 1928, a decade after Madge's visits to St. Louis, and Madge joined her for at least part of the honeymoon: There are snapshots in both women's photo albums of the three of them, Madge, Olguita, and her new husband, lounging in matching bathing suits on the beach at Le Touquet in northern France. Olguita's London homes appeared in *Britannia and Eve* twice in the 1930s—undoubtedly Madge's doing. But for both women, the meaning of their bond outlasted the friendship. Olguita married an Englishman and spent the rest of her life in London and Malvern, so Madge and she were never far away from each other, but they drifted apart and then there was a rupture, from which Madge never recovered.

In 1945, as the war was ending and Madge was about to leave for the United States, including a stay in St. Louis, she sat in the dining room at the Dorchester Hotel waiting for Olguita, who never arrived. The next day, she received Olguita's letter explaining why she had not kept their date and telling Madge that she would not see her again. Her reasons are obscure now, because Madge ripped up the first few pages of the letter when she received it. More than forty years later, sorting through her papers in preparation for a move, Madge found the remaining pages. Olguita's words now begin in mid-sentence on page four and go on:

> I somehow wish our lives fitted better, but my domestic schedule and your electrified one seem so far apart. We'd probably both find lots still in common, but the odd hour for lunch seems an unsympathetic and stilted allotment. One can hardly find pieces of treasure—in a hurry. I feel our friendship was too important to treat lightly, and I like keeping it the way I remember it . . . I'm rambling. I just wanted to say—I'm sorry—for bungling the chance of seeing you. You sounded remote and busy and I feel it was difficult to say on the telephone how tired and unavailable I was.

The shock of coming across this fragment in the 1980s was so great that Madge was moved to document her distress and try to explain their friendship. Writing in an almost illegible scrawl, when her eyesight but not her acumen was failing, writing when her sense of what she could say was still conflicted, veering between longing and disavowal, she produced two pages. She did not name Olguita.

It is 43 years since I sat in the Dorchester waiting for my luncheon guest. She never arrived. Next morning a letter arrived in the familiar spidery writing. Today I had the courage to ask my secretary to read it to me. Yes, I said, I know the first three pp. are missing (they had been torn up when the letter first arrived—too full of anguish, too acute to be born— [illegible] were [two words illegible] destroyed—p. 4 continued to explain, to attempt to describe a relationship so precious, so unique that it could not be related [sic] to a brief luncheon at the Dorchester . . . Our total innocence would be impossible today but we were [blank space] of illicit relationships and certainly had no such desires on either side. We loved each other, had perfect trust in each other and tho we were both so different.

Madge wrote that after this broken date they met again only twice, both times by accident. Once they ran into each other "in a quiet street not far from Sloane Sq. stopped under a lam[p]post and began to talk—we talked and talked as if our lives depended on our conversation—it began to rain and we went on talking. It grew dark and we parted, our eyes clinging to each others in an agony of betrayal." Denying "illicit" feelings, this writing—private yet seemingly composed with an audience in mind; fragmented, oblique, and direct; romantic and repudiating romance—was an attempt to come to terms with emotion that still had the power to derail her. The scrawled pages, her need to account for the conclusion of a friendship that had been of the utmost importance to her, the story she told about crying for three days when she learned of Olguita's marriage—all are of an intensity that makes the distinction between *innocent* and *illicit* irrelevant. Olguita died in 1983. It is possible that "~~the death of a~~ a great sorrow" that Madge wrote about in the essay about May was Olguita's death.

•

"Of course I am a feminist!" Madge exclaimed to a young reporter in the mid-1980s. She often paid tribute to the inspiration of Rebecca West's early feminist writing and brave life. When West married in 1930, Madge felt bereft and expressed her shock to others. "It is not a question of comparative affection," says Josephine Napier, in *More Women Than Men*, after the marriage of two teachers in her school. "That may be why we feel a faint resentment over people's marriages. Because I think there is no doubt that we do." Madge and West remained close, and late in their lives West was her only intimate who had also known and cared about Dody. "You are not one of the old friends who are merely a custom," West wrote; "you fascinate me just as much as you did when I first met you."

More women: When Madge talked about having known "most of the great beauties of my time," she meant the models, of course, but she was also thinking about the artists Marion Dorn and Lee Miller. The first time Madge visited Man Ray's studio, Miller opened the door: There was "this wonderful-looking creature: pale, pale blond hair; pale blue eyes; pale, pale peach skin; pale grey sweater; and pale grey velvet pants." Miller's beauty was exceptional; her clothes were unusual: Women still did not wear pants in Paris, only on the Riviera. "She was so beautiful—she was *so* beautiful," Madge said, expressively and redundantly, "that it was just a pleasure to be with her." Miller would reply to such appreciation by saying that she wanted "to break the beauty." She had moved to France from New York in 1929 to apprentice herself to Man Ray, and became his lover and model; she was also photographed, filmed, and painted by Edward Steichen, Picasso, Cocteau, and others. A superb photographer in her own right, she later produced some of the most crucial images of wartime and postwar London and Europe, including Dachau and Buchenwald. But in the years that followed, she did break herself: drinking heavily, no longer taking photographs, never speaking of her work, retreating to the farm in Sussex where she lived with her husband, the art historian Roland

Madge, "chez Rebecca [West] taken by her," at Ibstone House, in the 1960s (MGP)

Penrose, where Madge would visit her. At her death, she was known more as a model for famous male artists than as a photographer, and this relative obscurity persisted until her son stumbled on boxes of her work—an archive of some forty thousand negatives and hundreds of prints—and set about rescuing them and her reputation. Madge loved her, and although Miller rarely had women friends ("She was much more for the boys," said Madge), the feeling was mutual. "How are you honey? love + kisses—Lee," reads an undated note she wrote to Madge on the back of a snapshot.

Christine (Kitty) Salmond Pringle Mocatta was a paragon of elegant butch femininity, and her house in the Thames Valley was one of Madge's refuges during the war. From an artistic family (her brother was the cellist Felix Salmond; her sister was a partner in the Redfern Gallery), she left a miserable first marriage and supported herself and her young son as a music hall dancer until one of her stage door admirers, Edgar Mocatta, the heir to the Mocatta gold-dealing fortune, proposed marriage in 1940. Slim and tall, with striking violet eyes, Kitty was generous and she loved opulence. She had her suits made at Hawes and Curtis, clothier to the Prince of Wales: gray or navy blue, with double-breasted jackets and velour collars. She wore handmade shirts with French cuffs. She smoked her own blend of Egyptian (oval) cigarettes from a Bond Street tobacconist, wore Mitsouko or Jicky by Guerlain, carried crocodile handbags, and wore crocodile pumps. The only color in her ensembles came from her lacquered red nails, her substantial jewelry (sapphires by day, rubies and diamonds for the evening), and her handkerchiefs. Those *foulards*—in blue or pink, from a shop on the rue de Castiglione that sold nothing else—were a vehicle for the language of love, since Kitty and her intimates embroidered messages on everything. When she traveled, she carried these scarves in a pouch of silk satin, a gift from Madge. On its front, embroidered in petit point: "TO DARLING KITTY"; on the inside: "TO KITTY DARLING"; on the back: "YOURS, MADGE"; on one of the scarves: "FOR MY BELOVED, FROM KITTY TO MADGE." A *suivez-moi, jeune homme* (literally, a "follow me, young man") refers to a number of accessories meant to attract a man's attention—hat ribbons that flutter seductively at the nape of the neck, the handkerchief that a woman drops intentionally. "So these were what you might call *suivez-moi, jeune fille*" ("follow me, young woman"), said Colombe Pringle, Kitty's granddaughter and Madge's goddaughter, who was the editor of French *Vogue* from 1987 to 1994. They were "*des billet doux, mais en tissu*"—love letters inscribed on fabric.

And then there was Dody, whose traces are few after the 1920s, but whose end must be mentioned. *The New Interior Decoration*, by Dorothy Todd and Raymond Mortimer, was published in 1929. It is dedicated to Madge Garland. Dody ran a gallery for a short time in the 1930s, and she published an essay about Marion Dorn's work in *The Architectural Review*. During the war, she held a government job as a social worker. She made several attempts to reestablish herself in publishing, appealing to magazine editors for work. She published a translation of Le Corbusier's *Sur les Quatre Routes* in 1947 and a translation of a biography of Metternich in 1953. She might have published a memoir, through Virginia Woolf's intervention— the editorial roles briefly reversed—for the Hogarth Press. In June 1926, at a party at Edith Sitwell's Bayswater flat in honor of Gertrude Stein, Woolf had "proposed, wildly, fantastically, a book—which she [Todd] accepts!" Woolf was "in my new dress" (from a dress- maker Dody had recommended); Stein was "in blue-sprinkled bro- cade, rather formidable"; Madge, E. M. Forster, and Siegfried Sassoon were also at this party. In the course of the evening, Woolf's unease overwhelmed her. "Jews swarmed," she wrote to her sister; "Leon- ard, being a Jew himself, got on very well with her [Stein]. But it was an anxious exacerbating affair: . . . I was so morose that I flew to the bosom of Todd, and there reposed. I have asked her to write her life, but I gather that there are passages of an inconceivable squalor."

Dody never wrote this book. She remained a teacher, a seduc- tress, and a snob. She "hated the Cockney accent to a degree that was unbelievable," even phobic, recalled her grandson, Olivier. She peppered her conversation with Greek, Latin, and French and dur- ing the evening would read Shakespeare or T. S. Eliot to Olivier, who lived with her after the war. By this time, "she was a frail, scruffy little old lady" who lived in two messy, cat-dominated rooms off the King's Road and dressed in a motley outfit of floor- length skirt, flat sandals, white blouse, and man's tweed jacket, with pins holding her clothes together. She dropped names, lied, and drank. "She would say 'I'll be right back,' then go around the corner for a drink," recalled Olivier. But her generosity was intact: With virtually no money, she made it possible for him to attend Cambridge University. And she retained a sense of dignity: "Condé Nast she hated, but she never complained to me about the not altogether gentlemanly way people had treated her when she stopped being able to have *Vogue*. And she was always full of wild plans." An encounter with a Sitwell on the King's Road was the occasion for an awkward dance of pleasantries, prevarication, and avoidance. ("Dody, you must come to Renishaw." "Yes, of course, how lovely.")

She held on to the preferences that had served her well and ill: "Art came first, and then religion and philosophy." Her knowledge was obvious, despite her posturing, but it also seemed to her grandson that "below the varnish of genuine culture there was a terrible intellectual mess: socialism, plus Christian Scientism, plus Anglicanism, plus Cubism." Olivier, too, urged her to write a memoir. Instead, she worked intermittently on a project that she understood as a history of philosophy and key to all mythologies, and that he described as "merely accumulated quotations on yellowing pages, an incongruous jumble, fragments copied out from St. Theresa of Avila, Martin Buber, Alfred North Whitehead and Ludwig Wittgenstein." He eventually wrote several vivid, critical, affectionate portraits of her. In 1962, when the first of these, the novel *La Traversée de la Manche*, had been translated, Dody threatened to sue the publisher for libel if it appeared in England. The translation, already in galleys, never came out. She moved to Cambridge and became friendly with Iris Murdoch. She lived on a small government pension and still drew occasional income from her trust, "but was constantly borrowing one pound here, two pounds there." Her grandson, her daughter, and Madge helped to support her. She died in "extreme poverty" in Cambridge in the mid-1960s. Toward the end, she charmed a young Italian woman who left her husband for her.

Tracking discretion, one amasses a curious archive—fleeting details that do not necessarily have a "proper" place in a life story, but are

Elspeth Champcommunal, Worth of London, with models, British *Vogue*, March 1953 (© Norman Parkinson Archive / courtesy Norman Parkinson Archive)

essential to understanding it: the proud statement of one man that he had helped Madge in her old age by complying with her request that he dispose of many of her personal and professional papers; another informant's observation that homosexuality ran through the lives of Madge and her friends "like a green slime." There was Madge's own use, in an essay about the work of Evelyn Wyld and Eyre de Lanux, of the then-common term *nigger brown* to describe part of their palette. There was the disdain in the voices of some, and the intimate, thrilled quality in others'—the ways they radiated pleasure—when they spoke about Madge.

Often what flew up was the question of discretion itself. "We always knew, everybody in the inner circle" knew, said Chloe Tyner of Dorothy Todd. "But it had to be terribly discreetly handled . . . She couldn't go anywhere, like everybody can today. The whole situation is so open today. In those days it was still rather discreet. Companies wouldn't touch you if they had any feeling that—" she broke off. "It was very difficult, that." She was also speaking of, yet not mentioning, her mother, Elspeth Champcommunal. Discretion expressed itself in euphemism. Madge, describing a friend's lover of many years, referred to that woman's "great friend." In Shoreham, the current owner of Madge's house told me that Madge had bought the place from "two rather fruity old gentlemen." The garden was full of espaliered fruit trees, pear and apple, some of which Madge had planted. Discretion expressed itself in fascination. One woman said, "I know nothing," then went on to relate a great deal. Another suspected that Madge had had an affair with Marie Laurencin. Another was sure that Madge and Ivy Compton-Burnett had been lovers—why else would Ivy have left Madge all that money? Discretion expressed itself in disbelief: Madge's desire for Dody Todd was intellectual rather than carnal, some insisted, a distinction that would have been irrelevant if Todd had been an influential male magazine editor, the sexual appeal of whose power, intellect, and connections would have needed no explanation. And it expressed itself in flirtation. One observer was certain that Madge and Eyre de Lanux had been lovers. How do you know? I asked. How did she tell you this? Oh, it was the way she said it, this woman replied, lowering her voice, head, and eyelids, and looking up at me suggestively, to show me how Madge—or was it Eyre?—had looked at her and said, "We were *very* close friends." In her eighties, Madge herself still flirted and used clothes to do so. Discussing the growing use of color photography in art books with a young writer, she slid to a comment on her interviewer's blouse: "It has entirely changed our approach. *You* have *very* pretty colors on today."

LOOKING IS NOT VANISHING

She was inevitably a magnet for admiration and disdain. "She was intelligent and read everything," observed the writer and editor Francis Wyndham, but she was "rather too interested in what people looked like and what they were wearing." Her prose was "too frilly and feminine," wrote the *New Yorker* editor Katharine White, when Janet Flanner tried to get Madge work writing for the magazine in the late 1920s. And as Peter Ward-Jackson put it, "She has left no monument."

Madge Garland herself felt that she had left no monument and she wanted no memorial of any kind. She insisted to her friends that they hold no service in her honor. More disavowal, handwritten in old age on a scrap of paper:

NO HYMNS
NONE
I detest (church)
(religious)
music
AND WORDS

Her ambivalence came to a head in old age, in part because she continued to be well-known, into the 1980s, to curators, collectors, historians of design, and people in the fashion industry, as well as to ordinary women who had read her columns or seen her on television. Living in a country and traveling in circles where producing a written document about oneself—diary, letters, memoir—was common, she "never vaunted or validated what she did." A

biographer who tried to tell her story was unable to interest a publisher in the project. When she died, in July 1990, age ninety-four
(but admitting to ninety), one obituary referred to her as "a key figure in the history of British fashion journalism, the British fashion
industry, and the training of fashion designers" who "neither ex-
acted nor received the credit she deserved for her achievements."

In the 1960s, as the fashion world changed and designers' shows
became "explosive, fast," said one fashion journalist, "there was
Madge still impeccable in hat and gloves." She was of the past and
of the present—an anachronism to some and an inspiration to others. As interest in the 1920s grew and as Art Deco and modern design were reevaluated in the 1970s, writers came to interview her
about celebrated friends such as Nancy Cunard, Cecil Beaton, and
Frederick Ashton, as well as about more neglected figures (Marion
Dorn, Eve Wyld). Most of these writers were looking not at but
through Madge, an approach that may have been easier for her. Yet
she was also profiled in the newspaper, and pleased to be, as a new
generation of fashion journalists discovered her. She wrote and co-
hosted *Seven Ages of Fashion*, a television series broadcast in 1975.
She continued to publish into old age and, like any committed
writer, corrected her work even after it was in print; her own copies
of her articles and books are covered with revisions.

The Changing Face of Beauty, published in 1957, is a kind of up-
dated version of her childhood scrapbook-keeping—a collection of
images and commentary that she described as "not a reading book
at all, [but] a looking book." Like much of her journalism, the brilliant, short volume *Fashion*, published by Penguin in 1962, analyzes
and pays tribute to the industry and is full of telling detail. The
showings in the 1920s of the couturier Jean Patou were galas where
"only a few of the most important journalists were admitted,"
she writes, "but at the little tables, with champagne sparkling in
the glasses before them, sat the smartest and prettiest women in the
rich international set, complete with rows of diamond 'service
stripe' bracelets on their arms, surrounded by their gigolos and
titled husbands." Madge believed that *The Indecisive Decade: The
World of Fashion and Entertainment in the Thirties*, which appeared in
1968, was "valuable insofar as it doesn't deal with the major figures . . . Who would have heard of Allan Walton if I hadn't put him

in there?" she asked. "And [yet] he had a great influence, in his time."
(The strongest chapters of this book are those on fashion and decoration. The others are more enumerative than analytical.) She published *The Changing Form of Fashion* in 1970; *The Small Garden in the
City* in 1973; *A History of Fashion* (co-written); and a catalogue essay
for a major museum exhibit on prewar fashion in 1975. She continued
to publish book reviews into the 1980s.

She spent much of the last thirty years of her life, and increasingly after Ivy Compton-Burnett's death, away from England, looking for new visual excitement, further education, and warm weather.
She traveled—by cargo boat, not in luxury, and always with her
typewriter—to Spain, the Azores, Singapore, Bangkok, Hong Kong,
Shanghai, Macao, Manila, Sri Lanka, Penang, Kuala Lumpur,
Malacca, Israel, Egypt, Tangiers, Ghana (where she lectured at the
university), the Gambia, Nairobi and the interior of Kenya, Mada-
gascar, and South Africa. She lived in Marrakech for several winters. She wrote most of her books on these travels. She kept small
notebooks in which she recorded impressions of what she had seen,
proper spellings of place names, books to read, people to contact,
friends to whom to send cards, shopping lists, and reminders ("look
up Cicilia [sic] Vinitiana of Rome courtesan & lesbian 16th cent").
"She had a ferocious hunger for adventure and experience," said a
friend, and "put herself through degrees of discomfort which we
would wonder about now." She found pleasure in most of what
she saw. The architecture of the public buildings in Kuala Lumpur, such as the railway station and the post office, made "even buying a stamp great fun," she wrote in 1962. In an essay on travel by
cargo boat for the *Spectator*, she wrote, "Unexpected oddities of
no special importance, a remote port, a native village, a small dusty
museum, a temple of no aesthetic value are collector's items to the
truly curious," as are "the loading and unloading of the various
cargoes." The travel articles she wrote for British *Vogue* in the
1960s are full of admiration for the beauty of the textiles and
the women in these locales: "the panache of a race which goes
shopping in ankle-length gowns, draped over-skirts, low-necked

---

On the set for *Seven Ages of Fashion* with co-presenter Allan Hargreaves, circa 1975 (MGP)

bodices and two-foot high headdresses—plus all their glittering jewellery."

She admired, wryly, the women adventurers of the nineteenth and early twentieth centuries. One of the last books she planned to write was a series of profiles of these figures, travelers in North and South America, Asia, North Africa, Russia, Eastern Europe, and Nepal. When it became clear that she would not carry out this project, she gave her notes to a young friend and urged her to write the book. Her "real love was travel," she wrote of the voyager Isabella Bird, in a dazzling essay about four of these women.

> She had found the panacea which was to solve her problems for the rest of her adventurous life: to be in the centre of the stage, spot-lit by distance and danger, to describe at length to an admiring circle at home the appalling situations and discomforts which she surmounted with such remarkable poise; to remove herself from all domestic ties, yet cling to them with all the strength of her stubborn nature; to remain "a lady" but live the life of an adventurer—such contrasts almost completely obliterated from Isabella's mind the "spinal complaint" from which she suffered in the captivity of home-life. The cosy comfort of Victorian England must have been stifling to a woman who could with equanimity share a log-cabin with two male students, camp out in the mountains with a known murderer, and sleep soundly in a hut with "hairy Ainos."

These insights into "Isabella's mind" are also self-knowledge. Here is Madge describing her own back pain in 1970, after her return to England from a winter in North Africa: "It is lovely to be home and see friends and pictures and theatres but, alas, already I have begun to ache again and the sciatic nerve to become inflamed. It had quite vanished from my consciousness."

Over the next decade she became increasingly frail, but continued to travel. She made an excursion to the Indian subcontinent that would have been complicated for someone half her age, took a

---

With the Marie Laurencin portrait, 1986, photographed by Sue Adler (Courtesy Camera Press)

ride on an elephant, fell off, broke bones, and ended up in a clinic, in a room with a dirt floor, for weeks. She wanted to die far away from England, said Hilary Spurling, convinced that these later trips were suicide missions. "I've been in more hospitals than I have fingers on my hands," Madge said to friends in the 1980s, "including in Africa and America." When she could no longer travel—could no longer even leave home—she would sit for hours studying atlases.

At some point in the 1960s or '70s she began going to the Raja Yoga Center in northwest London to study meditation—Mercedes de Acosta had earlier introduced her to Bhagavan Sri Ramana Maharshi—and after a fall in her garden she had an out-of-body, near-death experience that she was moved to write about, "but despite this energetic adventuring to the Sufis, to the ashram, she still couldn't come to believe in any form of eternity," said a friend. When she talked about what might happen after death, she would say, "Darling, it's a huge, great abyss." She took herself to a convent nursing home, anticipating her imminent demise, then "spent five or six or seven years dying," said Peter Ward-Jackson, whom she asked to be her executor and next of kin. Still, "ill and bedridden and half-blind and miserable, she would pull herself together and talk, and talk in a very interesting way," for visitors. "I think that she felt if you were giving friendship to her she was very determined to be a friend back," said one young friend of her old age. "You came in the door and it didn't matter what sort of pain you could see on her face. Once you said hello, she rallied and put herself into a mode where she was delighted and interested." "She died in 1951," Madge wrote of Daisy Bates, another of those intrepid travelers, who spent most of her life in the Australian outback, "aged ninety-two, poor and alone, but believing that nothing is ever lost."

"Fashion is like air," Madge said. Many dresses, like those of the 1920s, depend "for their charm on the graceful movements of a supple body beneath." "I wish I had them now!"—that scarf, that skirt, that dress—she said. But she was devoid of nostalgia, and was never "not excited about the new season, and the new hat, and the new this, and the new that." She loved modern music and was thrilled when she discovered the work of Philip Glass. She illustrated an essay on men's beauty with a photograph of Mick Jagger. She was still attending fashion shows in the 1980s. Thinking through clothes was how she lived, and in extreme old age she still made it her business to be flawlessly put together: clothes, coiffure, the arrangement of her hands and feet, and makeup, although her poor eyesight meant that she made up her face (blue eye shadow, some rouge) not with the mirror but from memory. She sat on her sofa, her gray-and-white hair perfectly coiffed, the rest a confection of bows, ruffles, and shawls, more pale blues and pinks.

"What is there that can be both said and repeated about fashion?" Madge asked in her lecture to the Royal Society of Arts in 1951. "Even the most fragile *soufflé* leaves behind it a recipe, so that given the same ingredients we can make and enjoy it another day, but fashions once past can only be dowdy or amusing—it can never be fashionable again." Wear it now. "Whether we like it or not," she said, "we are given the possibility to live in only one age." In the 1970s, she said, "I don't like old costume, I like new clothes." She was referring to the academic study of fashion, which focused on the history of costume. The idea that "the 'Good Old Days' were somehow preferable to present ones" made no sense to her. "This nostalgia thing depresses me," she said of the vintage revival in the mid-seventies. "In the past fashion didn't look back." "I am incapable of living in other than the present tense (with occasional curious and anticipatory glances toward the future)," she wrote in *Britannia and Eve* in 1930. But "how miraculous it is," she said to an interviewer in 1979, "when you hear voices from the past." Over her lifetime, many of her dresses that did not wear out or were not superseded by new fashions were lost in catastrophic events: the sudden presence of bailiffs in the Royal Hospital Road flat; the bombing of her house and constant dislocations of the Second World War. In the 1970s and '80s, she patronized a high-end consignment shop in Sloane Square, placing old frocks there to raise funds for new ones. Out shopping, "bent as she was, blind as she was, she could just pick up from the hanger some limp-looking rag and drape it round herself and make it look as if it came out of Balenciaga." Suffused with light—like Woolf's Mabel Waring—she sprang into existence.

What remains is not an article of clothing. When the fashion school at the Royal College of Art marked its fiftieth anniversary, it commissioned a scent in her honor. Described as "feminine and sensual, with white hyacinth and lily of the valley, and bright top notes

of tangerine and rhubarb to bring it into the 21st Century," this eva-
nescent memorial was distributed to guests at the student fashion
show in 2000. Teddy Wolfe's painting of Madge hangs in the Gef-
frye Museum in London, to which Madge donated it in the 1970s.
Marie Laurencin's portrait of her belongs to Colombe Pringle.

What remains is writing that describes a commercial arena but
is often saturated with such feeling and vision that it conjures her
presence and experience. The postwar fashion shows in Italy, she
wrote, used

> the [Palazzo] Pitti as a showroom and the Strozzi as a meeting-
> place where the actual selling was done, while the Bobcli
> gardens were the scene of flood-lit fêtes for the buyers.
> Rarely have clothes been seen in more palatial surroundings
> than in the vast ballroom of the Pitti, air-conditioned against
> the summer's heat, its huge chandeliers winking in the
> lights, white-gloved attendants handing around iced drinks,
> a bar (free) in another room, the commentary spoken in
> four different languages, magnificent guards in the full pan-
> oply of Renaissance costumes to herald the lovely Italian
> model girls.

A monument sits solidly, referring to the past but defying time.
But velvet is very important, and Madge Garland's life attests to
something as powerful as monumentality. In their materiality and
their ephemerality, their capacity to make history present and to
index the passage of time, a dress and her story offer something that
a monument cannot: some mixture of the texture of daily life and
of the vertigo of history, with all of their immediacy and loss, and
all of their distortions.

Even in her eighties, loss and distortion still marked her relationship with Dody, any mention of whom would make Madge
blanch, snap at her interlocutor, and change the subject. When Olivier Todd was writing about his grandmother and inquired about
speaking with Madge, "she said, 'No, under no circumstances.'"
The refusal is even more striking, since she sought out Ewart Garland's son, Patrick, around the same time, wanting to know him—
but of course she had wounded Ewart, not been hurt by him. Dody

appears and recedes in the attempts at autobiographical writing that Madge imagined might be read by a public: missing, incompletely named (as "my friend" or "the English editor of *Vogue*"), or present only as a sort of implication. At no point in the drafts of her memoir does Madge indicate that the "friend" with whom she "shared a house" and "the English editor of *Vogue*" were the same person. In the 1950s, visiting the novelist Anthony Powell, she listened to him criticize the characterization of Pierre in *War and Peace* as implausible. She replied that Pierre—intelligent but highly irrational, and always searching for meaning—made sense to her; she had once known someone just like him. She did not go on, but Powell knew that she was referring to Dody. She spoke about Dody directly once, in the last year of her life, to Hilary Spurling, who insisted that she unburden herself and leave a record of that relationship and its rupture. "She was a brilliant woman, absolutely brilliant," Madge said. "But erratic. She was a very strange character, and she had a fearful end. She was *so* gifted. She had the best and kindest of hearts. But she was a woman who ruined herself."

She was able to speak publicly about that part of her life through clothes and the business of fashion journalism. Reviewing Caroline Seebohm's biography of Condé Nast in 1982, she commented on Nast's "less-than-always-honorable methods of dealing with staff" and described him as "a man whose whole life was based on pursuing an absolute balance of perfection: his own blinkered vision of what women *should* wear, what a page of the magazine *should* look like, the *exact* relation of illustration to text." In this book review, she was able to say that the magazine "smelled of snobbery so extreme that it [now] seems sometimes obnoxious, sometimes hilarious." In the process, she turned again to the question of importance and suggested what she considered the proper material and scope of a biography. This portrait was disappointing, she wrote, because the real substance of Nast's character—including threatening staff with "disclosure to avoid paying up for a broken contract"—was "glossed over here in two or three lines," whereas "trivia—the number of bottles of drink consumed at a party, or a three-line, conventional letter of thanks—are given in full."

Writing in the early 1960s, Madge had described Edna Woolman Chase as "the first journalist to foresee the influential rôle a fashion paper could play in commerce"; later she acknowledged all that she had learned from Chase. Reviewing Nast's biography, she did not say that he and Chase had broken her more than once. But she did write that it was a "relief" to emerge back into the present moment after having read at length about those potentates who had exercised such control over not just the fashion world but the lives of their employees, even to the point of dictating in which neighborhood they could reside. "One emerges from this world of false values, of rooms furnished by Elsie de Wolfe in false Louis XV style, into a world where young people today go about their business with carrier bags, wear no hats—and live where they like." Chase, she explained, used to insist that every woman working on the magazine wear a hat and clean white gloves, and Madge wrote that she regretted the disappearance of both. "But," she concluded, "one can pay too high a price for anything—even for clean white gloves."

NOTES

I have standardized the idiosyncrasies of Esther Murphy's writing in just one way: I have silently corrected her spelling, for ease of reading. In her hands *particular* was usually *particuliar* and *extraordinary* was *extradinary*, for example. She was also capable of misspelling the names of her closest friends (*Magaret* for *Margaret*) and of her subject (*Maintenon* was often *Maintainon*). I have let most her punctuation stand, because—odd as it sometimes appears to a contemporary eye, and although some of her habits were hers alone—some was common practice in her day.

ABBREVIATIONS

AFP Arthur Family Papers, Manuscript Division, Library of Congress

CBD Cecil Beaton unpublished diaries, courtesy of the Literary Executors of the late Sir Cecil Beaton

CNA Condé Nast Archive

EWP Edmund Wilson Papers, Yale Collection of American Literature, Beinecke Rare Book and Manuscript Library

GSMP Gerald and Sara Murphy Papers. I consulted this archive when it was still in possession of the family and known as the Donnolly Family Papers. It is now part of the Yale Collection of American Literature, Beinecke Rare Book and Manuscript Library.

IAP Isabelle Anscombe Papers. Consulted privately; now housed at the Newnham Literary Archive, Newnham College, Cambridge University.

JFP Janet Flanner/Solita Solano Papers, Manuscript Division, Library of Congress

JSP John Strachey Papers, private collection

MdAP Mercedes de Acosta Papers, Rosenbach Museum & Library, Philadelphia

MDP Muriel Draper Papers, Yale Collection of American Literature, Beinecke Rare Book and Manuscript Library

MEP Max Ewing Papers, Yale Collection of American Literature, Beinecke Rare Book and Manuscript Library

MGP Madge Garland Papers. Consulted in a private collection. Now acquired by the Royal College of Art Archives, London.

MHFP McHarg Family Papers, private collection

RCAA Royal College of Art Archives

RWP   Rebecca West Papers, General Collection of Rare Books and Manuscripts, Beinecke Rare Book and Manuscript Library
SBP   Sybille Bedford/Allanah Harper Papers, Harry Ransom Humanities Research Center

THREE LIVES

5 *"one likes romantically . . . gloom"*: Virginia Woolf, "Lives of the Obscure," *The Essays of Virginia Woolf*, vol. 4: 1925–1928, Andrew McNeillie, ed. (London: Hogarth, 1994), 119.

5 *"What is style? . . . thinking"*: Marguerite Young, "Inviting the Muses," in *Inviting the Muses: Stories, Essays, Reviews* (Normal, Ill.: Dalkey Archive, 1994), 114.

A PERFECT FAILURE

9 *"a nonstop conversationalist"*: Calvin Tompkins, *Living Well Is the Best Revenge* (New York: Viking, 1962, 1971), 13.

9–10 *"a wonder" . . . "a 'genius'"*: Patrick Murphy to Gerald Murphy, July 23, [1909], GSMP. He went on: "It has been remarkable: a continuous string of laurels."

10 *"with a dissertation . . . Turgenev"*: Quoted in Honoria Murphy Donnelly, with Richard N. Billings, *Sara and Gerald* (New York: Times, 1982), 130.

10 *"to several magazines . . . write!"*: Gerald Murphy to Sara Wiborg, July 28, 1913, GSMP.

10 *"ask[ed] why in . . . night"*: Max Ewing to parents, Wednesday May 9, 1928.

10 *"Bounding Bess, noted . . . Fact"*: Djuna Barnes, *Ladies Almanack* (New York: New York University Press, 1992 [1928]), 32.

10 *"I don't remember . . . talking"*: John Peale Bishop to F. Scott Fitzgerald, quoted in Elizabeth Carroll Spindler, *John Peale Bishop: A Biography* (Morgantown, W.V.: West Virginia University Library, 1980), 185.

10 *"But you were" . . . "'Esther'"*: Quoted in Edmund Wilson, *The Sixties: The Last Journal, 1960–1972* (New York: Farrar, Straus and Giroux, 1993), 210.

10 *"going through all . . . audience"*: Ibid., 207. He was reporting a story that Gerald told him and Dawn Powell, after Esther's death.

11 *"personally and professionally . . . arrogance"*: Dawn Powell to Gerald Murphy, December 13, 1962, GSMP.

11 *"it could be a . . . anything"*: James Douglas to author, interview, Paris, September 20, 2002.

11 *"All we know is"*: Sybille Bedford to author, conversation, London, June 28, 1999.

11 *"There has never . . . failures"*: Quoted in Richard Holmes, "Scott and Zelda: One Last Trip," *Sidetracks: Explorations of a Romantic Biographer* (New York: Random House, 2000), 322.

11 *"I am certain . . . failure"*: Gertrude Stein, "Portraits and Repetition," *Lectures in America* (Boston: Beacon, 1985 [1935]), 172.

12 *"fond of saying . . . failure"*: Gertrude Stein, *Everybody's Autobiography* (Cambridge, Mass.: Exact Change, 1993), 88.

12 *"the speeded-up . . . money"*: Edmund Wilson, "The Author at Sixty," *The Portable Edmund Wilson*, Lewis M. Dabney, ed. (New York: Viking Penguin, 1983), 23. Wilson considered his father an example of this phenomenon.

13 *"the most important . . . crash"*: EM to Leonie Sterner, November 11, 1930, MDP.

13 *"rescued the forgotten . . . Jansenists"*: EM to Sybille Bedford, n.d. (postmarked December 21, 1954), SBP.

13 *"Did she realize . . . failure?"*: EM, Madame de Maintenon drafts, GSMP.

13 *"with her usual historical gusto"*: Edmund Wilson, *The Fifties: From Notebooks and Diaries of the Period*, ed. Leon Edel (New York: Farrar, Straus and Giroux, 1986), 251.

13 *"was all about . . . research"*: Sybille Bedford to author, interview, London, March 30, 2000.

13–14 *"Statistics," wrote Dawn . . . "jewels"*: Dawn Powell, *The Diaries of Dawn Powell: 1931–1965* (South Royalton, Vt.: Steerforth, 1995), 249.

14 *"I will now . . . through"*: EM to Muriel Draper, April 27, 1933, MDP.

NO SUCH WORD AS FAIL

16 *"Esther is without . . . dialogue"*: Max Ewing to parents, March 7, 1927, MEP. Anna Murphy, he wrote, "finally wanders off to bed. Esther and her father linger for an hour or so at the table, and are an amazing pair."

16 *"so proud . . . straight"*: Anna Murphy to Gerald Murphy, June 24, 1909, GSMP.

16 *"life and . . . tragically"*: Gerald Murphy to Sara Wiborg, August 25, 1915, GSMP.

16–18 *"Mother was devoted . . . life"*: Gerald Murphy to EM [1957]. Gerald's biographer describes Anna Murphy as "devoutly Catholic," but Esther told Sybille Bedford that her mother was Protestant, which this letter seems to confirm.

18 *"Our father who . . . Europe"*: Donnelley, *Sara and Gerald*, 77.

18 *Born in Boston*: The facts about Patrick Murphy's early years are unclear. According to his descendants, he attended the academically rigorous, public Boston Latin School, but a contemporary source notes that he was educated "in the Quincy Grammar and English High Schools, Boston." (*Boston Morning Journal*, January 2, 1878, 4.) Most of Cross's fine harnesses and saddles were produced in the town of Walsall in the English Midlands, a center of leather goods manufacturing, and Murphy may have been apprenticed for a time at a Walsall factory. Before buying Mark Cross, he may have first started his own firm: In late 1891, he was writing on stationery headed "London Harness Agency—P. F. Murphy & Co.—Harness, Saddlery and Horse Furnishings." Gerald called Patrick Murphy a self-made man, but Murphy's own father must have had some means, because he is said to have loaned his son the $6,000 he needed to purchase the Mark Cross Company. One obituary of Murphy asserts, "Incidentally, the company never was headed by any one named Mark Cross, but it won that name by its practice of marking its shipments with a cross." ("Patrick Murphy Dies; Famed as Dinner Speaker," *New York Herald Tribune*, n.d., GSMP.)

19 *"was still a . . . Frenchman"*: Mrs. Winthrop Chanler [Margaret Chanler], *Roman Spring* (Boston: Little, Brown, 1934), 234, 238.

19 *"to be regarded . . . Association"*: "Horse Show Luncheon Prelude to Opening," *New York Times*, November 19, 1906, 10. At another of these early events, "loud cries of 'Murphy!' resounded through the dining room, which were renewed as the official orator arose to acknowledge the greetings of those present," "Horse Show Opens with a Luncheon," *New York Times*, November 18, 1907, 8.

19 *"clear fluent monotone"*: *New York Times*, n.d.

19 *"He who breeds . . . applause"*: "Horse Show Ready for Opening Today," *New York Times*, November 14, 1904, 7.

20 *"The art of . . . stop"*: Ms., GSMP.

20 *"Buying inferior articles . . . time"*: GSMP. "Many a False Step is made by Standing Still," read another ad. "This is a paradox. A paradox is 'truth standing on its head to attract attention.' Something seemingly absurd but true in fact. The purpose is to direct attention to the fact that Mark Cross Has Grown A New Branch At 175 Broadway." *Wall Street Journal*, October 10, 1923, p. 11.

20 *"Before we knew . . . her"*: Anna Murphy to Gerald Murphy, June 24, 1909, GSMP.

20 *"instigated"*: Anna Murphy to Gerald Murphy, August 1, 1909, GSMP. She also tells him that "Esther is upstairs writing—she has been asked to send something to the Paris 'Matin' and has been offered ten [?] cents a word for them."

20 *"Edgar Allan Poe-ish"*: Sybille Bedford to author, interview, London, March 29, 2000.

20 *"History is simply . . . history"*: "Fifteen Waggish Epigrams—Delivered at the Lambs' [Club] Spring Gambol by Patrick Francis Murphy," *The World*, Sunday, May 6, 1923.

22 *"Happily . . . fail"*: *New York Times*, November 18, 1907, 8.

22 *"He looked like . . . gloves"*: "Patrick Murphy Dies; Famed as Dinner Speaker," *New York Herald Tribune*, n.d., GSMP.

22 *"distinguished and remarkable . . . women"*: EM to Sybille Bedford, n.d. [postmarked July 3, 1959], SBP.

22 *"a clever and . . . Ma's"*: EM to Sybille Bedford, n.d. [1954], SBP.

24 *"the Black Service"*: Gerald Murphy to Sara Wiborg, Friday, n.d. [1915], GSMP.

24 *"a defect over . . . time"*: Gerald Murphy to Archibald MacLeish, January 22, 1931, Archibald MacLeish Papers, Library of Congress.

24 *"fail[ure] to grasp . . . married"*: Gerald Murphy to Sara Wiborg, August 26, 1915, quoted in Amanda Vaill, *Everybody Was So Young: Gerald and Sara Murphy, A Lost Generation Love Story* (New York: Houghton, Mifflin, 1998), 64.

24 *"a peculiar form . . . indigestion"*: Quoted in Vaill, *Everybody Was So Young*, 23.

24–25 *"My appearance is . . . attractions"*: EM to Gerald Murphy, n.d. [postmarked November 18, 1916], GSMP.

25 *"as light in . . . Amazon"*: EM to Gerald Murphy, July 6, 1915, GSMP.

25 *"I assure you . . . wandered"*: EM to Gerald Murphy, July 13, 1915, GSMP.

25 *"All the masculine . . . Gerald"*: Wilson, *The Sixties*, 62.

25 *"Come, brace up . . .* failure": Patrick Murphy to Gerald Murphy, November 20, 1909, quoted in Vaill, *Everybody Was So Young.*

26 *He died without . . . father:* "I have never ceased to regret that I was unable to bring Fred and Father into at least human terms at the last," Gerald Murphy to EM, September 9, 1937, AFP.

26 *"in a bad . . . alone":* EM to Gerald Murphy, n.d. [postmarked November 18, 1916], GSMP.

28 *"a more* completely *. . . again":* EM to Chester Arthur, June 17, 1943, AFP.

28 *"if you are . . . indelible":* Mary McCarthy, *Memories of a Catholic Girlhood* (New York: Harcourt, 1985 [1957]), 24.

28 *"it is also . . . civics":* Ibid., 25.

28 *"together with much . . . non-Catholics":* Ibid., 26.

28–29 *"knowing the past . . . own":* Ibid., 25.

TO FILL UP HER KNOWLEDGE IN ALL DIRECTIONS

30 *" 'The American Woman' . . . Magazine!":* EM to Gerald Murphy, April 13, 1917, GSMP.

31 *"I will limit . . . to":* EM to Gerald Murphy, November 21, 1916, GSMP.

32 *"You are my . . . robust":* Ibid.

32 *"both men and . . . it":* EM to Chester Arthur, June 15, 1936, AFP.

33 *"incontrovertible" proof of . . . "table":* Esther Arthur, "Have You Heard About Roosevelt," *Common Sense,* August 1938, 15.

33 *"of seeking to . . . aspired":* Esther Murphy, "The President's Appeal," Letter to the Editor, *New York Times,* October 22, 1920, 12.

33 *"normalcy" as his . . . "situation":* Esther Murphy, "Democracy in Action" an address by Mrs. Chester A. Arthur Delivered Before a Joint Breakfast of the Los Angeles Democratic County Central Committee and the Young Democrats of California, June 1, 1941, AFP.

35 *"rather monotonous sojourn[s]":* EM to Edmund Wilson, August 3, 1922, EWP.

35 *"nothing but other Americans":* Edmund Wilson, *The Fifties,* 254.

35 *"one of the . . . me":* EM to Edmund Wilson, n.d., EWP.

35 *"more and more devoted":* Edmund Wilson to John Peale Bishop, June 30, 1920 [1923], in Wilson, *Letters on Literature and Politics, 1912–1972* (New York: Farrar, Straus and Giroux, 1977), 106.

35 *"unclouded":* Edmund Wilson, "A Weekend at Ellerslie," *The Portable Edmund Wilson,* 194.

35 *" 'Victorian' article":* EM to Edmund Wilson, July 12, 1922, EWP.

35 *"the sheer intellectual . . . thing":* EM to Edmund Wilson, July 15, 1924, EWP.

35–36 *"We could discuss . . . done":* EM to Edmund Wilson, August 9, 1922, EWP.

36 *"the only complaint . . . to":* EM to Edmund Wilson, n.d. [circa September 1922], EWP.

36 *"ruthlessly in at . . . off":* T. S. Matthews quoted in Lewis M. Dabney, *Edmund Wilson: A Life in Literature* (New York: Farrar, Straus and Giroux, 2005), 130.

36 *"We fell on . . . chef":* Wilson, *The Fifties,* 251–52.

36 *"quietness and flatness . . . another":* Wilson, *The Fifties,* 375–6.

38 *"her gawky girlhood . . . York":* Ibid., 254.

38 *"the special characteristics . . . maturity":* Ibid., 253.

38 "*I had always . . . Divines*": EM to Sybille Bedford, August 15, 1956, SBP.
38 "*the Philistines are . . . them*": EM to Edmund Wilson, n.d. [circa September 1922], EWP.
38 "*redeemers of mankind . . . me*": EM to Edmund Wilson, July 15, 1924, EWP.
38 "*Perhaps he interests . . . need*": EM to Edmund Wilson, July 5, 1923, EWP.
39 "*among the greatest . . . choice*": Esther Murphy, "Books and Authors: 'Love and Friendship'" (review of *Love and Friendship and Other Early Works*, by Jane Austen), *New York Tribune*, September 24, 1922; Esther Murphy, "Jane Austen" (review of *The Watsons*), *New York Tribune*, April 29, 1923, 27. If she saw Austen as clear-sighted about literary and sexual politics, she shared the more standard view that the novels display no evidence of power and politics beyond the family circle, writing that Austen "entirely overlooked the fact that history was being made all around her." For the *Tribune*, Esther also reviewed biographies of Mrs. Humphry Ward and King Leopold of Belgium.
39–40 "*Hawthorne's animosity toward . . . contemporaries*": EM to Edmund Wilson, September 10, 1922, EWP.
42 "*the Great and . . . Wharton*": EM to Edmund Wilson, July 12, 1922, EWP.
42 "*I'm going to . . . me*": EM to Edmund Wilson, n.d., EWP.
42 "*the custodian of . . . dwelling*": All quotations from Edith Wharton, "The Angel at the Grave," *Scribner's Magazine* 29 (Feb. 1901): 158–66.
45 "*a dull enough . . . beauty*": EM to Edmund Wilson, August 3, 1922, EWP.
45 "*scheduled for future publication*": *Los Angeles Times*, April 22, 1928, C17.
46 "*demoted from a . . . kept*": Abby Slater, *In Search of Margaret Fuller* (New York: Delacorte, 1978), 3.
46–47 "*I did not . . . satisfactory*": EM to Edmund Wilson, October 5, 1951, EWP.

BACHELOR HEIRESS

48 "*decided to be . . . bottle*": Wilson, *The Fifties*, 254.
48 "*preliminary drinks . . . experience*": Wilson, "A Weekend at Ellerslie," 189, 191, 194.
49 "*would occasionally bring . . . eloquence*": Max Ewing to Mrs. Alice Manning [postmarked March 15, 1927], MEP.
49 "*moved absent-mindedly . . . sequins*": Max Ewing to parents, May 9, 1928, MEP.
49 "*magnificent as the . . . convent*": Max Ewing to parents, n.d. [postmarked January 28, 1930], MEP.
49 *he painted Mercedes*: These portraits and others appeared in Chanler's show at the Valentine Gallery in New York in 1929. "To be painted by Bob Chanler, says Carl Van Vechten, is to have a career, a social opportunity and an education," wrote the art critic Henry McBride, "Spirited Portraits by Squire Chanler Shown—Authentic Celebrity Conferred on Sitters by Singular Artist—Process Revealed by Mr. Van Vechten with Reckless Abandon—Painter Himself Clings to Larger Aspects," *New York Sun*, March 2, 1929, MEP.
49 "*stormed and raged . . . death*": Max Ewing to parents, Thursday, March 29, 1928, MEP.
49 "*indomitable, impetuous intransigent . . . me*": EM to Leonie Sterner, November 11, 1930, MDP.

49 *"Next to Muriel . . . known"*: EM to Sybille Bedford, September 2, 1954, SBP.

50 *"possessed of an . . . enthusiasm"*: Henry James Forman, "When All the Lions Came to Muriel Draper's House," *New York Times*, February 10, 1929, 62.

50 *"outrageous remarks and outrageous hats"*: "Edwardian Pink," *Time*, September 8, 1952.

50 *"It was an . . . artists"*: Paul Cummings, "Interview with Walker Evans," Connecticut, October 13, 1971, and New York City, December 23, 1971, Archives of American Art, Smithsonian Institution, www.aaa.si.edu/collections/interviews/oral-history-interview-walker-evans-11721.

50 *"Muriel Draper Dies"*: *New York Herald Tribune*, August 27, 1952.

50 *"You were superb . . . contemporary"*: EM to Muriel Draper, Wednesday, n.d. [mid-1920s], MDP.

50–52 *"stood up & looked . . . 'gang!'"*: Max Ewing to parents, January 17, 1928, MEP.

52 *"in pink spangles . . . flowers"*: Max Ewing to parents, Monday, n.d., MEP.

52 *"wonderful vitality and . . . mind"*: Teddy Chanler to EM, April 25, n.d., AFP.

52 *"a rather tormented . . . forty"*: Teddy Chanler to EM, July 5, n.d., AFP.

52 *"I'm so anxious . . . you?"*: Teddy Chanler to EM, September 3, n.d., AFP.

52 *"My boy friend . . . paradoxical"*: EM to Muriel Draper, Saturday, n.d. [circa 1926], MDP.

53 *"I have really . . . difficult"*: Teddy Chanler to EM, July 5, n.d., AFP. "(I wonder, by the way, if in future years, providing we're both famous, the history of Our Relationship won't constitute a separate course at Columbia.)" Teddy Chanler to EM, September 3, n.d., AFP.

53 *"a very usual occurrence"*: Teddy Chanler to EM, April 25, n.d., AFP.

53 *Esther would pass out*: She later told Sybille Bedford that she woke in their apartment one morning to see an enormous portrait of Queen Victoria over the bed, inscribed by the queen: TO MY DARLING GODDAUGHTER OLIVIA. Sybille Bedford to author, conversation, London, March 30, 2000.

53 *"the long-roofed . . . ship"*: F. Scott Fitzgerald, *Tender Is the Night* (New York: Scribner's, 1995 [1934]), 205.

54 *for whom she . . . "admiration"*: EM to Gertrude Stein, Tuesday, n.d. [circa 1929–30], Gertrude Stein and Alice B. Toklas Papers, Yale Collection of American Literature, Beinecke Rare Book and Manuscript Library, Yale University.

54 *"upbraid[ed]" her for . . . "Barney"*: Teddy Chandler to EM, August 6, [1926], AFP.

54 *"outlet for sensibility"*: EM to Gerald Murphy, November 21, 1916, GSMP.

54 *"could not be . . . themselves"*: Wilson, *The Sixties*, 289.

54 *"Her behavior . . . rebuke"*: Vaill, *Everybody Was So Young*, 348.

54 *"a process of . . . realities"*: Gerald Murphy to Archibald MacLeish, January 22, 1931, Archibald MacLeish Papers, Library of Congress.

55 *"full of homage . . . sure"*: William Carlos Williams, *The Autobiography of William Carlos Williams* (New York: New Directions, 1967), 228–29. Barney, Williams went on, "could tell a pickle from a clam any day in the week."

55 *"her strongest desire"*: Quoted in George Wickes, *The Amazon of Letters: The Life and Loves of Natalie Barney* (New York: Popular Library, 1978), 284.

55 *"entirely selfish . . . compass"*: Sybille Bedford to author, conversation, London, June 30, 2001.

55 *"vegetable-placid . . . really"*: EM to Muriel Draper, April 27, 1933, MDP.

55 *"Above all* don't *. . . novelist"*: Teddy Chandler to EM, April 25, n.d., AFP.

55–56 *"Natalie Barney lay . . . bed"*: Esther Murphy, untitled story, ms., 1926, MDP. The piece ends: "Get out the scarves[?] from my armoire and give them to me. Then take off your clothes and give yourself thirty lashes on the"

56 *"copiously"*: Esther Murphy, ms., n.d. [circa 1926], MDP.

56 *"We talked again . . . earth"*: Max Ewing to parents, Monday, March 7, 1927, MEP.

56 *"and by crazy . . . cuckoo"*: Max Ewing to parents, n.d. [circa May 1927], MEP.

56 *" 'She is not' . . . by"*: Barnes, *Ladies Almanack*, 33.

56 *"ON WAY TO CAPRICE"*: EM to Muriel Draper, June 2, 1927, MDP.

57 *"Miss Barney directs . . . troops"*: Max Ewing to parents, n.d. [August 1927], MEP.

57 *"Fancy Esther being" . . . long*: Dorothy Wilde to Natalie Barney, July 27, 1927, quoted in Joan Schenkar, *Truly Wilde: The Unsettling Story of Dolly Wilde, Oscar's Unusual Niece* (New York: Basic, 2000), 353.

57 *"strange stay with"*: EM to Sybille Bedford, February 10, [1949], SBP.

57 *"in a state of frenzy"*: Max Ewing to parents, "Sunday," n.d. [circa May 1928], MEP.

57 *"I suppose you're . . . wife"*: Hugh Thomas, *John Strachey* (London: Eyre Methuen, 1973), 70.

58 *"It was characteristic . . . all"*: F. Scott Fitzgerald, "Echoes of the Jazz Age" in ed. Edmund Wilson, *The Crack-Up* (New York: New Directions, 1993 [1945]), 14.

58 *"inabilities to act"*: John Strachey to EM, Tuesday, n.d. [circa winter–spring 1928–29], AFP.

58 *"startling and revelatory . . . ascertained?"*: Natalie Barney to EM, "late February" [1929], AFP.

58 *"She* dreamed *of being appreciated"*: Sybille Bedford to author, interview, London, March 29, 2000.

59 *"a sort of . . . purchase"*: John Strachey to EM, December 25, 1928, AFP.

59 *"You are truly . . . satisfying"*: John Strachey to EM, Tuesday, n.d. [circa 1928–29], AFP.

59–60 *"I'm going to . . . so"*: John Strachey to Yvette Fouque, February 22, 1929, quoted in Thomas, *Strachey*, 71–72.

60 *"Last night . . . elsewhere"*: Max Ewing, n.d. Thursday [postmarked March 7, 1929], MEP.

60 *"You would think . . . winter!"*: Max Ewing. n.d., Wednesday [postmarked March 13, 1929], MEP.

60 *"THINKING OF YOU CONSTANTLY"*: EM to Muriel Draper, March 28, 1929, April 4, 1929, April 23, 1929, MDP.

61 *"plunged into the . . . 1929"*: EM to Sybille Bedford, September 30, 1959, SBP.

61 *"To the Woman . . . Britain"*: Leaflet, "Parliamentary General Election, To the Woman Elector of Aston," signed Esther Strachey, MDP.

61 *"the swift 'transformation . . . Commonwealth' "*: Thomas, *Strachey*, 75.

61–63 *"the most important . . . hand"*: EM to Leonie Sterner, November 11, 1930, MDP.

64 *"second place . . . 'her'"*: Thomas, *Strachey*, 78, 71.

64 *"Remember, every upper . . . guilty"*: Ibid. 69.

65 *"Congratulations, John!" . . . "you"*: Sybille Bedford to author, interview, London, March 29, 2000.

65 *"It is not . . . them!"*: John Strachey to Yvette Fouque, August 13, 1929, quoted in Thomas, *Strachey*, 78–79.

65 *"Darling, darling Muriel . . . strange"*: EM to Muriel Draper, April 23, [circa 1930], MDP.

65 *"unbutton[ing] his fly"*: Mary McCarthy, "Fellow Workers," *Granta* 27 (Summer 1989): 107–23, 111.

66 *"forth on the . . . world"*: Max Ewing to parents, Tuesday, n.d. [postmark September 15, 1931], MEP.

66 *"The whole thing . . . money"*: Sybille Bedford to author, interview, London, March 29, 2000.

67 *"a living corpse"*: EM to Chester Arthur, June 10 [1936], AFP. Over thirty years after Anna Murphy's death Olivia Wyndham recalled "what [Esther] went through when her Mother was begging to die for months and Esther could do nothing about it." Olivia Wyndham to Sybille Bedford, July 26, 1964, SBP.

67 *"became ill with"*: Celia Strachey, unpublished memoir ms., JSP.

67 *"sympathy and understanding"*: EM to Muriel Draper, n.d., MDP.

67 *"does love you . . . this"*: Muriel Draper to John Strachey, April 6 and 15, 1932, JSP.

67 *"She is a . . . being"*: Amabel Williams-Ellis to John Strachey, n.d., AFP.

67 *"like a Victorian . . . her"*: Celia Strachey, unpublished memoir ms., JSP.

67 *"My heart quite . . . of"*: Amy Strachey to Gerald Murphy, November 23 [circa 1932], GSMP.

67 *"charming,—almost worthy . . . quite"*: Amy Strachey to EM, August 9, 1937, AFP.

68 *Left Book Club*: See Paul Laity, "The Left's Ace of Clubs," *The Guardian*, July 6, 2001. "It was 'the unorthodox political education of the Left Book Club,' Aneurin Bevan said, which 'prepared the way' for the Labour victory of 1945. . . . LBC monthly book choices helped to make full employment, proper housing, socialised medicine and civilised town planning axioms of general expectation, not only for an increasingly politicised working class, but for residents in middle-class and suburban constituencies which had seemed beyond the reach of Labour in 1935."

68 *"dotty . . . eccentric will"*: EM to Chester Arthur, 23 September 1945, AFP. The will also left control of the company to Murphy's mistress and secretary, who proceeded to run it into the ground.

68–69 *singer Spivy LeVoe*: LeVoe performed at the nightclub and restaurant Tony's and later ran her own boîte, Spivy's Roof. She was "famous in the elite gay world." George Chauncy, *Gay New York: Gender, Urban Culture, and the Making of the Gay Male World, 1890–1940* (London, Flamingo/HarperCollins, 1995), 349.

69 *"Never have I . . . depressing"*: EM to Muriel Draper, 27 April 1933, MDP.

69 *"I feel the . . . me"*: John Strachey to Joseph Brewer, April 27, 1932, quoted in Thomas, *Strachey*, 119.

THE RUMBLE OF THE TUMBRELS

70 *"saying, 'The Duke' . . . etc."*: Edmund Wilson, ed. Leon Edel, *The Twenties: From Notebooks and Diaries of the Period* (New York: Farrar, Straus and Giroux, 1975), 192.

70 *"celebrated for her . . . history"*: Esther Arthur, "Have You Heard About Roosevelt . . . ?," 15.

70 *"tall, gaunt, in . . . within"*: Powell, *Diaries*, 249.

71 *"or at any . . . self-destruction"*: EM to Janet Flanner, April 25, 1938, AFP.

71 *"To focus . . . her"*: Max Ewing to parents, n.d., [postmarked August 2, 1932], MEP.

71 *"At the close . . . them"*: Esther Strachey, "Godfather to American Corruption," *American Mercury* 32, no. 126 (June 1934): 170–79, 179.

71 *"were actually more . . . conspiracy"*: Esther Arthur, "The Politicos, 1865–1896, by Matthew Josephson," *Common Sense* (May 1938): 24–25, 25.

72 *"Grant's particular kind . . . America"*: EM, "Godfather," 170–71.

72 *"like the religious . . . Europe"*: EM to Janet Flanner, April 25, 1938, AFP.

72 *"I have just . . . them"*: EM to John Strachey, October 31, 1938, AFP.

72 *"Well," she wrote . . . "consequences"*: EM to Amabel Williams-Ellis, April 17, 1939, AFP.

72 *"the great prototype . . . failure"*: EM to Cliff McCarthy, May 4, 1938, AFP.

73 *"The Slippery Sam . . . History"*: EM to Sybille Bedford, n.d., SBP.

73 *"the uncertified lunatics . . . live"*: EM to Muriel Draper, September 1, 1938, MDP.

73 *"when she got . . . tell"*: Sybille Bedford to author, conversation, London, June 30, 2001.

73 *"I used to . . . Mary"*: James Douglas to author, interview, Paris, September 20, 2002.

73 *"flirted with me . . . party"*: EM to Sybille Bedford, April 4, 1950, SBP.

75 *"resembled nothing so . . . guns"*: EM to Gerald Murphy, June 20, 1958, GSMP.

75 *"that she traveled . . . 'illuminating'"*: Wilson, *The Fifties*, 377. Of this friend, Lorna Lindsley, Esther also noted, only partly in jest: "She went to the coronation [of Elizabeth II] where of course she caused the bad weather." EM to Sybille Bedford, June 14, n.d., circa 1953, SBP.

75 *"talking, her devouring . . . reality"*: Wilson, *The Fifties*, 254–55.

75–76 *"The Barney or . . . Nun"*: EM to Muriel Draper, Sunday, n.d.

77 *"animated by rhetoric . . . evidence"*: Jill Lepore, "Just the Facts, Ma'am: Fake Memoirs, Factual Fictions, and the History of History," *The New Yorker*, March 24, 2008, 80.

78 *"a landed proprietor . . . solicitude"*: EM to Muriel Draper, December 16, 1929, MDP.

78 *"the liberal . . . anachronism"*: EM to Muriel Draper, April 27, 1933, MDP.

78–79 *"that insidious charm . . . Gamp"*: EM to Chester Arthur, May 20, 1936, AFP.

79 *"whispering campaign . . . survive"*: Esther Arthur, "Have You Heard About Roosevelt . . . ?," 15, 16.

79 *"incalculable influence . . . own"*: EM to John Strachey, October 31, 1938, AFP.

80 *Esther's use of . . . to come*: I am grateful to Regina Kunzel for this insight.

80 *"a sort of . . . scene"*: EM to Carmel Snow, January 3, 1938, AFP.

80 *"curious and ambitious . . . so"*: Esther Arthur, "Mrs. Luhan and Rousseau," *The New Mexico Sentinel*, n.d. [1937], 6–7, MDP.

80 *"You live on . . . extirpated!"*: Quoted in Martin Duberman, *The Worlds of Lincoln Kirstein* (New York: Knopf, 2007), 234. Draper told Kirstein about this incident the next day, and he recorded it in his diary. Kirstein had been initially put off by Esther, "but before long," writes Duberman, he "grew to appreciate her tenderheartedness, intelligence, and loyalty"; when they were in Europe at the same time in 1933, Esther was "a generous source of contacts and introductions" for him (151).

81 *"as far as . . . years"*: EM to John Strachey, October 31, 1938, AFP. She noted that Wharton had also sent $5,000 to the cause of the Spanish government.

81 *"As the late . . . 'way'"*: EM to Muriel Draper, October 25 [1935], MDP.

81 *"one is forced . . . done"*: EM to Muriel Draper, December 1, 1938, MDP.

81 *"As one grows . . . 'sorrow'"*: EM to Chester Arthur, September 12, 1936, AFP.

ALL VERY QUEER AND A LITTLE DEPRESSING

82 *"You are too . . . me"*: EM to Muriel Draper, March 6, 1935, MDP.

83 *"the only two . . . South"*: Wilson, *The Fifties*, 252.

83 *"It is curious . . . Guermantes"*: Ibid.

83 *"a man whose . . . presidency"*: EM to Muriel Draper, September 11, [1935], MDP.

83–84 *"a marvelous character . . . selfish"*: Ibid.

84 *"almost died of . . . handicaps"*: Chester Authur to Morse Erskine, " 'Have the Sexes Achieved the Equilibrium of True Equality?' A Question Illustrated by a True Story," n.d. [May 1950], AFP.

84–85 *"sued him for . . . 'work'"*: *Time*, January 22, 1934.

85 *"a collective endeavor . . . Age"*: Norm Hammond, *The Dunites* (South County Historical Society, 1992), 31. A decade earlier, Cecil B. DeMille, filming the first version of *The Ten Commandments*, had built the set for the City of the Pharaoh nearby, making the area the staging ground for another kind of fantasy. This was a "a 720-foot-wide, 120-foot-tall set that required 1,500 workers, 500 tons of statuary, a half million feet of lumber and 75 miles of reinforcing cable . . . Over time, DeMille's Egyptian masterpiece became known as the 'Lost City,' buried by the shifting sands and forgotten by nearly everyone—except for the residents of Guadalupe who worked as extras on the film and knew all along that it had not been dismantled. To locals, it was simply 'the dune that never moved.' " "Do the Dunes," Santa Maria Valley press release, April 28, 2004.

85 *"a series of . . . society"*: John Marshall, "Passports to Utopia—II," *New International* 1, no. 5 (December 1934): 145–47. John Marshall was a pseudonym of George Novack. Accessed at www.marxists.org/archive/novack/1934/12/utopia2.htm.

86 *"full of a . . . idealism"*: Wilson, *The Thirties*, 508.

86 *"high-class old . . . crowd"*: Edmund Wilson to John Dos Passos, April 27, 1935, in *Letters on Literature and Politics*, 263.

86 *"The bride and . . . so"*: Wilson, *The Thirties*, 509.

86–87 *"ten days of . . . suffering"*: EM to Muriel Draper, April 17, 1935.

87 *"They are apparently . . . match"*: Gerald Murphy to Sara Murphy, February 15, 1935, in Linda Patterson, ed., *Letters from the Lost Generation: Gerald and Sara Murphy and Friends* (New Brunswick, N.J.: Rutgers University Press, 1991), 114.

87 *"promised to be . . . heterosexually"*: Chester Arthur to EM, August 16, 1961, AFP.

87 *"lonely, and . . . separately"*: Chester Arthur to Morse Erskine, "Part Two," January 1, 1948, AFP.

87 *"I feel that . . . physically"*: EM to Chester Arthur, Sunday, May 17 [circa 1936], AFP.

87 *"Are you disciplining . . . angel"*: Chester Arthur to EM, November 4, 1942, AFP.

87 *"more intimate than . . . anticipated"*: Havelock Ellis to Chester Arthur, May 2, 1935, AFP.

87 *"I know I . . . day"*: EM to Chester Arthur, Sunday, May 17 [circa 1936], AFP.

87 *"an enormous zig-zag . . . all"*: EM to Muriel Draper, September 11, 1935, AFP.

87–88 *"a slight nervous . . . kinds"*: Chester Arthur to Frank Palmer, September 4, 1935, AFP.

88 *"the most brilliant . . . York"*: Chester Arthur to Morse Erskine, n.d., AFP.

88 *"Do write me . . . man?"*: EM to Chester Arthur, May 17 [circa 1936], AFP.

88 *"various congressmen and . . . favorites"*: Chester Arthur to Rowena Dashwood Arthur, June 8, 1938, AFP.

88 *"Everywhere people were . . . knowledge"*: Dawn Powell, *A Time to be Born* (New York: Yarrow Press, 1991 [1942]), 279.

88–90 *"one of the . . . 1893"*: Esther Murphy, "Hetty Green," labeled "Esther's tryout for radio" by Chester Arthur, n.d., AFP.

90 *"a corrective biography"*: Chester Arthur to May Jackson, February 2, 1940, AFP. He did not write this book. Instead, several decades later, he produced a quasi-mystical study called "The Wavelength of History," which was mystifying to those who read it.

90 *"scenario for Pompadour . . . was!"*: Chester Arthur to Rowena Dashwood, January 26, 1940, AFP.

90 *"full of issues . . . radicalism"*: EM to John Strachey, October 31, 1938, AFP.

90 *"The Republican Party . . . ideas"*: Murphy, "Democracy in Action." Esther was working with Helen Gahagan Douglas, then vice chair of the state committee and chair of its women's division.

90 *"a superb political speaker"*: Chester Arthur to Morse Erskine, "Part III," May 1950, AFP.

90 *"You really might . . . it"*: Harry Howard to EM, April 22, 1942, AFP.

90–91 *"betrayed far more . . . it"*: EM to Muriel Draper, December 1 [1938], MDP.

91 *"the most charitable . . . world"*: EM to Amy Strachey, December 7, 1938, AFP.

91 *"Each new disaster . . . shock"*: EM to Janet Flanner, April 17, 1939, AFP.

91 *"a book on . . . 'Men'"*: Brenda Wineapple, *Genêt: A Biography of Janet Flanner* (Lincoln: Nebraska University Press, 1992 [1989]), 123. "I would give anything to have one book as my epitaph that I had written which was not concocted from other writings in newspapers . . . It makes me regret my

entire life, work & so called career." Janet Flanner to Sybille Bedford, June 8, n.d., SBP.

91–93 *"The 'recession' . . . it"*: EM to Janet Flanner, April 25, 1938, AFP.

93 *"the incorrigible optimism . . . voice"*: EM to Janet Flanner, April 17, 1939, AFP.

93 *"one of the . . . perpetrated"*: EM to Janet Flanner, April 25, 1938, AFP.

94 *"We are not . . . it"*: "Speech by Esther [1941]," AFP.

94 *"On the side . . . succeed"*: EM to Chester Arthur, January 19, 1943, AFP.

94 *"that poltergeist . . . undoing"*: EM to Muriel Draper, April 17, 1935, MDP.

94 *"all the fights . . . years"*: EM to Chester Arthur, January 30, 1943, AFP.

94 *"as close to . . . life"*: EM to Chester Arthur, n.d., AFP.

94–95 *"insatiable curiosity . . . acquaintances"*: EM to Muriel Draper, September 11, 1935, MDP.

95 *"The lonely eager . . . night"*: Chester Arthur to EM, n.d., AFP.

95 *"so bound by inertia"*: Chester Arthur to EM, February 26, 1943, AFP.

95 *"a huge & rather . . . work"*: Chester Arthur to EM, n.d. [circa 1939–1941], AFP.

95 *"You must really . . . talker"*: Chester Arthur to EM, February 26, 1943, AFP.

95 *"have confidence in . . . handicap"*: EM to Chester Arthur, December 10, 1942, AFP.

95 *"take heart and . . . failures"*: EM to Chester Arthur, Friday, n.d., AFP.

95 *"fundamental trouble . . . are"*: EM to Chester Arthur, June 17, 1943, AFP.

95 *"than to anyone . . . happens"*: EM to Chester Arthur, December 10, 1942, AFP.

96 *"She has seen . . . (Mexico!)"*: EM to Chester Arthur, December 23, 1942, AFP.

96 *"very kind and gracious letter"*: EM to Chester Arthur, Monday, n.d., AFP.

96 *"Some of the . . . country"*: EM to Chester Arthur, November 6, 1942, AFP.

97 *"A perfect memory . . . thought"*: Sybille Bedford to author, conversation, London, March 19, 1998.

97 *"very busy writing . . . work"*: EM to Mrs. Wheeler, April 18 [1944], AFP.

97 *"make a will . . . you"*: EM to Chester Arthur, September 23, 1945, AFP.

97 *"Gavin Arthur smiled . . . in"*: Allen Ginsberg, "To Gavin Arthur," in *Scrap Leaves: Tasty Scribbles*, handmade book, transcribed January 18, 1968; poem dated August 8, 1966. Accessed February 12, 2005, at www.levity.com/digaland /scrap/garthur1t.html. Ginsberg also used Chester to establish his queer literary lineage, telling an interviewer in 1973 that Neal Cassady, with whom he had had sex, had "slept with Gavin Arthur, who slept with Edward Carpenter, who slept with Whitman." "The Gay Succession," *Gay Sunshine* 35 (1973). Accessed February 12, 2005 at www.gaysunshine.com/exc_gaysuccess.html.

98 *"Gavin Arthur predicts . . . year!"*: Cited in "An Interview with Walden Welch, by Gina Cerminara." Accessed February 12, 2005, at www.wwastrologer .com/articles/mr_arthur.htm.

98 *"I have no . . . hippies"*: Chester Arthur to Janet Flanner n.d. [1967], AFP.

98 *"the social institution . . . ephemeral"*: Chester Arthur to EM, August 16, 1961, AFP.

98 *"may prove an . . . wealth"*: Chester Arthur to Morse Erskine, n.d., AFP. In 1949, for example, he claimed that her income was $1,000 a month and that he deserved half of it. Far from being her monthly income, it was more than a third of her yearly income, the total of which amounted to about $24,000 in today's terms.

98　"Homogenic, ambigenic, *and* . . . heterosexual": Gavin Arthur, *The Circle of Sex* (New Hyde Park, N.Y.: University Books, 1966), 19.

98　"paterfamilias, *completely heterogenic* . . . *not*": Ibid., 111.

98　*"female heterogenic category"*: Ibid., 27.

98–99　*"many business women . . . elements"*: Ibid., 83.

99　*"10 O'Clock . . . Type"*: Ibid., vi, 97–98.

99　*"my brilliant second wife"*: Ibid., 147.

99　*instances of the* . . . *"Courtesan"*: Ibid., 68.

99　*"a selfish Nine . . . it"*: Ibid., 92.

99　"As Mrs. Arthur . . . *adventuress*": Chester Arthur to EM, July 21, 1947, AFP.

99　"*I realized that* . . . *greatly*": Chester Arthur to Morse Erskine, "Part III," May 1950, AFP.

99–100　*"What a pair . . . collide"*: EM to Sybille Bedford, September 14, 1961, SBP.

100　"*in a crummy* . . . Hemingway": Alan Watts, "Introduction," in Arthur, *The Circle of Sex*, 8.

TOO LATE OR TOO SOON

101　*"a strange girl . . . men"*: Lloyd Morris, *This Circle of Flesh* (New York: Harper and Brothers, 1932), 52, 50, 52–53. See also Max Ewing's *Going Somewhere* (New York: Knopf, 1933).

101　"*Miss Bodicea Hangover* . . . *failing*": Max Ewing, "Thamar Tooting: Concerning Her Eccentricities and How She Achieved a Peculiar Success à Rebours— A Record of two New York Nights Entertainments as Ronald Firbank might have written it," *Inlander* (June 1930): 33–8, 37.

101–102　"A *very melodramatic* . . . *importance*": Max Ewing to parents, n.d. [postmarked April 1, 1929], MEP.

102　"*is one of* . . . *invent*": Martha Gelhorn to Sybille Bedford, April 11, 1953, SBP.

102　"*The wonderful thing* . . . *mouth*": Sybille Bedford to author, telephone conversation, September 10, 2005.

102　"*She* was *like that*": Sybille Bedford to author, interview, London, June 30, 2001.

103　"*free to indulge . . . anti-fascist*": Sybille Bedford, *Quicksands: A Memoir* (London: Hamish Hamilton, 2005), 39.

103　"*the* Partisan Review . . . *milieu*": Sybille Bedford to author, telephone interview, February 21, 2005.

104　"*I have never . . . this*": EM to Sybille Bedford, n.d., SBP.

104　"*elation, at the . . . existence*": EM to Sybille Bedford, Wednesday, n.d. [1945?].

104　"*that lost town . . . careful*": EM to Sybille Bedford, March 1, 1945, SBP.

104　"*super-naturally erudite*": Bedford, *Quicksands*, 13.

104　*Guilty about sitting out*: "I never felt at peace with the war," Sybille told a reporter at the end of her life, "but of course I felt we had to win this war, and so as a matter of conscience I felt I should have had to take the risks." Allison Hoffman, "Woman of Letters, Woman of the World," *The Forward*, May 19, 2006.

105 *"goodness of heart, her lovingness"*: Sybille Bedford to author, conversation, London, January 16, 2002. Sybille saw people as animals and called Esther "Horse." Esther signed many of her letters to Sybille with this name. She decided that Sybille was a version of the small hopping creature known as the Kangaroo Rat, and addressed her in correspondence thus.

105 *"the mind of . . . nature"*: Sybille Bedford to author, conversation, London, October 17, 2000.

105 *"She just swept . . . 'highballs' "*: Sybille Bedford to author, interview, London, March 29, 2000.

105 *"no aptitude whatsoever"*: Bedford, *Quicksands*, 64.

105 *"I thought I . . . work"*: Sybille Bedford to author, conversation, London, June 25, 2001.

105 *"writer manqué"*: Sybille Bedford to author, telephone interview, February 21, 2005.

106 *"much too much . . . books"*: Sybille Bedford, *A Visit to Don Otavio: A Traveller's Tale from Mexico* (London: Picador, 1997 [1953]), 36.

106 *"She hated to . . . 'life' "*: Sybille Bedford to author, interview, London, March 29, 2000.

106 *"eloquent on the . . . prostration"*: Bedford, *Don Otavio*, 229.

106 *" 'I will not' . . . Commons"*: Ibid., 105.

106 *"In my native . . . Niagara"*: Ibid., 293.

106–107 *"I laugh when . . . learned"*: Sybille Bedford to author, conversation, June 25, 2001.

107 *"stalked past it . . . Hebrides"*: Bedford, *Don Otavio*, 303.

107 *"In the spaces . . . Troy"*: Ibid., 61.

107 *"became governess to . . . marchioness"*: Ibid., 11.

107 *"side of the . . . '39?"*: Ibid., 226.

107 *"My father voted . . . woman."*: Ibid., 213–14.

107 *" 'I am an . . . around' "*: Ibid., 156.

108 *" 'Don Otavio,' said . . . 'in 1770' "*: Ibid., 146.

108 *"swinging a small . . . France"*: Ibid., 133–34.

109 *"staged" a "mad farewell party"*: Sybille Bedford to Margaret Marshall, May 28, 1957, SBP.

109 *"She came, she . . . plate"*: Bedford, *Quicksands*, 99.

109 *"part jubilant . . . traumatic"*: Ibid., 13.

109 *"infatuated with her . . . me"*: EM to Sybille Bedford, Friday, June 3 [1949], SBP.

109–110 *"the twenty years . . . hour"*: EM to Sybille Bedford, June 2, 1949, SBP.

110 *"I have played . . . revived"*: EM to Sybille Bedford, Friday, June 3 [1949], SBP.

110 *"clouds of talk . . . somehow"*: Sybille Bedford to Toni Muir, July 20, 1949, SBP.

110 *"I love you . . . soon"*: EM to Sybille Bedford, n.d. [circa March 1950], SBP.

110 *"only person"*: Noel Murphy to Gerald Murphy, January 26, 1958, GSMP.

110 *"Next to my . . . known"*: EM to Sybille Bedford, Monday n.d. [May 1, 1957], SBP.

110 *"table . . . now?"*: Allanah Harper to Sybille Bedford, October 13 [1950], SBP.

111 *"Sometime during the"*: All of the following citations are from the drafts of Esther Murphy's Madame de Maintenon book, ms. and typescript, GSMP.

112 *"With respect to . . . themself"*: She is citing La Beaumelle's *Mémoires pour servir à l'histoire de Madame de Maintenon, et à celle du siecle passé* (*History of Madame de Maintenon and Her Time*).

117 *she asked and . . . apartments*: Sybille Bedford recalled these arrangements. Mitford's Pompadour book appeared in 1953. Mitford's correspondence may suggest that she and Esther did not become friends until 1955.

117 *"The writing is . . . considerably"*: EM to Chester Arthur, January 19, 1943, AFP.

118 *"'My God, how' . . . that"*: EM to Sybille Bedford, May 25 [1949], SBP.

118 *"As Madame de . . . mankind"*: EM to Sybille Bedford, November 22, 1949, SBP.

118 *"that ex-Huguenot . . . of"*: EM to Sybille Bedford, Sunday, n.d. [1950], SBP.

118 *"many relics . . . world"*: EM to Sybille Bedford, November 17 [1950], SBP.

118 *"monarchy incarnate"*: Murphy, Maintenon drafts, GSMP.

119–121 *"Nearly all the . . . believed"*: Murphy, Maintenon drafts, GSMP. In the epigraph, Esther is quoting a conversation between Maintenon and her companion-secretary, Mademoiselle d'Aumale, recorded in the latter's *Souvenirs sur Madame de Maintenon*.

121 *"determined" that Esther . . . "self"*: EM to Sybille Bedford, March 19 [1955], SBP.

121 *"it would not . . . depressing"*: EM to Sybille Bedford, postcard, March 3, n.d., SBP.

121 *"fragment . . . Brace"*: EM to Sybille Bedford, n.d. [circa late March 1959], SBP.

121 *"The book is . . . whole"*: EM to Sybille Bedford, July [1956], SBP.

121–122 *"But the figure . . . Dear!"*: EM to Sybille Bedford, August 3, 1956, SBP. The idea that character is a "will-o'-the-wisp" (as Virginia Woolf puts it in the essay "Character in Fiction") that cannot be pinned down is one of the canons of modernist thinking about representation.

122 *"I am so . . . curiosity"*: EM to Sybille Bedford, January 5, 1959, SBP.

122 *"Madame de M. . . . 'poison'"*: EM to Sybille Bedford, Thursday n.d. [February 1959], SBP.

122 *"I am glad . . . 'being'"*: EM to Sybille Bedford, May 3, 1962, SBP.

122–123 *"She, stigmatized as . . . wars"*: Maud Cruttwell, *Madame de Maintenon* (London: Unwin, 1930), xvii.

123 *"step[s] on a . . . places"*: A.J.A. Symons, *The Quest for Corvo: An Experiment in Biography* (New York: New York Review Books, 2001 [1934]), 3.

123 *"biography alone has . . . show"*: A.J.A. Symons, "Tradition in Biography," in *Tradition and Experiment in Present-day Literature: Addresses Delivered at the City Literary Institute* (Oxford University Press, 1929; reprinted by Haskell House, New York, 1966), 149–50.

123 *"absorbed . . . continually"*: Julian Symons, "Introduction," A.J.A. Symons, *Essays and Biographies*, ed. Julian Symons (London: Cassell, 1969), vi.

123–124 *"showed an imbalance . . . success"*: Ibid., viii.

124 *"He never really . . . biography"*: Ibid., ix.

124 *"thirty pages of . . . prose"*: Sybille Bedford to author, interview, London, March 29, 2000.

THE GRAVE'S INTERCOM

125 *"sitting in triumph . . . her"*: EM to Sybille Bedford, n.d., [postmarked May 6, 1950], SBP.

125 *"some research . . . fruitful"*: EM to Gerald Murphy, July 29, 1952, GSMP.

125 *"work goes well this month"*: EM to Sybille Bedford, Tuesday, n.d. [July 1956], SBP.

125 *"Esther still believes . . . does"*: Wilson, *The Fifties*, 377.

125 *"In the 10 . . . 'now' "*: Hodgson, "Sublime Governess."

125–127 *"I am sorry . . . illness"*: EM to Gerald Murphy, September 9 [1949], GSMP.

127 *"that monument to the inessential"*: Gerald Murphy to Archibald MacLeish, February 8, 1943, quoted in Vaill, *Everybody Was So Young*, 319.

127 *"so changed, gay . . . people"*: Sybille Bedford to Allanah Harper, December 30, 1951, SBP.

127 *By the late 1950s:* "I have sold Allied Chemical stock & helped Esther momentarily," wrote Noel. "I fear it [is] not sufficient & will be lost. However, you & I knew this would happen but $80,000 in 5 years is quick work." Noel Murphy to Sybille Bedford, n.d. 1957, SBP.

127 *"blackmailing letters"*: Noel Murphy to Gerald Murphy, n.d., GSMP.

127 *"She should go . . . case"*: Noel Murphy to Gerald Murphy, n.d. [postmarked December 17, 1957], GSMP.

127 *"really sent more . . . publisher"*: Noel Murphy to Gerald Murphy, n.d., GSMP.

127 *"magnificent as far . . . secretive"*: Noel Murphy to Gerald Murphy, n.d., GSMP. Gerald hurt Esther and Noel by not contacting them on one of his postwar trips to Europe. In the summer of 1950, Esther wrote to Sybille that she had changed her travel plans to see him: "I loved having him here [in Paris] and we had a wonderful time and came to a new basis in our relationship. I hated to see him go." EM to Sybille Bedford, July 10, [1950], SBP.

127–128 *"a strange spiritual . . . lethargy"*: EM to Sybille Bedford, February 13, 1953, SBP.

128 *"a tail spin"*: EM to Sybille Bedford, May 5, [1950?], SBP.

128 *"an attack of . . . enjoyable"*: EM to Sybille Bedford, November 16, 1953, SBP.

128 *"I am rigidly . . . darling"*: EM to Sybille Bedford, January 5 [1959], SBP.

128 *" 'dishonoured and made' . . . indolence"*: EM to Sybille Bedford, March 19, 1955, SBP.

128 *"skeleton thin, & . . . sheets"*: Noel Murphy to Gerald Murphy, n.d. [circa December 1959], GSMP.

128 *"probably a pre-disposition . . . alone"*: Noel Murphy to Gerald Murphy, July 26, 1960, GSMP. Around this time, Alice De Lamar recalled that Esther had had the DTs in the 1920s—possible, or perhaps that episode (like the "wrongly diagnosed" cerebral hemorrhage Chester reported in 1935) was an epileptic seizure. Janet Flanner reported that "Esther's nearly fatal illness—& it was that—was like a gigantic purge that wiped out all her habits of exaggeration, mental & physical. She phones to me freely, is pathetically tender to Noel, reaches for her hand at the dinner table to squeeze it, talking only nearly all

the time, not entirely all, & with a moderation that is touching, brilliant in a new way because devoid of glitter." Janet Flanner to Sybille Bedford, June 8, n.d., SBP.

128 *"Her scrambled eggs . . . plate"*: Sybille Bedford to author, conversation, London, June 25, 2001.

128–129 *"Two things about . . . purpose"*: Wilson, *The Fifties*, 376–77.

129 *"inertia and cowardice"*: EM to Sybille Bedford, n.d. [1949], SBP.

129 *"situation that no . . . was!"*: EM to Sybille Bedford, February 13, 1953, SBP.

129 *"I have been . . . live"*: EM to Chester Arthur, June 17, 1943, AFP.

129 *"at home with . . . singularity"*: Wilson, "The Author at Sixty," 44.

129 *"She is perhaps . . . self-pity"*: Wilson, *The Fifties*, 254.

129 *"she would launch . . . McCarthy"*: Hodgson, "Sublime Governess."

129 *"Dulles thinks Communism . . . all"*: EM to Edmund Wilson, September 25, 1958, EWP.

130 *"I can't tell . . . her"*: EM to Sybille Bedford, September 30, 1949, SBP.

130 *"very few satisfactions . . . help"*: EM to Sybille Bedford, n.d. [postmarked September 1954], SBP.

130–131 *"I fear that . . . judgment"*: EM to Sybille Bedford, Monday, n.d. [circa April 1958], SBP.

131 *"my learned friend . . . Arthur"*: Charlotte Mosley, ed., *The Letters of Nancy Mitford and Evelyn Waugh* (London: Hodder and Stoughton, 1996), 367.

131 *"Alice De Lamar . . . entourage"*: EM to Sybille Bedford, July 10 [1950], SBP.

131 *"passing through [Paris] . . . astronomers"*: EM to Sybille Bedford, June 14 [circa 1951–52], SBP.

131 *Mary McCarthy and Esther*: In Carol Brightman's biography of McCarthy, *Writing Dangerously: Mary McCarthy and Her World* (New York: Harcourt Brace, 1992), Esther is the "unidentified woman" in a photograph of the group waiting for the wedding couple outside the *mairie*.

131 *"Noel brought me . . . books.)"*: EM to Sybille Bedford, Saturday, n.d., SBP.

131 *"She had a . . . ones"*: Alice De Lamar to Gerald Murphy, November 24, 1962, GSMP.

131 *"A whole part . . . memories"*: EM to Sybille Bedford, n.d. [postmarked February 3, 1954], SBP.

131 *"under Esther's influence . . . café"*: Wilson, *The Fifties*, 262.

131–132 *"They came for . . . them"*: Hodgson, "Sublime Governess."

132 *"She never woke . . . reviews?"*: Ibid.

132 *"Esther worries a . . . realities"*: Noel Murphy to Gerald Murphy, November 7, n.d., GSMP.

133 *"put [her] foot . . . Esther"*: Noel Murphy to Sybille Bedford, n.d., SBP.

133 *Gerald, who buried . . . headstone*: "Gerald's posthumous sentimentality revolts me," wrote Noel, "& the picturesque tomb, where Esther & I used to tell ghost stories—doesn't interest me." Noel Murphy to Sybille Bedford, n.d., SBP.

133 *"melancholy"*: Thomas, *Strachey*, 293.

133 *"Do you know . . . friend?"*: Mercedes de Acosta to Gerald Murphy, n.d. [postmarked November 30, 1962], GSMP.

133 *"My darling Sybille . . . man"*: Allanah Harper to Sybille Bedford, November 26, 1962, SBP.

133 *"The great tragedy . . . distinction"*: Janet Flanner to Gerald Murphy, November 25, 1962, GSMP.

133 *"I am sure . . . Documents"*: Dawn Powell to Gerald Murphy, December 13, 1962, GSMP. Gerald replied that he felt some remorse that he had not "share[d] more in her life" and worried that he had "urged her too much to write," when "she was no doubt not meant to." Gerald Murphy to Dawn Powell, December 17, 1962, quoted in Vaill, *Everybody Was So Young*, 348.

133 *"a large sandy . . . her"*: Mosley, ed., *The Letters of Nancy Mitford and Evelyn Waugh*, 469.

133–135 *"What's the use . . . sordidness"*: Sybille Bedford to author, telephone conversation, February 12, 2000.

135 *"Finishing a book . . . apprehensions"*: EM to Sybille Bedford, Friday, n.d., SBP.

135 *"facile gift for verbalization"*: EM to Sybille Bedford, n.d. [circa 1944–45], SBP.

136 *"I have never . . . pity"*: EM to Sybille Bedford, Wednesday [circa 1945], SBP.

136 *"She talks constantly . . . privacy"*: Powell, *Diaries*, 249.

136 *"ruined by Prohibition . . . writing"*: Sybille Bedford to author, telephone conversation, February 12, 2000.

136 *"She would talk . . . different"*: Allanah Harper to Sybille Bedford, September 16 [1945], SBP.

136 *"I am not . . . capable"*: EM to Chester Arthur, January 19, 1943, AFP.

136–137 *"Madame de Maintenon . . . mother"*: Murphy, Maintenon ms., GSMP.

137 *"If any one . . . intelligences"*: Jane Austen, *Mansfield Park* (London: Penguin Books, 1988 [1814]), 222.

137 *"For me, her . . . joyful"*: EM to SB, Thursday [circa September 1952], SBP. In the same letter, she noted that *Time* magazine's article about Draper was "far better and less flippant than I feared it would be and underneath their essential vulgarity of style and spirit, there seems to be a vague cognizance that they are dealing with a very extraordinary being who cannot be fitted anywhere in the framework of the only values that they recognize."

137 *"ageing but hopeful"*: EM to Sybille Bedford, October 20, 1953, SBP.

137 *"not historically possible"*: Esther Arthur, "The Politicos," 25.

140 *"the language of . . . businessmen"*: Scott Sandage, *Born Losers: A History of Failure in America* (Cambridge, Mass.: Harvard University Press, 2005), 4–5.

141 *"of a round . . . 'men' "*: Dabney, *Edmund Wilson*, xii.

141 *"that the twenties . . . time"*: Wilson, *The Fifties*, 519.

141 *"casualties"*: Wilson, "The Author at Sixty," 42.

141 *"My self-immolation . . . score"*: Fitzgerald, "The Crack-Up," 70.

141 *"I talk with . . . again"*: Fitzgerald, "Notebooks," in *The Crack-Up*, 181.

141–142 *"After 21 years . . . spotlight"*: Powell, *Diaries*, 236.

142 *"Failure frightened him . . . possible?"*: Dawn Powell, *A Time to be Born* (New York: Yarrow, 1991 [1942]), 130–31. In *The Happy Island*, the novel she had published four years before, Powell describes the collective reaction to one of her characters thus: "As the shabby dripping figure stalked through the lobby, people drew aside to let him pass, they snatched their skirts back, they glanced quickly away as if a look was contamination; here was Failure,

the Enemy, merely to brush against him was misfortune" (S. Royalton, Vt.: Steerforth, 1998) [1938]), 91.

142 *"confounded her friends . . . 'wanted!'"*: Dawn Powell to Gerald Murphy, December 13, 1962, GSMP.

143 *"the kindness that . . . understood"*: Hodgson, "Sublime Governess."

143 *"I don't know . . . appointment"*: EM to Sybille Bedford, April 26, 1953, SBP.

144 *In 1950 she sent*: Dr. A. Whitney Griswold, "Our Tongue-Tied Democracy," *New York Herald Tribune*, 1954, GSMP. Conversation, he wrote, "is forsaken by a technology that is so busy tending its time-saving devices that it has no time for anything else. . . . It is shouted down by devil's advocates, thrown into disorder by points of order. It is subdued by soft-voiced censors who, in the name of public relations, counsel discretion and the avoidance of controversy. . . . It languishes in a society that spends so much time passively listening and being talked to that it has all but lost the will and the skill to speak for itself."

144 *"Winter is come . . . misfortunes"*: EM to Sybille Bedford, June 14, n.d. [circa 1953], SBP.

144–146 *"As Muriel Draper's . . . 'Draper'"*: EM to Sybille Bedford, Friday, n.d., July [1956], SBP.

144 *"As a workman . . . 'lasse'"*: EM to Edmund Wilson, September 25, 1958, EWP.

146 *"relieved to have . . . 'goût'"*: Gerald Murphy to Richard Myers, July 22, 1958, Myers Family Papers, Yale Collection of American Literature, Beinecke Rare Book and Manuscript Library.

146 *"As Jane Bowles . . . us"*: EM to Sybille Bedford, May 3, n.d., SBP.

146 *"Joe Appiah wouldn't . . . apple!"*: Simon Hodgson, "Sublime Governess," *New Statesman*, February 22, 1963, 268.

146 *"what made it . . . 'cherub'"*: Powell, *Diaries*, 249.

146 *"We leave this . . . 'interesting'"*: EM to Sybille Bedford, October 13 [1956], SBP.

146 *"She has a . . . thoughts"*: Virginia Woolf, "Madame de Sévigné," *The Death of the Moth and Other Essays* (New York: Harcourt, Brace, Jovanovich, 1974 [1940]), 52.

147 *"Every book is . . . ancestors"*: Ralph Waldo Emerson, *Representative Men* (New York: Modern Library Classics, 2004 [1850]), 25.

147 *"'furnishes a key . . . superscription'"*: Susan Howe, *The Midnight* (New York: New Directions, 2003), 116.

147 *"Here is the . . . Esther"*: EM to Sybille Bedford, October 22 [1955], SBP.

FANTASIA ON A THEME BY MERCEDES DE ACOSTA

152 *"One never thinks . . . scene"*: *New York Times*, October 23, 1900, 6.

152 *lead in* Chantecler: In Edmond Rostand's *Chantecler*, the title character, a rooster, is hailed by another avian character as "My, thy, his, her, our, your, and their Cock!"

152 *"a structure unique . . . lighting"*: *New York Times*, January 16, 1908, X2.

152 *"seemed almost like . . . nature"*: "The Jesters," *New York Times*, January 5, 1908, 9.

152 *"had been technically . . . own"*: "Maude Adams Is Dead at 80," *New York Times*, July 18, 1953.

154 *"a real personal . . . audience"*: Issac F. Marcosson and Daniel Frohman, with an Appreciation by James M. Barrie, *Charles Frohman: Manager and Man* (New York and London: Harper and Bros., 1916), pp. 171, 170.

154 *"theatre car . . . existence"*: *New York Times*, April 15, 1906, 1. This front-page article is directly under the report of a lynching (hanging and burning) of two men in Springfield, Missouri, while a mob of three thousand watched "their agony."

154 *"You are not . . . you"*: "A Time of Years," *Time*, July 27, 1953. Accessed at www.time.com/time/magazine/article/0,9171,936102,00.html.

155 *"lived quietly with . . . McKenna"*: Ibid.

155 *"As long as . . . theatre"*: "Maude Adams Is Dead at 80."

155 *"the almost hysterical . . . charms"*: "Maude Adams, Beloved 'Peter Pan,' Dead at 80," *New York Herald Tribune*, July 18, 1953.

157 *"mon grand amour"*: Marlene Dietrich to MdA, September 23, 1932, MdAP.

157 *"I fear Janet . . . there"*: EM to Sybille Bedford, July 10 [1950], SBP.

157 *"Mercedes never lies"*: Sybille Bedford to author, conversation, London, June 28, 1999.

157 *"undeniable gifts . . . egotism"*: EM to Chester Arthur, September 12, 1936, AFP.

157 *either uncritical homage*: One notable exception is Patricia White, "Black and White: Mercedes de Acosta's Glorious Enthusiasms," *Camera Obscura* 15, no. 3 (2000): 226–65.

157 *"the first celebrity stalker"*: Daniel Jeffreys, *New York Post*, April 18, 2000, 7.

158–159 *"I often stood . . . heroic"*: Mercedes de Acosta, "Here Lies the Heart," typescript [1938], first draft, 29, MdAP.

160 *"the Spanish code . . . cloister"*: Daniel Schwarz, "Builder of the Eye Bridge," *New York Times*, November 2, 1947.

160 *"the most romantic . . . society"*: Cholly Knickerbocker, "Cholly Knickerbocker Says," *New York American*, March 1, 1935, MdAP.

160 *"Parents in the . . . convenient"*: Mercedes de Acosta, *Here Lies the Heart* (New York: Reynal, 1960), 109.

160 *"the country"*: Ibid., 18.

160 *"long religious essays . . . letters"*: Mercedes de Acosta, "Here Lies the Heart," typescript, [1938], first draft, 8, MdAP.

161 *"a suicidal mania"*: de Acosta, "Here Lies the Heart," typescript [1938], first draft, 229, MdAP.

161 *"put [her] face . . . moaned"*: De Acosta, *Here Lies*, 38.

161 *"craving for death . . . state"*: De Acosta, "Here Lies the Heart," typescript [1938], first draft, 231–32, MdAP.

161 *"the frustration and . . . men"*: De Acosta, *Here Lies*, 117.

161 *"without a shred . . . women"*: Ibid., 76.

161 *"my hair was . . . collapse"*: De Acosta, "Here Lies the Heart," typescript, [1938] first draft, 28, 30, 31, MdAP.

161 *"I am not . . . life"*: Ibid., 32, MdAP.

161 *"childhood tragedy"*: Ibid., 33, MdAP.

162 *"Every child was . . . ecstasy"*: De Acosta, *Here Lies*, 17.

162 *"like hunters out . . . Ethel"*: Ibid., 42.

162 *"too shy and . . . migraine"*: Ibid., 42–43.

162 *"would actually die"* . . . *room*: Ibid., 70.

162 *"Meeting these artists* . . . *life"*: Ibid., 42.

162 *"many celebrities other* . . . *Castellane"*: Ibid., 47.

162 *"persistently paragraphed and* . . . *photographed"*: Knickerbocker, "Cholly Knickerbocker Says."

162 *"magnetic personality"*: De Acosta, *Here Lies*, 5.

164 *"I have known* . . . *woman"*: Ibid., 5.

164 *"her presence raised* . . . *her"*: Ibid., 46.

164 *"a veritable museum"*: Frank Crowninshield, "The Fabulous Mrs. Lydig," *Vanity Fair*, April, 1940, 106, MdAP.

164 *In 1913 she* . . . *house*: The art dealer Joseph Duveen bought one of her Flemish tapestries for $41,000.

164 *"The curators of* . . . *taste"*: M.L.K., "Lady of an Antique World," *The New Yorker*, November 19, 1927, 28.

164 *"really works of art"*: Crowninshield, "The Fabulous Mrs. Lydig," 62.

164–165 *In 1940, Mercedes* . . . *Museum*: Parts of both these donations were on display in the 2010 exhibitions of the Metropolitan and Brooklyn museums' newly combined costume collections, American Woman: Fashioning a National Identity, and American High Style: Fashioning a National Collection.

165 *"mad extravagance* . . . *opinion"*: De Acosta, "Here Lies the Heart," typescript [1938], first draft, 197, MdAP.

165 *"rebellion against the* . . . *prudish"*: De Acosta, *Here Lies*, 67.

165 *"as if it* . . . *behind"*: Ibid., 85.

165 *a "minor" talent*: Ibid., 102.

166 *"feverishly compared notes* . . . *Duse"*: Ibid., 114.

166 *"I was in* . . . *development"*: Ibid., 109.

166 *Mercedes's sartorial predilections*: If Mercedes was attracted to icons of the stage and screen, "she also made *herself* iconic," notes Patricia White, in "Black and White."

166–167 *"She wears peculiarly* . . . *cap"*: "Daily Sketch" April 27, 1928, MdAP.

167 *"long-toed, silver-buckled* . . . *cape"*: Hugo Vickers, *Loving Garbo: The Story of Greta Garbo, Cecil Beaton, and Mercedes de Acosta* (New York: Random House, 1994), 253.

167 *"These were the* . . . *lives"*: De Acosta, "Here Lies the Heart," typescript [circa 1960] second draft, 221, MdAP.

168 *"despised distance and* . . . *flesh"*: Janet Flanner to MdA, n.d. [1927], MdAP.

168 *"The most talked-about* . . . *fears"*: Quoted in Karen Swenson, *Greta Garbo: A Life Apart* (New York: Scribner, 1997), 260.

170 *"Both idolized their* . . . *melancholia"*: Ibid., 250.

170 *"a cameraman who* . . . *Costa [sic]"*: "Daily Sketch," November 7, 1934, MdAP.

170 *"a sort of* . . . *tristesse"*: De Acosta, "Here Lies the Heart," typescript [circa 1960], second draft.

170 *"in depicting people* . . . *lives"*: MdA to Cecil Beaton, October 24, n.d., Cecil Beaton Papers, St. John's College, Cambridge University.

170 *"a self-effacement* . . . *saint"*: De Acosta, *Here Lies*, 71.

170 *"spiritual as well* . . . *footlights"*: Ibid., 138.

170 *"a deeply spiritual* . . . *public"*: "Here Lies the Heart," typescript [circa 1960], second draft, 515.

170–171 *"astrology, costmic-astrology . . . phenomena"*: De Acosta, *Here Lies*, 146.

171 *"a worshipper . . . through"*: Vincent Sheean, blurb on back of first edition of *Here Lies the Heart*; also used in display advertising in *New York Times*, March 8 and 20, 1960, MdAP.

171 *"Greta complained during . . . subject"*: De Acosta, "Here Lies the Heart," typescript [circa 1960], second draft, 415.

172 *"done as a . . . Francis"*: Elsa Maxwell, "Elsa Maxwell's Party Line: Mercedes de Acosta," *New York Post*, April 20, 1943, 12, MdAP.

172 *"Until I was . . . starlight?"*: Quoted in Maria Riva, *Marlene Dietrich* (New York: Alfred A. Knopf, 1993), 168.

172 *"Greta will come . . . it"*: Meher Baba to MdA, July 10, 1935, MdAP.

172–173 *"These past years . . . again"*: MdA to George Cukor, July 10, 1938, George Cukor Papers, Margaret Herrick Library, Academy of Motion Picture Arts and Sciences.

173 *"Though there may . . . part"*: De Acosta, "Here Lies the Heart," typescript [circa 1960], second draft, 514.

174 *"Don't let a . . . life"*: Cecil Beaton to MdA, April 25, 1958, MdAP.

174 *"gallantry . . . lovers"*: Cecil Beaton, unpublished diaries, May 1968, quoted in Vickers, *Loving Garbo*, 281.

174 *"The German people . . . always"*: This was Garbo's response to her reception in Berlin for "Gösta Berlings Saga," in *Photoplay*, May 28, 1924, quoted in Swenson, *Greta Garbo*, 69.

174–175 *"always was fond . . . trashy"*: EM to Chester Arthur, September 12, 1936, AFP.

175 *"sexual reaction[s]"*: De Acosta, "Here Lies the Heart," typescript [1938], first draft, 129, MdAP.

175 *"out on the astral plane"*: De Acosta, *Here Lies*, 39.

175 *"affected and excited . . . me"*: De Acosta, "Here Lies the Heart," typescript [1938], first draft, 129, MdAP.

175 *"slow breathing exercises . . . house'"*: De Acosta, *Here Lies*, 305.

175 *"a very different . . . sex"*: Ibid., 117.

175 *"disappeared one by . . . ports"*: Ibid., 95.

175 *"was crowded with . . . day"*: Ibid.

175 *"While this is . . . Acosta"*: *Des Moines* (Iowa) *Register*, April 3, 1960, MdAP.

176 *"met many of . . . knew"*: De Acosta, *Here Lies*, 140.

176 *"Friends were kind . . . others"*: Ibid., 206.

176 collector *Gabrielle Enthoven*: Mercedes notes that Enthoven acquired "thousands of engravings and photographs of actors and actresses, scenes from plays, interiors and exteriors of theatres, and a great many printed texts including 150 prompt copies of eighteenth-century plays used by the Theatre Royal, Drury Lane," de Acosta, *Here Lies*, 124. Enthoven donated this material to the Victoria and Albert Museum in 1924, but continued to collect until her death in 1950. Her collection formed the basis of the Theatre Museum in London.

176 *"part of the . . . twenties"*: De Acosta, *Here Lies*, 126.

177 *"in her personal . . . way"*: Ibid., 71–72.

177 *"so fat that . . . Hall"*: Ibid., 71.

177 drew *"from memory"*: Ibid., 357.

177 *"Let me tell . . . it"*: MdA to William McCarthy, June 27, 1960, MdAP.

177–178 *"Am sending you . . . them"*: MdA to William McCarthy, October 17 [1961], MdAP.

178 *"Utterly broke," she . . . "worries"*: MdA to William McCarthy, n.d. [postmarked September 20, 1961], MdAP.

178 *"I never get . . . people"*: MdA to William McCarthy, October 31, 1964; emphasis hers, MdAP.

179 *"My kisses like . . . hips"*: Isadora Duncan to MdA, n.d. [1927], MdAP.

179 *"with the eyelash . . . fly"*: De Acosta, *Here Lies*, 343.

179 *"A single stocking . . . note"*: Catalogue, Mercedes de Acosta Papers, Rosenbach Museum & Library.

179 *"wore during rehearsals . . . slippers"*: MdA to William McCarthy, Wednesday [postmarked September 20, 1961], MdAP.

183 *Sitting in the reading room:* The reading room has since been relocated.

183 *"Anyone determined to . . . 1960"*: Press conference, April 17, 2000, Rosenbach Museum & Library, Philadelphia, Pa.

183 *"Garbo Letters: Reveal . . . Lesbianism"*: *Metro*, Philadelphia, April 18, 2000.

183–184 *"No Hint of . . . Trove"*: *Philadelphia Daily News*, April 18, 2000, 6.

184 *"When we climbed . . . clasp"*: De Acosta, Poem no. 7, "Hollywood 1935," MdAP.

184 *"There is holiness . . . dreams"*: De Acosta, Poem no. 5, "Tistad 1935 Sweden," MdAP.

185–186 *"a lover of . . . years"*: Edwin Wolf, *Rosenbach. A Biography* (Cleveland: World Publishing, 1960), 7, 8.

186 *"The brothers loved . . . 'collection!' "*: "The Rosenbach Brothers: Collecting Their Collections," in The Rosenbach Collectors's Kit, educational material, Rosenbach Museum & Library.

186 *"11-year-old . . . DiCaprio"*: Carrie Rickey, "Garbo, Ever Guarded," *Philadelphia Inquirer*, April 18, 2000, F1, F3.

186–187 *"Acosta's fanatical devotion . . . point!"*: Press conference, April 17, 2000.

187 *"It was not . . . own"*: Quoted in Swenson, *Greta Garbo*, 225.

187 *"a great many . . . appeared"*: MdA to William McCarthy, July 25, n.d., MdAP.

187 *"because she insinuated . . . art"*: Carrie Rickey, "55 Greta Garbo Letters to Be Opened Here," *Philadelphia Inquirer*, March 19, 2000, A1, A18.

187 *"round[ing] out a . . . century"*: Rosenbach Museum & Library press release, March 2000.

187–189 *"a pre-Enlightenment . . . unrealities"*: Terry Castle, "Seductress Extraordinaire," *London Review of Books* 26, no. 12 (June 24, 2004).

189 *"Probability is not . . . dictionary"*: *Times Literary Supplement*, May 10, 1928, MdAP.

189 *"purple passages that . . . decade"*: *Weekly Dispatch* (London), June 24, 1928, MdAP.

189 *"amazed that the . . . window"*: De Acosta, *Here Lies*, 112.

189 *"Suddenly I thought . . . Infinite!"*: Mercedes de Acosta, *Moods* (New York: Moffat, Yard, 1919).

190–191 *"I have seen . . . them"*: EM to Chester Arthur, September 12, 1936, AFP.

191 *"so absurdly and . . . room"*: De Acosta, *Here Lies*, 70.

191 *"I do know . . . words!")*: Riva, *Marlene Dietrich*, 168.

193 *"Garbo Letters Leave Mystery Intact"*: *USA Today*, April 18, 2000.

194 *"One by one . . . everything"*: MdA to William McCarthy, n.d. [postmarked September 16, 1964], MdAP. She did not sell the Garbo papers, however; the Rosenbach has stated clearly that this material was a gift.

194 *"quite unique and . . . material"*: MdA to William McCarthy, June 29, n.d., MdAP.

VELVET IS VERY IMPORTANT

197 *"graver trouble . . . paranoia"*: All quotations from Madge Garland memoir drafts, MGP. She typed some of these pages herself, and some were typed from tapes she dictated.

198 *"as a pale . . . mother"*: Angela Neustatter, "The Magic Circle," *Guardian*, September 9, 1975, MGP.

198 *"rather excessive charm"*: Virginia Woolf, *The Diary of Virgina Woolf*, vol. 3: 1925–30, ed. Anne Olivier Bell, 5 vols. (New York: Harcourt Brace Jovanovich, 1977–84), 184 (May 31, 1928).

198 *"intellectual devotee of* couture": "Madge Garland," obituary, *Sunday Telegraph*, July 17, 1990, MGP.

198 *"meringue"*: Anne Scott-James to author, interview, London, December 9, 1997.

198 *"A bunch of froth"*: Helen Drummond to author, interview, London, December 8, 1997.

199 *"ideally cast . . . new"*: "Madge" [by Natasha Ledwidge], MGP.

200 *book after book*: See Madge Garland, *The Changing Face of Beauty: Four Thousand Years of Beautiful Women* (London: Weidenfeld and Nicolson, 1957); *Fashion* (Harmondsworth: Penguin, 1962); *The Indecisive Decade: The World of Fashion and Entertainment in the Thirties* (London: Macdonald, 1968); *The Changing Form of Fashion* (London: Dent, 1970); and Madge Garland and J. Anderson Black, *A History of Fashion* (London: Orbis, 1975).

200 *"I was never . . . independent"*: SaraJane Hoare, "Come into the Garland, Madge," *The Observer*, December 14, 1986, MGP.

200 *"She believes in . . . personality"*: "The Changing Face of Beauty, by Madge Garland," n.d., MGP.

200 *so-called minor arts*: See Isabelle Anscombe, *A Woman's Touch: Women in Design from 1860 to the Present Day* (London: Virago, 1984).

201 *"Fashion can be . . . personality"*: Madge Garland, "For Thousands of Years Women's Dress Has Proclaimed Her Status—Does It Now?" n.d., 64, MGP.

201 *"She really was . . . rebel"*: Sarah Stacey to author, interview, London, December 7, 1997.

201 *"kitten . . . ruffles"*: De Acosta, *Here Lies*, 133.

201 *"an exquisite piece of porcelain"*: Rebecca West to MG, February 25, 1980, RWP.

201 *"She was undoubtedly . . . monument"*: Peter Ward-Jackson to author, interview, London, September 17, 1997.

202 *"Fashion is both . . . worn"*: Madge Garland, "Artifices, Confections, and Manufactures," in *The Anatomy of Design: A Series of Inaugural Lectures by Professors of the Royal College of Art*, Delivered at the Royal Society of Arts, March 6, 1951 (London: Royal College of Art, 1951), 81.

202 *"Never in all . . . dress"*: MG memoir drafts, MGP.

202 *"a state in . . . time"*: Ibid.

203 *"cherished"*: MG to Isabelle Anscombe, interview, London, July 2, 1980, IAP.

203 *"futuristic"*: Cecil Beaton, *Photobiography* (New York: Doubleday, 1951), 42.

203 *"beautifully dressed in . . . make-up"*: "Dress Reformer," n.d. [circa mid-1940s], MGP.

203 *"wearing a Marimekko . . . pearls"*: Prudence Glynn, "50 Years On," *Times* (London), December 12, 1972, 18.

203 *"looking absolutely marvelous"*: Julia Burney to author, interview, London, January 22, 2002.

203 *"the most beautiful . . . outfit"*: Patrick Woodcock to author, interview, London, January 25, 2002.

203 *"as if she . . . archive"*: Selina Hastings to author, conversation, London, January 14, 1999.

I ABSOLUTELY REFUSED

204 *"horrid, thick . . . dresses"*: Madge Garland, "Children's Clothes," transcript, May 29, 1947, BBC Written Archives Centre.

204 *"My family didn't . . . all"*: MG to Flora Groult, interview, London, July 26, 1986.

204 *"I told them . . . 'no'"*: MG to Shaunagh Ward-Jackson, conversation, London, n.d.

204 *"I thought, 'No . . . won't!'"*: MG to Isabelle Anscombe, interview, London, October 8, 1979, IAP.

204 *"Millinery, Straws, Ready-to-Wears . . . Gloves"*: *Draper of Australia*, February 27, 1920, 70.

204 *"very, very fond of clothes"*: MG to Peter and Shaunagh Ward-Jackson, conversation, London, October 14, 1989.

205 *"just the stamp . . . colonist"*: "Colonial Industrie: Mr. Thos. Aitken's Victoria Parade Brewery, East Melbourne," *Carlton Advertiser and Trades Advocate*, April 8, 1882, MHFP.

206 *"the wilds of Hampstead"*: MG to Shaunagh Ward-Jackson, conversation, London, n.d.

208 *"always smelled delicious"*: MG memoir drafts, MGP.

208 *"beautifully dressed, always . . . buttoned"*: MG to Peter and Shaunagh Ward-Jackson, conversation, London, October 14, 1989.

208 *"pretty-mama" and . . . "neck"*: MG memoir drafts, MGP.

208 "My darling *Mama*": MG to Isabelle Anscombe, interview, London, July 2, 1980, IAP.

208 *"many fringes, fish-tails . . . hats"*: Garland, *Fashion*, 119–20.

208 *"at least I . . . home"*: MG to Peter and Shaunagh Ward-Jackson, conversation, London, October 14, 1989.

210 *"It is hard . . . hint"*: Garland, *Fashion*, 57.

210 *"for a Paris . . . weeks"*: Ibid., 60.

210 *"my helpless youth . . . body"*: Garland, "Children's Clothes."

210 *It was the claustrophobia . . . now*: Gwen Raverat, writing about her childhood
     as a member of the (in many other respects unconventional) Darwin family,
     observed that "for nearly seventy years the English middle classes were
     locked up in a great fortress of unreality and pretence; and no one who has
     not been brought up inside the fortress can guess how thick the walls were,
     or how little of the sky outside could be seen through the loopholes." Gwen
     Raverat, *Period Piece* (London: Faber, 1971 [1952]), 104.

210 *"If you want . . . Presbyterian"*: MG to Peter and Shaunagh Ward-Jackson, con-
     versation, London, December 28, 1987. She also said that her family attended
     church only in her early childhood.

210 *"Art and literature . . . all"*: MG to Isabelle Anscombe, interview, London,
     October 8, 1979, IAP.

210–211 *"Victorian Gothic . . . nothing"*: MG to Isabelle Anscombe, interview,
     London, July 2, 1980, IAP.

211 *The house was crammed . . . gadgets*: An auction catalogue from the 1938 sale of
     the McHargs' home in Melbourne gives an object-by-object view of Andrew
     McHarg's passion for accumulation. "If you were making a joke about Edwar-
     dian taste this is what you'd compile." Charlotte Gere to author, conversation,
     London, November 15, 2003.

211 *"extremely bad copies . . . for"*: MG to Isabelle Anscombe, interview, London,
     July 2, 1980, IAP.

212 *"a delight . . . star"*: MG memoir drafts, MGP.

212–213 *"Though married life . . . one"*: *The Encyclopædia Britannica: A Dictionary of
     Arts, Sciences, Literature and General Information*, vol. 28 (Cambridge, U.K.:
     University of Cambridge, 1911), 782, 785.

213 *"a very much . . . baby"*: MG to Shaunagh Ward-Jackson, conversation, Lon-
     don, n.d.

213 *"the problem . . . daughter"*: MG memoir drafts, MGP.

213 *"silly books . . . girls"*: Ibid.

213 *"I discovered that . . . going"*: MG to Shaunagh Ward-Jackson, conversation,
     London, n.d.

214 *Cheltenham Ladies' College*: Founded in 1841, this school was run from 1858 to
     1906 by Dorothea Beale, a pioneer of girls' education (she was also the foun-
     der of St. Hilda's Hall, later St. Hilda's College, Oxford) and an activist for
     women's rights who transformed Cheltenham from a school for the acquisi-
     tion of the ladylike skills of music, dancing, and drawing to a place that em-
     phasized rigorous academic training and had a reputation for scholastic
     excellence.

214 *"totally unaware of . . . girls"*: MG memoir drafts, MGP.

214 *"difficult and unruly . . . improved"*: MG to Shaunagh Ward-Jackson, conversa-
     tion, London, n.d.

214 *"they always knew . . . minute"*: Ibid.

215 *"jump through the window"*: MG to Flora Groult, interview, London, July 26,
     1986.

215 *"remote churches all over Paris"*: MG to Isabelle Anscombe, interview, Lon-
     don, October 8, 1979, IAP.

215 *"freedom of thought"*: MG to Flora Groult, interview, London, July 26, 1986.

215 *"prison-like after . . . Paris"*: MG memoir drafts, MGP.

215 *"was strictly limited"*: Glynn, "50 Years On."

215 *"You see my . . . 21"*: MG to Flora Groult, interview, London, July 26, 1986.

215–216 *"the most violent . . . secret"*: MG to Shaunagh Ward-Jackson, conversation, London, December 28, 1987.

216 *Virginia Woolf later argued*: Virginia Woolf, *Three Guineas* (New York: Harcourt Brace, 1966 [1938]).

216 *"After some months . . . implored"*: MG memoir drafts, MGP. The college was founded in 1849 by social reformer Elizabeth Jesser Reid.

217 *And she spent . . .* : Andrew McHarg may well have forced her to leave Bedford College, but if so, it was probably before 1917. The college records indicate that she completed the Cambridge Higher Local, a one-year course to prepare for a qualifying examination that would allow her to apply to Cambridge and Oxford; grades are recorded for her for each of the three terms in 1914/15. There is no evidence that she took the exam, however, and no record of her at the college beyond 1915. Her name does not appear in the surviving Newnham College files, but it is still possible that she applied and was accepted there. There is a family story that she attended Melbourne University, and while there is no record of her in the university's files, she might have enrolled in a course or two. Certainly it is easy to imagine her exacting this concession from her father in exchange for her company during those years.

218 *"clad in silken . . . wardrobe"*: MG memoir drafts, MGP.

218 *John Francis Queeny . . .* : Long before Monsanto was committed to plant biotechnology, it was making money on two of its earliest products, saccharin and caffeine—and when the war cut the United States off from European manufacturing, business boomed. In 1917, Monsanto started manufacturing aspirin; until the 1980s it was the world's largest producer of the drug. Queeny offered Andrew McHarg the Australian rights to the formula for acetylsalicylic acid, but the latter demurred and suggested some Australian colleagues, the Nicholas Brothers, who made their fortunes from it.

221 *"American girls . . . wanted"*: MG to Flora Groult, interview, London, July 26, 1986.

221 *"I wanted to . . . nothing"*: MG memoir drafts, MGP.

221 *"the piles of dead birds"*: Ibid.

221–222 *"She would talk . . . aborigines"*: Sarah Stacey to author, interview, London, December 7, 1997.

I WAS FREE

223 *"must make a . . . century"*: Virginia Woolf, *The Diary of Virginia Woolf*, vol. 2: 1920–24, Anne Olivier Bell, ed., Appendix 3, "The Intellectual Status of Women," 341. It is a letter to the editor of the *New Statesman*, October 16, 1920.

223 *"all the miseries . . . suffered"*: MG memoir drafts, MGP.

223 *"One of the . . . McHarg"*: "Miss McHarg of England, on Way Home from Australia, Is Much Entertained by Miss Queeny and Other Friends Here." St. Louis, Sunday Morning, December 1, 1918, no source, Olguita Monsanto Queeny Berington scrapbook, private collection.

223 *"rather special rather . . . more"*: Olguita M. Q. Berington to MG, n.d. [1945], MGP.

223 *"a relationship so . . . unique"*: Untitled, MGP.

227 *"the youngest Flight . . . horror"*: Ewart Garland war diary, courtesy of Patrick Garland.

228 *"Oh no, Ewart . . . that"*: Patrick Garland to author, interview, London, December 9, 1997.

228 *"not a matter . . . nothing"*: MG memoir drafts, MGP.

230 *"Well, it was . . . all"*: MG to Isabelle Anscombe, interview, London, October 8, 1979, IAP.

230 *"the suffragette generation . . . idol"*: MG to Flora Groult, interview, London, July 26, 1986.

230 *"It was* quite *. . . that"*: MG to Isabelle Anscombe, interview, London, October 8, 1979, IAP.

230–231 *"wanted somehow to . . . job"*: MG memoir drafts, MGP.

231 *"became an organization . . . editor"*: Edna Woolman Chase, *Always in Vogue* (New York: Doubleday, 1954), 150.

231 *"in a very dingy little office"*: MG to Flora Groult, interview, London, July 26, 1986.

231 *"I must go . . . o'clock"*: MG memoir drafts, MGP.

231 *"You see, I . . . pressed"*: MG to Flora Groult, interview, London, July 26, 1986.

231 *"replied that he . . . me"*: MG memoir drafts, MGP.

231 *"And that," she . . . "that"*: MG to Isabelle Anscombe, interview, London, October 8, 1979, IAP.

232 *"I was free . . . time"*: MG to Flora Groult, London, interview, July 26, 1986.

232 *"He never really . . . all"*: MG to Shaunagh Ward-Jackson, conversation, London, n.d.

232 *"What I did . . . hours"*: MG to Isabelle Anscombe, interview, London, October 8, 1979, IAP.

232 *"as a messenger boy"*: MG memoir drafts, MGP.

232 *"to get proofs . . . actress"*: MG to Isabelle Anscombe, interview, London, October 8, 1979, IAP.

232 *"I was very . . . England"*: MG to Flora Groult, interview, London, July 26, 1986.

232 *"I grew into . . . it"*: MG to Isabelle Anscombe, interview, October 8, 1979, IAP.

232–233 *"so-called English . . . snapshots"*: Ibid.

233 *"dreamt up by . . . artists"*: Garland, *Fashion*, 107.

233 *"who wore the . . . results"*: Ibid., 140.

233 *"though the First . . . predecessor"*: Garland, *Fashion*, 119–20.

233 *"immense and far-reaching . . . her"*: MG memoir drafts, MGP.

233 *"first editor British* Vogue, *1916–22"*: "Who's Who in Vogue 1916–66," British *Vogue*, October 1966.

235 *"the only Englishwoman . . . Paris"*: Madge Garland, typescript, slide lecture to the Design and Industries Association [circa September 1979].

235 *"a beautiful dress . . . Paris"*: MG to Flora Groult, interview, London, July 26, 1986.

235 *"a tea girl"*: MG to Flora Groult, interview, London, July 26, 1986.

235 *"the hideous laced-up . . . boots"*: MG memoir drafts, MGP.

235 *"Are you dressed . . . that?"*: MG to Flora Groult, interview, London, July 26, 1986. "Aldous had great eye trouble," Madge said, "but he managed, like a lot of people with eye trouble, to see what he wanted to see."

235–236 *"walking about and . . . little"*: MG memoir drafts, MGP.

236 *" 'Oh you won't . . . ill' "*: MG to Flora Groult, interview, London, July 26, 1986.

236 *"COME AT ONCE AND MARRY ME"*: MG memoir drafts, MGP.

WHO NEED NEVER BE MENTIONED

237 *"in anything as . . . parted"*: MG memoir drafts, MGP.

238 *"Madge has gone . . . do"*: Patrick Garland to author, interview, London, December 9, 1997. "He was very crushed by this episode," said Patrick Garland, Ewart's son by his second marriage; "he felt it as . . . a tremendous insult to his masculinity."

238 *"the absolute making . . . love"*: Chloe Tyner to author, telephone interview, May 19, 1997.

238 *"the only two . . . life"*: Chloe Tyner to author, June 5, 1997. Tyner was citing Madge's correspondence to her.

238–241 *"inexpressibly painful," she . . . "case"*: MG to Hilary Spurling, conversation, March 29, 1989.

241 *"When Miss Todd . . . mentioned"*: Gertrude Stein, *A Novel of Thank You* (Normal, Ill.: Dalkey Archive Press, 1994), 13. This book, written in 1925–26 but not published until 1958, is so full of names that when Carl Van Vechten edited *The Yale Gertrude Stein*, he felt compelled to "identif[y]" some of them. Todd's is not among these.

242 *"the bucket in . . . loneliness"*: Cecil Beaton, unpublished diaries, cited in Hugo Vickers, *Cecil Beaton* (Boston: Little, Brown, 1985), 80.

242 *"tremendous mind," remembered . . . "amusing"*: Chloe Tyner to author, telephone interview, May 19, 1997.

242 *"a shimmer of . . . it"*: Woolf, *Diary*, Saturday, February 18 [1928], 3:176.

242 *"a wasp's nest . . . character"*: MG to Hilary Spurling, conversation, London, March 29, 1989.

242 *his second wife*: They married in December 1881.

243 *"All that belonged . . . well"*: Olivier Todd to author, interview, Paris, September 23, 1997.

243 *"by friends or . . . life"*: MG to Hilary Spurling, conversation, London, March 29, 1989.

244 *"I never heard . . . things"*: Chloe Tyner to author, telephone interview, May 19, 1997.

244 *"the innumerable young . . . us"*: Helen Todd, unpublished ms., private collection.

245 *"accustomed to drunkenness . . . age"*: Ibid.

246 *"People disapproved of . . . hard"*: Rebecca West, in George Plimpton, ed., *Women Writers at Work: The Paris Review Interviews* (New York: Modern Library, 1998), 76.

246 *"normal" family life . . . "niece"*: Helen Todd, unpublished ms., private collection.

246 *"I see Dody's . . . niece"*: Hilary Spurling to author, conversation, London, September 25, 1997.

246 *"should have felt"*: Helen Todd, unpublished ms., private collection.

247 *"Other people will . . . repay"*: MG to Hilary Spurling, conversation, London, March 29, 1989.

247 *"It was entirely . . . London"*: Ibid.

247 *"for about four . . . London"*: MG to Isabelle Anscombe, interview, London, October 8, 1979, IAP.

247 *"two very remarkable . . . arts"*: Rebecca West, in Joan Russell Noble, ed., *Recollections of Virginia Woolf* (London: Peter Owen, 1972), 90.

249 *"not only [to] . . . Group"*: Chase, *Always in Vogue*, 151.

249 *"helped Roger Fry . . . Marais"*: West, *Recollections*, 90.

251 *"Vogue . . . is going . . . her"*: Woolf, *Diary*, October 17 [1924], 2:319.

251 an *"enthusiastic"* article: Alice B. Toklas, *What Is Remembered* (San Francisco: North Point Press, 1985), 118.

251 *their initial exposure*: As Rebecca West put it, Madge and Dody "gave young writers a firmer foundation than they might have had by commissioning them to write articles on intelligent subjects at fair prices." West, *Recollections*, 90. In Madge's words: "Dody had . . . an overwhelming generosity. In that way, she was a wonderful editor—she would give someone his head." MG to Hilary Spurling, conversation, March 29, 1989.

251 *"She . . . could have . . . water"*: West, *Recollections*, 90.

252 *"perfectly repellent Bayswater . . . Square"*: MG to Flora Groult, interview, London, July 26, 1986.

252 *"downright forthright manner"*: Ibid.

252 *"her curly hair . . . back"*: Frances Spalding, *Vanessa Bell* (New Haven and New York: Tichnor and Fields, 1983), 243. "In 1930 Clive and Benita spent six weeks at Cannes, at Madge Garland's villa in the rue d'Antibes, where they frequently entertained Raymond Mortimer Brian Guinness and John Banting who were staying near by."

252 *"a very forcible lady"*: Raymond Mortimer to Isabelle Anscombe, interview, London, March 21, 1979, IAP.

254 *"looked charming . . . well"*: Cecil Beaton, unpublished diaries, Thursday, October 21, 1926, CBD.

254 *"was received as . . . importance"*: Beaton, *Photobiography*, 40.

254 *"the Vogue gang"*: Cecil Beaton, unpublished diaries, January 23, 1926, CBD.

254 *"he concentrated . . . Garland"*: Hugo Vickers, *Cecil Beaton*, 67.

254 *"one or two . . . Bloomsbury"*: Cecil Beaton, unpublished diaries, February 21, 1926, CBD.

254 *"She absolutely knocked . . . star"*: Anne Scott-James to author, interview, London, December 9, 1997.

254 *"almost like an agency"*: Chloe Tyner to author, telephone interview, May 19, 1997.

255 *"Because I am one"*: Madge Garland, in Noble, ed., *Recollections of Virginia Woolf*, 174.

255 *"You'd never go . . . somebody"*: *A Salute to Marcel Boulestin and Jean-Emile Labourer: An Exhibition of Artists Associated with the Restaurant Boulestin* (London: Michael Parkin Fine Art, 1981), 26.

255 *"a beautiful house for parties"*: MG to Hugo Vickers, interview, London, March 8, 1980.

255 *"charming & very . . . out"*: Cecil Beaton, unpublished diaries, Sunday, November 7, 1926, CBD.

255 *"impromptu wild parties"*: Patrick Balfour [Kinross], *Society Racket: A Critical Survey of Modern Social Life* (London: John Long, 1933), 64. In this long list of some of the parties he attended in the 1920s—"Parties for the Blackbirds; an unforgettable Russian party in Gerald Road, with a Negro band, where a whole house and studio had been specially redecorated for a single night; the swimming party in the St. George's baths; David Tennant's Mozart party, where the eighteenth century was recaptured for a night; . . . impromptu wild parties, in fancy undress, in the Royal Hospital Road"—he is echoing Evelyn Waugh's catalogue in *Vile Bodies*: "Masked parties, Savage parties, Victorian parties, Greek parties, Wild West parties, Russian parties, Circus parties, parties where one had to dress as somebody else, almost naked parties in St John's Wood, parties in flats and studios and houses and ships and hotels and nightclubs . . .—all that succession and repetition of massed humanity. . . . Those vile bodies."

255 *"it was like . . . family"*: MG to Flora Groult, interview, London, July 26, 1986.

255 *"Several ultra smart . . . pearls"*: Cecil Beaton, unpublished diaries, Sunday, November 7, 1926, CBD. Wyndham was working with the American Curtis Moffat in his photography studio. During the war, after she moved to New York, she enlisted in the WACs and again worked as a photographer.

255 *"the thinnest person . . . waist"*: Anne Scott James to author, interview, London, December 9, 1997.

255 *"the people one . . . bacchanals"*: Vernon Duke, *Passport to Paris* (Boston: Little, Brown, 1955), 163–64. Duke was an old friend of Ewart Garland's.

257 *"The 'twenties in . . . dancing"*: MG to Flora Groult, interview, London, July 26, 1986.

258 *"the vein of poetry"*: MG to Isabelle Anscombe, interview, London, October 8, 1979, IAP.

258 *"eventually swept every . . . done"*: Garland, *Fashion*, 50.

258 *Yet it was . . . time*: As the philosopher and sociologist Georg Simmel observed at the turn of the twentieth century: "It is peculiarly characteristic of fashion that it renders possible a social obedience, which at the same time is a form of individual differentiation." Georg Simmel, "Fashion," *International Quarterly* 10 (1904): 130–55, 141. See this essay also for more on the relationship between fashion and shame.

258 *"look[ing] perfect in . . . pink"*: Cecil Beaton, unpublished diaries, Sunday, February 21, 1926, CBD.

258 *"patterned jumper [sweater] . . . forth"*: MG to Isabelle Anscombe, interview, London, October 8, 1979, IAP.

258 *"put the gramophone on and danced"*: MG to Flora Groult, interview, London, July 26, 1986.

258 *"whole school of Paris* artistes-decorateurs*"*: MG to Isabelle Anscombe, interview, London, October 8, 1979, IAP.

258–259 *"both Bohemian and . . . feminine"*: Madge Garland, "The World of Marie Laurencin," *The Saturday Book* 23, John Hadfield, ed. (London: Hutchinson, 1963), 46.

259 *"costumes for 'Les' . . . designs"*: Charlotte Gere, *Marie Laurencin* (London: Academy, 1977), 23.

259 *"both modern and exquisite"*: Sarah Stacey to author, interview, London, December 7, 1997.

259 *"in her espadrilles . . . bistro"*: Garland, "The World of Marie Laurencin," 59.

259 *"frock consciousness"*: Woolf, *Diary*, Monday, April 27 [1925], 3:12.

259 *her frequent despair*: See Lisa Cohen, " 'Frock Consciousness': Virginia Woolf, the Open Secret, and the Language of Fashion," *Fashion Theory*, vol. 3, no. 2 (May 1999): 149–74.

260 *"I have been . . . it"*: Woolf, *Diary*, April 27 [1925], 3:12–13.

260 *"My love of . . . discover"*: Woolf, *Diary*, Thursday, May 14 [1925], 3:21.

260 *"knew that she . . . was"*: MG to Isabelle Anscombe, interview, London, October 8, 1979.

261 *"So there is . . . outfit"*: MG to Flora Groult, interview, London, July 26, 1986.

261 *"a very beautiful . . . head"*: Garland, in Noble, *Recollections*, 171.

261 *"hilarious conversation about corsets"*: MG to Isabelle Anscombe, London, October 8, 1979, IAP.

262 *"I asked Todd . . . fee"*: Woolf, Friday October 17 [1924], *Diary*, 2:319.

262 *"the ethics of . . . Vogue"*: Virgina Woolf to Jacques Raverat, January 24, 1925, *The Letters of Virginia Woolf*, vol. 3, 1923–1928, 6 vols., Nigel Nicholson and Joanne Trautmann, eds. (New York: Harcourt Brace Jovanovich, 1977), 154.

262 *"Why," she wrote . . . "Toddery?"*: Virginia Woolf to Vanessa Bell, Saturday May 25 [1928], Woolf, *Letters*, 3:502.

262 *"perhaps worse than . . . petticoats"*: Virginia Woolf to Logan Pearsall Smith, Wednesday, [January 28, 1928], Woolf, *Letters*, 3:158.

262 *"And whats [sic] . . . Sup"*: Virginia Woolf to Vita Sackville-West, Tuesday, September 1, 1925, Woolf, *Letters*, 3:200.

262 *"I want as . . . wit"*: Woolf, *Diary*, Sunday, April 19 [1925], 3:9.

262 *"The New Dress"*: Virginia Woolf, "The New Dress," in *The Complete Shorter Fiction of Virginia Woolf* (New York: Harcourt, Brace, 1989, 1985), 170–77. All quotations of this story are from this edition.

263–264 *"Vogue is going . . . public"*: Harry Yoxall, unpublished diaries, Thursday, June 28 [1923].

264 *"naturally of a . . . out"*: Chase, *Always in Vogue*, 152.

264 *"the publisher, the . . . it"*: Carolyn Seebohm, *The Man Who Was Vogue: The Life and Times of Condé Nast* (New York: Viking, 1982), 80–81.

265 *"The world was . . . dressmakers"*: MG to Isabelle Anscombe, London, October 8, 1979, IAP.

265 *"difficult to find . . . fraught"*: Madge Garland, "Condé Charm," review of *The Man Who Was Vogue*, *Financial Times*, September 11, 1982, 10.

265 *"Miss McHarg (Mrs. . . . required"*: Harry Yoxall, unpublished diaries, Monday, September 13, [1926].

265 *"end on the . . . Nast"*: Harry Yoxall, unpublished diaries, Sunday, November 14, [1926].

266 *"This affair has . . . rupture"*: Vita Sackville-West to Harold Nicholson, September 24, 1926, quoted in Seebohm, *The Man Who Was Vogue*, 128.

266 *"It is said . . . action"*: Virginia Woolf to Vanessa Bell [end of September 1926], Woolf, *Letters*, 3:295.

266 *"So poor Todd . . . order"*: Vita Sackville-West to Harold Nicholson, September 24, 1926, quoted in Seebohm, *The Man Who Was Vogue*, 127–28.

266 *"immediately . . . representative"*: Seebohm, *The Man Who Was Vogue*, 130.

266 *"The lady [Dody] . . . formula"*: Chase, *Always in Vogue*, 152–53.

266 *"in the days . . . contract"*: Garland, "Condé Charm."

267 *"that filthy Editor . . . bit"*: Cecil Beaton, unpublished diaries, Sunday, January 10 [1926]; Wednesday, October 20 [1925], CBD.

267 *"Miss Todd the . . . Garland"*: Cecil Beaton, unpublished diaries, Thursday, April 8 [1926], CBD.

267 *"a brilliant evocation . . . youth"*: Quoted in Julie Kavanaugh, *Secret Muses: The Life of Frederick Ashton* (New York: Pantheon, 1996), 72.

268 *"both looking very . . . dressed"*: Harry Yoxall, unpublished diaries, Sunday, November 14 [1926].

268 *"to be Vogue, only quarterly"*: Virginia Woolf to Vanessa Bell, Tuesday, February 21, 1928, Woolf, *Letters*, 3:463.

268 *"trying hard to . . . pictorial"*: Cecil Beaton, unpublished diaries, Sunday, October 31 [1926], CBD.

268 *"a black toque . . . dress"*: Cecil Beaton to his sisters, January 14, 1927, quoted in Vickers, *Cecil Beaton*, 89.

268 *"I wanted to . . . flower"*: Cecil Beaton, unpublished diaries, Thursday, October 21, 1926, CBD.

268 *"Todd was a . . . normal"*: Cecil Beaton, unpublished diaries, Sunday, November 7, 1926, CBD.

268–269 *"rows in front . . . hours"*: Chloe Tyner to author, telephone interview, May 19, 1997.

269 *"in a state . . . tearful"*: Chloe Tyner to Shaunagh Ward-Jackson, April 2, 1991.

269 *"like some primeval . . . hirsute"*: Woolf, *Diary*, Saturday, February 18 [1928], 3:175–76.

269 *"The Todd ménage . . . ends"*: Virginia Woolf to Vanessa Bell, Saturday, May 25 [1928], Woolf, *Letters*, 3:501.

269 *"Todd's room; rather . . . Garland"*: Woolf, *Diary*, Thursday, May 31 [1928], 3:184.

269–270 *"She had been . . . awful"*: MG to Hilary Spurling, conversation, London, March 29, 1989.

270 *"I had never . . . remained"*: MG memoir drafts, MGP.

TO REMAKE MY CAREER

271 *"Dody went downhill . . . charming"*: Chloe Tyner to author, telephone interview, May 19, 1997.

271 *"it was much . . . London"*: MG memoir drafts, MGP.

271 *"almost anywhere"*: MG to Shaunagh Ward-Jackson, conversation, London, n.d.

271 *"miserable meals . . . eyes"*: MG memoir drafts, MGP.

273 *"One night we . . . flat"*: MG to Shaunagh Ward-Jackson, conversation, London, n.d.

273 *"sober habit . . . women"*: Iris Tree, in ed. Simon Fleet, *Sophie Fedorovitch: Tributes and Attributes; Aspects of Her Art and Personality by Some of Her Fellow Artists and Friends* (Bolton, printed for private circulation, 1955), 14.

273 *"feeling for ethereal . . . stage"*: Maude Lloyd, in ibid., 44.

273 *"my greatest artistic . . . adviser"*: Kavanaugh, *Secret Muses*, 73.

273 *"drinking tea and . . . hours"*: MG to Shaunagh Ward-Jackson, conversation, London, n.d.

273 *"the early beginnings"*: MG memoir drafts, MGP.

273 *"way of life and dress"*: Ibid.

274 *Illustrated Newspapers Group*: Their other papers included *The Illustrated London News, Tatler,* and *The Sphere.*

274 *"I can and I will"*: MG to Shaunagh Ward-Jackson, conversation, London, n.d.

274 *"Madge's two old . . . bed"*: MG to Flora Groult, interview, London, July 26, 1986.

274 *"what are called women's interests"*: MG memoir drafts, MGP.

274 *"knitting, and babies . . . saucepan"*: MG to Shaunagh Ward-Jackson, conversation, London, n.d.

274 *"such a challenge"*: MG memoir drafts, MGP.

276 *"I lived the fullest life"*: MG to Flora Groult, interview, London, July 26, 1986.

276 *"always very elegant . . . soignée"*: Anne Scott-James to author, interview, London, December 9, 1997.

276 *"always in a hat"*: David Sassoon to author, interview, London, September 22, 1997.

276 *"I thought I . . . not!"*: "Madge" [by Natasha Ledwidge], n.d., MGP.

276 *"Dark brown is . . . blue"*: "Madge Garland Writes a Forecast of Fashion," *The Bystander,* January 6, 1932, 35.

276 *"Pink and brown . . . shades"*: Madge Garland, "New Ways with Woollens," *The Bystander,* May 4, 1932, 230.

276 *"Sports clothes favour . . . divided"*: "Madge Garland Writes a Forecast of Fashion," 35.

276–277 *"For evening wraps . . . gowns"*: Madge Garland, "Madge Garland Brings Back News from Paris," *The Bystander,* January 20, 1932, 133.

277 *"copy of a . . . STOP"*: Madge Garland, "A Telegram from Paris," *Britannia and Eve,* March 1930, 76.

277 *"Don't you think . . . bustle?"*: Madge Garland, "A Fashion Questionnaire: A Few Pertinent Remarks on the High-lights of the 1931–1932 Winter Fashions," *Britannia and Eve,* November 1931, 54. She used this form several years before Diana Vreeland's "Why Don't You" column in *Harper's.* In fact, she and Vreeland knew each other when Vreeland lived in London and ran a lingerie shop in the early 1930s.

277 *"Which Would You . . . Tulle?"*: Madge Garland, "News and Novelties," *The Bystander,* October 5, 1932, 34–35.

277 *"A long dress . . . it"*: Gertrude Stein, "Tender Buttons," *Writings 1903–1932* (New York: Library of America, 1998), 318.

277–279 *"Practice measurement, practice . . . accentuation"*: Stein, "Tender Buttons," 319.

279 *"Looking is not . . . clothing"*: Stein, "Portrait of Mabel Dodge at Villa Curiona," *Writings 1903–1932,* 357.

279 *"For this is so. Because"*: Stein, "If I Told Him: A Completed Portrait of Picasso," *Writings 1903–1932*, 506.

279 *"Velvet is Very Important"*: Madge Garland, *The Bystander*, September 21, 1932, 561.

279 *"The ANGLE of . . . important"*: Garland, "Madge Garland Brings Back News from Paris," 130–31.

279 *"This insistence on . . . importance"*: Madge Garland, "What I Saw in Paris," *Britannia and Eve*, April 1930, 74.

279 *"Importance is given . . . gaillac"*: Madge Garland, "A Letter from Paris: Autumn 1933," *Britannia and Eve*, October 1933, 63.

280 *"There is a . . . frivolous"*: Mary Graham [Madge Garland], "The Psychology of Dress," *Britannia and Eve*, December 1930, 87. I have found no other trace of Graham, so I attribute the article to Madge, whose initials she shares.

280 *"it is the . . . 'trivial'"*: Virginia Woolf, *A Room of One's Own* (New York: Harcourt Brace Jovanovich, 1989 [1929]), 73–74.

280 *"the desire to . . . individual"*: Graham [Garland], "The Psychology of Dress," 87.

280–281 *"It is a . . . house"*: Madge Garland, "This Fashion Business," *Britannia and Eve*, November 1930, 140.

281 *"A huge modern . . . lamé"*: Garland, "Letter from Paris, Autumn, 1933," 9, 60, 86.

282 *"madly jealous of . . . hell"*: MG to Isabelle Anscombe, interview, London, July 2, 1980, IAP.

282 *She remained in France*: "England was unsuitable for their chosen way of life," as Wyld's niece put it. Biddy Kay to Isabelle Anscombe, n.d, IAP.

282 *"always set her . . . belts"*: Ibid.

282 *"the most austere . . . materials"*: Madge Garland, "Interiors by Eyre de Lanux," *The Studio* (1930): 263–65, 265.

283 *"was radical in . . . day"*: Isabelle Anscombe, *A Woman's Touch*, 121, 123.

283 *"the grain of . . . banal"*: Garland, "Interiors by Eyre de Lanux," 265.

283 *"grew up in . . . living"*: MG to Isabelle Anscombe, interview, London, July 2, 1980, IAP. Like Esther Murphy, Madge lost many friends of the 1920s to opium and other addictions; she believed that she had never succumbed to drugs because she had to support herself.

283 *"Give Madge what she wants"*: MG to Shaunagh Ward-Jackson, conversation, London, n.d.

284 *"toadied to in . . . princesses"*: Garland, *Fashion*, 100.

284 *"You will go far"*: "Madge Garland," obituary, *Telegraph*, July 17, 1980, MGP.

284 *"the rôle of merchandise-stylist"*: Garland, *Fashion*, 105–6.

284 *"looked on with . . . criticism"*: Ibid.

284 *"be the pivot . . . idea"*: Ibid., 106.

284 *"deals with the . . . stores"*: Jane Mulvagh, *Vogue Fashion History of 20th Century*, foreword by Valerie D. Mendes (London: Viking, 1988), 185.

285 *"Selfridges or Harrods . . . wherever"*: MG memoir drafts, MGP.

285 *"was the chicest . . . lot"*: Virginia Nicholson to author, telephone interview, May 26, 1998.

285 *"antennae"*: Anne Scott-James to author, interview, London, 9 December 1997.

285 *"bitterly anti-Garland . . . so"*: Harry Yoxall, unpublished diaries, September 2, 1935.

285 *"much more boring . . . reliable"*: Anne Scott-James to author, interview, London, December 9, 1997.

285 *"people who happened . . . homosexual"*: Jennifer Beattie to author, interview, London, December 9, 1997.

285 *"Claire [sic] Luce . . . star"*: Harry Yoxall, unpublished diaries, June 19 [1937].

285–286 *"and have cocktails . . . host"*: Harry Yoxall, unpublished diaries, Saturday July 8 [1939].

286 *"straight skirt, nice . . . spectacular"*: Jennifer Beattie to author, interview, London, December 9, 1997.

286 *"sorting out everyone's . . . own"*: Patricia Laffan to author, interview, London, March 21, 1998.

286 *"She had no . . . irony"*: Patrick Woodcock to author, interview, London, January 25, 2002.

286 *"a very complex . . . difficult"*: Sybille Bedford to author, telephone conversation, January 8, 2003.

286 *"quarreled . . . bitterly"*: Sybille Bedford to author, interview, London, December 7, 1997.

286 *"In a match . . . winning"*: Francis King to author, interview, London, March 21, 1998.

286 *"Here comes that . . . Garland"*: Patricia Laffan to author, interview, London, March 21, 1998.

287 *"until we see . . . war"*: Harry Yoxall to Condé Nast, November 4, 1938, CNA.

287 *"The clothes were . . . future"*: Madge Garland, "Introduction," *Fashion, 1900–1939*, Scottish Arts Council and Victoria and Albert Museum (London: Idea, 1975), 8.

287 *"The cost of . . . so"*: Harry Yoxall to Condé Nast, September 28, 1939, CNA.

287 *"reckless in the . . . met"*: Sybille Bedford, *Aldous Huxley* (New York: Carroll and Graf, 1985 [1973, 1974]), 308.

288 *"low in the . . . stress"*: Harry Yoxall to Condé Nast, October 11, 1939, CNA.

288 *"turned up trumps . . . brighter"*: Harry Yoxall, unpublished diaries, September 26, 1939.

288 *"It was a . . . well"*: Harry Yoxall, unpublished diaries, December 29, 1939.

288 *"to get rid of Madge"*: Harry Yoxall, unpublished diaries, October 31, 1939.

288 *"fundamentally artificial approach . . . conservatism"*: Elizabeth Penrose to Harry Yoxall, November 2, 1939, CNA.

288 *"contact with the . . . clothes"*: Condé Nast to Edna Woolman Chase, November 30, 1939, CNA.

288 *"difficult situation," wrote . . . "but . . ."*: Harry Yoxall, unpublished diaries, October 31, 1939.

288–289 *"There are to . . . anguish"*: Harry Yoxall, unpublished diaries, January 2, 1940.

289 *"swansong . . . trip"*: Harry Yoxall, unpublished diaries, February 6, 1940.

289 *"Then once again . . . friends"*: MG memoir drafts, MGP.

289–290 *"children's socks, or . . . thing"*: MG to Flora Groult, interview, London, July 26, 1986. Betty Penrose had also complained that Madge had no "practical, promotional sense," no "merchandising sense." "If I were a merchant looking for a sound fashion director," she wrote to Harry Yoxall, "Mrs. Garland would be the last person I would choose." Stafford Bourne had other ideas.

290 *"such trivial matters . . . moment"*: MG memoir drafts, MGP.
290 *Britain was far behind . . .* : When British industry groups finally develcped a sizing code derived from systematic measurements of the population, beginning in the 1960s, manufacturers still resisted using it.
290 *"a series of . . . etc.)"*: Garland, *Fashion*, 65.
290 *"the right type . . . size"*: MG memoir drafts, MGP.
290 *"began to dabble in design"*: Glynn, "50 Years On."
291 *"through shattered streets . . . glass"*: Vera Brittain, *Testament of Experience: An Autobiographical Story of the Years 1925–1950* (New York: Macmillan, 1957), 266.
291–292 *"I don't know . . . all"*: MG to Gerald McHarg, June 2 [1941], MHFP.
292 *"One can only . . . done"*: Ibid.
292 *"nowadays one only . . . seen"*: MG to Gerald McHarg, n.d. [postmarked March 12, 1942; received June 10, 1942], MHFP.
293 *"to restrict the . . . trimmings"*: Garland, *Fashion*, 61.
293 *"coupons, clothes, style . . . B. o. T."*: MG to Gerald McHarg, June 3, [1942], MHFP.
293 *"I never thought . . . it"*: MG to Shaunagh Ward-Jackson, conversation, London, n.d.
293 *"He had more . . . together"*: MG to Hugo Vickers, interview, London, March 8, 1980.
293 *"It was always . . . match"*: MG to Isabelle Anscombe, interview, London, October 8, 1979, IAP.
293 *"were backward in . . . fashion"*: Garland, *Fashion*, 61.
294 *"died a quick . . . war"*: MG to Isabelle Anscombe, interview, London, October 8, 1979, IAP.
294 *"Uncertainty with regard . . . acute"*: MG to Gerald McHarg, November 9, [1941], MHFP.
295 *"in the abstract . . . it"*: Violet Powell to Hilary Spurling, conversation, Somerset, January 2002.
295–296 *"very badly blitzed . . . disaster"*: MG to Gerald McHarg, September 30 [1944], MHFP.
296 *"planes in hundreds . . . wheels"*: Janet Flanner to Solita Solano, November 15, 1944, JFP.
296 *"The streets were . . . nothing"*: Jane Heap to Florence Reynolds, Holly A. Baggett, ed., *Dear Tiny Heart: The Letters of Jane Heap and Florence Reynolds* (New York: New York University Press, 2000), 136–37.
296–297 *"enough to live . . . resources"*: MG to Gerald McHarg, September 30, [1944], MHFP.
297 *"with rockets and sirens around"*: MG to Gerald McHarg, November 28, 1944, MHFP.
297 *"so that I . . . occasions"*: MG memoir drafts, MGP.
297 *"the greyness of London"*: Ibid.
298 *"pretty and gay . . . 'transformed'"*: Quoted in Bedford, *Aldous Huxley*, 442.
298 *"Talked with Madge . . . rugs"*: Hedda Hopper "Looking at Hollywood," *Los Angeles Times*, June 25, 1945, A2.

298 *"where I expect . . . day"*: MG memoir drafts, MGP.

298–299 *"colorful, impudently gay . . . America"*: "Dress Reformer," MGP.

299 *"this poverty stricken island"*: MG to Gerald McHarg, November 16 [1947], MHFP.

299 *"I have a . . . it"*: MG to Gerald McHarg, June 19, 1946, MHFP.

299 *"icy . . . With the . . . everywhere"*: MG to Gerald McHarg, January 25 [1947], MHFP.

299 *"epic: fourteen hours . . . horrible"*: MG to Gerald McHarg, n.d. [1946], MHFP.

300 *"the clothes in . . . interesting"*: Ibid.

300 *"to set up . . . center"*: *Women's Wear Daily*, September 5, 1947, MGP.

300 *"to remake my . . . up)"*: MG to Gerald McHarg, June 19, 1946, MHFP.

300 *"in the thick . . . do"*: MG to Gerald McHarg, September 18, 1947, MHFP.

PROFESSOR OF FASHION

301 *"as soft and easy . . . gloves"*: Quoted in www.exero.com/mastergate/secured/ fashion/ferragammo.htm.

301 *"high marriage wastage"*: "And by the Way . . . ," n.d., MGP.

301 *"London's most unusual professor"*: Fashion Professor to Marry Museum Director," March 7, 1952, MGP.

301 *"The First Professor of Fashion"*: Marjorie Beckett, "The First Professor of Fashion," *Picture Post*, February 19, 1949.

302–303 *"My dear Gerald . . . egotism"*: MG to Gerald McHarg, July 9, 1949. See *Times* (London) July 8, 1949, MHFP.

303 *"not only the . . . industry"*: *Harper's Bazaar*, n.d., 46, RCAA.

303 *"the civil servant stuffed shirts"*: MG to Isabelle Anscombe, interview, London, October 8, 1979, IAP.

303 She also hired . . . England: "She was open enough to employ . . . all kinds of people," Brogden recalled. "I can remember seeing the number tattooed on this woman's arm," she said of the Jewish refugee who taught lingerie, for example.

303 *"I wanted people . . . industry"*: Glynn, "50 Years On."

303 *"costume history, cutting . . . embroidery"*: *Harper's Bazaar*, n.d., 46, RCAA.

304 *"facts and technique . . . sophistication"*: Ibid.

304 *"to train you . . . awful"*: Joanne Brogden to author, interview, London, December 4, 1997.

304 *"She was an . . . go"*: David Sassoon to author, interview, London, September 22, 1997.

304 *"You had visits . . . time"*: David Watts to author, interview, London, June 13, 1998.

304–305 *"She wears clothes . . . wit"*: "Their Business Is Fashion," British *Vogue*, June 1949, 77. There is a "gaiety" to her style, "which is uncontrived, indefinable, but very much in character."

305 *"original approach to . . . individuality"*: "Two Names in London Fashion," n.d., MGP.

305 *"a very glamorous . . . sleeves"*: David Watts to author, interview, London, June 13, 1998.

305 *"She was what . . . heaven"*: David Sassoon to author, interview, London, September 22, 1997.

305 *"the way she . . . awe"*: Gina Fratini to author, interview, London, September 18, 1997.

305 *"Paris, Kensington"*: Foreword, Christopher Frayling, Royal College of Art Fiftieth Anniversary program.

305 *"We were a . . . own"*: Anne Tyrell to author, interview, London, June 15, 1998.

305 *"would invite all . . . people"*: Joanne Brogden to author, interview, London, December 4, 1997.

305 *"Madge's office I . . . all"*: David Watts to author, interview, London, June 13, 1998.

306 *"immaculate scarlet varnished . . . over"*: Joanne Brogden to author, interview, London, December 4, 1997. See also Marjorie Beckett, "The First Professor of Fashion," *Picture Post*, February 19, 1949.

306 *"addressed 600 locals"*: MG to Gerald McHarg, March 27 [1949], MHFP.

306 *"The early attempts . . . today"*: Garland, *Fashion*, 92.

306 *"staggeringly beautiful . . . houses"*: Joanne Brogden to author, interview, London, December 4, 1997.

306–308 *"the rigorous self-discipline . . . taste"*: "And by the Way . . ." n.d., MGP.

308 *"walking in one . . . 'off'"*: Joanne Brogden to author, interview, London, December 4, 1997.

308 *"We were 'her' . . . Vogue"*: Sheila Pearson to author, telephone interview, July 9, 1993.

308 *"I definitely would . . . her"*: David Sassoon to author, interview, London, 22 September 1997.

308 *"She was really . . . intimidate"*: Joanne Brogden to author, interview, London, December 4, 1997.

308–309 *"she thought she . . . warmer"*: David Sassoon to author, interview, London, September 22, 1997.

309 *"employing a designer . . . designer"*: Anne Tyrell to author, interview, London, June 15, 1998.

309 *"In 1948, when . . . energy"*: Robin Darwin to MG, May 9, 1956, Madge Garland personnel file, Royal College of Art.

309 *But they had . . . place*: "'We disagreed', said Darwin, cryptically," notes a recent history of the Royal College of Art, "and that was that." Christopher Frayling, *The Royal College of Art: One Hundred and Fifty Years of Art and Design* (London: Barrie and Jenkins, 1987), 154. Ironside remembered that Madge threatened to resign in a dispute with Darwin and that he accepted her resignation. Janey Ironside, *Janey* (London: Michael Joseph, 1973), 83.

309 *"She'd arrive staggeringly . . . around"*: Anne Tyrell to author, interview, London, June 15, 1998.

310 *Like Madge, she*: Fashion was "surely no more frivolous than architecture, to which it is closely related," Carter wrote in her memoir, Ernestine Carter, *With Tongue in Chic* (London: Michael Joseph, 1974), 181.

310 *"The proper function . . . 'present'"*: Garland, "Artifices," 82.

310 *"lack of professional . . . style"*: Ibid., 86.

310–311 *"most people think . . . 'collection'"*: Ibid., 82.

311 *"The fashion writer . . . fashion"*: Garland, *Fashion*, 105.

311 *"based on a . . . culture"*: Ibid., 32.

311 *"I went—not . . . 'shown?'"*: Garland, "This Fashion Business," 140.

312 *"The English have . . . knowledge"*: MG to Isabelle Anscombe, interview, London, October 8, 1979, IAP. Her analysis echoes Lytton Strachey's observation about the lack of support for literature: "The mere existence of a body of writers officially recognized by the authorities of the State [the Académie Française] has undoubtedly given a peculiar prestige to the profession of letters in France. It has emphasized that tendency to take the art of writing seriously—to regard it as a fit object for the most conscientious craftsmanship and deliberate care—which is so characteristic of French writers. The amateur is very rare in French literature—as rare as he is common in our own." From Lytton Strachey, *Landmarks in French Literature*, quoted in Michael Holroyd, *Lytton Strachey: The New Biography* (New York: Farrar, Straus and Giroux, 1994), 248.

312 *"how sensually she . . . samples"*: Ironside, *Janey*, 63.

312 *"What woman does . . . gown?"*: Graham [Garland], "The Psychology of Dress," 87.

312 *"There is a . . . in"*: Garland, "Artifices," 81.

312 *"I can, with . . . 'mode'"*: Ibid., 89.

312–313 *"We admire a . . . calculation"*: Ibid., 87.

313 *"Apart from money . . . thought"*: Madge Garland, "How to Dress on Nothing a Year," *Brittania and Eve*, September 1931, 76.

313 *"really hard work"*: MG to Isabelle Anscombe, interview, London, October 8, 1979. This friend was probably Kitty Pringle Mocata.

313 *"The selection of . . . salons"*: Garland, *Fashion*, 148.

313 *"match[ed] perfectly . . . way"*: MG to Isabelle Anscombe, interview, London, October 8, 1979, IAP.

313–314 *"In those days . . . money"*: Garland, *Fashion*, 148.

314 *"To consume without . . . lady"*: Madge Garland, "For Thousands of Years Women's Dress Has Proclaimed Her Status—Does It Now?" British *Vogue*, n.d. [circa 1960s], MGP.

314 *"as deceptive as . . . detail"*: Madge Garland, "Introduction," *Fashion 1900–1939*, 7.

314 *"the best life for women"*: MG to Isabelle Anscombe interview, London, October 8, 1979, IAP.

NOTES ON DISCRETION

316 *"a vibrant voice . . . flamboyant"*: Peter Ward-Jackson to author, interview, London, September 17, 1997.

316 *"Darling, I get . . . order"*: Hilary Spurling to author, conversation, New York, September 1993.

316 *"Sport is absolutely . . . away"*: MG to Shaunagh Ward-Jackson, conversation, London, December 28, 1987.

316 *"She used to . . . creature"*: Patrick Woodcock to author, interview, London, January 25, 2002.

316–317 *"My child, you . . . divine"*: David Sassoon to author, interview, London, September 22, 1997.

317 *"hysterical"*: MG to Peter Shaunagh Ward-Jackson, conversation, London, October 3, [circa 1980s].

317 *"it was interesting . . . room"*: Ibid.

318 *"The atmosphere is . . . answered"*: Garland, "This Fashion Business," 37.

318 *including one . . . period*: "These tiny Baby Simcas are barely larger than a perambulator and the first time I saw a Parisienne wearing her loose fitting coat, her feathered hat on the back of her head, and her bulky feet fold herself into one of the cars I laughed heartily." Madge Garland, "Fashion Today," typescript, BBC Home Service, London, January 16, 1947, BBC Written Archives Centre.

318 *"the way she . . . lesbian"*: Hugo Vickers, unpublished diaries, March 8, 1980.

318 *"She lived very . . . was"*: Francis King to author, interview, London, March 21, 1998.

319 *"revelations or insinuations . . . time"*: Anne Olivier Bell to author, September 16, 2004. The phrase is in Woolf's diary entry for February 18, 1928. Consulted at the Berg Collection, New York Public Library.

319 *"People of that . . . so"*: Francis King to author, interview, London, March 21, 1998.

319 *"It was in . . . discreet"*: Sybille Bedford to author, interview, London, December 7, 1997. Another example: Among the short autobiographical essays that make up the drafts of Madge's memoir are three and a half typed pages in which she recounts a momentous event that took place during her first years at *Vogue*: her interview with Radclyffe Hall. The novelist was then "the most scandalous woman in London," Madge writes.

> The permissive society of today can have no conception of the scandal caused by the publication of *The Well of Loneliness*—a book never to be seen on anyone's table or bookshelf but read by all in secret . . . And now I was to interview this famous—or infamous lady—but was she a lady? That was one problem but the main problem was that I had not the faintest idea of how to conduct an interview. How did one begin? Every subject seemed fraught with dangerous innuendos.

The interview was nevertheless a triumph—her first real piece of journalism and a coup that made her "the centre of attention" at a party that night. She is describing her life and work circa 1922, however, and *The Well of Loneliness* was published in 1928—one of several mysteries about this short document.

320 *"gestures full of duplicity"*: Susan Sontag, "Notes on 'Camp,'" *Against Interpretation* (New York: Farrar, Straus and Giroux, 1966), 281.

320 *"the impression of . . . boots"*: Graham Reynolds to author, telephone interview, January 12, 2004.

320 *"She was so . . . it?"*: Patrick Woodcock to author, telephone interview, January 22, 2002.

320 *"I wish I . . . darling"*: Shaunagh Ward-Jackson to author, interview, London, September 17, 1997.

320 *"ate next to . . . food"*: Sybille Bedford to Evelyn Gendel, January 13, 1957, in "A Bouquet for Sybille Bedford," *Five Dials*, March 18, 2011.

322 *"It was the . . . durable"*: De Acosta, *Here Lies*, 132.

322 *"It was the . . . feminine"*: De Acosta, "Here Lies The Heart," typescript (circa 1960), second draft, 271.

322 *"represented . . . figure"*: Patrick Woodcock to author, interview, London, January 25, 2002.

322 *"had this flair . . . on"*: MG to Isabelle Anscombe, interviews, London, July 2, 1980, and London, October 8, 1979, IAP.

323 *"seeing the world . . . phenomenon"*: Sontag, "Notes on 'Camp,'" 277.

323 *"taste is not . . . 'natural'"*: Susan Sontag, "The Double Standard of Aging," *Saturday Review*, September 23, 1972, 38.

323 *"like stage sets"*: Hilary Spurling to author, conversation, London, January 11, 2002.

323 *"painted elaborately by . . . daring"*: Cecil Beaton, unpublished diaries, Sunday, November 7, 1926, CBD.

323 *"in pink and . . . had"*: MG to Isabelle Anscombe, interview, London, July 2, 1980, IAP.

323 *"it looked like . . . different"*: MG to Isabelle Anscombe, interview, London, October 8, 1979, IAP.

323 *"was like going . . . beautiful"*: Gina Fratini to author, interview, London, September 18, 1997.

323 *"dead birds, surrounded . . . frames"*: Chloe Tyner to author, telephone interview, May 19, 1997.

324 *"She was the . . . 'that'"*: Isabelle Anscombe to author, conversation, London, January 2, 2002.

324 *"held that all . . . homosexual"*: Hilary Spurling, *Ivy: The Life of I, Compton-Burnett* (New York: Knopf, 1974, 1984), 279.

324 *"with a grey . . . coat"*: Peter Ward-Jackson to author, interview, London, September 17, 1997. Ward-Jackson went on to say that a taxi driver taking Roger's fare once said, "Cor blimey sir, you'll be wearing earrings next!" To which Roger replied, "Not with tweeds, my dear fellow!"

324 *"Purple Party"*: David Sassoon to author, interview, London, September 22, 1997.

324 *"my dears"*: Selina Hastings to author, conversation, London, January 14, 1999.

325 *"very bright star . . . world"*: Graham Reynolds to author, telephone interview, January 12, 2004.

325 *"his flair for . . . objects"*: Graham Reynolds to author, February 2, 2004.

325 *"Primary Galleries . . . time"*: Ibid. See also, Graham Reynolds, "Leigh Ashton," obituary, *Apollo*, May 1968.

325 *"it was a . . . seriously"*: Graham Reynolds to author, telephone interview, January 12, 2004.

325 *"Just read the . . . it"*: Allanah Harper to Sybille Bedford, February 27, [1952], SBP.

325 *"Fashion Professor to . . . Museum"*: Morna Condell, March 7, 1952, MGP.

326 *"A title draws . . . country"*: Isabelle Anscombe to author, conversation, London, November 10, 2003.

326 *"You can't even . . . fabric"*: Patrick Woodcock to author, interview, London, January 25, 2002.

326 *"She loved to . . . Ashton"*: Colombe Pringle to author, interview, Paris, December 5, 1997.

326 *"DEAR GERALD MARRIED . . . Madge"*: John McHarg to author, interview, Melbourne, September 10, 2003.

326 *"an ambition which . . . Leigh"*: Graham Reynolds to author, March 2, 2004.

327 *"a nice cosy . . . austerity"*: Ibid.

327 *"Don't marry," Madge . . . "regulations"*: MG to Isabelle Anscombe, interview, London, October 8, 1979, IAP.

327 *"drinking career . . . occasion"*: Graham Reynolds to author, telephone interview, January 12, 2004.

327 *"Dear Leigh," she . . . "agreement"*: Peter Ward-Jackson to author, conversation, London, January 4, 2002.

327 *"So the performance . . . months"*: Graham Reynolds to author, telephone interview, January 12, 2004.

328 *"for reasons of failing health"*: "Leigh Ashton," obituary, *Times* (London), March 17, 1983, MGP.

328 *As Lady Ashton . . . title*: Her snobbery had its most meaningful applications in England, but it was global in reach. When she traveled to India late in life, said her goddaughter, it was "not only for the gurus, but for the Maharajas." Colombe Pringle to author, interview, Paris, December 5, 1997.

328 *"because nothing was . . . sides"*: Spurling, *Ivy*, 506.

328 *"Ivy came to . . . again"*: Madge Garland, "A Friendship Without a Thorn," unpublished typescript, MGP.

328 *"one of the . . . life"*: Spurling, *Ivy*, 506.

328 *"Madge could do no wrong"*: Sybille Bedford to author, interview, London, December 7, 1997.

328 *"She was besotted . . . world"*: Francis King to author, interview, London, March 21, 1998.

328 *"although she belonged . . . it"*: Garland, "A Friendship Without a Thorn."

328 *"she knew that . . . dependable"*: MG to Flora Groult, interview, London, July 26, 1986.

329 *"had strong feelings . . . tone"*: Garland, "A Friendship Without a Thorn."

329 *"Madge is in . . . her"*: Barbara Robinson to author, telephone interview, July 30, 1998.

329 *"passion for clothes" . . . homosexual*: Spurling, *Ivy*, 263.

330 *"clothes-conscious"*: Ibid., 364. Spurling also argues that Josephine has strong affinities with her creator.

330 *"Oh, pray let . . . over-civilised"*: Ivy Compton-Burnett, *A Family and a Fortune* and *More Women Than Men* (New York: Simon and Schuster, 1965 [1933]) 434, 488, 311, 335.

330–331 *"I have said . . . women"*: Compton-Burnett, *More Women Than Men*, 489–90.

331 *"Ivy educated me"*: Garland, MG to Hilary Spurling, conversation, London, September 18, 1975.

331 *"The whole thing . . . anyone"*: Sybille Bedford to author, interview, London, December 7, 1997.

331 *"a wildly mixed . . . velvet"*: Garland, "A Friendship Without a Thorn."

331 *"in the end . . . drunk"*: MG to Hilary Spurling, conversation, London, September 18, 1975.

331 *"deep tenderness"*: MG to Barbara Robinson, September 22, 1969.

331 *"She might flay . . . safe"*: Garland, "A Friendship Without a Thorn."

331 *"I felt I . . . helplessness"*: Ivy Compton-Burnett to MG, June 7, 1968, quoted in Spurling, *Ivy*, 533.

331–332 *"that it prevented . . . was"*: MG to Barbara Robinson, September 22 1969.

332 *"submerged stones against . . . toe"*: MG to Hilary Spurling, interview, London, March 31, 1973.

332 *"Ivy said nothing . . . point"*: MG to Hilary Spurling, quoted in Spurling, *Ivy*, 352.

332 *"He's getting married . . . knows"*: Quoted in ibid., 438.

332 *"Will you come . . . coming"*: MG to Hilary Spurling, conversation, London, October 1974.

332 *"Come on Madge . . . hers"*: Francis King to author, interview, London, March 21, 1998.

333 *"discreet to the . . . obsession"*: Spurling, *Ivy*, 368.

333 *"she never, as . . . life"*: Francis King to author, interview, London, March 21, 1998.

333 *"didn't make any . . . it"*: Sybille Bedford to author, conversation, London, January 12, 1999.

333 *"tell her a . . . Lesbians"*: Cecil Beaton, unpublished diaries, September 2, 1927.

333 *"It wasn't Madge . . . married"*: Peter Ward-Jackson to author, interview, London, September 17, 1997.

333 *"She was always . . . women"*: Hardy Amies to author, interview, London, January 14, 1999.

333 *"a wonderful bridge . . . second-rate"*: "Madge Garland," obituary, *Sunday Telegraph*, July 17, 1990.

334 *"was so furious . . . quashed"*: Madge Garland, "Rose Bertin: Minister of Fashion," *Apollo* (January 1968): 40–45, 44.

334 *"Madge came down . . . work"*: Rebecca West to Janet Flanner, November 2, 1958, JFP.

334 *"What Camp taste . . . thing"*: Sontag, "Notes on 'Camp,'" 286.

335 *"great amount of . . . room"*: Peter Ward-Jackson to author, interview, London, September 17, 1997.

335 *"parchment velvet . . . gowns"*: Madge Garland, "A Portfolio of Fashion," *The Bystander*, September 20, 1933, 529.

335 *"terribly tough, with . . . fun"*: Sarah Stacey to author, interview, London, December 7, 1997.

335 *"the most percipient of friends"*: MG memoir drafts, MGP.

335 *"smug, self-assured . . . did"*: Hilary Spurling, "Madge Garland," obituary, *Independent*, July 17, 1990.

335 *"within two years . . . life"*: MG memoir drafts, MGP.

335 *"Everybody was one . . . flames"*: Sybille Bedford to author, interview, London, December 7, 1997.

337 *"one of the . . . life"*: MG to Hugo Vickers, interview, London, March 8, 1980.

337 *"was leaving me . . . man"*: MG memoir drafts, MGP.

337 *"The years passed . . . May"*: MG memoir drafts, MGP.

338 *"I cried and . . . crying"*: Peter Ward-Jackson to author, interview, London, September 17, 1997.

338 *"I somehow wish . . . was"*: Olguita Berington to MG, n.d., [1945], MGP.

339 *"It is 43 . . . betrayal"*: MG memoir drafts, MGP.

341 *"Of course I am a feminist!"*: Hoare, "Come into the Garland, Madge."

341 *"It is not . . . do"*: Compton-Burnett, *More Women Than Men*, 438.

341 *"You are not . . . you"*: Rebecca West to MG, n.d., RWP.

341 *"most of the . . . time"*: MG to Isabelle Anscombe, interview, London, July 2, 1980, IAP.

341 *"this wonderful-looking . . . beauty"*: MG to Flora Groult, interview, London, July 26, 1986.

341 *farm in Sussex*: Miller's photo essay about having friends and guests help run the property includes a photograph of Madge. "Working Guests," British *Vogue*, July 1953.

342 *"She was much . . . boys"*: MG to Flora Groult, interview, London, July 26, 1986.

342 *"How are you . . . Lee"*: N.d., MGP.

342–343 *"TO DARLING KITTY . . . tissu"*: Colombe Pringle to author, interview, Paris, December 5, 1997.

343 *"in my new . . . formidable"*: Woolf, *Diary*, June 9, 1926, 3:89.

343 *"Jews swarmed . . . squalor"*: Virginia Woolf to Vanessa Bell, June 2, 1926, Woolf, *Letters* 3:269–70.

343–344 *"hated the Cockney . . . lovely"*: Olivier Todd to author, interview, Paris, September 23, 1997.

344 *"Art came first . . . Cubism"*: Ibid.

344 *"merely accumulated quotations . . . Wittgenstein"*: Olivier Todd, *Year of the Crab*, trans. Oliver Ocburn, galleys to unpublished book [Henley-on-Thames: Aidan Ellis, 1975], 132.

344 *"but was constantly . . . poverty"*: Olivier Todd to author, interview, Paris, September 23, 1997.

346 nigger brown: Garland, "Interiors by Eyre de Lanux," 265.

346 *"We always knew . . . that"*: Chloe Tyner to author, telephone interview, May 19, 1997.

346 *"great friend"*: MG to Isabelle Anscombe, interview, London, July 2, 1980, IAP.

346 *"two rather fruity old gentlemen"*: Peter Schabacker to author, interview, Shoreham, October 19, 2000.

346 *"I know nothing"*: Patricia Laffan to author, interview, London, March 21, 1998.

346–347 *"We were very close friends"*: Isabelle Anscombe to author, interview, Wittersham, January 11, 1999.

347 *"It has entirely . . . today"*: MG to Isabelle Anscombe, interview, London, October 8, 1979, IAP.

LOOKING IS NOT VANISHING

348 *"She was intelligent . . . wearing"*: Francis Wyndham to author, telephone interview, January 14, 1999.

348 *"too frilly and feminine"*: Katharine White to Janet Flanner, September 7, 1928, *New Yorker* papers, New York Public Library.

348 *"She has left no monument"*: Peter Ward-Jackson, interview, London, September 17, 1997.

348 "NO HYMNS . . . WORDS": Madge Garland, ms., MGP.

348 *"never vaunted or . . . did"*: Hilary Spurling to author, conversation, London, September 25, 1997.

349 *"a key figure . . . achievements"*: "Madge Garland," obituary, *Times* (London), July 18, 1990.

349 *"explosive, fast . . . gloves"*: Serena Sinclair to author, telephone interview, July 15, 2002.

349 *"not a reading . . . book"*: MG to Flora Groult, interview, London, July 26, 1986.

349 *"only a few . . . husbands"*: Garland, *Fashion*, 45

349–350 *"valuable insofar as . . . time"*: MG to Isabelle Anscombe, interview, London, July 2, 1980, IAP.

350 *"look up Cicilia [sic] . . . cent"*: Notebook, MGP.

350 *"She had a . . . now"*: Sarah Stacey to author, interview, London, December 7, 1997.

350 *"even buying a . . . fun"*: Madge Garland, "Travel in Vogue: Malaya," British *Vogue*, December 1962, MGP.

350 *"Unexpected oddities of . . . cargoes"*: Madge Garland, "Cargo-Boats: It's a Gift," *The Spectator*, September 15, 1967, MGP.

350–352 *"the panache of . . . jewellery"*: Madge Garland, "I Speak of Africa and Golden Joys," British *Vogue*, October 1967, 62.

352 *"real love was . . . 'Ainos'"*: Madge Garland, "Four Fearless Females" *The Saturday Book* 24, John Hadfield, ed. (London: Hutchinson, 1964), 65.

352 *"It is lovely . . . consciousness"*: MG to Barbara Robinson, March 22, 1970.

354 *"I've been in . . . America"*: MG to Peter and Shaunagh Ward-Jackson, conversation, London, December 28, 1987.

354 *"but despite this . . . abyss"*: Sarah Stacey to author, interview, London, December 7, 1997.

354 *"spent five or . . . way"*: Peter Ward-Jackson to author, interview, London, September 17, 1997.

354 *"I think that . . . interested"*: Sarah Stacey to author, interview, London, December 7, 1997.

354 *"She died in . . . lost"*: Madge Garland, "Four Fearless Females," 71.

354 *"Fashion is like air"*: "Seven Ages of Fashion: The Regency," Thames Television, 1975, videocassette (VHS), 26 min.

354 *"for their charm . . . beneath"*: Garland, "Introduction," *Fashion 1900–1939*, 7.

354 *"I wish I . . . now!"*: MG to Isabelle Anscombe, interview, London, October 8, 1979, IAP.

354 *"not excited about . . . that"*: Sarah Stacey to author, interview, London, December 7, 1997.

355 *"What is there . . . again"*: Garland, "Artifices," 81.

355 *"Whether we like . . . age"*: Garland, "Artifices," 85.

355 *"I don't like . . . clothes"*: MG to Isabelle Anscombe, interview, London, October 8, 1979, IAP.

355 *"the 'Good Old Days'"* . . . her: Garland, "Condé Charm."

355 *"This nostalgia thing . . . back"*: Neustatter, "The Magic Circle."

355 *"I am incapable . . . future)"*: Madge Garland, "You May Still Be on Your Holidays," *Brittania and Eve*, September 1930, 72.

355 *"how miraculous it . . . past"*: MG to Isabelle Anscombe, interview, London, July 2, 1980, IAP.

355 *"bent as she . . . Balenciaga"*: Diana Scarisbrick to author, interview, London, September 26, 1997.

355–356 *"feminine and sensual . . . Century"*: Royal College of Art Fiftieth Anniversary program.

356 *"the [Palazzo] Pitti . . . girls"*: Garland, *Fashion*, 75–76.

356 *"she said, 'No . . . circumstances'"*: Diana Scarisbrick to author, interview, London, September 26, 1997.

357 *"my friend . . . Vogue"*: MG memoir drafts, MGP.

357 *"She was a . . . herself"*: MG to Hilary Spurling, conversation, London, March 29, 1989.

357 *"less-than-always-honorable . . . full"*: Garland, "Condé Charm."

357–358 *"the first journalist . . . commerce"*: Garland, *Fashion*, 108.

358 *"relief" to emerge . . . "gloves"*: Garland, "Condé Charm."

ACKNOWLEDGMENTS

My first thanks are to Hilary Spurling, Madge Garland's literary executor and friend, who trusted me with Madge's papers, shared her memories of her, and provided gracious guidance. In addition, I am deeply grateful to Peter and Shaunagh Ward-Jackson, Madge Garland's executors, for crucial sources and perspective on her life; to Brenda Wineapple, for encouraging me to write about Esther Murphy and for her early support of this project; to Laura Donnelly, for allowing me to consult and cite the Donnelly/Murphy family papers; to Olivier Todd, for sharing memories and documents about his grandmother, Dorothy Todd, and his mother, Helen Todd; to John McHarg, Madge Garland's nephew, for safeguarding and allowing me to quote the letters she sent his father; to Patrick Garland, for his memories of his father, Ewart Garland, and for allowing me to quote his wartime diary; to Elizabeth Al-Quadi and Charles Strachey, for kindly permitting me to quote material in the archive of their father, John Strachey; to Lindsey Pietrzak, keeper of the diaries of her father, Harry Yoxall; to Alexandra Berington, for access to the scrapbooks and photo albums of her mother-in-law, Olguita Monsanto Queeny Berington; to William Noone, Helen Todd's son-in-law, for sharing his research on Dorothy Todd; and to Hugo Vickers, ever generous steward of Cecil Beaton's legacy.

I am indebted to the following librarians, archivists, curators, and institutions for their expertise and assistance: Elizabeth Fuller, Judith Guston, and Karen Schoenewaldt at the Rosenbach Museum & Library, Philadelphia; Stephen Mielke and others at the Harry Ransom Humanities Research Center, University of Texas, Austin; Barbara Orbach Natanson, Prints and Photographs Division, Library of Congress; Patrick Kerwin and others, Manuscripts Division, Library of Congress; the National Art Library and the Archive of Art and Design, Victoria and Albert Museum, London; the British Library (Colindale, Bloomsbury, St. Pancras); the Chelsea Library, London; the Royal College of Art Archives, London; the Guildhall Library, London; Nancy Kuhl, Leigh Golden, and others, Beinecke Rare Book and Manuscript Library, Yale University, New Haven; Jonathan Harrison, St. John's College Library, Cambridge; Trish Hayes, the BBC Written Archives Centre, Reading; Charlie Scheips and Shawn Waldron, the Condé Nast Archive, New York; Camden Local Studies and Archives Centre, London; the State Library of Victoria, Melbourne; Chris Petter, Special Collections, McPherson Library, University of Victoria, British Columbia; Terence Pepper, National Portrait Gallery, London; Polly Thistlethwaite, Mina Rees Library, the Graduate Center, City University of New York; McCabe Library, Swarthmore College; the New York Public Library; Bobst Library, New York University; Olin Library, Wesleyan University; Peter Maplestone, St. Mary le Strand, London; Rebecca Mayne, Grand Rapids History & Special Collections Center; Nicky Sugar, Royal Holloway and Bedford College, London; Charlotte J. Kuhn, Monsanto family archives, St. Louis; Cynthia Curtner, Boston Latin School; Sharon Stearns, The Brearley School, New York; Anne Thomson, Newnham College Archives, Cambridge; Betsy Lowenstein, Special Collections, State Library of Massachusetts, Boston; The National Archives, London.

My research was supported by the Andrew W. Mellon Foundation and Swarthmore College; the Harry Ransom Humanities Research Center, University of Texas, Austin; the Center for Lesbian and Gay Studies, City University of New York; the Center for the Study of Gender and Sexuality, New York University; and Wesleyan University.

This book could not have been completed without the following people, who generously granted interviews and corresponded with me about my subjects: Jane Abdy, Hardy Amies, Jennifer Beattie, Wilder Luke Bernap, Moorea Black, Lesley Blanch, Joanne Brogden, Julia Burney, Francis Collin, Roderick Coupe, Anne Crosthwait, James Douglas, Helen Drummond, Sarah Drummond, Lila Duckworth, Gina Fratini, Mimi Hodgkin, Della Howard, Virginia Ironside, Chippy Irvine, Francis King, Patricia Laffan, Flora Groult Ledwidge, Frances Loyen, Robert Macpherson, Gerald McCann, Peter Miall, Barbara Morris, Diana Mosley, Veronica Nicolson, Bernard Nevill, Colombe Pringle, Tim Pringle, Carol Newman, Michael Parkin, Sheila Pearson, Ralph Pindar-Wilson, Tristram Powell, Violet Powell, Graham Reynolds, Barbara Robinson, George Rylands, David Sassoon, Diana Scarisbrick, Marian Seldes, Richard Shone, Serena Sinclair, Charles Sinnickson, Sarah Stacey, Quentin Stevenson, Chloe Tyner, Chris Tyner, Anne Tyrrell, Clive Wainwright, David Watts, Audrey Williams, Audrey Withers, Christopher Wood, Patrick Woodcock, and Francis Wyndham.

I am grateful to the editors who published early versions of some of this material: Tom Beer, Ann Cvetkovich, Annamarie Jagose, Sarah Pettitt, Frances Spalding, and Valerie Steele.

For consultation, inspiration, hospitality, and other assistance along the way, I thank Devon Allison, Hilton Als, Dag Bennett, Lauren Blumenthal, Hanna Bottomley, James Cohen, Sarah Cohen, Blanche Wiesen Cook, Caleb Crain, Christina Crosby, Prudence Crowther, Ann Cvetkovich, Richard Deming, Carolyn Dinshaw, Maureen Emerson, Eliza Gagnon, Victoria Glendinning, Camilla Grey, John Griffin, Selina Hastings, Peter Kurth, Magdalene Lampert, Linda Leavell, Carolyn Lesjak, Nicola Luckhurst, Risa Mickenberg, Lisa Moore, Mark Morelli, Barbara Piscitelli, Deborah Rothschild, Robyn Selman, Andrew Spindler, David Stenn, William Stowe, Judy Tucker, Amanda Vaill, Hella von Unger, Shelley Wanger, Steven Watson, Geoff Weston.

I will always be profoundly indebted to Ira Silverberg, formerly of Sterling Lord Literistic; Lorin Stein, formerly of Farrar, Straus and Giroux; Courtney Hodell, Mark Krotov, and Jonathan Lippincott, Farrar, Straus and Giroux; and Sarah Lutyens, Lutyens and Rubenstein. My thanks also to Charlotte Strick, Jim Rutman, Dwight Curtis, Stephen Weil, and Georgia Cool.

Without whom not: Sybille Bedford, Sylvia Brownrigg, Clifford Chase, Jill Ciment, Charlotte Gere, Isabelle Grey, James Lyons, Aliette Martin, Ann Reynolds, Matthew Sharpe, Siobhan Somerville, Andrew Spindler, Patricia White, Elizabeth Willis. And finally, with love: David K. Cohen and Vanessa Haney.

INDEX

Page numbers in *italics* refer to illustrations. Page numbers beginning with 360 refer to notes.

A NOTE ABOUT THE AUTHOR

Lisa Cohen's writing has appeared in *Fashion Theory*, *Bookforum*, *GLQ*, *Ploughshares*, *Boston Review*, and other journals and anthologies. She teaches at Wesleyan University.